# Fashion Education

# Fashion Education

## The Systemic Revolution

EDITED BY

*Ben Barry and Deborah A. Christel*

Bristol, UK / Chicago, USA

First published in the UK in 2023 by
Intellect, The Mill, Parnall Road, Fishponds, Bristol, BS16 3JG, UK

First published in the USA in 2023 by
Intellect, The University of Chicago Press, 1427 E. 60th Street,
Chicago, IL 60637, USA

A catalogue record for this book is available from
the British Library.

Copy editor: MPS Limited
Cover designer: Tanya Montefusco
Cover artwork: Hayden Stern
Production manager: Laura Christopher
Typesetter: MPS Limited

Print (h/bk) ISBN 978-1-78938-643-1
Print (p/bk) ISBN 978-1-78938-680-6
ePDF ISBN 978-1-78938-644-8
ePUB ISBN 978-1-78938-645-5

To find out about all our publications, please visit our website.
There you can subscribe to our e-newsletter, browse or download our current
catalogue and buy any titles that are in print.

www.intellectbooks.com

This is a peer-reviewed publication.

# Contents

# Acknowledgements

We are indebted to the educators who planted the seeds from which this book grew. We recognise their courage to advance social justice in fashion education, where many were unsupported, distrusted, contested and dismissed by their colleagues and universities. With all our hearts, thank you for creating the spaces for our authors to contribute their experiences and dream up the possibilities described in this book.

From the moment we shared our proposal, Jelena Stanovnik and Intellect Books fully supported this project. Jelena, alongside Laura Christopher and Tim Mitchell at Intellect, offered deep care, flexibility and generosity throughout the publication process. We are grateful to them and everyone at Intellect for their unwavering support.

Thank you to the contributors of this book. We know many of the chapters not only share your brave pedagogical interventions but also your experiences of ongoing pain. Thank you for entrusting us to hold them. Your collective care, support and patience made it possible to accommodate one another during the ongoing global pandemic, life shifts and a deep reckoning in fashion education that was not happening when we started this project. We stuck together, and for that, we are extremely grateful. Additionally, a special thanks to Hayden Stern, the most incredible cover artist we could ever imagine.

Individually, we each have others to thank as well.

### From Ben

I am grateful to the teachers who showed me what a liberatory classroom felt like. Thank you to my Women and Gender Studies undergraduate professors at the University of Toronto – especially Carla Rice, Mary Nyquist and Honor Ford Smith. The theories you introduced and the ways you taught forever shaped my life. My ideas about fashion and social justice are indebted to the many fashion students who I have had the privilege to teach. Learning from and with you has been the greatest gift. I am also grateful to my colleagues at Toronto Metropolitan University and Parsons School of Design; my perspectives and practices are always expanding because of our conversations about teaching fashion. Thank you for always challenging me with care and kindness. I grow each day because of these communities.

With all my heart, thank you to my mom Conny, my husband, Daniel and our pup, Apple, who bring so much love into my life and remind me to find balance. My model of pedagogy is inspired by how you, Daniel, teach. I am forever grateful to my co-editor, Deb Christel. Thank you for being the most generous collaborator and friend. I have learned so much from your wisdom, brilliance and kindness. I am thankful that I was on this journey with you.

## From Deb

I want to acknowledge that I live on the traditional homelands of the Puyallup Nation and have lived and worked on the lands of the Nimiipuu (Nez Perce), Palus, Shawnee and the Moneton peoples.

Thank you, Dr Patti Watkins, for introducing me to Fat Studies and forever changing my personal and professional life trajectory. Thank you to the students who believed in and fought for inclusive fashion – your voice matters. I remain grateful to the scholars, fat activists, fat models and allies whose daily work is devoted to increasing equality and equity in the fashion industry And the world; Kelly Reddy-Best, Susan Dunn, Dominique Norman, Charlotte Cooper, Esther D. Rothblum, Marilyn Wann, Sondra Solovay, Kelly Lenza, Aubry Gordon, Da'Shaun L. Harrison, Chelsie Roland, Julie Arsenault, Saucye West, Adrienne Bennett, J Aprileo, Ashley Morse and others whose names could fill this book many times over.

Thank you to my wonderful husband, Louis. From reading early drafts to being my sounding board and keeping the munchkins out of my hair so I could spend all day editing. Thank you so much, dear. Thank you, munchkins, Mikayla and Lucas, for being my cheerleaders and reminding me to find joy in the little things. And thank you to baby Sophia, who arrived in our family near the end of editing this book, for reminding me to slow down and be more present.

I particularly want to thank Ben Barry. None of this would have been possible without him. Thank you for all the brainstorming sessions, late-night read-throughs and your dedication to making the world a better place for all. Thank you for teaching me and sharing the gift of your time through the process of this book. You are an inspiration to me and countless others.

# Radical Fashion Educators Unite: An Introduction

*Barry Ben and Deborah A. Christel*

Have you ever seen a garment, accessory or fashion image that was racist, culturally appropriated, fatphobic, transphobic or ableist, and asked yourself: *what were the fashion creatives thinking?* As educators, we ask: *how did they learn to think like that?*

The summer of 2020 brought this question to the beating heart of fashion schools. The murders of George Floyd, Breonna Taylor and Ahmaud Ardery at the hands of white police officers sparked a resurgence of Black Lives Matter protests and inspired a deep reckoning about racism in fashion education. In response to these murders, fashion schools released statements on their social media platforms condemning anti-Black racism. However, thousands of students, staff and members of faculty called their bluff. They posted comments and created new accounts to document the myriad of ways in which fashion schools devalue and discriminate against Black lives. Their experiences of racism could fill this book many times over. Here is a sample:

> How many [Fashion Institute of Technology] FIT talks about European businesses promoting getting their goods being supposedly 'made fairly in Africa' do you have to have before having classes actually teaching about Black America, Africa and the diaspora?
>
> (comment posted on FIT's Instagram page)

> I've reported Blackface 'pieces' (TWICE NOW) and no student was reprimanded, punished or even demanded to issue a formal apology.
>
> (comment posted on Rhode Island College of Art and Design's [RISD] Instagram account)

> The whole 3 years I was there we were never taught about doing makeup on people of colour. It was always for white/light skin and they'd tell us that working on darker

skin is more challenging and it would be useful for us to find courses specialising in makeup for darker skin.

(comment posted on @ualtruth about the University of the Arts London [UAL])

*Fashion Education: The Systemic Revolution* is an intervention into the current state of teaching fashion that maintains and perpetuates white supremacy, racism, fatmisia, cis-heteropatriarchy, ableism and other intersecting systems of oppression. Through this book, our project is largely one of social justice and, more specifically, focuses on reframing fashion curricula in the global North. We offer a collection of seventeen essays by fashion educators and students in Australia, Canada, the United States and the United Kingdom who chronicle their teaching practices to foster equity, inclusion and social justice. Collectively these essays ask: what can fashion education do to create a more equitable fashion industry and world? We view the classroom as a site for the world-making of radically inclusive fashion systems because, while education has the power to reinforce systems of oppression, it also has the power to revolutionize them.

Following adrienne maree brown's (2017) 'emergent strategy', we recognize that small-scale actions can transform complex systems. brown's (2017: 59) framework heeds the strategies of the natural world, as she observes, 'When we speak of systemic change, we need to be fractal. Fractals – a way to speak of the patterns we see – move from the micro to the macro [...] We must create patterns that cycle upwards'. She notes that both galaxies and seashells have the same spiral shapes. As such, brown's (2017: 53) framework for systemic change is grounded in the principle that, 'What we practice at the small scale sets the patterns for the whole system'. brown (2017: 24) reminds us that change is a constant condition of the universe and we need 'to be in the right relationship with change' for our small-scale actions to create a more equitable world. Therefore, how we enter relationships with each other, our students and fashion itself can support a just fashion paradigm that moves from the classroom into the world. You – fellow fashion educators, students and professionals – are invited to join this conversation and mission.

This book's positioning of pedagogy as a practice of social justice honours activists and teachers who led the ongoing struggle to confront inequity and advance transformation through education. We credit Black and Indigenous educators, educators of colour, and feminist, 2SLGBTQ+, D/disabled and abolitionist educators who have challenged pedagogy beyond white supremacist, ableist, fatphobic and cis-heteropatriarchal framings. For them, education guides us towards revolution. In particular, *Fashion Education* is grounded in the wisdom of bell hooks and her book *Teaching to Transgress: Education as the Practice of Freedom*. As hooks shares:

The classroom remains the most radical space of possibility in the academy [...].
Urging all of us to open our minds and hearts so that we can know beyond the
boundaries of what is acceptable, so that we can think and rethink, so that we can
create new visions, I celebrate teaching that enables transgressions – a movement
against and beyond boundaries. It is that movement which makes education the
practice of freedom.

(1994: 12)

The classroom is where we, educators and students, can transgress what we have
been told and taught; we can think and rethink, and make and remake tender,
kinder or more just worlds (Freire 2000; hooks 1994). Extending hooks's approach
to the fashion classroom, this book explores strategies, struggles and possibilities of shifting, reclaiming and expanding fashion pedagogy beyond the narrow
Eurocentric canon.

## Rebuilding the house of fashion education

Focusing on the classroom does not deny that deeper institutional change is necessary to transform fashion education. Achieving social justice is impossible without
profound changes in university policies, practices and value systems. The modern
western fashion industry, and as an offspring of it, modern western fashion education, is a direct result of the transatlantic slave trade and European colonization.
These continuing legacies have entrenched a white supremacist, heteropatriarchal,
ableist and fatphobic worldview and associated practices in fashion education's
curricula and culture. Sabrina Strings (2019) explains how the modern obsession
with thinness originated through the Enlightenment era belief that fatness symbol-
ized Black women's gender and racial inferiority. Kyla Schuller (2018) charts how
the gender binary was constructed to mark white people as superior. Eli Clare
(2017) describes how white people created ableism to justify the enslavement and
control of Black people. As such, white supremacist culture created beauty standards and body ideals to oppress and dominate. Fashion education naturalized and
normalized these beliefs into every facet of their purview (e.g., Barry 2020, 2021;
Cheang and Shehnaz 2020; Christel 2018; Reddy-Best et al. 2018a).

Fashion design, illustration and merchandising textbooks feature people of
colour in less than 15 per cent of images, with little representation of non-binary
and fat people (Reddy-Best et al. 2018a; Reddy-Best et al. 2018b). Privileging
white bodies in fashion textbooks mirrors those deemed qualified to teach fashion. Most faculty job postings do not recognize how racism – and its intersections with classism, sexism and other systems of oppression – restricts who has

access to terminal degrees and senior jobs at fashion brands. Qualifications rarely value knowledge developed outside Eurocentric frameworks of success, such as community activism, youth mentorship and micro-entrepreneurship (Barry 2021). While data from fashion departments are unavailable, universities in the United States and the United Kingdom report that 75 and 77 per cent of full-time faculty members are white. Moreover, only 5.4 and 0.35 per cent of Black and Indigenous faculty members in the United States are full-time, and only 2.8 per cent of Black faculty members in the United Kingdom are full-time (Higher Education Statistics Agency 2021; National Center for Education Statistics 2019).

These oppressive epistemologies sanction the experiences of anti-Black racism documented at the start of this chapter. Fashion education, therefore, requires a radical redesign, not a modification of existing systems. As Monique Mulholland observes in the context of Indigenous models in Australia, current efforts to advance inclusivity in fashion must start afresh because the system is rooted in white supremacy:

Undoubtedly the fashion industry is becoming more 'inclusionary' and multicultural – however, colonial epistemologies construct the normative ground on which inclusion is granted. Discourses of 'whiteness' laid the foundations, built the house, and are now opening the door. As such, through the very logics of 'entrance' and 'invitation,' those entering can never be the same, not quite. History is not left at the door, and the house is maintained by the histories that construct it.

(2019: 213)

Mulholland's metaphor references Audre Lorde's (1984: 110) declaration, 'The master's tools will never dismantle the master's house'. Mulholland makes clear that as long as the dominant Western fashion system gestures toward inclusion, its hegemony remains and maintains because it is built on the logic of white supremacy. If incorporating inclusion into fashion education is akin to building an addition to the house, the exclusionary foundation continues to be at the centre and hold it up. Instead of a foundation built on dominance and discrimination, we need a new foundation constructed on social justice and collective liberation.

After a workshop on social justice at Toronto Metropolitan University (TMU), Rania El Mugammar – an anti-oppression educator, artist and organizer – shared with me (Ben), 'You can either come to the conversation or it comes to you'.[1] For FIT, RISD, UAL and many other schools, the conversation came to them. The flood of comments on their social media channels and the resurgence of Black Lives Matter awakened them to the institutional changes necessary to rebuild the house of fashion education. These schools started assembling equity committees, initiating cluster hires for under-represented faculty members and developing scholarships for racialized students. While these initiatives are essential to create lasting change, this complex work varies across institutions, hinges on the priorities of the current administration, and often leaves out the potential of each faculty member and their pedagogy. This book declares that educators can harness their classrooms to create systemic change in parallel to larger institutional transformations, even when their departments refuse to begin the deeper work of social justice. To echo brown, the micro-changes we make in our fashion classrooms now will cycle up into larger transformations in fashion education and the fashion industry.

To some readers, our focus on changing fashion pedagogy might appear to be reforming the current system rather than transforming it. Following Mulholland's observation, we need to dispense with the university in its current form to build a new house for fashion education. After all, universities are colonial institutions that developed theories of racism and, subsequently, provided grounds for dispossession, oppression and domination (Gebrial 2018). The university must begin anew (Dei Sefa 2016), and rethinking fashion pedagogy will lay the foundation for rebuilding fashion education and the fashion industry. We return to Lorde's provocation, which grounded Mulholland's metaphor, because it offers guidance that different pedological tools can start this rebuilding process. Lorde (1984: 110) observes, 'The master's tools will never dismantle the master's house'. In our context, fashion pedagogy rooted in Eurocentric logic will never dismantle the intersectional structures of oppression that construct white, thin, non-disabled, cisgender and heterosexual people as normative and superior in fashion schools. As such, radically different teaching tools that contest the terms upon which dominant fashion exists can equip us with the knowledge and skills to dismantle and rebuild the house.

There are challenges and complexities when endeavouring to bring about social justice and decolonization from within the academy (Cote-Meek 2020).[2] Indeed, the stories in this book are not those of utopia; social transformation is a painful, messy, contradictory and slow journey. The authors share their frustrations of doing this work inside higher education. Yet they also suggest that these moments open possibilities to rethink fashion pedagogy and enact change in the classroom. The more of us who 'chip, chip, chip' away at exclusion through our teaching, the more our collective teaching becomes a transformative force that can, ultimately, crack 'the old block' of the dominant fashion system (Ahmed 2016: n.pag.). Our pedagogical tools offer paradigms and practices that can be used to lay different blocks and build a different house.

## Situating ourselves as editors

For the past decade, we have been living in parallel: we worked to bring about change in our classrooms at different fashion schools and at different times.

We experienced different degrees of resistance and success, forcing us to take unique paths in our careers as educators. We connected over our mutual effort to make body inclusion standard practice in fashion education and came together to co-edit this anthology because we knew our efforts weren't isolated. Many of us believe pedagogy can transform fashion education, the fashion industry and the world. It was time to assemble, amplify our collective intelligence, exchange our knowledge and support each other to create new precedents for fashion education. Sarah Cheang and Shehnaz Suterwalla (2020) remind us that positionality must be foregrounded to transform fashion education away from Eurocentrism. Educators must work on vulnerability, accountability and relationships with one another. In this spirit, we locate ourselves and share how we have come to this book.

### Ben Barry

I am a white, queer, disabled, Jewish, thin, cisgender man who currently lives and creates on the land of the Lenape Peoples. In 2012, when I was just finishing my Ph.D., the School of Fashion at TMU hired me into a tenure-track position of assistant professor of Equity, Diversity and Inclusion. One of my first assignments was to redevelop and teach a mandatory first-year course on fashion theory. The previous syllabus focused on European narratives with little discussion around topics of social justice. I redesigned the course to challenge dominant Eurocentric fashion boundaries; to consider how our positionalities inform our thinking and design practices; and to centre worldviews and bodies that were marginalized. My objective was to work with students to expose taken-for-granted tropes and favour plural understandings of fashion. I also worked with senior colleagues to redesign the first-year fashion curriculum to introduce body size diversity across the foundational design and illustration classes. The outcome was that first-year students learned to draw, pattern-draft and create garments for people with various physiques.

In 2018, I was appointed as Chair of the School of Fashion at TMU after receiving early tenure three years before. I applied for this position with the intention of heeding the social justice frameworks that had shaped my teaching to help guide the school's overall curriculum and culture. After a year of consultations with faculty members, staff, students, alums and industry partners, we collectively developed three principles for the school: inclusion, decolonization and sustainability. These principles would guide our priorities and decision-making, including course development and delivery, faculty hiring, and student recruitment effects and support systems (Barry 2021). In July 2021, I was appointed Dean of the School of Fashion at Parsons School of Design. My goal is to draw on my experiences at TMU and support the community to centre social justice in the fashion curriculum and culture. To date, my colleagues and I have introduced a new school vision, completed a faculty cluster hire in fashion design and social justice, and launched new courses on topics including Indigenous fashion and fat fashion design.

As I write about my journey, it is evident that my academic experience has been relatively smooth and successful within a relatively short time. Senior colleagues supported me, and the administrators who hired me agreed to my proposed changes and provided the necessary resources. This is not to say that I did not face resistance. However, I overcame it because, in large part, my positionality has granted me structural privileges and societal benefits. My embodied privilege as a white, thin, masculine-presenting, cisgender man with limited care responsibilities conforms to the normative model of who is considered a leader and, as a queer man, who is considered a leader in fashion. My disability is not visible, and so colleagues might not know unless I disclose it to them. I also hold a Ph.D. in Management. This education further legitimizes my embodied recognition as a leader and reduces 'concerns' that my plans are 'radical' by enveloping the presentation of social justice within the logic of business.

For example, when I began at TMU, students had to classify their graduating collections as menswear and womenswear, but many students did not want to narrowly gender their work. When I advocated for a non-binary option, I was met with resistance: 'That is not how the fashion industry works'. I responded: 'The purpose of fashion education is not to serve the fashion industry; it is to lead it'. I think my framing of social justice as 'leadership in the fashion industry', as said by a white cisgender man with a Ph.D. in Management, carried with it a masculine authority and coding of dominance of education over industry. If the same response came from someone with a different positionality, it might have been perceived as challenging and threatening to the worldviews of those with more conservative values. I presented a more sanitized version of social justice that likely quelled unease about revolutionary change.

With this awareness, I do my best to always pay close attention to how my privileges grant me advantages as I move in fashion education. I am committed to leveraging my positionality to bring about structural changes as well as to make them visible to overturn this pattern of advantage. I approach my work with the intention of prioritizing the experiences of those who are the most marginalized and supporting their pathways in fashion school.

### Deborah A. Christel

In 2012, I started my academic career as an assistant professor in a small fashion department. Two years later, I relocated to a tenure-track position at a larger research institution. I was excited to shift to a research institution with more resources and eager to see their advancements in fashion education. As I familiarized myself with the curriculum, I realized that the faculty taught the same material I had studied a decade earlier as an undergraduate. Despite significant social movements and changes in the fashion industry, the curricula failed to keep up. Even more worrisome, the faculty seemed uninterested in updating course content to meet the demands of the industry.

In my attempt to forge ahead and contribute to building an inclusive department, I faced resistance, social isolation and a rigid hierarchical structure. Unfortunately, my age, gender and social justice pursuits pushed me out of academia. I think it began when students started advocating for more plus-size methods in other courses, but some faculty members perceived it as an annoyance or perhaps an attack on their competence. I received comments such as, 'That is not how the industry works, we make sample sizes in an eight', and other remarks that I 'shouldn't come on too strong about teaching plus-size'. A department chair told me to 'choose my battles carefully and to make sure the benefit of winning is worth more than the cost of possibly losing'. In hindsight, this was a threat to my existence in academia; as the youngest female and only junior faculty on the tenure-track, and at the time, a recent sexual assault survivor, I faced multiple obstacles in my pursuit of an academic career. While my thinness, whiteness and cisgender provided many privileges, I faced pushback, less than reasonable expectations as a junior faculty and disfavour when I did not meet them. I also felt incredibly frustrated with the dominance of white male definitions of scholarship, particularly the rationalist theoretical paradigm, and I felt my applied plus-size research was viewed with scepticism and devalued. Faculty told me that publications in high-impact journals were critical to tenure, and I should co-author with more established senior faculty. While my research was the first of its kind, it did not align well with my colleagues' areas of interest.

It was standard practice that senior faculty vote on who advances through the tenure process. Sadly, my third-year review stated that my research was not high-impact. Despite publishing several peer-reviewed articles, including my publication about the Average American woman's body size (Christel and Dunn 2017) that was referenced in the *New York Times*, on *Good Morning America*, by Tim Gunn on NPR, *Forbes* and several other well-renowned publications, my research was viewed as low-impact and inadequate for tenure. I questioned my ability to create social justice for fat bodies in academia.

As I write my story, I worry I may be perceived as an *angry woman* who is complaining. My purpose in sharing is not to de-emphasize those with more significant challenges. Women are viewed as emotional or unfounded when they express a negative experience. Men, in contrast, are perceived as goal-oriented and strategic in their response behaviour. I hope my story sheds light on the disadvantages experienced by myself and other junior faculty who research social justice and fashion. After three years, academia pushed me out for my unwillingness to comply with outdated practices taught by tenured faculty and under the guise that my research was not of value. I needed to choose; do I stay as an adjunct faculty or leave the institution. I agonized about abandoning students eager to learn; on the other hand, I knew I was not welcome by those in power. It was clear; fashion education was not quite ready to adapt. I decided to leave and start my own business, Kade & Vos.

If you are a faculty member feeling unsupported in your progressive agenda, connecting with other faculty in your situation will be invaluable. My network was limited to Fat Studies and Women Studies departments, with a deficient fashion network to lean on. I felt isolated trying to push for size inclusion in a discipline that was unwilling to modernize. Perhaps I would have further advanced inclusive fashion practices at a different institution or at another time. That is not to say my work is without value. While it feels small at times, when hearing from former students about their incredible progress in the fashion industry or academia, it reminds me that the ripples of our work are not lost.

We acknowledge our experiences are tethered to gender, race, class and other social locations of privilege and disadvantage, and changing systems is not a linear or quick process. While our experiences differ, we are cognizant of our shared privileges as white, thin and cisgender people. We realize that other folks might not have been hired into faculty positions due to racism, fatmisia and other forms of discrimination. We hope this book might inspire other fashion educators – particularly those without our privileges – to expand upon our aspirations and desires for fashion education.

## Style and structure of the book

This book bears witness to knowledge that comes from lived experience. Each of the following seventeen chapters subverts colonial academic practice by sharing emotion, vulnerability and personal narrative (Cheang and Suterwalla 2020). We hope these chapters amplify the possibilities, struggles and complexities of liberatory fashion education and cultivate a more inclusive field. To this end, we asked contributors to consider including 'calls to action' in which they offer guidance about how readers might advance social justice in their teaching and university. Some contributors offer support for introducing similar pedagogical changes in their classroom, while others recommend strategies to those experiencing resistance to their proposed transformations. Irrespective of the specific advice, the underlying message in the calls to action is that change happens when we share our experiences and learn from each other.

We originally divided this book into three sections, a common practice in edited collections. As the chapters developed, we discovered that the categories no longer represented the final contributions. There was no simple approach to divide this book because individual chapters discuss multiple oppressions, span subject areas and mobilize various pedagogical strategies. We also felt uncomfortable dividing chapters when the proposed pedagogies deeply resisted narrow classifications and manifestations of power, whether constructing or arbitrating knowledge. Therefore, we decided that each chapter should exist both independently and as part of the entire group. Heeding brown once again, we hope this micro-decision suggests a larger practice in which inclusive fashion education breaks free of narrow categorizations and empowers us to make our own connections between subjects, practices and experiences.

In Chapter 1, 'Humanizing Blackness in fashion education', Krys Osei shares her lived experience navigating anti-Black racism within predominantly white fashion institutions while also championing fashion pedagogy that centres the multiplicity of Black fashion narratives. She shares her pedagogical approach of advising Black fashion students and working with them to document the histories of Black creatives at Central Saint Martins. In Chapter 2, 'Indigenizing fashion education: Strong hearts to the front of the classroom', Riley Kucheran hosts a roundtable with two student teaching assistants, Isabella Pellegrino and Cindy Wu. Their conversation explores Riley's first year as a faculty member, where they revised and designed four fashion courses to apply a decolonized philosophy and centre Indigenous ways of knowing.

In Chapter 3, 'Queering the fashion classroom: Intersectional student perspectives', Michael Mamp shares how he teaches fashion history through inter-sectional LGBTQ+ perspectives. Co-authored with students from the course–Alicia Johnson, Alexis Quinney, Austin Reeves and Joshua Simon–the students describe how the class impacted them. Lauren Downing Peters offers a re-thinking of the current fashion theory curriculum in Chapter 4, 'Theorizing fat oppression: Toward a pedagogy of empathy, inclusion and intentional action'. Desiring to create fashion pedagogy as a tool for fat liberation, she notes that fashion theory can help students gain a critical and embodied understanding of systemic size oppression. In Chapter 5, 'Reflections of a fat fashion faculty member', Carmen N. Keist shares her lived experience as a self-identified fat fashion professor. She analyses survey results from students to understand their perceptions of her and provides examples of how she has addressed their fat stigma.

In Chapter 6, 'Pattern-cutting without cultural appropriation', Greg Climer and Kevin Almond explore how they have taught fashion design students to address cultural appropriation in pattern-cutting courses. They recount how most pattern-cutting courses rarely question how common western pattern-cutting practices benefit from cultural hierarchies and colonialism. They offer creative approaches to interrogate and intervene in these exploitative practices. In Chapter 7, 'Diversity in fashion illustration: An oxymoron, don't you think?', Colleen Schindler-Lynch explores her process of developing a fashion illustration course that includes fat, disabled and other bodies. She examines the standardization of proportion in fashion illustration and provides pedagogical strategies for inclusive fashion illustration.

In Chapter 8, 'Fashion pedagogy and disability: Co-designing wearables with disabled people', Grace Jun recounts her work developing and teaching fashion courses that centre disability experiences. She offers strategies for how faculty members can facilitate equitable and accessible collaboration between fashion students and disabled people in the classroom. In Chapter 9, 'Decolonizing the mannequin', Tanveer Ahmed describes how dress-form mannequins legitimize societal and cultural hierarchies. Within an undergraduate fashion course, her chapter reveals how traditional fashion tools perpetuate racist and heteronormative ideals. She teaches students to question the roots of the methods and tools used in fashion school.

In Chapter 10, 'A starting point for fat fashion education', Deborah A. Christel highlights the dominance of weight bias in fashion curricula. She shares her experience teaching a plus-size swimwear design course and the process of guiding students to address their implicit beliefs about fat people. Her chapter offers a starting point for teaching fat fashion design and shares strategies for educators who encounter resistance in working for systemic change. In Chapter 11, 'Black Lives Matter: Fashion liberation and the fight for freedom', co-authors Brandon Spencer and Kelly Reddy-Best describe their experience co-developing a course about Black fashion histories and cultures at a primarily white university in the rural United States. Spencer shares his experiences as a Black male fashion student, and Reddy-Best shares her experience as a white female faculty member who is committed to anti-racist allyship. Together, they document their process of co-creating this course and its impact on students and the community.

In Chapter 12, 'Designing for drag', Sang Thai uses the format of a podcast interview to share his experience teaching a fashion design course in which students collaborated with emerging Indigenous drag queens in Australia to create costumes for the queens' performances. Thai shares how the course helped students have meaningful conversations about gender binaries, body proportions and cultural appropriation. Chapter 13, 'Curating empowerment: Negotiating challenges in pedagogy, feminism, and activism in fashion exhibitions', is written from the perspectives of faculty member Denise Nicole Green and five graduate students, Jenny Leigh Du Puis, Rachel Getman, Chris Hesselbein, Victoria Pietsch and Lynda Xepoleas. They reflect upon Green's course in which the students curated a fashion exhibition about how women have used dress to assert their political rights and occupy their rightful positions in public space.

In Chapter 14, 'Beauty to be recognized: Making the fashion show accessible', Ben Barry and five students – Johnathan Clancy, Bianca Garcia, Robin Chantree, Avalon Acaso and Anna Pollice – describe a course where students designed a fashion show that was grounded in access. They illuminate how fashion educators can expose ableism in fashion event planning courses and combine theory and practice to advance social justice. Mal Burkinshaw shares his strategy to embed inclusion into fashion education in Chapter 15, 'A diversity network: Industry and community collaboration for inclusive fashion design education'. He describes the evolution of his work from redesigning fashion curriculum to developing a network of fashion educators, creatives and professionals.

In Chapter 16, 'Redesigning dignity: A collaborative approach to the universal hospital gown', Brittany Dickinson and Lucy Jones highlight how inclusion is incorporated into a functional fashion design course – a context that is unique from ready-to-wear apparel. They describe their course in which students partnered with a health-wear company to redesign the standard patient hospital gown. By creating an emotional connection with patients, the students developed designs that met the needs of the wearers and caregivers. Lastly, in Chapter 17, 'Fashion exorcism: A journey in community-centred design', JOFF recounts his transition from a Jehovah's Witness to a fashion design creative to faculty member. He describes his development of a collaborative fashion design course where marginalized voices drive the design process. The chapter reviews three iterations of this course where students collaborated with incarcerated youth in Rikers, trans youth in Harlem, and fat, disabled and older people.

## *Join the revolution for inclusive fashion education!*

Transformation in fashion education is underway. The small-scale actions presented here are among the first efforts taken to change archaic practices of inequality in our field. Each chapter shares inclusive fashion pedagogies that value a plurality of worldviews and bodies and use fashion as an act of politics and world-making. brown (2017: 18) shares, 'Imagination gives us borders, gives us superiority […] I often feel I am trapped inside someone else's imagination, and I must engage my own imagination in order to break free'. While a narrow and harmful imagination has constructed most fashion curricula, each chapter demonstrates how the classroom can engage students' imaginations – exposing and freeing them (and us) from the dominance of thinness, whiteness, Eurocentrism, hetero-patriarchy and non-disabled supremacy.

The chapters open spaces for dissent by proposing different content and methods for teaching fashion. *Fashion Education* offers a different vision of fashion education – a vision of what fashion education ought to be.

Undoubtedly, we have fallen short in presenting this vision. Our positionalities and privileges have given us the time to work on this book while also, we know, limiting our perspectives. The narratives and strategies shared in this book are by no means exhaustive. Voices and viewpoints are missing. We think of colleagues whose work, teaching loads, financial and professional precarity, exhaustion and burnout, the COVID-19 pandemic and health concerns have made writing impossible at this time. In particular, we know these experiences are lived disproportionately by women and femme people, queer and trans people, disabled people, Black, Indigenous and people of colour and especially people at these multiple intersections. Moreover, this book is written from the position of educators and students at universities in the Global North. It contributes to the project of social justice by sharing fashion education interventions originating from this context. Future volumes should amplify narratives that centre fashion pedagogies from Latin America, Asia and Africa.

Pedagogical resources exist to support fashion educators in general (Kent 2018) and those who want to ground curricula in environmental sustainability in particular (Gwilt and Rissanen 2011; Fletcher and Grose 2012). *Fashion Education* is uniquely grounded in social justice and woven with anti-racist, fat, crip and decolonizing pedagogical approaches for fashion design, business, communications, theory and history. We hope you try out and build upon the practices shared in this book. By assuming these practices and making them your own, you will enrich them and, as brown (2019: n.pag.) observes, 'make critical mass solid enough not just to demand change, but to become change'.

*Fashion Education*, therefore, does more than document the individual journeys of faculty members who teach fashion through the lens of social justice; it seeks to scale them into a revolution by fostering a space for educators to share their struggles, successes and strategies. We hope their courage invites and inspires new practices for navigating our universities. You might be the only person advocating for inclusion in your department, but you are not alone in this work. We are a united movement of fashion educators bringing about systemic change. May the following chapters 'map out terrains of commonality' that ignite new pedagogies of transgression in your fashion classroom (hooks 1994: 130). Now that this book is in your hands, on your screen or in your ears, let it serve as proof that our critical mass is building and transforming fashion education, one classroom at a time.

## NOTES

1. Toronto Metropolitan University was formerly called Ryerson University. The previous name valorized a creator of the Canadian Government's Residential School System that forcibly removed Indigenous children in Canada from their families with the aim of

assimilating them into Euro-Canadian culture. The children were subject to torture, physical and sexual abuse and death, and the schools enacted the attempted genocide of Indigenous people in Canada.

2. We recognize the contested, plural and contextual meanings of decolonization (Gebrial 2018). On Turtle Island, where we are located, decolonization must prioritize Indigenous land and sovereignty in North America (Tuck and Yang 2012).

## REFERENCES

Ahmed, Sara (2016), 'Feminism and fragility', 26 January, https://feministkilljoys.com/2016/01/26/feminism-and-fragility. Accessed 17 December 2010.

Barry, Ben (2020), 'How fashion education prevents inclusivity', *Business of Fashion*, 6 January, https://www.businessoffashion.com/opinions/workplace-talent/op-ed-how-fashion-educationprevents-inclusivity. Accessed 6 July 2021.

Barry, Ben (2021), 'How to transform fashion education–A manifesto for equity, inclusion and decolonization', *International Journal of Fashion Studies*, 8:1, pp. 123–30.

brown, adrienne maree (2017), *Emergent Strategy: Shaping Change, Changing Culture*, Chico: AK Press.

brown, adrienne maree (2019), 'Build as we fight', 10 November, http://adriennemareebrown.net/2019/11/10/build-as-we-fight-remarks-from-the-2019-american-studies-association-annual-meeting/. Accessed 6 July 2021.

Cheang, Sarah and Suterwalla, Shehnaz (2020), 'Decolonizing the curriculum? Transformation, emotion, and positionality in teaching', *Fashion Theory*, 24:6, pp. 879–900.

Christel, Deborah A. (2018), 'Fat fashion: Fattening pedology on apparel design', *Fat Studies*, 7:1. pp. 44–55.

Christel, Deborah A. and Dunn, Susan C. (2017), 'Average American women's clothing size: Comparing national health and nutritional examination surveys (1988–2010) to ASTM international misses & women's plus size clothing', *International Journal of Fashion Design, Technology & Education*, 10:2, pp. 129–36.

Clare, Eli (2017), *Brilliant Imperfections: Grappling with Cure*, Durham: Duke University Press.

Cote-Meek, Sheila (2020), 'From colonized classrooms to transformative change in the academy: We can and must do better', in S. Cote-Meek and T. Moeke-Pickering (eds), *Decolonizing and Indigenizing Education in Canada*, Toronto: Canadian Scholars, pp. xii–xxiii.

Dei Sefa, J. George (2016), 'Decolonizing the university: The challenges and possibilities of inclusive education', *Socialist Studies*, 11:1, pp. 23–61.

Fletcher, Kate and Grose, Lynda (2012), *Fashion and Sustainability: Design for Change*, London: Laurence King Publishing.

Freire, Paulo (2000), *Pedagogy of the Oppressed*, 30th-anniversary edition, New York: *Continuum*.

Gebrial, Dalia (2018), 'Rhodes must fall: Oxford and movements for change', in G.K. Bhambra, D. Gebrial and K. Nişancıoğlu (eds), *Decolonising The University*, London: Pluto Press, pp. 18–36.

Gwilt, Alison and Rissanen, Timo (eds) (2011), *Shaping Sustainable Fashion: Changing the Way We Make and Use Clothes*, London: Routledge.

Higher Education Statistics Agency (2021), 'Who's working in HE?: Personal characteristics', https://www.hesa.ac.uk/data-and-analysis/staff/working-in-he/characteristics. Accessed 6 January 2022.

hooks, bell (1994), *Teaching to Transgress: Education as the Practice of Freedom*, New York: Routledge.

Kent, Holly (2018), *Teaching Fashion Studies*, London: Bloomsbury.

Lorde, Audre (1984), *Sister Outsider: Essays and Speeches*, Berkley: Crossing Press.

Mulholland, Monique (2019), 'Sexy and sovereign? Aboriginal models hit the "multicultural mainstream"', *Cultural Studies*, 33:2, pp. 198–222.

National Center for Education Statistics (2019), 'Full-time faculty in degree-granting post-secondary institutions, by race/ethnicity, sex, and academic rank: Fall 2017, fall 2018, and fall 2019', https://nces.ed.gov/programs/digest/d20/tables/dt20_315.20.asp?current=yes. Accessed 6 January 2022.

Reddy-Best, Kelly L., Choi, Eunji and Park, Hangael (2018a), 'Race, colorism, body size, body position, and sexiness: Critically analyzing women in fashion illustration textbooks', *Clothing & Textiles Research Journal*, 36:4, pp. 281–95.

Reddy-Best, Kelly L., Kane, Laura, Harmon, Jennifer and Gagliardi, Nika R. (2018b), 'Critical perspectives on fashion textbooks: Representations of race, gender, and body', *International Journal of Fashion Design, Technology & Education*, 11:1, pp. 63–75.

Schuller, Kyla (2018), *The Biopolitics of Feeling: Race, Sex and Science in the Nineteenth Century*, Durham: Duke University Press.

Strings, Sabrina (2019), *Fearing the Black Body: The Racial Origins of Fat Phobia*, New York: New York University Press.

Tuck, Eve and Yang, Wayne K. (2012), 'Decolonization is not a metaphor', *Decolonization: Indigeneity, Education & Society*, 1:1, pp. 1–40.

# 1

# Blackness in Fashion Education

*Krys Osei*

## Genesis

The beauty that resides in and animates the determination to live free, the beauty that propels the experiments into living otherwise. It encompasses the extraordinary and mundane, art and everyday use. Beauty is not a luxury; rather it is a way of creating possibility in the space of enclosure, a radical art of subsistence, an embrace of our terribleness, a transfiguration of the given. It is a will to adorn, a proclivity of the baroque, and the love of too much.

(Hartman 2019: 3)

Beauty provides the template for my existence. It is a luscious imaginative dream-scape that offers solace in a world that was not built to accommodate my presence (Hartman 2019). As a young Black girl who grew up in the Washington, DC metropolitan area, born to a Ghanaian father and a Cameroonian mother, the curation of my aesthetic presentation was fashioned by two of my favourite artists and their transcendent music video catalogues. Whether it was the soul-tingling gospel poetics of Mariah Carey's flawless *Butterfly* album or basking in Missy Elliott's futuristic delight and iconography in *The Rain (Supa Dupa Fly)*, my journey of being and becoming was rooted in their audiovisual portraits of womanhood, as I made sense of the world and wove a tapestry of belonging through their discographies. As an adult, my love for Mariah Carey and Missy Elliott still runs deep. Even now, there are certainly moments when I wrestle with how significantly commercial aesthetics have shaped the contours of my existence. It is a laborious undertaking to push beyond the confines of its trivialized and superfluous subjection, as the master narrative of beauty relentlessly criticizes my (and other Black women's) desire for beautification, reducing the essence of such embodied intergenerational practices to mindless – if not immoral – conspicuous consumption (Hernandez 2020).

I am writing this piece in the final year of my Ph.D. at Goldsmiths, University of London, and as a fashion educator at two creative arts and design colleges that are part of the University of the Arts London: Central Saint Martins (CSM) and London College of Fashion. I actively dedicate my self-reflexive intellectual labour to mapping geographies of how diasporic Ghanaian women in London, Accra and Washington, DC use glamour, fashion, and self-styling practices to cultivate beauty in their lives while faced with brutality (Hartman 2019: 32). Although purpose, charisma and whimsical joy animate this experimental scholarship that harvests memory from material objects and divests from conventional paradigms of knowledge production, I am often stifled by the everyday ricochet of violence that envelopes my existence and the lives of Black people in different parts of the world. Tethering these words together in May 2020, the relentless spectacle of the Black death plays on loop at whirlwind speed like a collective circuit of unimaginable grief. In tandem with the destabilizing effects of a global pandemic, which has magnified inequalities and disproportionately claimed the lives of Black people, writing this contribution is no easy feat. Yet, the trajectory of calculated assault on Black lives is nothing new. Instead, the systemic devaluation of our lives, this 'pervasive climate of anti-Blackness' (Sharpe 2016: 106), is part and parcel of the white supremacist organizing principles of the world. Engineered by what Black feminist literary scholar Saidiya Hartman (2007: 7) refers to as the afterlife of enslavement as 'a racial calculus and a political arithmetic that were entrenched centuries ago'. Hartman shows beyond doubt how the afterlife of enslavement manifests its wrath through 'skewed life chances, limited access to health and education, premature death, incarceration, and impoverishment' (Hartman 2007: 6).

And still somehow, I remain propelled by hope through the pockets of rebellion that sprout and build an archival presence of otherwise – propelled by the innovation and ingenuity of our collective self-preservation and how the syncopated rhythms of Black futurity (Campt 2017: 2019) incubate the lineage and legacy of our cultural expression. Propelled by the Black imagination that dares to hold on tight to the transformative, yet fleeting, moments of joy and beauty that unhinge us from the brutal dispossession and harm that we continue to endure in our inhabited geo-cultural settings. Although my tethered desire for beauty and fashion cannot rectify these relentless state-sanctioned atrocities, it does carve out crucial moments of reprieve that are vital to surviving the friction of interlocked oppressive frameworks – both in my personal life and within the context of my role as a fashion educator.

I fought through a suffocating battle of enclosure while teaching conventional Media Studies during the 2017-18 academic year as a graduate teaching assistant in the Department of Media, Communications and Cultural Studies at Goldsmiths, University of London. In conjunction with my Ph.D. studies, I pursued teaching at the undergraduate level to gain the necessary experience and pedagogic guidance and to assemble the diasporic Ghanaian beauty archives. I wanted to know if a traditional learning environment would effectively receive my transatlantic mixed method and world-making approach. While I did not have the opportunity to deliver lectures in this entry-level position, I was encouraged to incorporate my research on geographies of Black fashion cultural heritage in seminars to generate student debates concerning the relationship between the sociopolitical construction of identity through popular culture. Week by week, I was met with heated sparks of resistance from white students who were uninterested, if not repulsed, by the idea of validating fashion as an everyday 'incubator of possibilities' (Hartman 2019: 348). Week by week, I was met with hostile opposition to entertain foundational discussions about fashion's unique vantage point in tethering threads of belonging in cross-cultural diasporic visual communication beyond material consumption. Week by week, my frustrations abounded with the rigid barriers of the enclosure from a conventional Media Studies year group writing off fashion as a minor figure, a deficient power structure that is exclusively to blame for the ongoing ecological crisis, and an optical machine that wreaks unforgivable havoc on human self-esteem.

On the one hand, I applaud my seminar students for remaining steadfast in their valid critiques of the fashion system and its detrimental impact, inextricably tied to capitalist modes of destruction that shapeshift across time and space. However, their rapid-fire teardowns were void of openness and alarmingly failed to grasp the multiplicity of truth that marks the vitality of Black cultural identity and diaspora (Hall 1990). Their persistent inability to engage in rich and generative conversations about the dynamics between fashion, race, ethnicity, gender, social class, sexuality and cultural geography flattened the capacity to facilitate a horizontal pedagogic space that recognizes beauty as the antidote to violence in the lives of Black folks who 'create life and make bare need into an arena of elaboration' (Hartman 2019: 6). Their holistic disillusionment with centring fashion as a communal dreamscape circuit; a toolkit for people to author themselves into the world, levitating into the possibility of personhood that no longer is defined by the social space in which they have been placed (Tulloch 2016; Hall 2016) was lost in total rejection. This underappreciated quiet material revolution in the lives of Black folks showcased an inability for students to read between the lines, as their prescriptive gaze of what constitutes revolutionary ideals was unable to reconfigure fashion as a political tool of (de)construction and (re)configuration in the survival and imagination of the African diaspora (Tulloch 2016). There were no luscious dreamscapes of beauty and imagination to be found within this claustrophobic ring of the enclosure; a bizarre teaching experience that taught me the power of standing firm in my convictions. As a Black woman scholar and educator, I refuse to be riddled with shame in dispensing beauty and fashion as my executive assistants to rewrite the terms of what is possible, to improvise and outwardly challenge the social and political construction of my identity that is sentenced to dwell in a looming house of servitude and bondage in whatever direction I travel (Hartman 2019: 228). Aesthetics and self-styling – in theory and embodied practice – make up my quintessential toolkit to birth freedom against the waves of totalizing pillage and destruction; such is 'the untiring practice of trying to live when you were never meant to survive' (Hartman 2019: 228).

## Central Saint Martins: Resuscitating beauty from enclosure

The terms of teaching within a traditional Media Studies context were fixed with little to no room for flexible dialogue that detracted from essentializing the field of critical beauty and Fashion Studies. As I sit and reflect on the volatile and emotionally taxing encounter as a seminar leader at Goldsmiths, perhaps my expectations from students were misguided while teaching in a university where a fashion concentration is not offered. Redirecting my specialist knowledge and teaching efforts to a notable fashion education institution, Central Saint Martins, was a necessary manoeuvre that offered a refreshing learning atmosphere where fashion and creative arts degree programmes are the focal point of the student experience. It was riveting to join CSM in September 2018 as an associate lecturer in Cultural Studies for the Fashion, Textiles and Jewellery Programme. The moments I cherish forever are rooted in becoming a dissertation supervisor for a majority Black British student cohort completing their final year on various Fashion Design and Communication Pathways. The culmination of my story at CSM is about excavating documentation from nowhere, about breathing life into an archive that descended from somewhere. It is a collaborative story about generating beauty from a two-fold sense of enclosure. It is a story about a horizontal pedagogic practice that recognizes teachers and students as co-curators of freedom (hooks 2003). Together, we move with the audacious spirit that orchestrates a resounding chorus of Blackness at CSM, effectively holding space for current Black fashion students and the cohort of Black graduates that once occupied the corridors before them. Collectively, we have birthed a space of communion that will serve as more than a footnote in the master repository of fashion's cultural history.

I was giddy and intrigued two weeks before the first round of face-to-face meetings with my dissertation students in October 2018. Simply reading through their various fashion degree pathways caused a wave of exhilaration: Fashion

Communication and Promotion, Fashion Journalism, Fashion Design with Marketing, Fashion Knit, Fashion Womenswear and Fashion Menswear. As I continued to scroll through the proposals with delight, their working abstract descriptions stopped me in my tracks. From Humane Afrofuturism, to Caribbean migration transfiguring Black British beauty narratives; to an interrogation of the Americanization and fetishization of Black masculinity in contemporary British popular culture; to the systemic whitewashing and commodification of sustainability in high and fast-fashion; to inventive Black British sonic epistemologies of transcendence through sound and sociality in London through the work of director Jenn Nkiru; to a self-reflective photo-essay dismantling colourism and ethnic hierarchies in Peru through fashion, art, sexuality and religion; to a cross-cultural examination of intergenerational African diasporic visual communication through Black British fashion designers, Grace Wales Bonner and Mowalola Ogunlesi, and African American visual artists, Kerry James Marshall and Faith Ringgold – I was awe inspired and deeply moved by my soon-to-be students and their critical engagement with beauty, fashion and aesthetics as incubators of possibilities, *'yielding a thousand new forms and improvisations'* (Hartman 2019: 230, original emphasis) to contextualize cultural geographies of Blackness in motion.

### Inhale, exhale, repeat

I smiled ear to ear in my southeast London flat that evening and processed the forthcoming energized reintroduction to teaching. Inklings of hope were set on autopilot for the next two weeks as I eagerly awaited to concretize what already appeared to be a transformative teaching experience on paper. Thursday, 11 October 2018, marked the first day of my dissertation tutorials and the onset of my career at CSM. The time on my vintage gold-tone Casio watch read 10:23a.m. when I noticed the abstract echo of bustling footsteps alongside group chatter ricocheting from the adjacent corridor into my booked tutorial room, D122. A handful of final-year Black fashion students peeped their heads into the space on a mission to verify that I was indeed a Black woman. An awkward five-second pause became a symphony of laughter unleashed by our disoriented amusement. The kind of inimitable laughter that possesses your entire body. The kind of laughter that unleashes a reservoir of tears. The kind of laughter that erupts from the deepest wells of sadness and blossoms into immeasurable zeal. This laughter was the kind that brings you back to life after you have died from a thousand heartbreaks within the circle of enclosure and have now located sanctuary in communal endurance – you see, 'inside the circle it is clear that every song is really the same song, but crooned in infinite variety, every story altered and unchanging: *How can I live? I want to be free. Hold on*' (Hartman 2019: 349, original emphasis).

Our two-fold inventory of suffering on the margins as teacher and student was catalogued on that inaugural day of dissertation tutorials and updated in the following months. Yes, I was ushered to the forefront of representation for my students. Still, I welcomed it with open arms following the scolding anti-fashion brigade of white students I faced weekly within a conventional Media Studies environment in the prior academic year. It was fabulous to no longer feel like an academic outcast. It was a beautiful and collaborative undertaking that satisfied our joint appetite for interactive dialogue – with a Black fashion scholar-educator and Black fashion students unearthing a rarity of intellectual counselling in the enclosure of British academia. Free from razor-sharp stares of contempt and whiteness doubting our capacity to teach and learn, we were each other's mirror, an overdue reflection saturated with the cultural competence to co-curate a moving portrait of freedom.

In the transcript below, two of my former dissertation students graciously reflect on their experiences at CSM – Rhea Dillion (she/they) is an interdisciplinary artist who graduated from the BA Fashion Communications and Promotion Programme, and Kacion Mayers (he/him), a fashion journalist, graduated from the BA Fashion Journalism Programme. They reflect on me as their supervisor and the multi-layered anti-Black racism they faced within the imperial enclosure of CSM.

**KACION:** I had students that literally compared me to a slave when I was a student at Central Saint Martins, literally [...] white students joking about comparing me to a slave [...], and no one said a thing. It was a roller coaster; it was intense. Going into that space as a Black student, you must really know yourself. If you don't, [CSM] can really play with you. There were instances where I could have just questioned myself until the point where I crumbled. I worked through a lot of imposter syndrome. CSM was a completely bizarre world that was new, and I welcomed it, but there was also this friction of never completely belonging. I always felt a bit uncomfortable in terms of how people would perceive me, or I was always very conscious of how I would come across, no matter what, you know? I thought that there was always a special or different kind of perception when I did things in comparison to students that weren't Black. It was so, so wild.

**RHEA:** So wild! And actually, going through this process of reflection, we're both now able to contextualize and find the language for the treatment that we experienced. I realized the other day that I was bullied for a period of time with people in my class. That's wild. I've had friends say to me, coming to apologize on the behalf of other people [...] being like: 'By the way, how you were treated for this period of time wasn't cool, and I just wanted to say

21

something about it'. And I'm like, wow, thank you… you know? I hadn't even found the language for the treatment I received that was so …

**KRYS:** Normal?

**RHEA:** Yeah, super normal [because we were studying fashion], but it also feeds into racist tropes because white students are able to talk freely, while I'm expected to be able to fend for myself in any space because I'm the tough darker-skinned girl who has carried the weight of the world since eternity and it's disgusting. The entire teaching philosophy at CSM is to really break you down and then build you back up … but it was very much more apparent that Blackness (and I guess we'll say a non-whiteness) was really in charge of its own rebuilding. I really do think that there were so many more ways the university could have assisted with our process of rebuilding.

**KRYS:** I cannot deny the emotional shock after meeting a group of you before my first official [dissertation] tutorial. It was hilarious, terrifying, magical – all the mixed bag of feels when you know something is going to be a moment […] a life-altering encounter to cherish for years to come. I do have to say that at that moment, I instantly felt the need to be inadvertently tied to CSM for the foreseeable future, even though it was literally my first day on the job [group laughter].

**RHEA:** Oh my God, I feel like we scared you! Because I swear Kacion had his dissertation meeting first and came to tell me all about it, and I was like: 'No way!' I was really excited to have a Black woman, yeah. And then it all got around to the other Black students, and we were like: 'Oh my God!!' It was so wild […] you were the first teacher that was a Black person, let alone a Black woman, that I had for a sustained period of time.

**KRYS:** And did you feel that it was easier to talk through your dissertation themes with me? In terms of not having to explain your Blackness and/or the reasons you choose to equally platform race, gender and queerness into your writing and creative practice?

**RHEA:** Yeah, of course. It was also a form of counselling, you know? [Laughter] There's no question about the importance of having you in our final year. I think when you've gotten to the final year of university, we've finally figured out who we are and what we're about […] and it was helpful to have those conversations beyond the theoretical level of the dissertation by talking to someone who understood us. Like, finally, you know? I don't know [...] we shouldn't have even had to wait for that long. But since we did, the final year was definitely the best time to have your input, support and guidance.

**KACION:** The best quote I've ever read concerning the argument of representation is by Junot Diaz. This is paraphrasing because I can't remember exactly what he says, but it's something along the lines of: If you look in the mirror and you don't see your reflection, it's almost like you're a vampire, you're a monster, and when you do see a reflection it's like you become human again (Stetler 2009). I do exist, we do exist, and we are not monsters hidden in the shadows somewhere and can't come out in the daytime. We need to see ourselves, and white students take that for granted because they always see themselves. It's vital because a lot of our work is very personal and self-reflective – it was such an important experience. So major. But despite it all, CSM has shaped me; it made me. It broke me down and put me back together again completely. That school [...] switched the way I thought about things and completely flipped the way I approach things. It made me a lot more open. It made me question a lot of good and bad things. It was necessary. In order to be where I am today, it was necessary.

I sit back and process the parallel, yet contradictory, worlds of enclosure that fostered our gravitation to build a community space as dissertation supervisor and dissertation student. I entered the walls of CSM in October 2018 urgently seeking to escape the frustrating tensions that ensued from having to conceal fashion as the centrepiece of my life for the sake of surviving within a university department dominated by whiteness, masculinity, and age-old existing paradigms that were incompatible to bring both my thesis to life, alongside effective pedagogic practice led by matters of the heart (Hall 1990: 223). With swift abruptness, my body had reached its cutoff point where it could no longer inhabit the violence of being made to obscure an essential part of my everyday life. Self-fashioning is a necessary, daily sensory aesthetic experience in which the materiality of textures, silhouettes and fabrics that glimmer with the spectacle of adornment tend to the ruptured complexities that encompass my past, present and future diasporic existence as a Black woman. At CSM, I shed the deadweight of feeling like an academic outcast from the eternal validation of fashion education. Within lectures and seminars, I could openly teach how postcolonial fashion narratives catapult themselves into the political sphere, reckoning with the horrors of colonialism and intergenerational memories of geographic violence. My transcendent dissertation experience of supervising students who mirrored my reflection was boosted by the freedom to encourage cohorts of fashion students to think more expansively about Black identity. It has been truly rewarding to expose these curious minds, whose curriculum design is rooted in the Eurocentric canon of visuality, to the dynamic tapestry of Black diasporic fashion systems and aesthetics. From Windhoek, Namibia, to Kinshasa, the Democratic Republic of Congo, to Accra and Ghana, I remain delighted and fulfilled at the immeasurable impact of teaching transnational cultural geographies of fashion, which break open new pathways for understanding the beauty of dispossessed communities that refuse Blackness as a monolith and the centuries-old tales of inferiority that populate the consciousness of fashion education.

## Building the archive: Thinking through cultural expression

Becoming a fashion educator at CSM has allowed me to flourish personally and professionally. I write these contemplations no longer as an associate lecturer but as a full-time faculty member at the University of the Arts London – with my position divided between lecturer of Cultural Studies at CSM and practitioner in Fashion Media Production at the London College of Fashion. Within British academic universities, it is abnormal for Black women to hold a job with such security. The vast majority of Black women struggle to navigate the whiplash of precarity through the cycles of hourly paid fixed-term contracts that are unclear about career advancement opportunities. As an associate lecturer, I exchanged this raincloud of uncertainty by remaining present in the heartfelt resonance and the knowledge exchanged between my Black dissertation students and me. I teamed up with Rhea Dillion and Kacion Mayers to assemble our incubator of possibilities before their time at CSM closed as 2019 graduates (while my endpoint also loomed in the balance).

This incubator came to life as a labour of love – a passion project woven together through a series of conversations devising ways to improve the Black student experience at CSM. After reporting the racial violence experienced by my students to senior management, there was an outpour of support for my advancement to assume the role of academic lead for the initiative. Funded by the programme director for fashion and the associate dean of student experience and enhancement, *Building the Archive: Thinking through Cultural Expression (BTA)* was born in the summer of 2019. As a collective, we platform Black creative practitioners and their contributions to visual culture, often overlooked and under-acknowledged in arts and design higher education. With a specific focus on Black CSM graduates, we are establishing a lineage of Black past, present and future that healthily challenges the colonial constructs of fashion education. We encourage students through engagement with personal examples of career success in the creative arts while widening students' knowledge of contemporary legacies of Black cultural expression. We are not seeking to actively disrupt the notion of the university as a safe space; instead, we are creating our own space that shakes the room with the audacity to tap into the pulse of the radical Black imagination, envisioning a better, more sustainable future.

The conversation within the *BTA* is about the futurity of Blackness at CSM. At the same time, it pays homage to those who have survived and continue to survive under the western governance of the university landscape. This incubator of possibilities pays respect to those who have had the boldness to craft exquisite beauty while working against engrained oppression systems that manifests in the air we breathe. We have existed and will continue to exist, sharing the energy and spirituality that ensues by constructing our own portrait of fashion education that ruptures the master narrative of whiteness. This resounding chorus of Blackness is 'a vehicle for another kind of story [...] an assembly sustaining dreams of the otherwise' (Hartman 2019: 348).

> **KACION:** It's really difficult to locate these histories with the Black student population at Central Saint Martins [...] we're still struggling to establish that repository of Black students. And it's like, why? You can all look up to Galliano; you can all look up to all these other alumni and everyone else [...] all the way back to before CSM was even called CSM, before the school became part of University of the Arts London. It's interesting that you can locate that documentation from all the way back, but to search for one Black student from the 1980s, it's like: 'Oooof [...] hmm ... let me get back to you in two weeks with that' [laughter]. But why? Why is that?

The inaugural *BTA* conversation took place on Wednesday, 20 November 2019. Osei Bonsu, Curator of Modern and Contemporary Art of Africa at Tate Modern, graced us with his presence to discuss his journey into creatively embracing his Welsh and Ghanaian cultural heritage, his artistic inspirations and his motivations. After the reception at the King's Cross site, I was astonished to learn this was the first time Osei was invited to speak about his extensive career as a London and Paris-based programmer, cultural critic and art historian since he graduated from CSM with a BA in Culture, Criticism and Curation in 2013.

> **KACION:** Osei is literally heading up the Tate [...], redefining the museum experience! And yet, we don't appear to have any Black role models that are invited to come back to speak about their success stories. It's always white students or white people in the industry. And don't get me wrong [...] that engagement is still inspirational, but we do need to see ourselves.

**RHEA:** Bringing our voices together was nothing short of magical, and the tone that was set with Osei was liberating. It's funny because we thought Osei would be more reserved because of the Tate Modern and it being another colonial institution, but he was just so open and happy to be in the space of community, which is what we had hoped for anyone that is invited to speak. It was really magical how naturally all of our voices came together so perfectly to facilitate that.

Black students filled the room to capacity and intently listened as Osei delivered an energized discussion about the healing power of creating a community with other Black students – just as he did with Ibrahim Kamara, the Sierra Leonean stylist, former Senior Editor at Large at i-D Magazine, and current Editor-in-Chief of Dazed Magazine. He delved into the importance of following your intuition and taking advantage of student resources to minimize the expensive cost of materials. Furthermore, he passionately unearthed his greatest rewards and challenges in the whitewashed curation profession. Our second *BTA* conversation occurred on Wednesday, 26 February 2020, with the charismatic British-Ghanaian multidisciplinary artist, photographer and filmmaker Campbell Addy, who graduated in 2016 with BA in Fashion, Communication and Promotion. In line with sentiments expressed by Osei in November, Campbell also voiced an interest in being more engaged with CSM to dismantle the hierarchy of gatekeeping in the industry. Jessica Gianelli (she/her), a Caribbean American student from New York City in the MA Fashion Image programme, heartwarmingly reflected on attending the talk with Campbell Addy and the impact of seeing him front and centre stage as one of CSM's iconic success stories (Figures 1.1–1.3).

**JESSICA:** I knew who Campbell was, but growing up in the US, with a Caribbean background [...] there was always a stigma around what Black people can and can't do, especially in terms of school and career – the traditional idea of being a doctor or a lawyer, etc. It was so motivating to hear about the similarities with him growing up in a Ghanaian family [...] wanting to pursue photography and working in fashion. Seeing Campbell there, like actually seeing him in person [...] because yeah, you see stuff on the internet, but seeing him there [...], he seemed like such a super normal guy [laughter] in comparison to other practitioners that I've seen talk. He was so open and down-to-earth, and it made me feel like of course, I can do it too. You know what I mean? And just to be in the room full of people that were like me as well was really comforting. I don't think I had ever sought out a space in London that was for Black creatives, but being there felt really, really inspiring to see what he does and the raw

FIGURE 1.1: Group of students seated listening to Campbell Addy, 2020. Courtesy of photographer Caleb Azumah Nelson.

honesty he brought by talking about the difficulties of attending CSM, the racism he's fought through to get to where he is...the experience was incredibly empowering. I really did walk out of the door and thought to myself: Okay, I can do this too.

My beautiful and transformative experience as a fashion educator at CSM will stay with me forever. It has been a place of ascension, a culmination of gorgeous encounters with my Black dissertation students that have laid the groundwork for a pedagogic approach rooted in the spirit of 'Black aliveness, or the poetics of being' (Quashie 2021). My dissertation students from 2019 and 2020 continue to grow and pursue their creative desires, and our teaching dynamic has blossomed into meaningful friendships that expand beyond the physical boundaries of the classroom. One day we'll look back at this learning community and the students who have taken flight from the corridors of CSM. We saw how the connection created from our archive of overlooked people reinvigorated Black fashion students and filled their hearts with hope for the future.

FIGURE 1.2: CSM graduates; Rhea Dillon, Campbell Addy and Kacion Mayers, 2020. Courtesy of photographer Caleb Azumah Nelson.

As a Black woman fashion scholar and educator, I learned that experimentation and openness cultivate possibilities for more equitable learning and teaching environments. I did not embark on this journey into fashion higher education with a blueprint for establishing and developing an initiative such as *BTA*. In collaboration with Black students who gravitated towards resuscitating memories from the ruptures, silences and misconstrued narratives that obscure the multiplicity of who we are, I leaned into the essence of invention and improvisation. In March of 2021, I attended an online nonfiction writing workshop by Nadia Owusu, a Ghanaian-Armenian-American writer and urbanist, entitled 'Healing the Body, Reimagining the World'.

She encouraged us to embrace authorship as an open-ended portal where we can revise harmful narratives into something transformative. To Black fashion educators seeking to plant seeds of optimism, I offer you this: 'The only ground firm enough to count on is the one we write for ourselves. What would the world [of fashion education] look like if we were to illuminate the truths that have been purposefully hidden?' (Owusu 2021: n.pag.). Guided by the urgency to shuffle the arrangements of what is possible within the confines of my authority, it must be noted that this exercise of the invention does not majestically blossom without

FIGURE 1.3: CSM graduates; Rhea Dillon, Campbell Addy and Kacion Mayers, 2020. Courtesy of photographer Caleb Azumah Nelson.

the imminent threat of discipline. But, if we understand the language of fashion as an extension of ourselves, an encryption of beauty that hosts ancestral codes of imaginative subsistence, I will remain hopeful while harvesting the tangible increments of our collective (re)imaginative and healing efforts in worldmaking.

> All meaningful love relations empower each person engaged in the mutual practice of partnership. Between teacher and student love makes recognition possible; it offers a place where the intersection of academic striving meets the overall striving to be psychologically whole.
>
> (hooks 2003: 136)

## REFERENCES

Campt, Tina Marie (2017), *Listening to Images*, Durham: Duke University Press.

Campt, Tina Marie (2019), 'Black visuality and the practice of refusal', *Women & Performance: A Journal of Feminist Theory*, 29:1, pp. 79–87, https://doi.org/10.1080/0740770X.2019.1573625.

Hall, Stuart (1990), 'Cultural identity and diaspora', in J. Rutherford (ed.), *Identity: Community, Culture, Difference*, London: Lawrence & Wishart.

Hall, Stuart (2016), *Cultural Studies 1983: A Theoretical History*, Durham: Duke University Press.

Hartman, Saidiya (2007), *Lose Your Mother: A Journey Along the Atlantic Slave Route*, New York: Farrar, Straus and Giroux.

Hartman, Saidiya (2019), *Wayward Lives, Beautiful Experiments: Intimate Histories of Social Upheaval*, London: Profile Books.

Hernandez, Jillian (2020), *Aesthetics of Excess: The Art and Politics of Black and Latina Embodiment*, Durham: Duke University Press.

hooks, bell (2003), *Teaching Community: A Pedagogy of Hope*, New York: Taylor & Francis.

Owusu, Nadia (2021), 'Healing the body, reimagining the world', seminar delivered online, 9–30 March, https://catapult.co/Nadia-Owusu/past_classes. Accessed 28 March 2023.

Quashie, Kevin Everod (2021), *Black Aliveness, Or A Poetics of Being*, Durham: Duke University Press.

Sharpe, Christina (2016), *In the Wake: On Blackness and Being*, Durham: Duke University Press.

Stetler, Carrie (2009), 'Junot Diaz: Man in the mirror', nj.com, 26 October, https://www.nj.com/entertainment/arts/2009/10/junot_diaz_man_in_the_mirror.html. Accessed 22 January 2022.

Tulloch, Carol (2016), *The Birth of Cool: Style Narratives of the African Diaspora*, London: Bloomsbury.

# 2

# Indigenizing Fashion Education:
# Strong Hearts to the Front of the Classroom

*Riley Kucheran*

## Introduction

The name of this chapter plays off a phrase often attributed to Tȟašúŋke Witkó (Crazy Horse), but came to me via Anishinaabe comedian and writer Ryan McMahon. The full version goes: 'It is a good day to fight! It is a good day to die! Strong hearts, brave hearts, to the front! Weak hearts and cowards, to the rear!' (McMahon 2018). This version, spoken before the Battle of the Little Bighorn in 1876 (Ambrose 1989), is a tragic reminder of the violent dispossessions of Indigenous territories during colonization. Yet the words still offer teachings about bravery, humility and care. Reflecting on the complex and emotional work required for reconciliation or decolonization McMahon said,

> those of us with strong hearts, that hold strong hearts, come to the front of the line and lead, show us, do something, anything. But when you get tired and when you get hurt, take a break and be good to yourself, be kind to yourself. This work burns you out and it will burn you out, it should, it's hard, it's heavy, if you're doing it right.
>
> (McMahon 2018: 9)

My first year of teaching definitely burned me, and while the politics of this burn-out requires attention, McMahon reminds me that strength requires care, and with care comes a sense of hope and a desire to get back up.

The following chapter introduces my journey as a Nishnaabeg (Ojibwe) student, teacher and fashion researcher; how I developed my decolonizing teaching philosophy; and how I applied it to my first year of teaching as an assistant professor of design leadership in fashion at The Creative School, Toronto Metropolitan University. Furthermore, part of the positionality includes a roundtable with two graduate assistants, Isabella Pellegrino and Cindy Wu, who discussed how I designed or refreshed four fashion courses, the effectiveness of the changes and how other fashion educators could follow this path. The courses covered a broad range of fashion design, history and management topics and thus represented the field's interdisciplinarity. My mission was to inspire the next generation of fashion leaders with Indigenous knowledge. My challenge was thinking about fashion education through a decolonizing lens and implementing radical shifts. My priority during this first year was survival.

Linda Tuhiwai-Smith (1999) observed in *Decolonizing Methodologies* that we need to transcend 'survival mode' and make space for creativity and innovation (159). My privileged position in the academy afforded me the creative space to test four new courses, to attempt the kind of 'epistemic reconstitution' that exposes students to the 'cracks in the colonial matrix of power' (Mignolo and Walsh 2018: 228), and then follow-up with practical ways in which we might dismantle the colonial, capitalist and hegemonic fashion system through resistance, refusal and *resurgence*. I can claim some success with the former, but the latter is ongoing.

## *Author location*

At the beginning of any course, I ask students to *locate themselves*, an Anishnaabe ethical practice that identifies where someone's voice comes from (Absolon and Willett 2006). Location often includes a snapshot of one's relationships to community, land and spirit, and the political, economic, environmental and social elements that shape one's life. Doing honestly with good intentions can establish a trusting relationship (98). It encourages self-reflection and reaches students at a deeper level, and here it also introduces my collaborative, student-centred approach to teaching. I identify as someone who came into my Indigeneity later in life: I was raised as an assimilated Canadian in a middle-class suburban household and then spent a decade in urban Toronto. I have mixed Ukrainian-Ojibwe heritage, but I did not grow up connected to the culture of my mother's community, *Biigtigong Nishnaabeg* ('Pic River First Nation'). Intergenerational traumas disrupted cultural knowledge transmission, particularly in the residential school system, detailed in the Truth and Reconciliation Commission (2015). The commission's final report was released when I was a master's student, and it made me deeply confront my family histories, previously unspoken and filled with shame. I often conceptualize my location within the Anishnaabe theory and practice of *biskaabiiyang*, ('a kind of personal decolonization or returning to one's self, in which someone looks back on their life, identifies how they've been colonized, and then reinterprets traditional teachings to promote a better way of life that nourishes ourselves and our communities') (Simpson 2011: 50–1). Biskaabiiyang is a daily practice of affirmation and commitment, an individual and collective process – both personal and necessarily public and political. Through biskaabiiyang I started to come into myself as a Two-Spirit person, a unique gender category with specific ceremonial and social roles. Cree scholar Harlen Pruden gave me a teaching about Two-Spirit people as powerful mediators or translators, which deeply resonated with me. I consider myself a connector with an intense commitment to centre the voices of others — which comes from profound humility. When I think about the enormous brilliance of 'traditional' or 'Indigenous knowledge', I recognize my ignorance and position myself as a co-learner.

I further locate my decolonizing perspectives with a professional background in fashion retail and interest in luxury management research. Before academia, I worked in the fashion industry and saw first-hand the well-oiled machines of global fashion brands. While gaining an appreciation for management, I also saw the industry's dark side. I realized I was part of the problem and contributing to the environmental damage and social inequity that fashion creates. I became deeply motivated to fix the fashion industry and found a community of critical thinkers and practitioners who had laid the groundwork. I then gained new insights from Indigenous perspectives, which I was denied growing up. I realized I needed to be at the intersection of dismantling mainstream fashion systems and supporting Indigenous designers in rebuilding our systems. Indigenous fashion, I learned, nurtures better relationships with the land and its relations through environmentally sustainable and socially responsible practices rooted in Indigenous values like respect and reciprocity (Kucheran et al. 2021). My background in retail and luxury saw the enormous potential of Indigenous fashion in economic terms with important cultural value because Indigenous fashion embodies our epistemologies and mobilizes relations needed for decolonization.

## On decolonizing fashion education

In a recent manifesto for equity, inclusion and decolonization, the former department chair of Fashion at The Creative School declared, 'fashion education is in a state of emergency', in part because 'our curricula and culture are grounded in the continuing legacies of the transatlantic slave trade and European colonization' (Barry 2021: 124). I wholeheartedly agree and make concerted efforts to unpack the deplorable ideological origins of Fashion Studies as a precursor to any study of fashion. Still, the urgency of this work cannot detract from the slow, strategic and systemic movement needed. To be clear, we can have both. Barry points to immediate steps institutions can take to cease ongoing and redress historical harm in fashion education. It reminds me of Indigenous approaches that foreground care and consensus, which takes time. Historical Nishnaabeg social movements like *Chibimoodaywin*, a migration of Nishnaabeg people across the Great Lakes region, took ten generations over 500 years. It was a resistance, mobilization and resurgence that involved sacrifice, persistence, patience and slow and painful movement (Simpson 2011). I tell students it took more than 500 years of colonization to get us here, and while I hope it doesn't take another 500 years to decolonize, it will still take generations. Chibimoodaywin required spiritual vision, intellectual and political leadership, and 'skills to excite, inspire and illuminate our peoples to unite and commit to transforming that vision into sustained and committed action' (67). Therefore, I characterize my teaching approach as long-term 'seed planting', which Cree Elder Joanne Dallaire told me is akin to the adage that 'wise people plant trees for shade they'll never sit in'. Seed planting is an exercise in groundwork, nurturing and patience. It requires that conditions are right and a safe space is created for students to receive key ideas and unlearn hard truths. Then, we must equip them with individual and collaborative tools to tend to these ideas with an acknowledgement that they won't bear fruit immediately.

I fear that a new 'decolonizing fashion' is itself re-colonizing. In a rush to claim decolonization as a hot new disciplinary pursuit, I wonder what structural inequities are reproduced by the academy, which, as Andrea Smith points out, is a 'structurally colonialist, capitalist, and white-supremacist institution' (Smith 2014: 214). The danger is that domestication turns an overtly political movement into a 'culturalist project of representation' (Simpson and Smith 2014: 11). In fashion, this could mean an uncritical inclusion of Indigenous students in inherently violent and anti-Indigenous colonial fashion systems. It becomes essential that any decolonizing discourse does not act as settler moves to innocence (attempts to alleviate settler guilt) by focusing solely on decolonizing the mind without direct material consequences like repatriation of stolen Indigenous land and reinstatement of Indigenous sovereignty (Tuck and Yang 2012: 19). Decolonized fashion is, therefore, a lofty goal: arguably incommensurable and something we cannot take lightly.

How do we get there if we accept that decolonization does not happen in the academy and is not achieved by encouraging Indigenous participation in destructive fashion systems? I describe decolonization as a dual process – a simultaneous dismantling of colonial systems and a rebuilding of Indigenous worlds. I urge non-Indigenous allies to focus on the former, see their role in decolonization as harm reduction, and shift power and resources to the Indigenous leaders working on the latter. It's critical to understand that decolonization is already happening on the ground and in communities, generated from the everyday practices of Indigenous individuals and collectives that are actively building decolonized futures. It is primarily up to Fashion Studies to get out of the way, listen and support Indigenous fashion resurgence, and create and hold space for Indigenous leadership without co-option and commodification. Decolonization must be recognized and understood as an expressly material process that involves financial reparations and the return of stolen and occupied Indigenous land – at a minimum. No notions of 'reconciliation' or repair can meaningfully begin until the deep inequities caused by colonization are addressed[1]. I think decolonized fashion education looks like a 'bush school'. Inspired by my time at *Dechinta* ('in the bush'), a Dene land-based institute (Ballantyne 2014), I now see Indigenous fashion education not bounded by walls and Eurocentric ideologies but grounded in land-based epistemologies[2]. Rebuilding this world encapsulates ideas of resurgence, a set of decolonizing theories from the latest generation of English-speaking Indigenous academics that are separate but aligned with the decoloniality thinkers of Latin America (Wilson 2006: 55–53, or see Simpson 2017 and Corntassel 2018). Full immersion on the land was not possible in the immediacy of developing new courses, so I introduced students to *resurgence*, an Indigenous 'strategic concession' (Kovach 2009: 40), but the Indigenous fashion bush school remains my guiding compass.

## The courses

FS8001: Graduate Methodologies courses cover survey theories, methodologies and methods from a wide range of creative, humanities and social scientific perspectives. My main addition to the syllabus was a *decolonizing methodologies* week, but we also used decolonizing perspectives to think about all methods. We began with the assumption that western research has historically weaponized marginalized communities, which set the stage to think about Indigenous research design and ethical protocols as a model for fashion research that contributes to a more inclusive, equitable and sustainable fashion system. FDL140: Managing Small Enterprises is a broad introduction to running Small and Medium-sized Enterprises (SMEs), a business model that lends itself to more environmentally conscious and socially responsible ventures. I introduced students to various skills needed to craft a business plan. Simultaneously, the tone was set by exploring Indigenous approaches to management, SMEs in 'the social economy', and learning from BIPOC entrepreneurs and case studies (Klassen and Taylor 2019). I substantially redesigned the next course, *FSN203: Design History*. Previously, the class took a chronological art history approach focused exclusively on the European *canon of good design*. The revised course kept some of this content on iconic nineteenth and twentieth century British and American design. I added critical design history and decolonization and used a variety of designed objects to thematically study colonialism, capitalism, industrialization, racism, gender and sustainability in design and design history. *FSN502: Fish Skin Tanning* was originally a studio course for producing leather and fur accessories. I shifted to focus on fish skin, a globally accessible Indigenous materiality. We learned how to respectfully engage in a spiritually and politically significant practice that offers a sustainable solution to textile production and food waste. Importantly, we discussed the intricacies of cultural appropriation and students were encouraged to engage their own cultural heritage so that we could incorporate Nordic, Mediterranean and Asian fish skin tanning traditions.

## Roundtable

**RILEY:** *Boozhoo* ('hello')! Let's start with introductions now that you've both read my 'location'.

**ISABELLA:** Sure, my name is Isabella Pellegrino. I was born and raised in Canada; however, all my grandparents immigrated here from Italy in the late 1950s. Therefore, I connect deeply with Italian culture, its sense of community and family values. Sustainability has always been at the forefront of my mind, specifically because of the gardens my grandparents make every summer and the fond memories I have playing in them, picking the food and watching my grandmothers cook. So the idea of slow fashion, based on ideals of the slow food movement, which originated in Italy, really resonates with me (Clark 2008: 428). Over the last year, my interest changed to focus on dismantling capitalist western beauty ideals that the media continues to portray and how fashion trends shape what's considered beautiful rather than any inherent being. I found myself bringing your decolonizing knowledge, Riley, into this work and my everyday life. I loved spreading important teachings to undergraduates, like how to think critically not only about design, fashion, history, etc. but also about our broader economic systems. I got to see change happening through your teaching methods. I read the essays of the fashion industry's next generation, and we saw some powerful ideas taking shape.

**RILEY:** *Miigwech* ('thank you')! That's really the point: decolonial processes like resurgence are about the personal, intimate, daily acts that contribute to a revitalization of traditional lifeways or the restoration of relationships

(Corntassel 2018: 29), so in your case, it might be a matter of returning to growing your own food or rekindling the relationality you shared with your grandparents. Of course, resurgence is always restricted by our embeddedness in systems of oppression, like colonialism and capitalism, so that dual process of dismantling and rebuilding systems is needed. And your story reinforces that decolonizing processes are for everyone. I'm reminded of the negative feedback when I used the term 'White', but here you are, a White/Italian person who can see the need to dismantle systems built with ideologies of white supremacy. Cindy?

CINDY: I'm Cindy Wu, I am Chinese-Canadian, born in Montreal, raised in Ottawa, and I'm currently based in Toronto. I majored in economics and minored in psychology. I did a year in the MA fashion programme before switching to an MA in media production. I'm currently working in a business-to-consumer marketing role outside of academia. There always seems to be an overarching people-centric theme throughout my research and work. As a graduate assistant, I've helped with two *Creative Industries* courses and two *Design Leadership* courses, all of which I quite enjoyed. I think being a graduate assistant puts you in an interesting position between students and professors, so you get to empathize with both. Especially this year, you could tell that everyone was having a really difficult time. I've learned how important it is just to be accommodating and empathetic whenever possible. At the same time, I've realized it's also impossible to have a course and teaching style that appeals to everyone. While the content of your course was fantastic on its own, it was also inspirational to see how well the material was received by students and the types of SME projects they were pitching as a result of the course.

RILEY: That's great. I think it's interesting and important that even though you're no longer in this academic space, your people-centric work aligns with decolonization. It reminds me that everyone has a role when integrating decolonizing pedagogies. Whether you're a fashion designer, a marketer, or in human resources, everyone can cultivate better practices to care for 'all our relations' — to use an expression from the Indigenous people in North America and Hawaii (LaDuke 1999). In your case, communication (or perhaps an urgent lack of communication?) is an important issue to grasp and work on from the industry.

CINDY: Yes, I'm in the tech-startup space, but it's important to me that the company I work for has values aligned with my own. For example, inclusivity is not only something we promote internally, but it's also something we project outwardly. When clients make certain asks that are discriminatory or exclusive in nature, we push back rather than accept everything to appease the client.

**RILEY:** You're not just embodying those good values but educating others. And that's actually the takeaway I wanted for students, too, to leave our school with a set of values or critical competencies to lead the industry with.

## *Graduate Methodologies – Fall 2020*

**RILEY:** Let's start with our seminar on methodologies because, in that course, we think through the application of decolonizing theoretical frameworks. I approach methods with a more unified decolonizing praxis, in which theory and practice inform and complement each other. I always see research through a lens of colonization, informed by personal experiences and resurgence theories. I'm open and honest about seeing every method in a particular way. When I use ethnography, I'm acutely aware of the harm that researchers inflict on Indigenous peoples globally. I work hard to correct the inherent power imbalances by collaborating with participants as much as possible and encouraging a reciprocal relationship. In my methodology training, I often ask, 'how can we fix this method' so that it stops inflicting harm or so that Indigenous people can use the method for Indigenous goals of sovereignty? I believe any method can be approached in this kind of way, with a more caring and empathetic lens. I find it difficult to approach fashion methods objectively, given my location, but I don't think that's a bad thing. Isabella, how did you receive this? Were you happy with the perspective on methods?

**ISABELLA:** I was, and I believe these perspectives should be taught alongside many more courses. My past experience stressed that everything must be objective when in reality, nothing is. This western, linear form of research is very one-sided. Whereas your class set the tone for decolonizing research and the value of voice. The very first thing you did was take a long time to locate yourself, and listening to your experience really stuck with me. It broke down the barriers between professor and student and inspired conversations to get to know and better understand the different parts of our classmates. It allowed us to centre ourselves and make us think about why we're here as students and individuals. It fostered a deep reflection that became the grounds for our future research goals.

**RILEY:** The word 'honesty' comes to mind? Locating ourselves is a deeply honest ice-breaker activity. I'm glad it inspired conversations within your cohort outside of the classroom. Collaborations and mutual support are so important in graduate school, so those, along with a solid foundation of who you are and where you want to go, are a potent combination. Let's talk about my choice not only to add an *Indigenous week* or *decolonizing week*, which I felt was too isolated and tokenistic. I think a targeted week is a good first step, but it can't be one module. How did decolonization frame other parts of the course?

**ISABELLA:** In *oral history week*, you taught us that getting to know someone or learning something within an hour-long interview is impossible. It takes several hours or days, weeks, months for a good relationship to form and for knowledge to transfer. So, the decolonizing perspective allowed us to place ourselves within research that encourages respect and that respect produces better research. It drew our attention to the power relationship between the participant and the person holding the clipboard during interviews. We talked about co-creation and working with participants to co-create the best data rather than just interviewing them.

**RILEY:** And collaboration can happen at all stages of the research process: identifying goals, coming up with research questions, analysing data, writing. This level of participant involvement is difficult when you can't offer compensation, which is another power dynamic that needs addressing, but a heightened level of care and respect for participants that recognizes power is a good place to start. And Cindy, you took an older version of the course a few years ago; what do you remember?

**CINDY:** This was almost three years ago, so I don't recall there being much on Indigenous perspectives or decolonizing fashion specifically. We read papers mostly from a western context or perspective. In terms of course content, what I remember most is learning about autoethnography, social media research and conducting semi-structured interviews with 'wardrobe analyses'. These tangible examples of methods in practice or with popular cultural contexts were key for my comprehension.

**RILEY:** The wardrobe interview assignment (wardrobe analyses) has been a staple of the MA fashion programme, and I think it works because the best way to learn about methods is to start doing them. If you want to learn about interviewing, conduct an interview, and you will learn quickly what to say and what not to say. I'm now thinking about how Indigenizing or decolonizing a course or curriculum takes time and collaboration between instructors who 'leave their mark' over the years. Ben Barry's work on diversity and body inclusivity expanded our notions of how bodies are fashioned – and that's still reflected in the course. I do wish there was more collaboration or even more communication between instructors and across semesters! I received old syllabi but never checked in with those instructors to ask 'how did it go? What would you change?' Part of the problem is that we're all stressed by the pandemic, but I think we should work towards better relations with colleagues. I have a lot of experience with ethnography and oral history, but I don't do social media research or quantitative research, so I would love to bring in more expertise. We did have some guest speaker specialists, but I had a small honorarium budget, another barrier to bringing people into the classroom. I think this is tied to humility; if I don't know something, I shouldn't pretend to. We should have twelve different instructors with special expertise if there are twelve weeks of methods.

### Managing Small Enterprises – Fall 2020

**RILEY:** This course was brand new and also part of the new fashion management curriculum, which is still being mapped. In that respect, piloting was a great opportunity to test the application of decolonizing theories. The course is an introduction to planning and managing a small enterprise, and I start by recognizing that business schools have fingerprints on a number of ecological crises, 'both a tool for, and product of, shareholder-centric, profit-maximizing and extractionist economics' (Kelly and Hrenyk 2020, n.pag). So, I had specific goals about learning from more diverse and sustainable businesses and encouraging students to propose business plans that address systemic issues in fashion.

I took cues from critiques of power structures inherent in business from Critical Management Studies, which assumes that something is *very wrong* with mainstream business education – that old models based on scientific knowledge and instrumental rationality were too effective (Alvesson and Willmott 1992). One Critical Management Studies suggestion is including more collaboration between critical academics and management practitioners (Perriton and Reynolds 2018: 523) and with pedagogy, a collaborative and concurrent critical reading that provides students with a lens to see structural challenges and disrupt management sensibilities (King and Learmonth 2015: 364–67). This opens space for theory, which has historically been

Marxism, more recently degrowth theory, and I'm now proposing decolonizing theory. Critical reading for us meant global Indigenous management perspectives such as *Nuu-chah-nulth-ah* ('economic systems that take aim at the necessity of growth in capitalism') (Atleo 2015); the Indian concept of *jugaad*, ('a kind of frugal innovation and creative adaptation'), and the South African concept of *ubuntu* ('the recognition that people are inextricably bound in each other's humanity') (Holtbrügge 2013: 4). We looked at enterprises in the social economy that prioritize the social well-being of communities and marginalized individuals without the profit logic of markets (McMurty and Brouard 2010). The tradeoff is that more time spent on theory means less time working on practical applications. Generally, students are quite *woke*, but progression is needed here; it's big-picture thinking before practical application. I wanted to introduce some theories at the front of the course and then get into more details about financial planning, building your team, marketing, supply chain management, product design and retail. There are many components to being an entrepreneur or running a fashion business, so I think that students just got a taste of fashion management. What do you think Cindy?

**CINDY:** I think the outcomes matched your intentions. This was clearly reflected in the types of projects the students pitched at the end and the feedback they left. Many SMEs embodied slow fashion and social or circular economy frameworks, and a lot of students mentioned how much they enjoyed learning about Indigenous management philosophies. In terms of how they were thinking about management, they were asked to think about which industries interested them, what consumers they wanted to appeal to, and what values they held. Many knew they wanted to work with sustainable materials and dyes, but they weren't yet researching which materials and how to source them. They were thinking about the roles in the management structure but weren't at the stage of defining the responsibilities and how the roles interact. This was expected in an introductory course. But several students were thinking a few steps ahead and asking questions like 'what comes next?' and 'how do I implement these strategies?' But upper-level courses can teach those skills.

**RILEY:** We tried to create a *resource bank* for those who wanted more in-depth training, and next year I'll add more. I regret that we might not have progressed as far as some students hoped, I was ready to argue that capitalism is bad, but some students are already coming into the programme with that assumption. Perhaps that's a recommendation for educators; assume your students already want to create slow-fashion, upcycling, non-binary or more inclusive collections. What else?

CINDY: The proposed SMEs were really great overall. It was such a pleasure to see the evolution of their 'lean canvas' business plan (Maurya 2012) and then the 'pitch competition' to see where their minds went after this course. We saw lots of social missions; a not-for-profit closet consulting service that declutters while providing good clothes for homeless populations, a tailoring factory that provides jobs for people who've been displaced by war in Cameroon. Lots of sustainability; denim recycling, T-shirt upcycling, natural skincare, clothing lines with new sustainable fabrics. And inclusivity; adaptive clothing, lingerie with more size range, accessible Black hair care, and a shop for Somali brides.

RILEY: That team had such gorgeous imagery of wedding gowns and the retail environment they wanted to create, full of family-vibes and commitment to celebrating Somali beauty. I think that was inspired by the 'ethnic enclaves' (an outdated term) that we examined, those tight-knit communities like Little Jamaica or Chinatown, which are socially embedded with access to customers, resources and the cohesive identity that encourages solidarity (Brush et al. 2007). The students scouted a perfect location for their bridal shop in an area with many Somali-Canadian businesses. I also remember a proposed e-commerce platform for stores in the fabric district because so many of the owners are seniors who are presumably not tech-savvy. A website would be helpful for fashion students, especially when shopping for fabric online during the pandemic, but I mostly loved their intergenerational commitment. The business was framed as a way to support struggling fashion Elders. We saw so much care and heightened ethics in a lot of these business proposals.

CINDY: Earlier, we were thinking about a resource bank, and having a list of mentors, SME founders willing to have students reach out to them could be beneficial. Many students were pitching SMEs they were currently building or planning on building, so they'd likely be more invested if there was a stronger personal attachment to the material.

RILEY: Which relates back to wishing I had more budget to bring in entrepreneurs and guests with different kinds of expertise. A related key takeaway was not to attempt things you're not good at, but instead to bring in part-time financial officers and part-time human resource representatives and outsource graphic design. A fundamental hope is that students build their own teams while at school. We have skilled designers, communicators, historians, material experts and management students; what if they assembled to launch a business? This returns us to Indigenous approaches that are more community centred and collaborative. Entrepreneurship and the fashion industry are so individualistic – there is that neo-liberal ethos of *doing it for yourself* or the belief in *star designers* who make it big. Students had so many great ideas for businesses. Perhaps the role of the fashion school is to incubate – to facilitate connections and support the launch. I remember telling some students to not let this be just another assignment, to actually do it. Maybe we need a part-two for this course.

**CINDY:** It is really important that students are exposed to these new perspectives. They need a space to dream big, pitch ideas and test concepts with room to make mistakes and not worry about the nitty-gritty. Some of the feedback wished for more detail because they realized 'oh, I'm actually really into this, but what's the next step?' They're already asking for a *Managing Small Enterprises 2*, (part-two).

**RILEY:** Perhaps the bigger theoretical picture comes in part-one when you form teams, ideate some business plans and then in part-two, you start researching and writing. This hints at the overwhelming pace of learning: we simply don't have enough time. Slowing down is an essential component to building a better fashion academy.

## *Design History – Winter 2021*

**RILEY:** For nearly two decades, this course was taught in a very Eurocentric way. It used a single textbook authored by the professor that committed students to memorizing key European designs, a standard chronological art-history approach that began with Victorian England and waded through design movements like Arts and Crafts, Art Nouveau, Modernism, Futurism etc. I tried to completely rewrite the course, which was a bold move that challenged and pushed me. My intention was to start by disrupting that canon of good design and think about design history more critically. I selected new designs for object-based analyses that illuminated themes of Indigeneity, colonialism, capitalism, industrialization, power, racism, gender and sustainability. We started by naming this as a critical challenge to the *traditional approach* of design history. I asked students to (quickly) grasp an entire field, recognize it as problematic, and trust me with this journey pursuing a more critical cultural history of design. I think they did?

ISABELLA: Yes! The student experience was overwhelmingly positive except for that *one* student. Maybe we should start with their negative feedback and get it over with; rip off the BandAid.

RILEY: It does provide some good context. One student took great offence at my course redesign. They called me biased, political and a white-bashing propagandist. They dismissed the content as unfactual, attacked the course structure and organization, called me incompetent, questioned my credentials and said I was 'incapable of forming insightful interpretations'. In retrospect, I learned a lot; there's a lot to unpack. A colleague let me vent and pointed me to Rosenberg's (2015) *Nonviolent Communication*, which reminded me that when students communicate violently, there's something deeper going on behind the scenes. Cheang and Suterwalla (2020) identify the issue succinctly:

trying to engage students in the reasons why they should care about decolonizing involves initiating and supporting difficult conversations that tread a delicate line between enabling White students to face the implications of their whiteness whilst ensuring the emotional labour of providing and receiving call outs is recognized and shared more equally.

(893)

This brings attention to the added emotional labour Indigenous fashion educators will endure: it was bad. I was crushed. Interestingly, their critique latched onto something I said in week one: from a place of humility, I was forthcoming and told students I have some knowledge of design and training in history, but I'm not a design historian per se. Perhaps I was too honest or modest, or maybe that student mistook my humility for lack of qualification. Importantly, I'm not going to revert any of my changes. I found it comforting that others have been thinking about this (Zinga and Styres 2019), so I'll approach white supremacy with a bit more clarification and delicacy, but students still need to understand the factual reasons why Eurocentric design history is dangerous. I'm reminded of titles by DiAngelo (2018), Anderson (2017) and Eddo-Lodge (2017) on white fragility, white rage, and refusing to talk to White people about race, but if I recall my teaching philosophy, I'm here to build Indigenous worlds, not re-centre Whiteness.

44

**ISABELLA:** And that was the response of one person out of 200 students. And as the other feedback shows us, most thoroughly enjoyed this new approach and felt more seen. Can you describe what the course redesign looked like on a weekly basis?

**RILEY:** Well, the heart of the course was object-based analyses that I would conduct every week and discuss with students. My first designed object was the iconic BIC pen. I just went down a design history rabbit hole and came out of the research with a new perspective on the pen, informed by the sociocultural context in which it was designed. Designed in the 1950s and marketed as an essential office tool, the BIC pen reflects the post Second World War economic recovery and expansion, a shifting job landscape to the office, the rise of white-collar professionalism, white flight, the rise of suburbia, racial segregation and the heteropatriarchal nuclear family dynamic. Every week, I included design history that integrated a critical perspective and various cultural intersections. I also introduced Indigenous design philosophies – reciprocity and nature with engineering, for example. We watched a great video about weaving the Q'eswachaka rope bridge (SmithsonianNMAI 2015), which introduces Indigenous values such as honouring Elders and Knowledge Holders, respecting land and waters, community collaboration, ceremony and celebration. And then, we reflected on how the Q'eswachaka rope bridge resists design tendencies like commodification and replication. We further reflected on why Indigenous design is not respected, despite being environmentally and socially sustainable.

We looked at the intersections of design and empire and how important designed objects like ships used to carry enslaved people and the printing presses exported to the empire. There was a week about *capitalism and the Industrial Revolution*, but I highlighted inequities caused by new industrial designs, like the automatic loom, which required child labour to operate. The week on *design and race* helped to locate design as an extractive practice. We spent a substantial amount of time learning about the cotton gin, invented by enslaved Black people but patented by a white American man. Interestingly, we returned to the patent system a few times. I identified it as one of those *cracks* in the colonial matrix of power. I realized it's a key mechanism to maintain power: we saw patent holders take ownership of Indigenous designs based on nature or designs by women. That was a big *a-ha moment* as it explains current situations. In one of the most important years for racial reckoning, we went back in time to see how the cotton gin, which went on to launch the Industrial Revolution, made white men wealthy and left no recognition or compensation for enslaved Black people. We were connecting these dots weekly, each object was an exercise in design's socio-cultural context, and we did some hard work, some unlearning and shaking our acceptance of current systems of oppression.

**ISABELLA:** That overall aim was achieved. I saw it reflected in assignments. You were exploring contexts of objects and concepts you picked, and students were mirroring your methods in their papers. Many shared your critical edge. Two analyses that stood out were the cotton gin patents and cabinets of curiosities. You mentioned them in the week on *Indigenous design* when we started seeing objects being *collected* and then copied for mass production. So much of fashion history is tied to museums; it was fascinating to learn about the awful origins of collections. The idea of colonizers going around the world collecting Indigenous objects to display – that mental image of buildings filled with stolen objects was a major crack that stuck with me.

**RILEY:** That week we explored the design history of kayaks. I contrasted a Eurocentric design history of the kayak, where it gets *discovered* in a European ethnology museum, is re-produced and patented, and eventually becomes a billion-dollar aquatic sporting industry – with an Anishnaabe design story of the kayak; In which *Nanabozho* ('the first being') journeys around the world to build relations and in the process designs a canoe based on observations of the natural world, the hull shape of *gich-manameg* ('whale') and *amik* ('beaver's') paddle-shaped tail. In that story are lessons about the Indigenous design philosophy and being in respectful, recipro-cal relations with nature. There are two very different worldviews here, two approaches to design, and we paused to reflect on inequitable power imbalances created when those worlds clashed. It's not Indigenous peoples profiting off that billion-dollar kayak industry, that's for sure.

**ISABELLA:** Do you want to talk about your memes?

**RILEY:** Yes! Every *Design History* lecture began with *memes of the week*, a new pedagogical tool. I came across so many fire memes on various social media platforms, and I started noticing memes related to course content. Weekly, I'd screen-grab them for lectures. I was hoping to accomplish a few things, like introducing key concepts in an engaging and light-hearted way. Memes encapsulate so much in an instant; there's so much irony, humour and history. The medium says a lot about the state of communica-tion, the fast-paced bites of information that get disseminated widely – but I think it's a medium students will remember, especially if it inspires critical thinking. The 'American textbooks' meme (Figure 2.1) speaks to so many issues. There's this whitewashing of elementary-level history (that I personally grew up with) – it's true that all our textbooks look like that, which speaks to those deeper layers of epistemological Eurocentrism to the issue of power, like who writes textbooks, from what perspective?

**ISABELLA:** I think students needed the memes to make key themes more memorable. It lets you laugh at something stupid or ironic, or even laugh at a hard truth, and for a quick second, there's this simultaneous discomfort, perhaps a release of pain? It was an engaging way to introduce students to tough ideas, like the fact that most history is whitewashed.

**RILEY:** The 'Bilbo Baggins why not' meme (Figure 2.2) was used when we arrived at climate change with the consumerist design boom in the 1980s-90s. We had already discussed the concept of planned obsolescence in relation to Apple's endless release of new products rife with bad design (Bogost 2017), but here we focused on consumer electronics waste, the intersections between design and destroying the environment. So many of us have those

No one:

American Textbooks:

FIGURE 2.1: *White Egyptian / American Textbook — Pharaoh Dudebrotep IV of the Chadite dynasty,* 2017. Colour meme photograph. (dontcryformeargentina 2020).

FIGURE 2.2: Stevensongs, *Bilbo Baggins why not meme,* 2021. Colour meme photograph. (stevensong 2021).

drawers – filled with old smartphones and tangled cables – and I wanted to reflect on the disposability of design as an intentional design flaw.

We looked at IKEA's iconic 1996 'chuck out your chintz' advertisement (Fairs 2014), and I tried to propose a holistic understanding of the design's lifespan, to instil a sense of responsibility in design that doesn't prescribe to planned obsolescence or trend-driven seasonality. What if we start from the assumption that we absolutely must consume less?

**ISABELLA:** It helps that you identify the origins of that hyper-consumer disposability, right? There are clear connections to that 1980s-90s tech-era and its associated consumer boom. It's recent. And yes, because we've all generated that electronics waste, there's an emotional reaction.

**RILEY:** Not all memes were related to course content. There was Paul Noth's (2011) 'Nobody ever asks *"How's Waldo?"*' cartoon that was reproduced in countless memes, and we used it to launch a discussion about mental health, slowing down, reducing expectations during a pandemic and taking care of ourselves. Memes were also about keeping things topical – I remember the Bernie Sanders inauguration meme that was combined with the 'This is Fine' meme. I used that to just hit pause and recognize yet another bad piece of news in an unprecedented academic year. To introduce decolonizing theories like 'Land Back', I shared striking graphics of Indigenous-controlled land slowly disappearing from the centuries of colonization until there was only 0.2 per cent of left in Canada. Perhaps I benefit from being a millennial and having some insider perspective on forms of communication that resonate with students, so I'll absolutely continue the practice. I now have a 'meme folder'. Next year I'd like to even assign meme-making as a component of assessment. I'd love to get students to a place where, after writing a lengthy essay, they can articulate the essence of their argument with a single meme. All the better if the meme can go viral and disseminate their learning, which relates to my decolonizing teaching philosophy of enabling education every-where, not just within the academy.

**ISABELLA:** Should we talk about their final assignment?

**RILEY:** I was inspired by a quote from the film *Objectified* (Hustwit 2009), that 'every object tells a story, if you know how to read it'. This encapsulated our study of *Design History* and the object-based approach to revealing cultural history. It connected beautifully to Indigenous methodologies of storytelling. 'Storywork' for Archibald (2008) encodes knowledge or 'the consciousness of people' (26). It's central in the decolonization process of challenging dominant western research in content and form (Archibald et al. 2019; Kovach 2009). I told students that 'yes, every object has a story, but certain stories are marginalized and neglected and those need to be told urgently'. I tried to model that, hoping that students would do this them-selves, with objects and intersections that mattered to them.

**ISABELLA:** I learned so much from students. My favourite were everyday objects. Like your BIC pen, one student wrote about the Maybelline Ultra-Lash Mascara from the 1960s from a feminist perspective. The company was founded on the idea that a woman's worth was based on her beauty and ability to attract men by playing into the male gaze. The student analysed advertisements that included messages about transforming women into ideals, realized that they also encourage gender binary-based consumption, and finished with a critique of capitalizing feminine inse-curities. Another eye-opening paper was about the Skin-Tone Crayola crayon colour, a deceptively simple design and label rooted in racism. The student traced the history to 1903 when the design embodied the belief that people of colour were second or third class citizens, to 1956 when the Crayola Skin-Tone colour name was changed to Peach and how that signalled a change in racial dynamics and then cited contemporary studies about how skin tone consumer labels internalize oppressive racial beliefs and perpetuate white supremacy. It was an incredible story, all through a lens of design history.

**RILEY:** I was also deeply moved and proud of the students. We collectively abandoned that old way of celebrating the canon on aesthetic grounds because even when students did select iconic designs like Marianne Brandt's Bauhaus teapot or an Eames moulded plastic chair, they added critical layers, like the erasure of women from design history (in both cases), or the environmental impact of cheaply made disposable Eames-replicas. My favourite papers came from students who reflected on their heritage, and I think we saw this because I was forthcoming about location and honouring our cultures. One student, inspired by rising anti-Asian sentiments and the racially-motivated Atlanta shooting, told the story of the Mandarin or Chop Suey font. Through graphic design history, they recalled 200 years of Orientalism, the Chinese Exclusion Act, the concept of model minorities, cultural loss and anti-Asian hate, and ended by musing on what Asian solidarity could look like in dismantling American imperialism. Another told the story of the *Bahay Kubo*, (a 'traditional Filipino stilt house'), and beautifully illustrated the tragic loss of architecture rooted in biophilia and kinship by urban planners who 'made colonialism concrete' with city grids, grand imperial outposts and neo-colonial luxury homes; and cognitively through the colonial mentality and a kind of self-exoticism. In the end, they called for a return to a multiplicity of Filipino design identity. Again, incredible.

There were many more: Hollywood villain lairs, environmental domination and the failure of organic design; the hot comb and the complex intersections between upholding racist structures and Black entrepreneurship; plastic bendy straws, ableism and misplaced environmentalism; fitness apps and the neo-liberalization of health. I learned so much, and these examples will make the course much richer next year.

**ISABELLA:** Another example of co-creating course content? I see this intergenerational aspect of 'paying it forward' and improving the course for the next cohort. I gathered that most students enjoyed having autonomy and room to explore critical design history themselves.

**RILEY:** I loved the ability to pick topics that interested me and dive down rabbit holes. But I can see how some might want more structure. To accommodate both, I'll create a bank of objects to choose from. We have lots of examples from this past year. Any other feedback?

**ISABELLA:** The introduction of critical thinking made an impact, and many of the students said they were going to engage with design very differently now. They said the course influenced their design process and inspired them to dive deeper, to design for purpose and with the bigger picture in mind. The ability to contextualize objects rather than simply memorize details about them was most appreciated, so much so that they recommend introducing more critical perspectives and cultures into the course. Overall, students ended the course eager to make changes within the design or fashion industry. Some students wanted more information on how to make careers out of implementing these changes, and a few asked for guest lectures from industry professionals working towards decolonizing goals or perhaps design historians who could touch on scholarship.

**RILEY:** With retrospect, it's unsurprising that students were looking for more tangible ways to fix these broken systems. We looked at really heavy content (colonialism, racism, patriarchy, misogyny, climate change), and it was perhaps hard to grapple with the idea that design, which you might think is about making the world a better place, has actually done enormous damage. It's absolutely fair to say students need more hope and ways of positively impacting design and design history. Dori Tunstall's (2021) lecture 'A change is gonna come: Black speculative futures for the Cooper Hewitt Design Museum' was a great example – she rethinks and inserts Black design into that museum – but I shared this in our penultimate week and class attendance was dropping. More is needed anyway.

**ISABELLA:** By the end of the course, you said you hoped students understood the rationale behind a critical approach to studying design history, as opposed to just celebrating the canon purely on aesthetic grounds. Do you think that came across?

**RILEY:** I think so. By only studying a European canon and celebrating good design like a Bauhaus chair, you're just going to encourage students to walk the same path. Clearly, we've identified how oppressive and how environmentally damaging design is, so if we celebrate design without taking a step back and looking at these important sociocultural impacts, nothing is going to change. We need better, more socially-aware and ethical designers, and students want to be better designers. Learning some hard truths about design history can get us there. I learned so much from this course, and think it's important that students play an active role in teaching me and teaching each other about these hidden histories in design objects.

## Fish Skin Tanning – Winter 2021

**CINDY:** Neither of us were graduate assistants for your final course, but do you want to describe your experience and maybe we can reflect on connections?

**RILEY:** Maybe this chapter also needs a part-two; there's so much to say about this course. It was absolutely my favourite because it took us closer to that bush school I dream about. Originally, I wanted to do hide-tanning, which is a brilliant and beautiful Indigenous material practice. We've brought hide tanning to our campus before, for our university's *Pow Wow* ('an Indigenous event for dancing, singing, renewing friendships and making new ones') (Figure 2.3), and it's always a transformative experience.

**RILEY:** It's a radical act, seeing hide fleshed, stretched and scraped in an institutional setting. It's surprising. The smell of hide and smoke from the fire transports you from this mostly concrete landscape to the bush. Hide tanning 'camps' are appearing all over, and it's a powerful act of Indigenous reclamation. For non-Indigenous students, it's an eye-opening experience to see the amount of labour that goes into producing leather by hand (it's really, really difficult!), so they gain a new appreciation for the material. The camp setting itself holds a lot of teachings about community and collaboration and how necessary everyone's roles are. When you're learning in the literal bush, like at Dechinta, the person chopping wood or collecting water is just as important as any professor or Knowledge Holder. The Elders would probably point to the cook if you asked who's in charge. The immersive experience of a camp teaches you about survival and governance, but due to the pandemic, this was not possible. I tried to replicate the feeling of camp a little bit: we went through a lot of imagery and videos of hide tanning camps, including the *Stoodis Science Virtual Hide Camp* (SciXchange 2020), facilitated by Amber Sandy, who joined to help facilitate the course. Amber is an incredible Anishnaabe Knowledge Holder and coordinator of Indigenous science outreach and programmes. Inspired by

FIGURE 2.3: Amber Sandy (left) stretching and scraping a hide during tanning at the Ryerson University Student Pow Wow in downtown Toronto (Dalton 2019).

a series of stories on her Instagram (ambersandy 2020), I decided to pivot to tanning that students could do from home in their kitchens (Figure 2.4).

**RILEY:** This was a beautiful experience. Each week we would gather in our kitchens to physically work on creating fish skin leather. I would have loved to forage my own tannins and catch my own fish, but we mostly used tea for tanning, and I used grocery store fish fillets. Still, here the seed planting was both metaphoric and literal; in this course, we discussed the interconnectedness between resurgent fashion practices and regrowing traditional food systems, we incorporated a lesson on gathering tannins respectfully and natural plant dyes. This literal planting speaks to that *everydayness* of Indigenous resurgence, and I saw this change my own life. I started looking at food scraps differently, wondering if I could use them to make dyes. I'll never look at fish the same way, and I'll always make sure skins aren't wasted. That was another caveat – students had to procure their own skins, and many went to sushi restaurants on Amber's suggestion because a lot of skins are thrown out. This pushed them out of their comfort zone, which

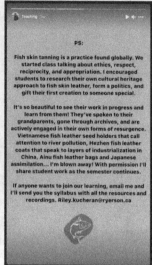

FIGURE 2.4: Riley Kucheran, *Instagram Story Highlights Documenting the Course*, 2021, (Kucheran 2021). Three colour photographs.

takes guts (pun intended). I think there were a lot of lessons in this course about resourcefulness and collaboration. It was one big experiment (I was learning this technique too), so it needed communication, checking-in on each other's skins, sharing knowledge and best practices and troubleshooting issues as they came up.

**CINDY:** We've reflected a bit on remote, online learning and teaching in a pandemic, and I think this course presents a really interesting case?

**RILEY:** Student engagement was much higher with *Fish Skin Tanning*. I had fewer blank Zoom screens, likely because the content was so hands-on. Classes were mostly studio time with some lectures, but we were literally scraping and holding up fish skins to cameras. It was bizarre and oddly comforting. I think there will be a lot more hybrid learning in the future and adding elements of what we've learned from the pandemic to in-person learning. People were tanning at their own pace, so they appreciated recordings to go back to.

It also made me reflect on potential ways to engage a global community of students. We had students from Europe, the Middle East and Asia, so how can we radically rethink a fashion school if anyone from around the world could attend? What if a truly global community of students create a fashion business together? Or bring diverse perspectives to design history or materiality? There was a beautiful diversity of student work in *Fish Skin Tanning*. The point of the course wasn't to teach students Indigenous techniques so they could become Indigenous designers, the ubiquity of fish skin tanning meant that most cultural heritages could be investigated. I mentioned Indigenous, Nordic, Mediterranean and Asian fish skin tanning traditions, and it was fascinating to watch students compare their research findings and gain inspiration for the accessories they ultimately created. In line with my decolonizing teaching philosophy, many of these accessories were also highly political. Some of my favourites included an anti-capitalism leather logo sleeve for a Starbucks thermos. Another student spoke with their Vietnamese grandparents, who recalled fish skin tanning from decades ago. They ended up creating a seed pouch out of fish leather because their grandfather is a farmer who's trying to save seeds before river pollution in the Mekong Delta ruins vegetation beyond repair. So instantly, in one accessory, we see connections between fish, river pollution, farming, family and intergenerational cultural legacies. I always love when students engage with family, especially when they speak to grandparents. Another student learned about Italian fish skin tanning traditions and produced a beautifully constructed bag inspired by and gifted to her Nonna (Figure 2.5). It's such an incredible piece with a history and message behind it. I'm so happy with how this course turned out. I want to keep refining it. It's world-building.

FIGURE 2.5: Emilia Deprisco, *La borsa di Nonna Rosa (Nonna Rosa's Purse)*, 2021, handcrafted fish skin bag. Courtesy of Emilia Deprisco (De Prisco 2021).

**CINDY:** Any final thoughts? Conclusions or recommendations for educators?

**RILEY:** One common theme I noticed was how much students appreciated reduced expectations during the pandemic and my acknowledgement of the mental health challenges. Every week there was something shocking in the news. We went through multiple waves of cases. Some students got COVID-19 or their family members got COVID-19, and they would e-mail me because they were worried about completing the assignment! I took a completely accommodating stance and did not question anything. I tried to build in as much flexibility with deadlines as I could. I think that's something that shouldn't go away post-pandemic. I guess the argument is that if you give students an inch, they'll take a mile? But, I went through mental health challenges in my undergraduate degree. I once reached out to the professor for accommodation but didn't have a doctor's note to prove I was having issues. I could have failed a course and lost my scholarship, but they accepted my assignment and passed me. That could have been devastating, and it wasn't. I remember that so clearly, so now I'm firm on accommodating students. You just don't know what they're going through.

**CINDY:** I see slowing down as a key factor. Too often the discussion is on how to prioritize or how to do things more efficiently, but a lot of the de-stressors people turn to have been unavailable for over a year, like hanging out with friends and family, going out for meals, vacations or fitness classes. I think slowing down is really important, especially now.

## Conclusion

I want to thank Isabella and Cindy for joining me in this whirlwind first year, for their dedication to students and for the time they spent with me afterwards thinking about pedagogy. I started this year with the ambitious goal of integrating my decolonizing praxis into four different (virtual) classrooms. Decolonization and massive material projects, like 'Land Back', may seem like insurmountable challenges and when I get discouraged by the complexity or immensity of undoing the destructive effects of colonialism, I return to the everydayness of resurgence. As Simpson (2017) reminds us, resurgence begins with Indigenous individuals returning to their culture and working in meaningful relationships to collectivize its decolonizing effects. It can be as simple as being on the land, growing our own food, making our own clothing or relating to each other more meaningfully.

A decolonizing praxis takes time and care, but it is the prerequisite for decolonization. This year I applied Nishnaabe practices and perspectives to the research methods and theories used to study fashion, including the businesses and organizations we build, designs we create and then venerate in history and the materiality of fashion itself. Four classrooms, four small cracks in that colonial matrix, and four groups of students with new worldviews who will hopefully cultivate more of that good work.

I don't think Witkó actually said, 'weak hearts and cowards, to the rear!' Or perhaps, if he did, his words were mistranslated and the nuance lost. At the Battle of the Little Bighorn, Witó defeated and killed George Armstrong Custer, but this triggered greater expansion into the Black Hills of the United States – a won battle in the lost Sioux War. Witó needed strong warriors that morning in 1876, but I believe he also knew he needed those at the rear. The caretakers and healers, carriers and nourishers, visionaries and mobilizers, teachers and supporters, youth and Elders. In other words, we all have a role to play. Our fashion institutions are inherently colonial, racist and capitalist. And institutions are made of relations. People, all of us healing, doing our best to improve this place. We've inherited unjust systems, but together we can change them. It takes heart to stand at the front of the classroom, and it takes many hearts to dismantle the classrooms, so there are no fronts.

## NOTES

1.  See the Yellowhead Institute (2019, 2021) on 'Land Back' and 'Cash back' about repatriation and reparations.
2.  See Coulthard (2014) on 'grounded normativity' (13) and Barry et al. (forthcoming) for a spirited panel discussion on Indigenous fashion education and 'Land Back' during Indigenous Fashion Week Toronto 2020.

## REFERENCES

Absolon, Kathy and Willett, Cam (2006), 'Putting ourselves forward: Location in Aboriginal research', in L. Brown and S. Strega (eds), *Research as Resistance: Critical, Indigenous, & Anti-Oppressive Approaches*, Toronto: Canadian Scholars' Press, pp. 97–126.

Alvesson, Mats and Willmott, Hugh (1992), *Critical Management Studies*, Thousand Oaks: Sage.

ambersandy (2020), 'Fish leather', Instagram, 31 May, https://www.instagram.com/stories/highlights/18099860746153951/?hl=en. Accessed 9 December 2020.

Ambrose, Steven (1989), 'Crazy horse: The legend', *Windspeaker*, 7(17), https://www.ammsa.com/publications/windspeaker/crazy-horse-legend. Accessed 11 June 2021.

Anderson, Carol (2017), *White Rage: The Unspoken Truth of Our Racial Divide*, New York: Bloomsbury.

Archibald, Jo-ann (2008), *Indigenous Storywork: Educating the Heart, Mind, Body, and Spirit*, Vancouver: University of British Columbia Press.

Archibald, Jo-ann, Ziiem, Qu'm, Morgan, Jenny Bol, Jun Lee and De Santolo, Jason (2019), *Decolonizing Research: Indigenous Storywork as Methodology*, London: Zed Books.

Atleo, Clifford (2015), 'Aboriginal economic development and living Nuu-chah-nulth-aht', in E. Coburn (ed.), *More Will Sing Their Way to Freedom: Indigenous Resistance and Resurgence*, Halifax: Fernwood, pp. 150–62.

Ballantyne, Erin Freeland (2014), 'Dechinta Bush University: Mobilizing a knowledge economy of reciprocity, resurgence and decolonization', *Decolonization: Indigeneity, Education & Society*, 3:3, pp. 67–85.

Barry, Ben (2021), 'How to transform fashion education: A manifesto for equity, inclusion and decolonization', *International Journal of Fashion Studies*, 8:1, pp. 123–30.

Barry, Ben, Keene, Adrienne, de Loggans, Regan, Ottman, Shawkay, Tunstall, Dori and Kucheran, Riley (forthcoming), 'Indigenous fashion education: Supporting the next generation', *Fashion Studies*, 5:1.

Bogost, Ian (2017), 'The myth of Apple's great design', *The Atlantic*, 9 February, https://www.theatlantic.com/technology/archive/2017/02/the-myth-of-apples-great-design/516093/. Accessed 21 November 2020.

Brush, Candida, Monti, Daniel, Ryan, Andrea and Gannon, Amy M. (2007), 'Building ventures through civic capitalism', *The Annals of the American Academy of Political & Social Science*, 613:1, pp. 155–77.

Cheang, Sarah and Suterwalla, Shehnaz (2020), 'Decolonizing the curriculum? Transformation, emotion, and positionality in teaching', *Fashion Theory*, 24:6, pp. 879–900.

Clark, Hazel (2008), 'SLOW + FASHION–An Oxymoron–Or a promise for the future… ?', *Fashion Theory*, 12:4, pp. 427–46.

Corntassel, Jeff (2018), *Everyday Acts of Resurgence: People, Places, Practices*, Olympia: Daykeeper Press.

Coulthard, Glean Sean (2014), *Red Skin White Masks: Rejecting The Colonial Politics of Recognition*, Minneapolis: University of Minnesota Press.

Dalton, Kaytee (2019), 'Amber Sandy (SciXchange) hide tanning at the 2019 Pow Wow', X University Pow Wow, 20 September, https://www.torontomu.ca/powwow/. Accessed 28 March 2023.

De Prisco, Emilia (2021), 'La borsa di Nonna Rosa (Nonna Rosa's purse)', Unpublished undergraduate work shared with author's permission.

DiAngelo, Robin J. (2018), *White Fragility: Why It's so Hard for White People to Talk about Racism*, Boston: Beacon Press.

dontcryformegiratina (2020), 'Pharaoh Dudebrotep IV of the Chadite dynasty', r/HistoryMemes Subreddit, 18 August, https://knowyourmeme.com/memes/white-egyptian-american-textbook#fn5. Accessed 12 February 2021.

Eddo-Lodge, Reni (2017), *Why I'm no Longer Talking to White People about Race*, New York: Bloomsbury Circus.

Fairs, Marcus (2014), 'IKEA's Chuck out your chintz' ads changed British taste, says the man who wrote the slogan', *Dezeen*, 22 February, https://www.dezeen.com/2016/02/22/ikeachuck-out-your-chintz-1996-advertising-campaign-changed-british-taste-says-naresh-ramchandani-design-indaba-2016/. Accessed 16 April 2021.

Holtbrügge, Dirk (2013), 'Indigenous management research', *Management International Review*, 53:1, pp. 1–11.

Hustwit, Gary (2009), *Objectified*, UK: Swiss Dots Limited.

Kelly, Dara and Hrenyk, Jordyn (2020), 'A call to decolonize business schools, including our own', *The Conversation*, 22 October, https://theconversation.com/a-call-to-decolonizebusiness-schools-including-our-own-145915. Accessed 22 May 2021.

King, Daniel and Learmonth, Mark (2015), 'Can critical management studies ever be "Practical"? A case study in engaged scholarship', *Human Relations*, 68:3, pp. 353–75.

Klassen, Robert and Taylor, Kelsey (2019), 'World tailors: Stitching together a plan for growth', https://www.iveypublishing.ca/s/product/world-tailors-stitching-together-a-plan-for-growth/01t5c00000CwofhAAB. Accessed 20 March 2023.

Kovach, Margaret (2009), *Indigenous Methodologies: Characteristics, Conversations, and Contexts*, Toronto: University of Toronto Press.

Kucheran, Riley (2021), 'Teaching', Instagram, https://www.instagram.com/stories/highlights/17861652254465407/. Accessed 31 January 2021.

Kucheran, Riley, Clark, Jessica P. and Lezama, Nigel (2021), 'Luxury and Indigenous resurgence', in J. P. Clark and N. Lezama (eds), *Canadian Critical Luxury Studies: Decentering Luxury*, Bristol: Intellect, pp. 275–54.

LaDuke, Winona (1999), *All Our Relations: Native Struggles for Land and Life*, Boston: South End Press.

Maurya, Ash (2012), 'Why lean canvas vs business model canvas?', Leanstack blog, 27 February, https://blog.leanstack.com/why-lean-canvas-vs-business-model-canvas/. Accessed 24 August 2020.

McMahon, Ryan (2018), 'Red man laughing: Reflections on reconciliation', Lecture, 6 April, Montreal: Initiative for Indigenous Futures, Concordia University, https://indigenousfutures.net/wp-content/uploads/2019/06/Indigenous-Futures-Cluster-Presents_-Ryan-McMahon-1.txt. Accessed 11 June 2021.

McMurtry, John Justin and Brouard, François (2015), 'Social enterprises in Canada: An introduction', *Canadian Journal of Nonprofit and Social Economy Research*, 6:1, pp. 6–17, https://doi.org/10.22230/cjnser.2015v6n1a199.

Mignolo, Walter and Walsh, Catherine (2018), *On Decoloniality: Concepts, Analytics, Praxis*, Durham: Duke University Press.

Noth, Paul (2011), 'Nobody ever asks "How's Waldo?"', *The New Yorker*, 7 February, https://knowyourmeme.com/memes/nobody-asks-how-is-x. Accessed 16 March 2021.

Perriton, Linda and Reynolds, Michael (2018), 'Critical management education in challenging times', *Management Learning*, 49:5, pp. 521–36.

Rosenberg, Marshall (2015), *Nonviolent Communication: A Language of Life*, Encinitas: Puddle Dancer Press.

SciXchange (2020), 'Stoodis science virtual hide camp', Video Series, 1 December, https://www.ryerson.ca/scixchange/indigenous-outreach/stoodis-science-hide-camp-2020/. Accessed 12 December 2020.

Simpson, Audra and Smith, Andrea (2014), *Theorizing Native Studies*, Durham: Duke University Press.

Simpson, Leanne Betasamosake (2011), *Dancing on Our Turtle's Back: Stories of Nishnaabeg Re-Creation, Resurgence and a New Emergence*, Winnipeg: Arbeiter Ring Publishing.

Simpson, Leanne Betasamosake (2017), *As We Have Always Done: Indigenous Freedom Through Radical Resistance*, Minneapolis: University of Minnesota Press.

Smith, Andrea (2014), 'Native studies at the horizon of death', in A. Simpson and A. Smith (eds), *Theorizing Native Studies*, Durham: Duke University Press, pp. 56–98.

SmithsonianNMAI (2015), 'Weaving the Bridge at Q'eswachaka', YouTube, 5 June, https://www.youtube.com/watch?v=dql-D6JQ1Bc. Accessed 3 January 2021.

stevensongs (2021), *Bilbo Baggins why not meme*, Twitter, 28 February, https://twitter.com/stevensongs/status/1365997780842422281/photo/1. Accessed 12 March 2021.

Truth and Reconciliation Commission of Canada (2015), *Truth and Reconciliation Commission of Canada: Executive Summary*, Winnipeg: National Centre for Truth and Reconciliation.

Tuck, Eve and Yang, K. Wayne (2012), 'Decolonization is not a metaphor', *Decolonization, Indigeneity, Education & Society*, 1:1, pp. 1–40.

Tuhiwai-Smith, Linda ([1999] 2012), *Decolonizing Methodologies: Research and Indigenous Peoples*, New York: Zed Books.

Tunstall, Dori (2021), *A Change Is Gonna Come: Black Speculative Futures for the Cooper Hewitt Design Museum*, New York: The Morse Historic Design Lecture.

Wilson, Shawn (2006), *Research Is Ceremony: Indigenous Research Methods*, Halifax: Fernwood, pp. 53–55.

Yellowhead Institute (2019), *Land Back a Yellowhead Institute Red Paper*, Toronto: The Faculty of Arts at Ryerson University.

Yellowhead Institute (2021), *Cash Back: A Yellowhead Institute Red Paper*, Toronto: The Faculty of Arts at Ryerson University.

Zinga, Dawn and Styres, Sandra (2019), 'Decolonizing curriculum: Student resistances to anti-oppressive pedagogy', *Power & Education*, 11:1, pp. 30–50.

# 3

# Queering the Fashion Classroom: Intersectional Student Perspectives

*Alicia Johnson, Michael Mamp, Alexis Quinney,*
*Austin Reeves and Joshua Simon*

I am a white, gay, Jewish, cisgender man, and I developed and taught the first semester-long undergraduate *Queer Fashion* course in the United States. The course is described as 'an examination of LGBTQ+ experiences via historical fashion analysis; emphasis on LGBTQ+ identity fashioned through sartorial choice; gay aesthetic, camp culture, and LGBTQ+ designer contributions'[1]. My aim is to introduce students to fashion history from a queer perspective of the eighteenth to twentieth century. My approach to developing and delivering this course is informed primarily by queer theory in an attempt to consider fashion, identity and gender outside of the heteronormative status quo perpetuated by typical fashion education and industry practice.

Many years ago, as an openly gay undergraduate student, it was often an isolating experience. Although I came out at age 19 in a very public way in the school newspaper, there were no coming out experiences that I was able to emulate or other gay men with whom I was able to discuss my journey. Even more bleak was the classroom experience that discussed every topic from a heterosexual point of view. The opportunity to develop and deliver this class which centres queer identity and considers fashion from a broader perspective about gender and sexuality, has been a full-circle process for me. My goals were to, in some way, provide a classroom experience for young queer folk to see and learn about people like themselves and to create a less isolating experience for the next generation.

Gathering the material necessary for the course was challenging; I spent several years collecting sources. The course starts with the impact of men milliners in the eighteenth century, like the hairdresser to Marie Antoinette Monsieur Leonard, and then examines cross-dressing masquerade parties and mollies and molly houses prevalent in cities such as London. In the nineteenth century, we explore how dandyism was used as a means of variable representation of masculinity from the very macho Beau Brummel to the aesthetic sensibilities of Oscar Wilde. The twentieth century portion of the class covers a variety of topics; how mannish lesbians of the early twentieth century dressed, the phenomenon and powerful artistry of drag, sexual sartorial signifiers such as red ties and suede shoes, queer art and performance that explored femme identity and sexual fetishes through dress, the contributions and impact of gay male designers and ultimately how subculture impacts mainstream fashion. I began the course by using two books: *A Queer History of Fashion: From the Closet to the Catwalk* and *Queer Style*. I have since developed a course reading and film list instead of textbooks. This more promising approach allows me to update the content as new scholarship is published in this evolving area of inquiry.

The course begins with an introduction to queer theory to help students understand the performative nature of gender perpetuated by society and achieved in part through sartorial choice (Butler 1999). Using lectures, planned class discussions and assigned readings and films, students understand how members of the LGBTQ+ community have used dress to shape identity and form community while influencing mainstream fashion. Students complete various small assignments, including annotated citations of assigned readings, and the semester culminates in a group queer styling project. In this applied project, students style looks and collaboratively complete photoshoots to consider appearance and dress from a queer perspective. Students create looks inspired by historical representations of queer fashion reviewed in the course. Many take their cues from important readings and classroom topics. For example, students enjoy learning about queer designer, performance artist and activist Leigh Bowery (Bancroft 2011; Figure 3.1).

My diverse students' voices and presence make the course a transformative space. Since the course began in the spring of 2018, it has been offered every semester to an average of 40 students in face-to-face, Hyflex, and online asynchronous formats. I am happy to share specific details of course content with anyone who is interested[2]. However, for this essay, I thought it would be more compelling to hear directly from my students what the course meant to them. Included are the voices of my insightful former students who speak to their experiences in a queered classroom.

### *Reconciling my identities through fashion (Alicia)*

I identify as a Black lesbian woman. I feel most aware of my identity as a 'Black' 'woman', and as such, it feels very important to understand Black history. I feel

FIGURE 3.1: Leigh Bowery inspired image from student queer styling group project. Bowery often created elaborate costumes that entirely covered his body, intending to illustrate that gender is a construct that can be manipulated through appearance. Photograph courtesy of Autumn Pickney.

like I belong because of my experiences in childhood and adolescence with strong Black female protagonists like my mother, grandmothers and school friends. As a Black lesbian woman, I have often felt made to choose between blackness, femininity and being gay in order to help others avoid confusion and to, at times, avoid difficult questions regarding my identity.

I came out during my first year of college. It was a scary but liberating experience, and I was left with a 'what's next?' or 'now what?' feeling. Other than my physical attraction to other women, I knew very little about what it meant to be lesbian. I did not know the culture, the history, the communities I could connect with, the verbiage or definitions. Therefore, I did not know how to take this identity that millions of others hold close and make it my own. I spent time and energy attempting to prescribe to society's idea of a lesbian. At this time, I found most online imagery and information primarily featured masculine presenting lesbians. An online quiz entitled 'Which Lesbian Stereotype Are You?' is a prime example of this. The quiz featured several curated outfits to pick from, with only two of seven being feminine and all others featured menswear or hypermasculine clothing. Quizzes like these increased the pressure I felt to subscribe to specific masculine lesbian stereotypes. The modification of my self-presentation through clothing and appearance to align with images I encountered of masculine present-ing lesbians in popular culture artificially led me to believe that strangers would know I was a lesbian. Then I'd feel affirmed and acknowledged. This was how I practiced representing my identity as a lesbian in the public sphere for a year or so, but I then realized that this did not matter because I still did not know what it meant to be lesbian. So, I tried to understand gay culture and history but did not get very far. I felt stumped and needed more. I began to question my place in the LGBTQ+ community.

On my journey, I also encountered homophobia in the Black community. When I initially came out, not only did I feel a lack of belonging in the LGBTQ+ community, but I also experienced alienation from Black social groups. It became harder to find support and friendship when the Black community does not accept you for being gay. Rachel Haug researched the increased psychological distress experienced by LGBTQ+ minorities for her dissertation. According to Haug, minority groups experience greater distress and lack of belonging than their majority counterparts because of added discrimination and harassment (Haug 2018). Furthermore, DeMarquis Clarke urged people to understand a multicul-tural perspective by stating, 'Those who have multiple positions of powerlessness and lack of privilege experience oppression from multiple sources [...] [which] is threatening for a queer person of color who is already facing racial discrimina-tion' (Clarke 2011: 5).

My college campus was not visibly diverse so I did not know who to ask for help. When I heard about a new *Queer Fashion* class, I leapt at the opportunity to enrol. I was not completely sure what it would entail, but I knew it was a start, and I wanted to be a part of it. What made me even more excited to take the class was that it discussed not only LGBTQ+ history but also its connection to fashions past and present. Once receiving the syllabus, I got even more excited, particu-larly by the unit covering lesbianism. In our *Queer Fashion* class, we had in-depth conversations about lesbian sartorial choices and ways of dress ranging from the mannish styles of the early twentieth century to the handsome revolution of the twenty-first century.

In Katrina Rolley's article 'Cutting the dash: The dress of Radclyffe Hall and Una Troubridge', we learned how two twentieth century women used dress to convey their identities as lesbians. According to Rolley, Radclyffe Hall's modernity resulted from her need to express her sexual identity through 'masculine' dress and appearance. For her, every change in fashion that allowed women to wear clothes formerly designated 'male' was important (Rolley 1990). Troubridge's more feminine sartorial choices still expressed her sexuality but in relation to Hall's hyper-masculinity. We also learned about how, Miki Vargas' twenty-first century photography project, *The Handsome Revolution* explored the projection of a masculine identity achieved partly through dress. Vargas proudly displayed masculine presenting women in the project and created a transformative affirming space for her subjects (Reddy-Best 2017).

While reading about the history of lesbian styles, I started to understand how my appearance evolved. I took this class in my senior year of college and, by this point, had strayed away from a hyper-masculine mode of dressing and sat more comfortably in my femininity. For me, femininity is not just dresses, skirts and pretty patterns; it is also the accentuation of my figure. I changed from wearing button-down shirts and bowties that I did not feel the best in, to wearing dresses and jewellery every day that I felt celebrated in. Seeing different women embrace their own sense of style and their queer identities throughout history allowed me to feel more comfortable expressing my identity through dress.

The highlight of the entire course was our final project. The assignment was to creatively portray our version of different themes and styles reviewed in the course. One theme my group chose was the mannish lesbian style of the early twentieth century. I volunteered to style and model this look for the project even though I no longer identified with this way of dress. Donning the slacks, button-down shirt and oxford shoes from the back of my closet for the photo shoot was liberating because it reminded me of who I was trying so hard to be. Wearing masculine or feminine clothing does not erase my lesbian or feminine identity, nor excludes me from my Black identity. Seeing the final images from the photo shoot of a smiling and happy Black lesbian woman (me) was very self-affirming.

The *Queer Fashion* classroom was more diverse than any other course I had taken. It was refreshing being surrounded by other students, queer or not, who were interested in the subject. Hearing the stories of fellow Black students, even Black queer women, during class discussions made the class an instant safe haven for my peers and me. Finally, I felt like I had a space to explore my blackness, queerness and femininity without judgement and among those with shared experiences. This class showed other struggling students and me that we had a community on a predominately white heteronormative campus. Furthermore, the people I met in our class did not prescribe to any stereotypes; they existed on their own as queer or as people of colour and stood strong in those identities. Minority representation in a class discussing queer history finally gave me the sense of belonging that I always yearned for, the feeling that I have a voice in this community under all intersections of my identity, a voice that deserves to be listened to and affirmed.

## Queer fashion: Discovering me (Austin)

You might be wondering who I am. I am a Black, cisgendered male from Detroit. I graduated from college in 2018 with a degree in Business Administration focused in marketing. Not your typical student demographic for a *Queer Fashion* class. You might be thinking … 'why did he take this course?' Let me tell you the story.

Throughout my college career, I developed an interest in the fashion industry while simultaneously becoming more comfortable with my sexuality and identity as a gay male. However, I knew nothing about my community's history. I grew up in a Christian Baptist household where being gay wasn't accepted. My parents enrolled me in a private Christian school where nothing was ever said about gay history because of the heteronormativity of the curriculum. The school's culture was that the students would bully you if you were openly gay. With those experiences in my past, I thought that the *Queer Fashion* class would be the perfect opportunity to learn more about fashion and the history of my community. The course also fulfilled my remaining requirement for the university's general education programme.

The first day of class was a little intimidating. I felt somewhat comfortable but also felt like a fish out of water. Most of the students were cisgender women in the Fashion Merchandising and Design programme. Yet the room was full of people that looked like me: Black and brown folks as well as larger-sized people. As a plus-sized individual, I thought that was really important to see in a fashion class because the industry doesn't particularly cater to all body types.

Throughout the semester, we had many discussions. One discussion that stood out to me was the course's gay sexual liberation component. We learned about how the LGBTQ+ community often connected with each other using sartorial signifiers when being gay was taboo. This conversation led to further discussion about how gay men interact with each other in present times via dating apps and the profile tagline of 'No Fats, No Fems, No Asians, No Blacks'. This was important to me because it highlights the experience of queer people of different races and body types. This line of thinking within gay male communities supports further 'marginalization of fat, femme and/or racialized queer bodies and identities within queer communities […] that is, the white, masculine and muscular queer man who is understood and represented as being the right kind of Queer' (Conte 2017: 1). When I came out my sophomore year of college to my friends, some individuals in the Black community treated me differently once I started living my truth. I learned that it's even harder for some Black queer men to find acceptance.

Another important section of the course for me was entitled, *The Power of Drag: Intersections of Race, Gender, Sexuality, Style and Performance*. This was when I really started to become proud of my queer history. Growing up, the school system only taught Black history for Black History Month, but there is so much about our culture that is not taught in school. This section of the course really demonstrated how much Black members of the LGBTQ+ community have contributed to popular culture. For example, the men and women of the Ballroom Scene of the 1980s influenced fashion and popular culture. This was a place in particular for Black, LatinX and trans people of the LGBTQ+ community to come together and express their identities in the runway categories of ball competitions. According to Marlon Bailey, 'houses provide a space for queer youth to feel supported' (Bailey 2011: 367). Furthermore, 'the balls resist these gender norms by gender-bending through both the outfits and the mannerisms of the queens and kings' (Buckner 2020: n.pag.). Personally, this course section had the most positive impact on my self-confidence.

This class was really the first time I could learn about my queer history and be fully proud of it. I was able to learn a great deal about the contributions and impact of the LGBTQ+ community on both fashion and mainstream culture. It also really strengthened what I want my purpose in life to be. This *Queer Fashion* course reiterated the importance of representation and self-confidence. Everyone should be able to live fully and confidently so they can do whatever they set their minds to (Figure 3.2).

### New perspective: History, gender and intersectionality (Joshua)

When presented with the opportunity to take a newly developed course entitled *Queer Fashion*, I was very enthusiastic. As an aspiring scholar of dress history, I assumed it would provide opportunities to study dress history from an LGBTQ+ perspective. Personally, I hoped to learn more about myself; as an individual who had come to terms with and explored his own queer identity a few years before taking the class. I also desired to find connections to people in the past that shared thoughts and experiences similar to mine. *Queer Fashion* did that, providing a sense of validity via historical context. Before taking the course, I had never learned about members of the queer community in any class (other than sporadic mentions of the AIDS epidemic). Sometimes, it felt as though LGBTQ+ identities were a relatively new concept, that I was part of a group that found its origins within the past 30 years. This bothered me; sometimes, it even made me question

FIGURE 3.2: Queer fashion student Austin Reeves explores the push–pull of identity through styling. Photograph courtesy of Autumn Pickney.

if something was wrong with me. *Queer Fashion* changed this feeling for me. Our learning about queer history and fashion began in the eighteenth century with discussions of molly-houses, macaronis and the practice of masquerade. Almost immediately, it became clear that individuals with queer identities have existed throughout history. Tracing origins related to one of my identities created a larger context in which I felt more grounded and valid. Rather than a relatively new concept, queerness finds its origins in the further away past, providing hundreds, if not thousands, of years of history to learn about, develop a deeper understanding of, and be proud of.

The course also provided me with a deeper context and understanding of my identity as a man as well as what masculinity means. Prior to taking the class, while educating myself about who I am in relation to my queer identity, I had also found material discussing topics related to the construction of gender. *Queer Fashion* included discussions of masculinity and femininity, their relationship and histori-cal context and the idea of stepping outside these binary ideas. An introduction to feminist and queer theories truly expanded my own understanding as it related to my identity. I also learned the importance of understanding the privilege associated with my identity as a white, cisgender man. Even queer-related topics or histories can be problematic as particular identities were also disenfranchised; one example would be dandyism. Despite the queer interpretations of dandyism by individuals like Oscar Wilde and Quentin Crisp, 'the male dandy does little to challenge a long cultural history of misogyny' (Cerankowski 2012: 232). Exploring this has continued to deepen my understanding of the privilege of being a cisgender white man, despite also being queer.

From this, I developed a deeper understanding of intersectionality. I had heard of and had a basic understanding of this concept prior to taking *Queer Fashion*; I served as a resident assistant for three and a half years, and this topic frequently came up during our professional development and training sessions. However, *Queer Fashion* aided me in the development of a better understanding. I am a queer, cisgender man; however, I am also White, Agnostic and an American citizen. All these identities intersect and interact with one another and form my unique life experience; it is impossible to remove an identity and discuss it individually without talking about how other identities impact it. In *Queer Fashion*, intersec-tionality was stressed, for example, when we discussed the style of Black women who were also queer, like famed blues singer Gladys Bentley who often wore a top hat and tails when she performed, presenting in a very masculine way. This opened the door to new discoveries as 'intersectionality itself is constantly under construction' rather than a finished, stagnant concept (Hill Collins and Bilge 2020: 15). Consequently, I was able to improve the facilitation of programmes in my resident assistant role. I also talked about how all of our identities are inherently connected. For me, it is impossible to separate my queerness from my gender, race, citizenship and the privileges afforded me.

## *Intersectionality: Acknowledging your privilege (Alexis)*

In my final semester, my advisor introduced a new *Queer Fashion* course into the curriculum. The first of its kind in the programme and at our university, I was excited to learn about fashion history through a new lens. Most instruction about historical dress is taught solely from the perspective of heteronormativity. Examining LGBTQ+ identities via fashion history was initially an opportunity for me to learn about gay aesthetics, camp culture and LGBTQ+ designer contri-butions. Yet over the semester, it turned into a much more personal and profound experience for me as a Black, non-disabled, middle-class, heterosexual, cis-woman. This course and, more importantly, the space this course provided challenged me to reconsider my thoughts on diversity and representation in the classroom.

This course explained how minorities have greatly impacted fashion and culture as we know it. The course content included scholarly works, culture-defining films and queer fashion history. We also covered dress and identity, the relationship between gender expression and appearance, and gender and race inequalities in society. For many students, it was their first time learning about people with whom they identified, which was a rare and precious opportunity for those focused on fashion merchandising and design – a discipline dominated by a homogenous group of individuals. I looked forward to every class period; the discussions were a highlight. It was the most diverse place on campus I had ever been in, encompassing various backgrounds, races, sizes, ages and majors, where students of varying views and backgrounds found common ground. The course broadened my viewpoints on topics I have always felt a strong connection to, such as critical race theory (CRT) and the theory of double consciousness. CRT is a theoretical framework that examines depictions of race relations within cultures. It explores how systemic racism informs cultural perceptions of race and how people present themselves to counter bias (Crenshaw et al. 1996). According to W.E.B. Du Bois, the theory of double consciousness is the sensation 'of always looking at one's self through the eyes of others' (Du Bois 1903: 3). In some cases, this can cause extreme harm to the self-worth of those in minority groups. They tend to take on the beliefs or biases of the dominant culture and contribute to systemic racism within their own communities.

The introduction of queer and feminist theories broadened my viewpoints to include issues of gender expression and homophobia in the Black community (Jagose 2009). To learn more, I researched Blaxploitation films from the 1970s to the end of the twentieth century. I focused on how queer characters dressed compared to the uber-masculine main characters. I analysed the appearance of 23 characters. I found that dress was used to convey cultural messages of gender expression for the Black queer and heterosexual males. The visual representation of queer characters prompted, for me, complex cultural meanings regardless of how long or how brief the audience saw them. The images or symbols displayed by their dress and appearance are then 'encoded into the cultural framework' in which people form beliefs, opinions and learn social structures (Harris and Mushtaq 2013: 4). Queer characters were portrayed as sexual pariahs, one-dimensional jesters, opposing the ideal sexually desired, macho, leading man; further contributing to the othering of queer folks.

As a Black woman, I have always felt I brought a diverse perspective to every course I took, every group project I was a part of and every class discussion.

My view was black and white in a literal sense. I was constantly aware of my inter-sectionality, but only as Black and female. I saw this as the short end of the stick for both race and gender. My existence itself was a protest to the injustices I felt in every interaction; I felt it was my place to challenge those who may have opposed me based on my identities. Constantly on the defence, in my mind, I thought I knew everything about diversity and inclusion. It was not until after reading Katrina Rolley's writing on the dress and identity of Radclyffe Hall and Una Troubridge, and listening to my classmates, that the idea that my intersectionality included privilege occurred to me (Rolley 1990).

The concept that I held any privilege was so foreign to me. Privilege is inherent; without actively engaging in it, I would never have been aware of how it informed my life. I was ashamed of the sudden realization that I, a cis-hetero woman, who considered herself an ally, was not aware of the hardships experienced by my queer counterparts. I have never been judged or feared for my life when it came to how I dressed and who I chose to love. I had never thought about holding hands, hugging or displaying affection in public. I had never had a second thought when mentioning a boyfriend at work or thought about the assumptive questions about who people may find attractive. Heterosexuality was the default, and I never noticed because it fit into my life perfectly. Acknowledging my privilege was at first jarring but one of the most expansive experiences for me in the class. The discussions and openness lent tremendously to my growth as an ally. A tough class period for me was when I offended a trans person with my outdated language. While discussing the read-ing, I used a term and was unaware of the weight it held for people in the room. This interaction would have been negative in any other space and ended without a clear understanding on both sides. The instructor used this moment to teach us how learning and unlearning are both important and take time. I was given the grace to make mistakes and to learn without fear of being wrong, and many times, I was. I now have the basic building blocks to better support and advocate for the LGBTQ+ community. I am aware that though this class profoundly impacted me, it had an even greater impact on those represented. I will never be able to under-stand fully, but I must continue to learn and share with those who will never be able to experience this class and the growth I had because of it.


### Call to action

The student perspectives shared here illustrate how impactful a queered fashion classroom can be for many reasons. These student voices are a testament to how the diversification of the fashion curriculum can create transformational spaces that expand knowledge and provide an affirming space and room for critical discourse. While I had hoped this *Queer Fashion* course would appeal to students who identify as LGBTQ+ and their allies, I was pleased to find that the classroom became a haven for students of colour, both LGBTQ+ and heterosexual cisgender. Granted, it took the perfect storm; a gay man with the desire and opportunity to propose a course about *Queer Fashion* and the willingness to complete the substantial extra labour to do so. Aside from a course about queer fashions, styles and bodies developed by Kelly Reddy-Best at Iowa State University, I am unaware of any other semester-long curriculum related to queer fashion offered by our field in the United States (Reddy-Best and Goodman 2020). While many fashion programmes have some type of dress and culture or diversity class, which may mention sexuality or gender, there remains a significant opportunity to understand LGBTQ+ identity and experience further using a lens of fashion (Reddy-Best and Mamp 2018). As indicated from the student perspectives, adding a *Queer Fashion* course to the curriculum can provide an affirming, safe and transformative space for students.

## NOTES

1. For the master course syllabus, see: https://team.cmich.edu/sites/MCS/Shared%20 Documents/FMD/FMD280.pdf.

2. For further discussion of my experiences developing *Queer Fashion* over five years, see: Mamp, M., Elia, A. C., Bernstein, S. T., Brewer. L. A. and Green, D. N. (2018), 'Engaging labor, acknowledging maker', *Dress: The Journal of the Costume Society of America*, 44:2, pp. 133–51.

   Reddy-Best, K., Keist, C., Ellington, T. N., Deihl, N. and Mamp, M. (2019), 'Scholar's roundtable presentation: Do we study diversity in dress', *Dress: The Journal of the Costume Society of America*, 46:2, pp. 141–57.

## REFERENCES

Bailey, Marlon M. (2011), 'Gender/racial realness: Theorizing the gender system in ballroom culture', *Feminist Studies*, 37:2, pp. 365–86.

Bancroft, Allison (2011), 'Leigh Bowery: Queer in fashion queer in art', *Sexualities*, 15:1, pp. 68–79.

Buckner, Rachel (2020), 'Underground ball culture', Subcultures and Sociology, https:// haenfler.sites.grinnell.edu/subcultures-andscenes/underground-ball-culture/. Accessed 25 August 2020.

Butler, Judith (1999), *Gender Trouble: Feminism and the Subversion of Identity*, New York: Routledge.

Cerankowski, Karli June (2012), 'Queer Dandy style: The cultural politics of Tim Gunn's asexuality', *Women's Studies Quarterly*, 41:1&2, pp. 226–44.

Clarke, DeMarquis (2011), 'Growing up gay in Black America: An exploration of the coming out process of Queer African American youth', Ph.D. thesis, Syracuse: Syracuse University.

Conte, Matthew (2017), 'More fats, more femmes, and no whites: A critical examination of fatphobia, femmephobia and racism on Grindr', Ph.D. thesis, Ottawa: Carleton University

Crenshaw, Kimberlé W., Gotanda, Neil, Peller, Gary and Thomas, Kendall (eds) (1996), *Critical Race Theory: The Key Writings that Formed the Movement*, New York: The New Press.

Du Bois, W. E. B. (1903), *The Souls of Black Folk: Essays & Sketches*, Chicago: A.C. McClurg & Co.

Harris, Angelique and Mushtaq, Omar (2013), 'Creating racial identities through film: A Queer and gendered analysis of Blaxploitation films', *Western Journal of Black Studies*, 37:1, pp. 28–38.

Haug, Rachel Mary (2018), 'Perceived belongingness, self-esteem, and outness level on psychological distress among lesbian, gay and bisexual individuals', Ph.D. thesis, Greeley: University of Northern Colorado.

Hill Collins, Patricia and Bilge, Sirma (2020), *Intersectionality: Cambridge and Medford*: Polity Press.

Jagose, Annamarie (2009), 'Feminism's Queer theory', *Feminism & Psychology*, 19:2, pp. 157–74.

Reddy-Best, Kelly (2017), 'Miki Vargas: Queer Fashion photographer and the handsome revolution', *Clothing Cultures*, 4:2, pp. 153–70.

Reddy-Best, Kelly and Goodin, D. (2020), 'Queer fashion and style: stories from the heartland authentic Midwestern queer voices through a fashion exhibition', *Dress: The Journal of the Costume Society of America*, 46:2, pp. 115–40, https://doi.org/10.1080/03612112.2019.1686875.

Reddy-Best, Kelly and Mamp, Michael (2018), 'Queering the classroom: Intersections of fashion and the LGBTQ+ community', *International Textile & Apparel Association Annual Conference*, Cleveland, OH, 18 November.

Rolley, Katrina (1990), 'Cutting a dash: The dress of Radclyffe Hall and Una Troubridge', *Feminist Review*, 35, pp. 54–66.

Steele, Valerie (ed.) (2013), *A Queer History of Fashion: From the Closet to the Catwalk*, New Haven and London: Yale University Press.

# 4

## Theorizing Fat Oppression: Towards a Pedagogy of Empathy, Inclusion and Intentional Action

*Lauren Downing Peters*

To say that fashion and fat make uneasy bedfellows would be an understatement. Although some scholars have taken a romantic view of fashion history, arguing that, at different moments, a 'voluptuous' ideal was *de rigueur* (Almond 2013, emphasis added), overt fatness has never been in fashion. While there have been periods during which the fashion industry seemed to embrace the fat female consumer – as, for example, with the emergence of the stoutwear industry in the early twentieth century (Keist 2012; Peters 2018) and, in the 1980s, plus-size fashion (Peters 2017) – she has essentially remained fashion's forgotten 'other', relegated to ghettoized corners of department stores and all but absent within the fashion media. Looming large over all of this is that the slender body – an ideal deeply rooted in systemic racism and oppression – persists as the proper, if not *sole*, model of feminine embodiment in the West (Strings 2019: 6–7, emphasis added).

These circumstances make fat challenging to discuss in the fashion classroom. As those who have curricularized fat liberation can attest, we must handle the topic with great care, compassion and, perhaps more than anything, patience (Cameron 2015; McPhail et al. 2017; Watkins et al. 2012). This is because "obesity"[1] discourse has been normalized in western society to such an extent that some regard it as the last bastion of socially acceptable prejudice (Brownell et al. 2005). In my own experience, I have found this work is made doubly hard within the context of fashion programs where the industry's biases are reified through a curricular model that has evolved very little over the last half-century, and that prioritizes 'hard' design skills over the 'softer' skills of critical thinking and reflection and in which primary and secondary resources for studying the history of fat fashion are scarce to non-existent. While challenging, it is nevertheless incumbent upon fashion educators – especially those who make claims to diversity and inclusion – to overcome the discomforts of talking about fat if they expect students to transform a system that, for all intents and purposes, is profoundly broken.

Indeed, it is no secret that the fashion industry has a diversity and inclusion problem; the issues that pervade plus-size fashion expose these failings. For too long, however, fashion educators have been content to assign blame to editors and designers without examining how and to what extent their curricula and pedagogies support and uphold the fashion system's values and hierarchies. Much like the rest of higher education, fashion schools have become 'transactional laboratories' that prepare students to be compliant managers and executives while 'setting aside humanitarian ideals [...] [and] any collective responsibility for marginalized and vulnerable groups' (Damianidou and Phtiaka 2016: 236). A critical re-thinking of the entire fashion school model is long overdue; however, few institutions are well positioned to engage in curricular overhauls, fund new research initiatives or invest in diverse tenure-track faculty who can do this challenging work. Historic drops in enrollment and budgetary shortfalls in higher education have all but ensured that fashion programmes remain frozen in a mythic past. Therefore, the burden of curricular reform has largely fallen upon the shoulders of individual instructors who, as the title of this section suggests, have thrown out the textbook and, with it, the old ways of teaching fashion.

In the realm of plus-size fashion specifically, scholars and practitioners have only recently begun to develop critical construction and design pedagogies. The supermodel Emme, for instance, developed a plus-size design course in partnership with Syracuse University (Schlossberg 2015), while Deborah Christel's 'fat Fashion pedagogy' (FFP) addresses and provides strategies to overcome the structural inequalities that pervade fashion design education (Christel 2018). Less attention, however, has been paid to critical Fat Studies and size-inclusive pedagogies in the expanded field of Fashion Studies – the interdisciplinary field of study that examines the history, theory, social functions, mediation and aesthetics of fashion and dress.

In this chapter, I aim to fill this gap by fleshing out a pedagogy of *empathy, inclusion and intentional action* for the interdisciplinary Fashion Studies classroom[2] that exposes students to Fat Studies concepts and activism, which is rooted in fashion theory. Drawing upon bell hooks's essay, 'Theory as liberatory practice', fashion theory is framed here as a 'location for healing', as 'a way to challenge the status quo' and a 'necessary practice within a holistic framework of liberatory activism' (1994: 59–60, 69). In the following pages, I argue that fashion theory – which helps students gain a critical and embodied understanding of the mechanisms of systemic size oppression – can lay the groundwork for meaningful activist fashion practice. Thus, fashion theory is presented as a *conduit of empathy* through which students may gain a deep understanding of the lived realities of fat embodiment. Having embraced the title of 'fashion activist', my goal is to bring fat from the margins to the centre of Fashion Studies curricula. Therefore, I use the idea of 'centring' to present my scaffolded approach in what I hope is valuable and actionable for other activist Fashion Studies educators.

## One: Centring ourselves

In their article, 'Exposed social flesh: Toward an embodied fat pedagogy', McPhail et al. reflect on their embodied experience teaching critical Fat Studies. Too often, they write, 'fat – the material-hugging-on-the-bones-softness of it, the fluid abject-ness of it – can [...] be jettisoned from the very space in which it is to be centred and reimagined' (McPhail et al. 2017: 18). This is problematic for a number of reasons, not least of which is the fact that the body itself can function as a site of learning, or what Beasley and Bacchi refer to as a 'social flesh' (Beasley and Bacchi 2007). To resist discussions of embodiment instates a problematic Cartesian mind/body split that negates the embodied realities of fat (McPhail et al. 2017: 18). In her survey of Fat Studies instructors, Cameron found that the majority of respondents recognized the need to centre fat-as-flesh and therefore took pains to address their own embodiment, whether or not they identified as fat (2015: 32–33). While most found this strategy useful – one that opened the door to more honest and empathetic dialogue – some of Cameron's study participants remarked that such disclosures left them feeling vulnerable or, worse, undermined their credibility (2015: 33).

Valerie Steele famously referred to fashion as the 'F-Word' within the academy (1991: 17–20); however, one could argue that fat is deserving of this designation, too, given the extent to which fat is pathologized in western culture. The practice of 'outing' oneself as fat or, conversely, as thin privileged in the classroom is not entirely without risk and therefore has to be handled with great care. Here, however, fashion educators are perhaps at a marked advantage over colleagues in adjacent fields because of the embodied nature of self-fashioning. As Entwistle has observed, 'human bodies are *dressed* bodies', and in addition to making the body 'appropriate' for the social world, dress imbues bodies with meaning and an identity (2000: 6–7, original emphasis). While non-fashion educators risk 'exposing' themselves when discussing their bodies, fashion educators can use the medium of dress to reflect on and facilitate meaningful discussions about dress as an embodied practice, opening the door to more critical investigations into weightism and size bias in fashion.

In my teaching, this manifests in the initial observations that we all have bodies and that we are all dressed. I explain to students that whether we identify as fashionistas or subscribe to the edicts of anti-fashion, we all participate in and are subject to the caprices of the global fashion system. Standardized sizing is one small but highly significant aspect of this system that touches everyone's lives and materializes the relationship between dress and the fleshy body. Most everyone can recount a painful moment when they couldn't slide a well-loved pair of jeans over their hips or zip up a favourite dress. When there is a disconnect between our sense of self and our fleshy embodiment, we are often forced to confront uncomfortable thoughts about how and to what extent our bodies satisfy normative standards of beauty. Because clothing mediates our sense of self and experience in the world, moments such as these provoke what Eco has referred to as 'epidermic self-awareness', or a state in which one grows aware of the relationship between the garment, the self and society (1986: 192). Within the fashion classroom, the concept of epidermic self-awareness can be employed as a first step towards understanding that there is nothing neutral nor 'standard' about clothing sizing while also opening up what Zembylas describes as affective spaces of empathy and understanding (2012: 113–14). In my experience, however, few students possess the discursive toolkit that would enable them to critically reflect on their embodied dress practices. So as not to throw them into the proverbial deep end, I first share a bit about my own relationship to fashion and sizing in order to both destigmatize 'fat talk' (Gruys 2012: 485) and set the parameters for our discussion.

Although my body size has fluctuated over the years, causing me to have a somewhat complicated and non-linear relationship to fat oppression, I do not currently present or self-identify as fat. Even when my body size has necessitated that I wear plus-sizes, I did not align myself with individuals whose bodies are the targets of 'the daily microaggressions and systemic oppression that fuels the 'war' on fat bodies' (McPhail et al. 2017: 24). Even at my largest, I inhabited an unquestionably privileged body; however, this does not mean that I have not been subject to the fashion industry's inconsistent and biased sizing standards. One painful moment I have curricularized in the classroom occurred in the fitting room at my favourite boutique, where I got physically stuck in a dress. With the rigid fabric and unyielding seams straining and pulling on my flesh, I had no choice but to tear myself out of the dress by breaking the zipper. It was a moment of great personal shame. The $200 dress I had ruined was the store's largest standard size, a US size 12. Not only had I made a costly mistake (How had I not noticed my weight gain? Why did I force the dress over my too-large stomach?), but I had crossed the symbolic threshold between standard and plus-sizes, which begin at a US size fourteen. Officially, I was plus-size, at least according to the fashion industry's standards; however, I did not *feel* or outwardly identify as such.

This moment of cognitive dissonance holds a place of great importance in my sartorial biography but also in my practice as a fashion scholar and activist. After sharing this story with students, I then wonder out loud if I, as a person inhabiting a privileged body, was considered plus-size or 'non-standard' according to industry conventions; 'what must people who fall on the higher end of the size spectrum feel and experience daily?' While my story brings fat back into the classroom (McPhail et al. 2017: 32), this question is asked to nurture empathy by connecting my experience to those of people who are at a greater disadvantage while at the same time avoiding drawing an equivalency (Damianidou and Phtiaka 2016: 238).

After sharing my story, I then ask students to complete an exercise in which they reflect upon 'pain points' or moments of disappointment, bias or frustration they have experienced when shopping for clothing or getting dressed. This exercise can take the form of a short reflection paper, a small group discussion or independent journaling followed by a class discussion. In recent semesters, I have found the latter to be the most productive, as students seem to feel emboldened and eager to share once they have had a moment to gather their thoughts. For many undergraduate students (especially non-fashion majors), this is perhaps the first time they are asked to critically reflect upon their self-fashioning practices and the first time they have heard about others' fitting room frustrations. While uncomfortable at times, discussions such as these that delve into and dismantle 'troubled knowledge' are necessary components of activist and social justice pedagogy (Zembylas 2012: 114).

In my classrooms, this discussion establishes a united front and a shared activist agenda amongst myself and the students. It does so by instituting a baseline acknowledgement that the fashion industry's sizing practices are discriminatory and arbitrary. Perhaps most importantly, however, it engenders the understanding that sizing issues are not the proprietary concern of fat people but something about which we should all care deeply. Suddenly, fat stigma doesn't seem like an isolated problem but a powerful force that touches all of us and shapes everything from garments to retail geographies to the media we consume.

While this exercise has proven to be incredibly productive in facilitating discussion and identifying how the fashion industry marginalizes and oppresses people based on their body size, it fails to get at the *whys* and *hows* of these unjust systems and, therefore, falls short of fostering genuine empathy and understanding. This is where fashion theory comes into play.

## Two: Centring Theory

Although the past decade has witnessed the flourishing of the interdisciplinary field of Fashion Studies through the establishment of international MA and Ph.D.

programmes (Jenß 2016: 2), Fashion Studies has yet to find a home within under-graduate fashion programmes, due, perhaps, to its perceived remove from fashion practice. Theory is commonly understood as an intellectual device that merely explains phenomena. Amongst some scholars working in the sister disciplines of dress history, fashion design and fashion merchandising, Fashion Studies has become synonymous with fashion theory. This reductive perspective problemat-ically glosses over the field's interdisciplinarity while also positioning it as elitist, abstract, inaccessible and 'removed from the real world' (Rocamora and Smelik 2016: 3). This perspective on theory is not entirely unfounded, however. Indeed, as hooks observes,

> It is evident that one of the many uses of theory in academic locations is in the produc-tion of an intellectual class hierarchy where the only work deemed truly theoretical is work that is highly abstract, jargonistic, difficult to read and containing obscure references.
>
> (1994: 64)

Outside of the ivory tower – or in spaces that uncomfortably straddle the worlds of higher education and the industry, as is the case with fashion departments – theory can be perceived not only as useless but as 'a kind of narcissistic, self-indulgent practice that […] seeks to create a gap between theory and practice so as to perpetuate elitism' (hooks 1994: 64). Indeed, theory, when applied too bluntly and without regard for students' lived experiences can leave them 'stumbling and bleary-eyed', or worse, alienate them (hooks 1994: 65). What then is the function of theory in undergraduate fashion design programmes? Why muddy the curric-ular waters with theory when resources and energy can be directed to the more utilitarian and productive pursuit of career readiness? I have struggled to answer these questions since joining a faculty largely composed of practitioners. Part of my struggle arises from the fact that these questions – however well-meaning they may be in their centring of student employability – incorrectly presume that theory and practice are unrelated. In 'Theory as Liberatory Practice', hooks argues that theory is actually 'a necessary practice within a holistic framework of liberatory activism' (1994: 69). Continuing, she explains how theory can be a 'healing place' for students – one that enables introspection, self-recovery, collec-tive liberation and, perhaps most importantly, the ability to imagine different futures (hooks 1994: 61). Part of the reason theorizing can be intimidating is that it requires one to cast off old ways of thinking and to question established social norms (Eagleton 1990: 34–35). On the one hand, this is decidedly uncomfortable work. On the other, theorizing can be a joyful practice that is not entirely anti-thetical to the practice of fashioning itself. In *Women and Fashion: A New Look*,

Evans and Thornton describe fashion as a 'field in which women have found pleasure in the elaboration of meaning – meaning which is there to be taken and used' (1989: xv). In the same way that the wardrobe functions as a site of creative identity play and experimentation, theories can be employed to 'try on' different ways of thinking, which in turn can be used to transform and revolutionize fashion practices. Thus, a better question than, 'What is the point of theory in the fashion classroom?' might be, 'How can we build a more equitable and inclusive fashion industry *without* theory – without thinking outside the box or understanding the underlying mechanisms that made it so?'

To theorize fashion is to unpack, comprehend and analyse the social and cultural dynamics of fashion, dress and appearance (Rocamora and Smelik 2016: 1). As mentioned previously, fashion (as industry and practice) is deeply rooted in racism and oppression. For our students, this is not an abstract concept. They experience the fashion industry's biases daily, whether through retail discrimination or by simply not seeing people that look like them in the fashion media. These phenomena merits our attention, and theorizing can be one conduit through which we, as educators, can investigate and disrupt the exclusionary mechanics of the fashion system. However, one of the challenges of theorizing fashion lies in the fact that many of our field's key theorists do not, themselves, write about fashion. For the handful of scholars who have placed fashion at the centre of their theorizing, they often build upon and extend the work of familiar twentieth century thinkers. As Rocamora and Smelik observe, 'Theorizing does not happen in a vacuum', but rather, 'in critical dialogue with existing works and theories' (2016: 4). Because it can be difficult for undergraduates to, for example, make the ontological leap from discussing Michel Foucault's writings about the panopticon as a metaphor for social surveillance and the ways that it ensures the automatic functioning of power, to the ways that the fashion industry polices fat bodies through standardized sizing, I tend to teach theories that centre fashion.

Two theories useful in this pursuit are Joanne Entwistle's theory of 'dress as a situated bodily practice' (2000: 11) and Kawamura's theory of fashion as an institutionalized system (2005: 39). Because fashion, even more so than other cultural realms, 'consists of material objects and involves a bodily practice', to theorize fashion requires the weaving together of multiple strands of thought (Rocamora and Smelik 2016: 14). In thinking through how the fashion industry marginalizes fat bodies, Entwistle's theory of dress as a situated bodily practice helps students understand the relationship between the body and society and the fact that 'bodies are socially constituted, always situated in culture and [are] the outcome of individual practices directed toward the body' (Entwistle 2000: 11). Kawamura's discussion of fashion as an institutionalized system recognizes that the very functioning of the fashion system relies upon a collective belief in the idea of fashion. In order for the system to function, individual actors must work together to produce and perpetuate the ideology of fashion (Kawamura 2005: 39). While Entwistle's and Kawamura's theories draw upon the work of prominent post-structuralist French thinkers such as Michel Foucault and Pierre Bourdieu, my decision to foreground their work over those whom they quote is intentional. Entwistle's and Kawamura's focus on fashion helps students to 'unlock' the theory because they can always refer back to those moments of epidermic self-awareness or to their work experiences. Student insights and reflections by way of brainstorming and discussion are essential to this process. Indeed, as hooks writes, 'Personal testimony, personal experience, is such fertile ground for the production of feminist liberatory theory because it usually forms the base of our theory making' (1995: 70).

These theories help me dismantle fat stigma within the classroom, specifically any lingering ideas that fat people do not deserve equal access to fashion. Entwistle and Kawamura underscore that fashion (as an embodied practice and as a system) is a form of power: Garments give shape to bodies and make them culturally legible, while fashion's gatekeepers determine what gets produced and who has access to it. Critically analysing the systems that create and perpetuate bodily ideals and which determine who can participate in fashion, the focus shifts from the culpability of individuals to the role that designers, buyers, editors, sales associates and advertisers play in implicitly and explicitly perpetuating size bias. What, however, are students to do with these new perspectives?

### Three: Centring intentional action

In writing this chapter, I struggled with whether or not I should share my projects and deliverables because I have come to regard theorizing as not a means to an end but as an end unto itself. Said differently, I believe the ultimate goal of theorizing fashion (and thus the role I occupy within my department) lies in giving students ample space and time to critically reflect on the place they occupy in the fashion system and how fashion mediates their experience of being in the world. While I take it as a win if students walk out of the classroom buzzing with ideas and troubled by the fact that that there is an internal, if flawed, logic to the functioning of the fashion system, I also acknowledge that I work within the context of the neoliberal university in which assessment is based on measurable standards (or learning outcomes), essays and examinations (Damianidou and Phtiaka 2016: 236). However, these conventional modes of assessment have proven to be flawed and, perhaps more problematically, have the potential to alienate BIPOC and disabled students, as well as first-generation college students (Kitano 1997a: 1–17).

Particularly concerning my institution, Columbia College Chicago has an acceptance rate of over 80 per cent and historically (and proudly) has welcomed students who might otherwise struggle to find an academic home. In each of my classes, some students are exceptionally well-prepared for college, and some had never imagined themselves setting foot inside a lecture hall but *love* fashion. The long research essays I had written in college and graduate school, and that I had initially assigned to my students, simply weren't serving their purpose at Columbia; my students' understanding of the mechanics of academic writing was too all over the place to fairly assess their mastery of concepts. When grading my student's work, I had to confront the hard truth that their work had more to do with my assessment modes than their preparedness or lack thereof. Over the last year, I have therefore begun to overhaul the projects and deliverables I assign.

Following Morey and Kitano's framework for multicultural course transformation (1997), I have moved away from essays and exams toward assignments based on different ways of thinking about concept mastery. As Kitano explains,

> In classrooms where it has been established that knowledge is socially constructed, mastery refers to students' development of the ability to make meaning, or increasingly more sophisticated connections with topics, often through interaction with peers. This type of mastery is better assessed through [...] projects that empower students to apply their new learning in ways that produce change.
>
> (Kitano 1997b: 28)

The emphasis that Morey and Kitano place on students' ability to affect meaningful change aligns well with hooks's observations about theory as going hand-in-hand with activist practice, as well as with what it means to be a fashion activist more generally. In terms of assignment redesign, the shift occurred when I moved from essays written essentially for their own sake (and read only by myself) to projects that are more outward looking and where students are placed in positions of influence. In her anti-racism teaching, Cargle has described this as a pedagogy of 'intentional action' bolstered by 'radical empathy' (2020). Like Cargle, I have come to value unconventional deliverables that perhaps ask more questions than they answer over the polished sheen of the research essay.

In my course, *Creative Communities: Fashion Ethics and Aesthetics*, which I piloted in the Spring of 2020 and included two units on plus-size fashion, students participated in an end-of-semester zine sprint. A zine (pronounced *zeen*) is a self-published, non-commercial, independent magazine. Zines were a crucial element of the countercultural press that emerged in the 1960s and have been utilized to centre marginalized voices, build creative networks and raise awareness of social and political causes. In my class, students were invited to reimagine the medium of the fashion magazine as a critical vehicle to effect change in the fashion industry. In preparation for the zine sprint, students wrote two critical reflection papers where they synthesized the theories learned throughout the semester with what they hoped to achieve with their publication.

The sprint itself occurred in one three-hour class period, during which the students worked collectively to conceptualize and execute a critical fashion zine based on topics addressed in class. In order to give the students editorial *carte blanche*, I had them name the magazine (they chose *un-fashion*) and devise its structure. They agreed that each student would create three pages responding to the following prompts: reflect, educate and rise-up. Students were permitted to work in their medium of choice (i.e. illustration, collage) to create pages that reflected their ethics and aesthetics. With this project, the student's goal was to address the most urgent issues facing the fashion industry today while engendering more ethical and empathetic consumption habits among their peers.

Although this project did not explicitly focus on plus-size fashion, a handful of students chose to use their pages to call out the fashion industry for its treatment of fat consumers in order to, as Kitano writes above, 'apply their new learning in ways that produce change'. Although these pages do not directly quote Entwistle or Kawamura, they demonstrate a tacit understanding that there is nothing just or natural about the industry's marginalization of fat people. Beyond the students' evident mastery of the concepts presented in class, what I found most remarkable about these pages was that many were created by students who did not self-identify as plus-size but rather as newly-minted allies in the fight against fat oppression. I find this shift remarkable because, as recently as five years ago, fat allyship was a foreign concept to most of my students. Therefore, the burden and emotional labour of addressing fat sigma used to fall solely on the shoulders of students who had experienced various forms of fat oppression.

While recent mainstreaming of the body positivity movement has brought these issues into clearer focus for students (Johnston and Taylor 2008: 954), within the context of this project, the students' use of fat liberationist discourse upends the assumption that students in positions of power and privilege do not care about the wellbeing of marginalized people. Indeed, it has been inspiring and energizing to witness students who do not self-identify as fat align themselves with the fat liberationist cause. In keeping with the punk aesthetics of zine making, this project certainly lacked polish; however, if this work was to engender empathy within the students while moving them to action, I believe it was an unbridled success. Even so, I nevertheless struggle with the fact that my class is often the first and sole point of contact students have with fashion theory during their education. Critical Fashion Studies is often relegated to one (often elective) class taught by a single instructor, and my experience is no exception. As common as it might be, this siloing of fashion studies and practices within fashion curricula undermines the importance of theory in fashion education. Where, then, does that leave us?

## Call to action

In presenting this framework, I do not claim to have all of the answers, nor have I settled upon a single approach for theorizing fat oppression in the undergraduate fashion classroom, as each semester has presented different challenges. I will say, however, that talking about fat oppression with students has gotten easier with each passing year. Students in 2022 are much more open to inclusive and body positive discourse than when I started teaching in 2010. Along with the students, I, too, have grown and evolved over the past ten years. While I once believed it was my duty to ensure that all students left my class with a strong command of academic writing and a rote knowledge of the great designers, I have come to embrace what Garland-Thompson describes as a 'methodology of intellectual tolerance'. This method, she writes, 'asks difficult questions but accepts provisional answers' while allowing us to 'teach with authority at the same time we reject notions of pedagogical mastery' (Garland-Thompson 2002: 28). Essentially, the pedagogy of empathy, inclusion and intentional action presented here is provisional and unfinished.

Thus, my call to those reading this chapter is not to be content with my approach. (The practice of adopting and canonizing tried approaches to teaching fashion got us into this mess in the first place!) Instead, I challenge my peers (especially those teaching design) to:

- *Curricularize your embodied dress practices.* Do so by sharing your own experiences with fashion and sizing in the classroom. The body can function as a site of learning or a 'social flesh'.
- *Get comfortable in your discomfort.* It is not easy to talk about fat, but if we truly commit to diversity, equity and inclusion, we have to destigmatize 'fat talk'(Gruys 2012: 485).
- *Embrace theory as a necessary component of liberatory activism.* Rather than a way to explain away phenomena, theory should be understood as a way to challenge the status quo and as a location for healing.
- *Design assignments with intention.* Beyond mere skill mastery, consider how modes of assessment can put students in positions of influence and embolden them to be agents of change.

## NOTES

1. Members of the fat acceptance movement and scholars in the field of Fat Studies agree that the term 'obesity' medicalizes naturally occurring bodily differences and should only be used in scare quotes when used at all.
2. This framework has been applied in lower and upper-level courses such as *Introduction to the Fashion Industry, Clothing and Society, Creative Communities: Fashion Ethics and Aesthetics, Fashion History: Global Perspectives* and *Fashion and Dress Beyond the West*.


## REFERENCES

Almond, Kevin (2013), 'Fashionably voluptuous: Repackaging the fuller-sized Figure', *Fashion Theory*, 17:2, pp. 197–222.

Beasley, Chris and Bacchi, Carol (2007), 'Envisaging a new politics for an ethical future: Beyond trust, care, and generosity toward and ethic of "social flesh"', *Feminist Theory*, 8:1, pp. 279–96.

Brownell, Kelly, Puhl, Rebecca, Schwartz, Marlene and Rudd, Leslie (eds) (2005), *Weight Bias: Nature, Consequences and Remedies*, New York: Guilford Press.

Cameron, Erin (2015), 'Toward a fat pedagogy: A study of pedagogical approaches aimed at challenging obesity discourse in post-secondary education', *Fat Studies*, 4:1, pp. 28–45.

Cargle, Rachel Elizabeth (2020), 'Public address on revolution: Revolution now', YouTube, 30 May, https://www.youtube.com/watch?v=leBPMyQ60HM. Accessed 19 October 2020.

Christel, Deborah (2018), 'Fat fashion: Fattening pedagogy in apparel design', *Fat Studies*, 7:1, pp. 44–55.

Damianidou, Eleni and Phtiaka, Helen (2016), 'A critical pedagogy of empathy: Making a better world achievable', *Pedagogies: An International Journal*, 11:3, pp. 235–48.

Eagleton, Terry (1990), *The Significance of Theory*, Oxford: Blackwell.

Eco, Umberto (1986), *'Lumbar thought', in Travels in Hyperreality (trans. W. Weaver)*, San Diego, New York and London: Harvest, pp. 191–96.

Entwistle, Joanne (2000), *The Fashioned Body: Fashion, Dress and Modern Social Theory*, Cambridge: Polity.

Evans, Caroline and Thornton, Minna (1989), *Women and Fashion: A New Look*, London: Quartet Books.

Gruys, Kjerstin (2012), 'Does this make me look fat? Aesthetic labor and fat talk as emotional labor in a women's plus-size clothing store', *Social Problems*, 59:4, pp. 481–500.

Garland-Thompson, Rosemarie (2020), 'Integrating disability, transforming feminist theory', *Feminist Theory Reader*, 14:3, pp. 181–91.

hooks, bell (1994), *Teaching to Transgress: Education as the Practice of Freedom*, New York: Routledge, pp. 61–70.

Jenß, Heike (2016), 'Introduction: Locating fashion studies: Research methods, sites and practices', in H. Jenß (ed.), *Fashion Studies: Research Methods, Sites and Practices*, London: Bloomsbury, pp. 1–18.

Johnston, Josnée and Taylor, Judith (2008), 'Feminist consumerism and fat activists: A comparative study of grassroots activism and the dove real beauty campaign', *Signs*, 33:4, pp. 941–66.

Kawamura, Yuniya (2005), *Fashion-ology: An Introduction to Fashion Studies*, Oxford: Berg.

Keist, Carmen Nicole (2012), 'The New Costumes of Odd Sizes: Plus sized women's fashions, 1910–1924', Ph.D. thesis, Ames: Iowa State University.

Kitano, Margie K. (1997a), 'A rational and framework for course change', in M. Kitano and A. Morey (eds), *Multicultural Course Transformation in Higher Education: A Broader Truth*, New York: Pearson, pp. 1–17.

Kitano, Margie K. (1997b), 'What a course will look like after multicultural change', in M. Kitano and A. Morey (eds), *Multicultural Course Transformation in Higher Education: A Broader Truth*, New York: Pearson, pp. 18–30.

McPhail, Deborah, Brady, Jennifer and Gingras, Jacqui (2017), 'Exposed social flesh: Toward an embodied fat pedagogy', *Fat Studies*, 6:1, pp. 17–37.

Peters, Lauren Downing (2017), '"Fashion plus": Pose and the plus-size body in *Vogue, 1986–1988*', *Fashion Theory*, 21:2, pp. 175–99.

Peters, Lauren Downing (2018), 'Stoutwear and the discourses of disorder: constructing the fat, female body in American fashion in the age of standardization, 1915–1930', Ph.D. thesis, Stockholm: The Centre for Fashion Studies at Stockholm University.

Rocamora, Agnès and Smelik, Anneke (2016), 'Thinking through fashion: An introduction', in A. Rocamora and A. Smelik (eds), *Thinking through Fashion: A Guide to Key Theorists*, London: I.B. Tauris, pp. 1–27.

Schlossberg, Mallory (2015), 'Emme and fashion without limits', *Business Insider*, 25 July, https://www.businessinsider.com/emme-and-fashion-without-limits-2015-7. Accessed 16 October 2016.

Steele, Valerie (1991), 'The F-Word', *Lingua Franca*, 1 April, pp. 17–20.

Strings, Sabrina (2019), *Fearing the Black Body: The Racial Origins of Fat Phobia*, New York: New York University Press.

Watkins, Patti Lou, Farrell, Amy E. and Hugmeyer, Andrea Doyle (2012), 'Teaching fat studies: From conception to reception', *Fat Studies*, 1:2, pp. 180–94.

Zembylas, Michalinos (2012), 'Pedagogies of strategic empathy: Navigating through the emotional complexities of anti-racism in higher education', *Teaching in Higher Education*, 17:2, pp. 113–25.

# 5

# Reflections of a Fat
# Fashion Faculty Member

*Carmen N. Keist*

I am fat, short and pale; the antithesis of fashion. My love of fashion started at an early age. I am a fashion historian because dead people can't judge you. Loving fashion history, you didn't have to be fashionable or know what was going on with current trends. It was fantasy. The clothing that people wore in the nineteenth century looked ridiculous in the first place, so I didn't have to worry about it. I am not fashionable. I don't care about high fashion or the latest trends. My quasi-uniform includes Birkenstock sandals, jeans and hooded sweatshirts.

I have always been fat. I struggle with accepting my body for what it is, and I don't know if teaching fashion helps or hurts this struggle. I remember reading *Teen Vogue* with a neighbourhood friend as a child and dreaming of the day that I would grow into my 'grown-up lady body' (Simpson 1993). I would naturally have a flat stomach, tan skin and nice perky boobs. This obviously didn't happen (I'm still waiting for my boobs to grow).

By looking at these fashion magazines and growing up in the United States in the 1990s when 'heroin chic' models were popular, I was under the false impression that since this is what women were supposed to look like, I would automatically have this body when I grew up and hit puberty. Growing up, I heard many times, 'Are you going to eat all of that?', 'You shouldn't eat all of that', or from my father, 'You eat so many chicken nuggets you are going to turn into one'. I believe, or at least hope, he was trying to be helpful, but it wasn't. My mother unintentionally taught me to eat my feelings, something I still do today. Habits are hard to break. I have a lot of feelings, and I still eat every one of them. I do not know how many times I have been told that I would be pretty if only I lost weight. Guys in school told me that they would like me if only I were not fat. I desperately wanted to fit in and be popular, but no one wants to be the fat kid or be friends with one, or at least this was my experience. My best friend from Kindergarten to 5th grade dumped me before 6th grade because she knew I wasn't going to be popular (she was right) and didn't want to be associated with a loser. My mother had to shop in the junior's department to find pants that would fit my round body because I had outgrown *children's* clothing way before I *should have*.

Fast forward to me mothering my 6-year-old son in 2020. We were watching a Marvel Avengers movie, and Black Widow came on the screen. My son exclaims, 'Black Widow is so beautiful, and I like her because she is skinny'. My heart dropped. I try very hard to set a good example for him. I do not share negative thoughts about my body or weight; I do not focus on his or others' appearances, and I do my best to teach him how to have a healthy relationship with food. But with this statement, I truly realized that society's rules for beauty have a bigger sway on him than what he learns at home. We talked about these comments; I asked why he thought he liked Black Widow because she was skinny. He said he didn't know why he thought that or where he could have heard such statements. I reminded him that his Mama is fat and that he loves his Mama. We need to love and see people for who they are; not what they look like or how fat they are. Just recently, he asked if fat people were bad. I asked him what he meant by this. He said that people make fun of fat people, so he thought fat people were bad. I gently reminded him that his mother was fat and asked if I was a bad person. He said no (thank goodness!), and I tried to reinforce that people are different and everyone has value.

Society doesn't let me forget that I'm fat. For me, clothing is ill-fitting and ugly; college desks and restaurant booths are too small for my girth to fit comfortably. It encourages me that if I had self-discipline and more control, I could lose weight and be my best self. The phrase 'there is a thin person living inside every fat person' always makes me laugh. Diet culture perpetuates the myth that self-discipline and control will help you lose weight. It doesn't consider my heredity or that I have PolyCystic Ovarian Syndrome (PCOS). Having PCOS makes it very easy for me to gain weight and hard for me to lose it.

I use self-deprecating humour as my coping mechanism. It's my protection against how cruel people can be. I learned this technique in high school to confront the teasing I endured. Luckily, I didn't grow up with social media. Facebook wasn't a thing until I reached college; by then, I was more comfortable with who I was becoming. I can't imagine being a teenager today; bullying behind screens is so vile. Matwick and Matwick said it best in their 2017 article, 'Self-deprecatory humor on TV cooking shows', that 'humorous self-deprecation is self-directed critique done in a humorous way to minimize possible value judgement that the self-revealing information might provoke' (33). I feel like I must mention that I'm fat so others feel 'comfortable' knowing that I know I'm fat. My self-deprecating humour comes from a place of acceptance. This statement is further enforced by

Chaerani and Junaidi (2019: 55), who stated that 'self-deprecation is utilized as a tool to speak up what becomes somebody's physical imperfection that needs to be accepted'. I know I'm fat; the audience can see that I'm fat, and I want everyone to be okay with it. I hope it helps lessen the stigma associated with the word. First, let us talk about the elephant in the room (it is me!) so we can start talking about important topics.

I use the word fat to describe my body, and this tends to make people feel uneasy because society has made us feel that word is bad. It conjures up negative associations and makes people think that I am being mean to myself. I want to take that power away from the word. I make fun of my fat body, and 'to elicit laughter is to exert control, even power' (Russell 2002: para. 11). Just as a colour is used to describe an object, fat is simply a descriptor used to describe my body shape. It's true. I'm fat.

After changing majors several times and dropping out of the first undergraduate school I attended, I moved back home, took a semester off, and started again at Illinois State University in my hometown as a Family and Consumer Science major in Apparel Merchandising and Design. Looking around the classroom at my peers, I was the fattest student. I felt I didn't fit in with my peers or look like the ideal fashion student. Luckily, neither my professors nor my peers ever made me feel this way; I put this pressure on myself. Alternatively, society's perceptions of fat people made me feel this. I loved my fashion classes. I finally felt like I had found something I enjoyed and was good at. I decided to continue my education to pursue a master's and, eventually, a Doctorate. I attended Iowa State University for both degrees and was the fattest of my peers. During graduate school and now, when I tell people that I teach fashion, I get looked up and down, and people say, 'Really?' It used to bother me, but now I laugh at how superficial people can be.

The two main career choices with fashion history degrees are working in a museum setting or teaching. With my degrees, I knew my career had to be something with fashion history. As museum jobs are very hard to come by, I began applying for university faculty positions. If I couldn't work with historical clothing, I could teach it, where I find myself now – the 'authority' in the classroom and teacher of apparel merchandising students. As a fat professor, I hope to dispel some of the stereotypes surrounding fat and fashion. Based on previous experiences in the classroom as a student, I try to focus on all aspects of clothing. On the first day of my introduction course, I tell my students I use 'apparel' instead of the word 'fashion' as apparel encompasses everyone, though not all people are considered fashionable (Figure 5.1). Deborah A. Christel's (2014: 309) article on fat discrimination of college apparel students points out '67 per cent of scores [Beliefs about "Obese" People Scale] are below twenty, indicating that the majority of fashion and merchandising students have negative attitudes about "obese[1]" bodies'.

FIGURE 5.1: Dr Carmen Keist points out fat-shaming comments while teaching. Photograph courtesy of Carmen Keist.

As a fat college professor teaching in an apparel merchandising programme and researching fat fashions for twentieth century American women, this statistic is alarming. Fat women have always existed, of course. However, they are not always visible (well, obviously physically visible as you can't miss them because they take up space) in popular culture and the media. Bringing visibility to this diverse and marginalized group is important for the industry's future, for designers, merchandisers and beyond. The Centers for Disease Control and Prevention reports that the average American woman is a size fourteen and weighs 166 pounds. By 2030, the Trust for America's Health and the Robert Wood Johnson Foundation estimates that half of the adults in the United States will be "obese" (Begley 2012). The apparel industry must consider how they discuss bodies and shame fatness in the design, promotion and merchandising processes.

As a college professor, I am seen as the 'authority' on the subject matter. I often question whether or not a self-described unfashionable woman can be the authority on fashion. However, 'authority can be subverted through laughter' and boy, am I funny. I give them the good ol' razzle-dazzle. One criterion tenure-track faculty are evaluated by is student evaluations. Past studies have found that students who perceive their faculty as more attractive tend to receive higher evaluations. Escalera (2009) states, 'Professors who dress in formal or stylish attire are also likely to receive better evaluations' (205). Escalera (2009) reported from previous studies that stigma threat can interfere with a professor's effectiveness in the classroom, which impedes the learning process. I encountered this first-hand. During my first semester teaching, a comment on my student evaluations said, 'Needs to dress and wear attire/do makeup and hair in order to represent the fashion department. Very inefficient'. I wanted to say, 'I am sorry my hideous appearance makes it difficult for you to learn effectively.' Besides this one interesting student evaluation, I have found this is not true. My student evaluations tend to be high, and students report that I am knowledgeable. While writing this chapter, I extended an invitation to my former students to take a survey about their perceptions of my teaching and weight. The survey consisted of quantitative and qualitative questions. Students strongly agreed that 'Fat people have a right to wear clothing that is fashionable/trendy' (mean = 4.98) and strongly disagreed with the statement 'Fashionable clothing is only for slender and "average" sized people' (mean = 1.43). Although I am fat, my influence as the 'authority' on fashion works.

Students repeatedly stated that I looked comfortable and confident in my appearance and teaching, which is what mattered to them most. Many students said they noticed how confident I was after having a class with me and that it inspired them to be confident in themselves. Students stated, 'She's a great role model for advocating for inclusive fashionable clothing!', 'She had the most enjoyable class [...] who cares what her weight is' and 'She is the most confident woman I know. She taught me how to wear confidence.' An exceptionally impactful comment was,

> She has become one of the most inspiring people during my college career. Finding something that I am as passionate about as Dr Keist is about teaching and sharing her knowledge despite what the rest of the world says or thinks that she should look like while teaching, is a goal I have for my life. She has changed my views on fashion and how you have to be the skinniest person in the room to look the best. She has made me more comfortable in my own skin, while also allowing me to follow my love of fashion while not being the skinniest person in the room.

Escalera (2009) also states that 'an instructor who is a member of a stigmatized group [fat people] can create anxiety and distress in the students' (206) and uses the example of fat people teaching courses related to health. However, I would also apply these feelings of anxiety to apparel courses. Under the ideology that thin equals health, in American society, thinness and fashion go hand-in-hand. To help reduce stigma threat, Escalera (2009) encourages dispelling stereotypes by teaching students common misperceptions about weight. I think this is great advice and something that all students, not just students pursuing a fashion degree, need to consider. My programme is housed in Family and Consumer Sciences, including hospitality, dietetics and public health education degrees. I hear from colleagues who teach dietetics that many of their students have skewed views on health and weight. Many students enter dietetics to teach people to 'eat right' to help combat America's "obesity" problem. This narrow view reinforces the assumption that fat people cannot be healthy. It assumes that fat people do not eat healthily and are uneducated. I am educated and enjoy Bon Bons, but I do not spend all day lounging on the couch eating them.

## Call to action

Currently, I believe that most colleges and universities have generalized merchandising and design programmes and do not offer Fat Fashion Studies. Some courses might have a fat fashion component, but the inclusion of fat fashion needs to be infused across the curriculum. But more than body issues and weight acceptance need to be covered. The apparel curriculum needs to focus on all bodies because almost everyone wears clothes.

The industry will change when our graduates change. How can we expect anything to change if we keep the status quo in the classroom? There is a big discrepancy in the apparel industry. If the ones designing our clothing continue to discriminate against most of the population, how can we foresee a viable fashion industry in the future?

### Inclusion for all apparel curricula

- Include images of fat people in your lectures, including images of all races, sizes, gender identities and disabled people. Search the internet for these images. Do not rely on images from the runway that reinforce the current beauty ideal of Euro- and thin-centric. I have found many fantastic models on Instagram who don't fit into the 'stereotypical' model mould. Follow these influencers and encourage your students to do the same. Or even better yet, have students provide examples of who they want to see on the screen. I know from my experience that students are much more up-to-date on who is a style leader for their demographic.

Society tends to focus on female celebrities' body weight more than most topics. For example, Rebel Wilson and Adele both lost weight during the COVID-19 pandemic; this is the only thing the news focused on. On 5 November 2020, when I typed in the Google search bar 'Rebel Wilson', the top ten news stories reported she was seen on the beach wearing a one-piece green swimsuit. Breaking news! A woman is wearing a swimsuit on the beach! What happens when they potentially gain the weight back? What will the conversations be then? Will society find them less valuable?

- Start a body positivity movement on campus. Bradley University has The Body Project (https://www.bradley.edu/sites/bodyproject/), a hub of resources that challenge the current body ideal. Peer leaders can hold Body Project workshops on campus to encourage confronting the body ideal.
- Have guest speakers come to class and provide different viewpoints on body shape and body acceptance. I presented for the Women and Gender Studies Lecture Series on the history of plus-size women's fashions. I also included topics such as body positivity and size inclusivity. The audience consisted of many students and faculty outside of our fashion programme, and the feedback I received from them was very positive. One student commented after the lecture,

It was my privilege that I got an amazing opportunity to go to the presentation by Dr Carmen Keist [...]. She reminded me to love myself and not worry about what others think about my looks or the way I dress. I believe that having that attitude not only helps the person themselves but also the people around them because I know for sure that she affected the way I think about my body and myself. She positively made me feel good about my body and the way I dress [...] Hopefully, she does more research before the time I graduate from Bradley so I can get more chances of going to her presentations or talks.

- Have panels of students comfortable talking about their weight come to classes to discuss weight bias and how retailers/ clothing make them feel. By hearing others and empathizing, hopefully, students can see a person without judging their body size. This should coincide with weight sensitivity training for all majors.
- Work with retailers that support size inclusion and encourage internships at these places. Maurices is inclusive and offers clothing up to a size 24. Their plus-size clothing does not look different from the 'straight' sizes and is offered on the same racks. Modcloth, Eloquii and Universal Standard are just a few retailers focusing on clothing to fit more body sizes and be fashionable. Seeing this type of retailing is encouraging, especially for teens and young adults who might not be confident in their skin yet.

As a teenager, I was always embarrassed to go shopping with friends. I was a teen in the 1990s when American Eagle, The Limited and Abercrombie & Fitch were extremely popular. I could not wear these clothes because they did not offer my size. I would always make excuses as to why I did not want to try on anything or purchase clothing.

- I teach a course called *Survey of Fashion Designers* as a twentieth century fashion history course, and I use the term 'fashion designer' very broadly in this course. This course is half lecture and half discussion. The lecture portion is, for the most part, a typical fashion history course focusing on historical silhouettes and influential fashion designers from each decade. On discussion days, we focus more on culture and topics rarely covered in fashion history books. These topics include design piracy, feminism, LGBTQIA+, cultural appropriation, designers of colour and fat fashions. The students are asked to read articles posted online and bring discussion questions prior to class. Students are arranged in small groups with a discussion leader during class. The students discuss in their small groups while I go around the room and listen briefly to conversations. I write themes or phrases I hear on the whiteboard, and then we discuss them as a class. Students love this portion of the class; it is eye-opening for them and me. Their experiences inform the rest of the class on issues they face in the apparel industry and their daily lives. I have provided a sampling of potential articles for discussion on fat bodies and fashion at the end of this chapter.

- Have students take other classes to consider perspectives about the body, their body and other bodies. Body size and other sociocultural issues were rarely covered in my undergraduate and graduate education. Not only would apparel students, but all students would benefit from these classes. I am currently talking with the director of the Women's and Gender Studies programme to create a course like this.

## Inclusion for fashion design courses

- Include fat bodies in introductory clothing construction courses. When I took clothing construction as an undergraduate student, we received extra credit for wearing the clothing we had constructed. I purchased a sewing pattern in the largest size, and the clothing would still not fit; it was always too small. It was embarrassing because I did not have the skills to make it fit correctly or the voice to question the authority.

- Have students grade patterns to fit fat bodies. If your institution can't afford larger dress forms, find students on campus. Recruit students of different sizes and shapes. Not only would design students benefit from working with different body types, but I'm sure they would appreciate learning more about how to fit clothing for their bodies. During my patternmaking and draping courses, clothing was made for a sample size ten and graded down or up, but never into what would be considered plus-sizes. I cannot believe I never questioned this practice when making clothing that would never fit me.

I know from experience that accurate fit can be challenging for fat bodies. I understand that everyone has issues with fit, but coming from a person whose body shape is a heavy bottom pear, it can be near impossible. I have a small chest, a big stomach and very large hips. Most retailers think that with large hips, I must also have a large chest. American society presents the ideal female body as tall, thin, ample chest, slim waist and proportional hips. However, friends with large chests complain that their backs hurt and how frustrated they get about being objectified. People ogle over large breasts and many associate large breasts with promiscuity.

For me, shirts are the worst. They are either too baggy in the chest or too tight in the hips. I can't win, so for the most part, I give up. I have no option but to give up shopping for plus-size clothing. As clothing for fat people has not been readily available, I end up purchasing clothing that fits poorly or not buying clothing at all. I make do with what I have. I don't make time to find fashionable, well-fitting clothing for fat people. Many of these retailers are online and/or too expensive for a budget-conscious consumer. If I do find something I feel 'good' in, I tend to buy multiples of these garments, so my wardrobe doesn't have much variety. I often threaten to take a twin flat sheet, cut a head hole in the middle, and belt it to make an updated toga. Maybe the Ancient Greeks were on to something?

• Along with grading patterns for fat bodies (and other body shapes and sizes), do not let students design different clothing styles for different sizes.

Fat people want to be fashionable too! I am still disappointed when I see brands offering plus-size clothing but not all the styles or colours in larger sizes. For example, Levi's X Star Wars clothing collection featured galaxy and specialty printed items — jeans, denim jackets, sweatshirts, t-shirts, hats — but they only offered jeans up to a 31 inch waist. I would have purchased the denim in every design if they had them in my size. When companies are not inclusive, first, they lose out on customers and, second, profits. Use clothing companies, like LOFT and Madewell, as examples of stores trying to get it right. They don't have all styles in larger sizes, but they are starting to have a good selection.

## Implications and recommendations for the future

- Hire fat faculty.
- Encourage fat students to join apparel design and merchandising programmes. When I was in school, I felt like I was the only overweight student. This was very isolating. I have students who told me they would be a fashion student but do not feel like the major is for them because they don't 'look' the part. Unfortunately, many fashion design and merchandising programmes are perceived as superficial, one of the biggest stereotypes that need to change. We need to change our image and encourage everyone to join our discipline.
- Move away from the term plus-size or extended sizes! I'm fabulous and fat, but I'm not more (or less) than anyone else.

## Resources to use in the classroom

The following are resources I suggest including in your course reading list. There are many out there, but I have found these to be most useful in my classes.

- Aagerup, Ulf and Scharf, Edson R. (2018), 'Obese models' effect on fashion brand attractiveness', *Journal of Fashion Marketing and Management*, 22:4, pp. 557–70, https://doi.org/10.1108/JFMM-07-2017-0065.
- Bickle, Marianne C., Burnsed, Katherine A. and Edwards, Karen L. (2015), 'Are U.S. plus-size women satisfied with retail clothing store environments?', *Journal of Consumer Satisfaction/ Dissatisfaction & Complaining Behavior*, 28, pp. 45–60.
- Cain, Patricia and Donaghue, Ngaire (2018), 'Political and health messages are differently palatable: A critical discourse analysis of women's engagement with health at every size and fat acceptance messages', *Fat Studies*, 7:3, pp. 264–77, https://doi.org/10.1080/21604851.2018.1448174.
- Christel, Deborah A. (2014), 'It's your fault you're fat: Judgements of responsibility and social conduct in the fashion industry', *Clothing Cultures*, 1:3, pp. 303–20, http://dx.doi.org/10.1386/cc.1.3.303_1.
- Christel, Deborah A. (2016), 'Obesity education as an intervention to reduce weight bias in fashion students', *Journal of Education and Learning*, 5:2, pp. 170–79, http://dx.doi.org/10.5539/jel.v5n2p170.
- Christel, Deborah A. (2018), 'Fat fashion: Fattening pedagogy in apparel design', *Fat Studies*, 7:1, pp. 44–55, https://doi.org/10.1080/21604851.2017.1360669.

- Clayton, Russell B., Ridgway, Jessica L. and Hendrickse, Joshua (2017), 'Is plus size equal? The positive impact of average and plus-sized media fashion models on women's cognitive resource allocation, social comparisons, and body satisfaction', *Communication Monographs*, 84:3, pp. 406–22, https://doi.org/10.1080/03637751.2017.1332770.
- Czerniawski, Amanda M. (2012), 'Disciplining corpulence: The case of plus-size Fashion models', *Journal of Contemporary Ethnography*, 41:2, pp. 127–53, http://dx.doi.org/10.1177/0891241611413579.
- Gruys, Kjerstin (2012), 'Does this make me look fat? Aesthetic labor and fat talk as emotional labor in a women's plus-size clothing store', *Social Problems*, 59:4, pp. 481–500, http://www.jstor.org/stable/10.1525/sp.2012.59.4.481.
- Keist, Carmen N. and Marcketti, Sara B. (2019), 'Supporting acts: Patents for undergarments for stout women, 1891–1956', *Clothing & Textiles Research Journal*, 37:3, pp. 200–14, https://doi.org/10.1177/0887302X19836513.
- Keist, Carmen N. (2018), 'How stout women were left out of high fashion: An early twentieth-century perspective', *Fashion, Style & Popular Culture*, 5:1, pp. 25–40, https://doi.org/10.1386/fspc.5.1.25_1.
- Keist, Carmen N. (2017), '"Stout women can now be stylish": Stout women's fashions, 1910–1919', *Dress*, 43:2, pp. 99–117, https://doi.org/10.1080/03612112.2017.1300474.
- Keist, Carmen N. and Marcketti, Sara B. (2013), '"The new costumes of odd sizes": Plus-sized women's fashions, 1920–1929', *Clothing & Textiles Research Journal*, 31:4, pp. 259–74, https://doi.org/10.1177/0887302X13503184.
- Reddy-Best, Kelly L., Keist, Carmen, Ellington, Tameka N., Deihl, Nancy and Mamp, Michael (2020), 'Scholars' roundtable presentation: Do we study diversity in dress?', *Dress*, 46:2, pp. 141–57, https://doi.org/10.1080/03612112.2020.1715675.
- Stevens, Corey (2018), 'Fat on campus: Fat college students and hyper(in)visible stigma', *Sociological Focus*, 51:2, pp. 130–49, https://doi.org/10.1080/00380237.2017.1368839.
- Woodson, Ariel (2018), 'I love fashion, but fashion doesn't love me back', *Racked*, 5 June, https://www.racked.com/2018/6/5/17405966/plus-size-shopping-fashion-struggles Accessed 15 September 2021.

This is my truth and just one fat faculty member's perspective. I invite other fat fashion faculty members to contact me to investigate this phenomenon and our experiences further.

## NOTE

1. Similar to my colleagues, I retain the word "obese" when citing literature or quotes using this word, placing it in scare quotes to denote what Fat Studies scholars consider medicalizing terminology.

## REFERENCES

Begley, Sharon (2012), 'Fat and getting fatter: U.S. obesity rates to soar by 2030', Reuters, 18 September, https://www.reuters.com/article/us-obesity-us/fat-and-getting-fatter-u-s-obesityrates-to-soar-by-2030-idUSBRE88H0RA20120918. Accessed 15 September 2020.

Chaerani, Astrid Restu and Junaidi, J. (2019), 'Does diet start tomorrow? A discourse analysis of self-deprecating humor against diet culture in diet starts tomorrow', *Celtic: A Journal of Culture, English Language Teaching, Literature and Linguistics*, 6:2, pp. 51–62.

Christel, Deborah (2014), 'It's your fault you're fat: Judgements of responsibility and social conduct in the fashion industry', *Clothing Cultures*, 1:3, pp. 303–20.

Escalera, Elena Andrea (2009), 'Stigma threat and the fat professor', in E. S. Rothblum and S. Solovay (eds), *The Fat Studies Reader*, New York: New York University Press, pp. 205–15.

Matwick, Keri and Matwick, Kelsi (2017), 'Self-deprecatory humor on TV cooking shows', *Language & Communication*, 56, pp. 33–41.

Russell, Danielle (2002), 'Self-deprecatory humour and the female comic: Self-destruction or comedic construction?', *Third Space: A Journal of Feminist Theory and Culture*, 2:1, https://journals.lib.sfu.ca/index.php/thirdspace/article/view/d_russell/3117. Accessed 31 August 2022.

# 6

# Pattern-Cutting without Cultural Appropriation

*Kevin Almond and Greg Climer*

This chapter considers how cultural appropriation can be minimized in the fashion design pattern-cutting process. In the creative arts, cultural appropriation is the adoption of certain creative elements, by members of another creative yet more dominant culture, from a non-dominant culture without the consent of people who belong to that culture. This can involve using concepts, objects, emblems and other facets of visual or non-visual artefacts associated with a particular culture. Cultural appropriation is widespread in the fashion design process, and we can easily find examples in design, textiles, silhouettes, models and patternmaking. Many current fashion teaching methods comply with, normalize and perpetuate cultural appropriation. For instance, fashion design students are often instructed to gather images from different cultures and pull elements together to create a narrative for a design and, subsequently, a pattern-cutting idea. There is often little regard or depth of understanding for the significance of the people or customs presented in the cultural images. This perpetuates the oppression of minority cultures and allows the empowered culture to profit from the ideas of the minority. Doing so can diminish the importance of the minority's cultural knowledge, visual identity and craft practices, even though the dominating culture may retain admiration and respect for the plundered nation's traditions.

Fashion education has not addressed cultural appropriation on a grand scale because it exists within a system that benefits from cultural hierarchies and colonialism. Historically, there has been no financial motivation to change this system within the fashion industry because we have trained students to work within cultural confines, whether developing design and pattern-cutting ideas or showing work with mood boards and technical illustrations, etc. To minimize cultural appropriation in the future, it is essential to teach students to be aware of its negative connotations throughout their fashion education to redress this balance of power when entering the industry.

A literature search ascertained that across the globe, pattern-cutting methods taught in most fashion schools are largely based on western traditions. This approach revolves around flat pattern-cutting where a shape is drafted on a flat surface using measurements and darts and seaming to create the silhouette. Pattern-cutting methods in Asia, including China and Japan, are more fluid and utilize the kimono shape, without darts. This method is unstructured and involves wrapping and draping fabric on the body to create a silhouette. It is also noteworthy that cultures with their own pattern-cutting traditions teach the craft using a western methodology. For instance, Bunka Fashion School in Japan teaches western pattern-cutting despite Japan's rich history of garment making, where cutting emanates from eastern traditions. Examples such as this suggest there is a global dominance of western culture in pattern-cutting; however, the west appropriates global cutting approaches. Although a greater awareness of cultural appropriation has recently been added in global fashion design curricula, fashion education has not fully embraced this in teaching patternmaking. This skill is integral, as a pattern is the first stage in transforming a design idea into a three-dimensional garment. Patternmaking is often taught separately from design; however, it can also be a source of inspiration for the design. Teaching students to rebalance their reliance on cultural appropriation in pattern-cutting is essential as they can be encouraged to begin the process with *minimal reference points* in order to diminish bias. It also boosts a greater ethical awareness of the activities involved in this process.

Within this chapter, we explore a pedagogic case study, which evaluated pattern-cutting initiatives that minimized and shifted cultural appropriation within the classroom. The motivation for this project came from conversations at *The First International Symposium for Creative Pattern-Cutting*, held at The University of Huddersfield in the United Kingdom in 2013 (Almond 2013). We initially discussed cultural appropriation within design and referred to European colonization in American history and the subsequent limitations placed on Indigenous people in the North Americas. The conversation shifted to a discussion about pattern-cutting craft. Here, we were talking about the theft of ideas and the erasure of cultural craft traditions, but now there was a relatable skill set on which to hang our discussion. From a personal perspective, our investment in the project meant we had to critically observe our own culture and learn from others as we investigated cutting practices that acknowledge a variety of cultural references. Decentring western patternmaking approaches within the fashion industry can create opportunities for new knowledge in the discipline and ethical cross-cultural collaboration.

Fashion embraces the new and unexpected, yet the teaching of pattern-cutting tends to perpetuate methodologies without interrogating their underlying logic.

Creative approaches to pattern-cutting challenge assumptions about our traditions, not eradicating them but unpacking them. We recognized that designing and creating patterns without any reference points was challenging because our ideas and imagination are influenced by what we have seen in popular culture, the fashion industry and through lived experiences.

The aims of the chapter are to:

- Discuss and evaluate pattern-cutting initiatives that minimize cultural appropriation.
- Initiate a globally diversified approach to pattern-cutting where innovation in the cut is explored through craft approaches and the possibilities inherent in the fabric.
- Establish a globally significant reference point of lasting influence and a catalyst for new thinking in pattern-cutting to transcend cultural appropriation and bias.

## Literature review

Within the literature review, we explored the broader significance of cultural appropriation (Hall 1997; Vasalou et al. 2014). The *Oxford English Dictionary* defines it as, 'The unacknowledged or inappropriate adoption of the practices, customs, or aesthetics of one social or ethnic group by members of another (typically dominant) community or society' (2018: 1). This definition hints at the negativity behind appropriation, suggesting that removing an object or image from a country or culture and placing it within another context is both unfitting and inapt. The United Nations supports the concept and is guided by the principles of their charter, the: *Declaration of the Rights of Indigenous Peoples*, which seeks to protect human rights that maintain standards for the dignity, welfare and survival of Indigenous peoples globally. Article 31 of the declaration states, 'Indigenous peoples have the right to maintain control, protect and develop their cultural heritage, traditional knowledge and traditional cultural expressions' (Cultural Survival, n.pag.). This authenticates the cultural identity of different ethnicities. Sociologist Steve Bannon described how identification with an ethnic group involves retaining a shared ancestry, national and regional origins and a sense of language (Fenton 1999). The embezzlement of aspects of an ethnicity occurs when it is appropriated and exploited within another culture. Writer Rebecca Naughton observed, 'Cultural appropriation affects a culture such as an ethnic group, whether that be an ethnic group currently habituating in their country of origin, or whether a group retain ancestors from that ethnicity' (2019: 10).

Within design and pattern-cutting activities in the fashion industry, the cultural appropriation of an ethnic group is where the brand or designer utilizes an ethnic visual source that belongs to another culture, religion or country but has not sought the correct permission to do this. The visual source is subsequently used in the brand's designs to gain a profit for the company (Green and Kaiser 2017; Knox; 2011; Pham 2014; Vasalou et al. 2014). Cultural appropriation within the fashion industry has been prevalent throughout history; however, questioning its ethics has become topical because it is, in effect, theft. Some fashion scholars have considered how we can move away from cultural appropriation by shifting power structures; Green and Kaiser (2017) emphasized how the many strata and appropriation levels need careful consideration. Media Studies expert Minh-Ha T. Pham (2014) explored how designers could benefit from a deeper historical exploration of indigenous regions to inspire instead of appropriating ideas. These concepts are further explored in the students' multifaceted approaches to their work.

There has been an increase in internet articles about cultural appropriation within fashion houses (Gharib 2018; Gorrie 2017; Manning 2013). Naughton discussed design appropriation in Riccardo Tisci's Autumn/Winter 2015 collection *Chola Victorian*, for the French fashion house Givenchy (Armstrong 2015). The collection was controversial because, in Mexico, *Chola* is ('an expression used to describe a dog and is a negative slur to describe Mexican immigrants living in the United States'). The hair styling during the fashion show was inspired by immigrants but they failed to use any Hispanic models (Picardi 2015). Naughton described how the designer appropriated a style from their culture but had not involved them in aspects of the restyling. The journalist Alice Thompson, writing for a British daily national newspaper, *The Times*, described how accusations of cultural appropriation had gone into overdrive with the example of *Papercut Patterns*, a New Zealand pattern cutter for the online sewing community who 'Had been shunned by some craft people for copying Japanese culture by suggesting that its followers try a "Kochi Kimono" pattern' (Thompson 2019: 25).

Pattern-cutting involves the three-dimensional interpretation of a design idea to manufacture the final garment, and the merger of cultural approaches has informed many different pattern-cutting methods. There is a fundamental difference in pattern-cutting in eastern and western cultures (Almond 2010; Almond and Power, 2016; Almond and Power, 2018; Fox and Sissons 2016: 28; McQuillan et al. 2013; Nakamichi 2010, 2011). The differences, for example, are evident in the bodice and kimono block. The western bodice block relies on darts and seams to create its shape, whereas the eastern kimono block has a built-in sleeve and relies on wrapping the fabric around the body. A synthesis of these two approaches can create exciting results, as emphasized by fashion journalist Brenda Polan,

My admiration for the Japanese designers of the last decades of the twentieth-century, from Kenzo, through Miyake to Kawakubo and Yamamoto and their inheritors is rooted in their respect for the craft traditions of all cultures and the creativity expressed in their East meets West sensibility.

(2019: n.pag.)

Furthermore, we included an in-depth review of pattern-cutting taught in most global fashion schools that included an analysis of contemporary and historical literature related to pattern-cutting methods (Carr et al. 2016: 15; Page 2013; Plummer 2016: 25; Waugh 1968). The purpose was to identify if a bias towards teaching is based on eastern or western traditions. The findings identified little bias within most approaches converging on three methods: flat pattern drafting, cutting on the stand and two-dimensional and three-dimensional pattern development software. Flat pattern drafting uses body measurements and a pre-formulated draft; the pattern is drawn upon paper in a two-dimensional format and is altered to form the style lines required to interpret the design idea (Aldrich 2002, 2008; Bray 1986; Fischer 2009; Joseph-Armstrong 1999). Making the garment with cheap fabric, such as calico, allows the shape to be refined and altered when fitting it on the body. Draping on the stand is a three-dimensional approach to creating garment ideas (Joseph-Armstrong 2008; Kiisel 2013). It involves the manipulation of fabric on a three-dimensional form to achieve a shape which allows for greater experimentation. The draped pieces are laid onto pattern paper and then traced to create a pattern. Then, before a final pattern is created, a toile is produced and fitted on a model to test the pattern. Two and three-dimensional computer-aided design pattern-cutting has developed significantly in the last decade. The advantages of computerized pattern-cutting lie in the saving of time and the ability to view and manipulate ideas on a screen (Fang 2003; Hardaker and Fozzard 1998; Jefferson et al. 2012; Power et al. 2011; Sul and Jin Kang 2006). Pattern designs are displayed on avatars in various poses with realistic drapes.

We identified a recent body of pattern-cutting literature from Japan which explores a creative approach to cutting that appropriates both eastern and western influences. Pattern-cutting manuals published by a former Professor Tomoko Nakamichi from Bunka College in Japan, documented the results of research she carried out developing pattern-cutting instruction for her students (Nakamichi 2010, 2011). A reviewer of Nakamichi's books described her approach as, 'Intimidating and inspirational at the same time, *Pattern Magic* is not so much a "read" as a "see" and ponder' (Shea 2018: 1). The author shows how complex sculptural effects can be added to simple garments through experimental manipulation of paper. These books also document some of the sculptural techniques of influential Japanese designers such as Comme des Garçons and Yohji Yamamoto.

When they began showing their collections in Paris in the 1980s, their extraordinary shapes were soon appropriated by western designers inspired by their creations. The transformational reconstruction techniques introduced by the Japanese pattern cutter and designer Shingo Sato popularized the elimination of darting with seam lines, which is considerably different from conventional western approaches to pattern-cutting because the garments are constructed in three dimensions (Sato 2014). This process follows neither a western or eastern approach to cutting (Figures 6.1 and 6.2).

Some literature considers how the discipline of pattern-cutting has been taught and practised through innovative and interdisciplinary approaches. Researchers investigated the approaches through a meta-review of research papers presented at the second *International Conference for Creative Pattern-Cutting* in 2016 (Climer 2016: 17; Harding 2016: 21; Hardingham 2016: 21; McQuillan 2016: 26; Lindqvist 2016: 25). This conference was significant as it was an international platform for presenting and discussing research related to pattern-cutting. Each of the authors explored new ways to practice and teach pattern-cutting that, 'Blur the boundaries between different disciplines, mediums and techniques, introducing reflective practice to underpin learning by doing and encouraging the exploration of novel techniques and their benefits to learning' (Almond and Power 2018: 34). However, none of these papers explored issues related to cultural appropriation

FIGURE 6.1: Pattern workshop by Shingo Sato. Photograph courtesy of The British Fashion Council.

FIGURE 6.2: Interdisciplinary approach to cut – How Does a Box Become a Garment (Hardingham, 2016: 22). Photograph courtesy of Laura Hardingham.

in pattern-cutting. Ultimately, we identified a scarcity of work that documented cutting approaches devoid of cultural references. Therefore, the purpose of this chapter is to record the results of the pedagogic case study, which explored a culturally bereft approach. These results are evaluated as a catalyst for new thinking in pattern-cutting that will transcend cultural appropriation, be globally significant and fill a significant gap in pattern-cutting literature.

## *Methodological approach*

We selected a qualitative methodological approach because it allows the researcher to get close to the heart of the subject. As Denzin and Lincoln said 'Qualitative researchers stress the socially constructed nature of reality, the intimate relationship between the researcher and what is studied, and the situational constraints that shape inquiry' (2005: 10). We wanted the process to be both exploratory and observational in order to consider the characteristics, descriptions and definitions of cultural appropriation and pattern-cutting in the classroom. The first research method was the pedagogic case study evaluating if pattern-cutting initiatives minimize cultural appropriation and bias among fashion students. We chose a case study approach because they comprehensively and thoroughly analyse a subject within its contextual setting. They also inform a practice, such as pattern-cutting, by recording what has been achieved, what is currently working and what issues or areas need improvement.

Our methodology required us to omit the purpose of our study; 'Do limited cultural references in a pattern-cutting class affect cultural appropriation?' While the students knew they were participating in a research project, we did not make students aware of our approach because that might have altered their responses or influenced their creative thinking. Instead, we presented it as a *minimal reference project*, the student's only tools being their pattern-cutting equipment and the shapes they were provided to work with. The project was titled, *Creative Construction: Explorations in Pattern-Cutting* and asked the students to create patterns and evaluate the initiatives. We explained that we would explore fashion concepts and design practices outside the constraints of building a 'collection'. Initially, as an exercise, we asked students to consider how any two shapes with the same perimeter could fit together, and they may not lie flat, but they could come together.

With this basic rule, each student was asked to work with a single shape, repeated in multiple. It was suggested that this could be a rectangle, a square, a triangle, or a more complex shape. From this, they created a sculptural shape. New seam lines could be introduced to the shape, allowing the structural technique to influence the silhouette while not dictating style lines, print or colour, etc. The students were challenged to consider how to finish them and how they would fit the human body and begin to emulate the look of a garment. In order to troubleshoot these questions, we asked each designer to completely finish the prototype garments with facings or linings and seam finishes. The garments were made of inexpensive muslin and needed to be of high fidelity in their make and finish. Various exercises with shapes were completed throughout the course.

As well as evaluating pattern-cutting initiatives that minimized cultural appropriation and bias, the learning objectives of the project were to:

- Demonstrate methodologies in which pattern-cutting can be used as a design process either alone or in tandem with other design processes such as drawing or draping.
- Demonstrate how explorations with non-traditional shapes can be transformed into fully functional garments.
- Develop creative innovation and experimentation in the application of pattern-cutting.
- Develop the critical and reflective skills required to translate explorations into fashion design.
- Develop an independent approach to design.

In this educational context, the case study incorporated practice-led activities in the pattern-cutting studio. Practice-based research involves work carried out in order to gain new knowledge by utilizing the practice and examining the outcomes of that practice. At the beginning of the activities, we discussed with the students how different cultures cut garments in different ways. Then we explained that the approach revolved around creating algorithms for cutting, including using shapes on the human form to create ideas without visual references from other sources or, more specifically, in the case of this research, cultural references.

Instead, we asked the students to explore what was possible by manipulating fabric. The aim was to initiate a diverse approach where innovation in pattern-cutting is explored through craft approaches and the possibilities inherent in the fabrics. We also introduced an object-based approach, allowing an article to be closely analysed. This allowed the students to study their work's ongoing progression and results through observation and handling (Kawamura 2011; Kim and Mida 2015; Taylor 2002).

For instance, we presented garments from different countries to demonstrate how various cultures arrived at similar shapes and how each culture has its unique approach. As the idea was to focus on the garment's cut, we discouraged any reference to pattern-cutting manuals from the East or West. Initially, students were enthusiastic; however, they quickly became frustrated because they could not reference the literature. We discussed this with students at the beginning of the project as we identified the challenges in eradicating cultural bias. We recognized that we could rebalance power in pattern-cutting through minimal physical reference of visual sources from books, magazines, the internet, etc. Therefore, the students had to drape shapes on the human form to create ideas and explore what was possible through fabric manipulation. Draping initiated a problem-solving exercise between the tutee and the student to understand the qualities in the cut of the garments they began to create. We identified the value of this at the end of the project. Students felt a sense of achievement because they evaluated how each stage of the cutting process worked and extrapolated this new knowledge into the development of their patterns. Cultural appropriation and bias were minimized because no visual culture was emphasized as the ideal.

The case study also opened up opportunities to better understand the body and create clothes for body diversity, as the class included individuals with different body shapes, ethnicities and genders. Therefore, the students were encouraged to think beyond the traditional shape and sizing of the dress mannequin or the pattern block by draping the fabric on each other and comparatively considering how the fabric hung. We devised the project to free students from relying on cultural or other pattern-cutting references apart from the subconscious visual influences gathered from their lived experiences. It was, therefore, essential for them to consider their learning from this shift in reference points.

## Findings

### Appropriation or appreciation: The pedagogic approach to cut

Seven different versions of the class, delivered to different sets of students, were analysed at Parsons School of Design and California College of Arts. The approach to cut in the project began with an acknowledgement that the pattern-cutting would initially be created from western knowledge. Although the students were not allowed to reference pattern-cutting manuals, we discussed a modicum of selected literature at the beginning. Using *Cut My Cote* by Dorothy Burnham (1973), the students were shown how different cultures cut garments based on the width of their traditional looms. Burnham was a curator at the Royal Ontario Museum, in Toronto, Canada – she published *Cut my Cote* as an exhibition catalogue to accompany a curated exhibition with the same name in 1973 and was one of the first to emphasize the proficiency of cut as essential to the interaction between fabric width, garment cut and the resultant waste of fabric.

We also showed students patterns for garments from other countries to demonstrate how many cultures arrived at similar shapes, yet each culture had its own unique approach. Much of this information was derived from a book by historian Max Tilke entitled, *Costume Patterns and Designs: A Survey of Costume Patterns and Designs of all Periods and Nations from Antiquity to Modern Times* (1974). This sourcebook is widely used within the theatrical costume industry as it contains a complete series of costume patterns and designs from many time periods and nations. This initial research created algorithms for cutting, and algorithms are instruction sets which are repeatable with different variables. For example, as mentioned earlier, one exercise challenged students to use one shape repeatedly.

The students cut multiple rectangles, circles or hexagons, which were pinned together to create three-dimensional volume and these were taken to the dress form to begin draping (Figure 6.3).

This exercise forced them to step away from the conventional mindset of, for example, a bodice or a skirt. The shapes, when pinned together, created unexpected volumes, which meant the students had to think beyond their understanding of traditional silhouettes (Figure 6.4). Another short exercise began with an A4 piece

FIGURE 6.3: Multiple rectangles. Photograph courtesy of Greg Climer.

FIGURE 6.4: A student draping with only rectangles, exploring unexpected drapes, which occur on the body as a result. Photograph courtesy of Greg Climer.

of paper, cutting it once or twice and connecting it to create volume. The students had to identify one shape that could be imagined as a garment, enlarging it to a garment size and then draping with the shape. The underlying idea behind these exercises was to let the students drape with something other than a rectangle of fabric. Whether it was shapes sewn together or a rectangle with cuts, it disrupted more conventional approaches to draping. However, some students began to pin the shapes into a skirt or bodice shape to control the volume. When faced with draping on a human form with fabric, designers often go towards the garments they are familiar with (skirt, bodice, jacket, etc.) to bring order to the shapes created. The students naturally reflected on their prior knowledge of garments; however, the various cutting activities in the project disrupted this.

The students wanted to produce conventional pattern pieces but were prevented from doing so because they started with other shapes that needed to be placed on the human form (in this case, the dress stand or their own bodies). Established approaches to pattern-cutting were disrupted and the students were forced to be creative in order to find new outcomes. These outcomes were built in the moment, and the shift in approach, from using visual references to using shapes on the human form, limited cultural appropriation from happening. The designers could not reference a culture (or other pattern-cutting manuals) but explored what was possible through craft techniques and understanding the fabric's possibilities (as well as limitations). In the classroom, the project broke down into three three-hour sessions, once a week for four weeks. In the first week, we introduced the concept. The notion of identical shapes being sewn together was demonstrated using squares cut from calico fabric. If two identical squares were sewn together and simply stacked, one on top of the other, the result was a pillow. However, if they were offset, so the corner of one square was sewn to the middle of the other square's edge, then volume was produced. The next demonstration considered how this could be expanded. Six squares would produce a cube if they were aligned, corner to corner.

However, if they are offset, the resulting volumes are more dynamic. As fabric has a unique ability to drape and flow or hold its form, the outcomes were still able to adapt to the overall shape of the human body. Having shown the students this basic concept of creating volume, we asked them to begin exploring shapes more abstractly. Each student was instructed to select a shape and cut it in multiples. As the creative volumes evolved from how the shapes were connected and not from the inherent complexity of the shapes, we encouraged the students to start using – a square, a triangle, a rectangle or a circle. However, they often wanted to work with a symbolic shape, such as a star or a heart. While the initial explorations were trickier with these more complex shapes, they resulted in equally compelling work. The students pinned shapes together on the table, not the dress form. They were asked to continually pick up the piece, hold it from different directions, and observe how it draped when held each way. They were searching for forms that would inspire them to create clothes. This continued for most of the first session as the students gradually moved from the table to the dress stand, with a rough idea of what form the garment was beginning to take.

As the project evolved, creating garment shapes with minimal cultural reference proved challenging, if not impossible. We are surrounded by the vocabulary of many different cultures and their clothing – something we are visually conscious of. Therefore, an individual student's project could evolve into a shirt shape and the student had to decide if a western men's collar and button front placket was appropriate or perhaps fronts that cross and tie like an eastern kimono. In this context, it was necessary to remember that there was a difference between minimizing cultural appropriation and bias and attempting to ignore all cultures and their influence on our daily lives. We identified that design and pattern-cutting are problem-solving forms, and learning how to decide upon a shape that could become a garment is far from appropriating the aesthetic of another culture; it is multifaceted and more subtle.

Emphasized by Green and Kaiser, 'Appropriation is a complex political and ethical discussion with many nuances and layers that require careful and critical unpacking' (2017: 145). Within the case study, students had to find new ways to engage with garment creation and their findings evolved from their own practice and consideration of how the shapes they created would impact upon the human form. Therefore, the student's subconscious awareness of cultural influences acquired through their lived experiences needed to disregard the wider impact of appropriation on Indigenous identities, aesthetics and their resultant economies to be truly original. During a group feedback session in the second week, the students discussed their pinned-together prototypes. (Figures 6.5 and 6.6).

The variety of ways they designed known garments or parts of garments: shirts, sleeves, skirts, dresses, etc. was considered. Conversation focused on the overall aesthetic as well as the unique solutions to shaping fabric to the body. The discussions unfolded in different ways because each student's work was unique. We wanted to identify clear examples of how they created new or unexpected ways of forming shapes. For example, a sleeve might exist set into an armhole. However, neither the sleeve cap nor the armscye follow traditional patterns (the armscye is the circumference of the armhole measurement). Although the project did not specifically reference ideas from other cultures, we discussed how ideas found in different cultures had subconsciously and organically collided on the garments.

For instance, as taught by western pattern cutters such as Winifred Aldrich (Aldrich 2002, 2008), a straight band may have been used as a collar reminiscent of a Japanese kimono that is used on a neckline cut to the curve. We identified these

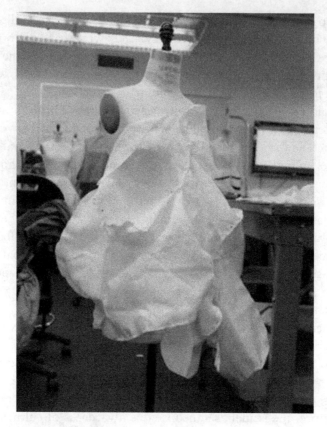

FIGURE 6.5: An example of a pinned together garment made of shapes on a dress form. Photograph courtesy of Greg Climer.

moments as opportunities to discuss how creating patterns are problem-solving exercises. What are the benefits of rectangle collars versus those of shaped collars? Which patterns create more waste and which patterns value the qualities inherent in the textiles more? How did the ideas impact on the overall aesthetic or the ability to move in the garment?

The conversations led to an understanding of how the students could put themselves into a new mindset. It was perceived that it is simplistic to believe we can follow the thoughts of an entire culture's evolution through a few questions about how a garment works. However, the question of *why* different shapes have evolved is an important step towards understanding other cultures. Therefore, we agreed that this technique could be used in a serious and rigorous study of another culture to inspire pattern-cutting instead of appropriating cultural ideas. This concept, suggested by Minh-Ha T. Pham, described how media criticism had not stopped

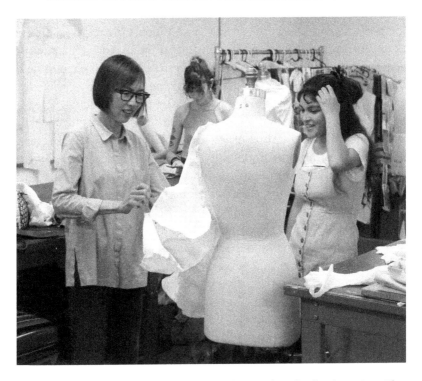

FIGURE 6.6: Pinned together prototype discussed in student feedback session. Photograph courtesy of Greg Climer.

fashion designers from continuing to appropriate ideas from other cultures. She said, 'Critics should change the subject by examining the histories of what gets swiped – and more importantly, what doesn't' (2014: n.pag.). In pattern-cutting, instead of simply appropriating a pattern idea from another culture, a much deeper analysis of its Indigenous visual heritage could result in a greater depth of original ideas instead of commandeering them.

## *Student feedback and observations*

The focus of the case study evolved organically out of an ongoing exploration of creative pattern-cutting in both of our individual research ventures (Almond 2010, 2016; Climer 2013, 2016). As a result, the emphasis on cultural appropriation was not built into the exit interviews with students and this allowed them to consider what they had achieved with minimal reference to other cultural artefacts (Almond and Climer 2019).

At the project's end, we emphasized to the students the relationships between minimal cultural appropriation and bias and a creative approach to pattern-cutting. The students also acknowledged that minimal reference points encouraged greater creativity in thought processes and practice. Upon completing the case study, we sent an online, anonymous exit questionnaire to the students. The questionnaire asked them to write their thoughts about the project and what they had learned without referencing our practice of minimizing cultural references in pattern-cutting. We think the anonymity allowed the students to consider their exploration of creative pattern-cutting organically.

Totalling all seven versions, the course questionnaire averaged a 50 per cent response rate, with a range of 11 to 64 per cent. The question that brought about the most insightful response was, 'What were the most effective aspects of this project?' One student commented that it, 'Taught me how to start a project from nothing. Now I know I can figure out the design through the experimenting process' (respondent 1). This points towards the idea that successful designing can begin from a place other than cultural reference and in this case the inspiration was in the shapes given to the students as a starting point. Other students reiterated this idea. The challenge of finding forms in the fabric, evolving from the initial experiments opened the students up to new possibilities. One commented, 'It gave me a totally new aspect for developing a pattern. Very inspiring and helpful for my future work. Also, the project was very challenging, but it made me want to improve for the better' (respondent 2). This highlights how many fashion students consider design and patternmaking to be a defined process of viewing inspiring images and then reimagining them as clothes. The new aspect of developing a pattern from shapes refers to designing and pattern development being the same process. The clothing design is a result of the pattern-cutting and the two activities are merged.

Throughout the project, we identified how the pattern-cutting approach required the designer to respond to the fabrics in their hands instead of cultural imagery. Criticism from some students was that we, as tutors, did not teach from the full extent of our own pattern-cutting knowledge and experience. As one said, 'The tutors introduced ideas and let the students utilize the ideas in a rather open-ended manner' (respondent 3). This was intentional on our part, aimed at generating creative freedom and encouraging the exploration of many possibilities.

We considered this to be critical to the project's success because if the goal had been to generate referential shapes, the end goal's foresight would have been counterproductive. This also suggests opportunities for future iterations in the project when we emphasize its pedagogic aims and objectives with the students. By introducing this meta-level discussion, related to how we learn and how this fits into a play-based and creative freedom model of learning, the frustrations expressed by the student's criticism could be alleviated. Reframing the struggle and frustration at failed iterations is, therefore, a crucial part of the process in which we learn.

Based on our observations during the project delivery, the initial minimal reference point pattern-cutting approach was a struggle for the students. The results of draping on the dress stand or the human body are fleeting unless each change to the garment is carefully documented. Often students would express dismay that they had found and lost a beautiful shape and could not quite recreate it. This style of cutting is a skill which needs to be developed.

Creating habits within the students, where each change is photographed or recorded in other ways, such as drawing or note-taking. In future projects, we will teach students to habitually photograph, record, draw or take notes to document each change to the design. Our classroom observations also identified that many students struggle to think outside their known vocabulary of clothing. Indeed, it is not easy to think outside any vocabulary, whether language, clothing or otherwise. What can be encouraged is an awareness of choices and to continually ask: 'Is this choice because I know about established garment shapes

FIGURE 6.7: Student outcome of creative pattern-cutting project. Photograph courtesy of JunLin He.

or because it is the best choice for this new garment?' The students did not artic-ulate these observations in the exit interviews although one commented, 'One of the things I really like about the project is how easy it is to start over, even just how easy it is to make a new model because I love the feeling of going back to the start' (respondent 4). Overall, we identified that future project delivery would include a more direct discussion of the appropriation of, and use of, the student's established knowledge and how this influences the subsequent learning style. It was also considered that minimal reference to cultural appropriation and bias at the project's onset would continue to be an important element in its continuous delivery, so the student's creative thinking is unprejudiced from the outset (Figure 6.7).

## Call to action

As fashion wakes up to the negative consequences of cultural appropriation, we need to seek out new ways to work which are equitable. The project explored is one entry point into pattern-cutting (as well as designing) that seeks to minimize cultural reference and bias. However, we do not advocate for a fashion industry devoid of cultural influences and cultural cross-pollination. There is an argument that without cultural appropriation and admiration for different cultures, the arte-facts and clothing of oppressed peoples would have disappeared with no hope of revival; however, this does not mean the practice is acceptable. It also needs to be recognized that many other visual sources inspire designers. As the fashion jour-nalist, Brenda Polan pointed out,

> Designers have just as often been inspired by the clothing of the 'dead' or at least past cultures – by ancient Greece and Rome of the Republic, by Mediaeval, Renais-sance and Directoire, by operetta milkmaids and opera queens, archaic pirates and matelots, soldiers and streetwalkers. Is that cultural appropriation? Or is it OK because there's no one left to whine that it is.

> (2019: n.pag.)

It is questionable whether patterns are ever cut without a reference point, as our ideas and imaginations are always influenced by what we have already seen. Ulti-mately, as instructors, this was the main thing we learnt. It also presents a challenge for the future development of the project and the possibility of beginning from zero instead of minimal cultural appropriation and bias. We were also conscious of our own identities in the process of thinking through cultural appropriation and our own analysis of pattern-cutting and how we taught it. As Caucasian males, one

British and one American, our critique of students' work came from that point of view. We openly discussed our identities with the students as a factor that influenced how we viewed the work.

We conceded that if we had been raised in a culture with different traditions from those we taught, we would have been more aware of cultural appropriation in patternmaking. Instead, the clothing we were surrounded by was initially the clothing we had taught our students to design and pattern-cut; therefore, we had been unaware of these missing aspects in pattern-cutting education for a long time. The case study project presented an opportunity to discuss inherent bias, which might not have otherwise been addressed, as we both recognize that you can not change what you do not acknowledge. In conclusion, it is necessary to empower and collaborate with cultures and their heritage when referenced in pattern-cutting and design approaches. New entry points into design, such as the minimal reference cutting project, are a starting point for new ways of thinking about form and pattern-cutting. Suppose these ideas are combined with equitable cross-cultural collaborations. In that case, there is a possible future in which pattern-cutting and, subsequently, design evolves beyond an overreliance on cultural influences, subconscious or otherwise.

When student patternmakers reference other cultures, using that culture's imagery or knowledge, they should be encouraged to ask: '*Is this culture benefitting from this as much as I am?*' This may entail rethinking approaches to the design process, such as sourcing fabrics from artisans in other countries instead of appropriating their patterns and ideas. For example, Siki Ims Menswear Autumn/Winter 2011 collection collaborated with Navajo textile artist Tahnibaa Naataanii, and her fabrics were an integral part of the designs (Designers Party 2011). This is an example of how designers can actively work with the cultures which inspire their imagination in a way that is respectful and mutually beneficial. We suggest watching and discussing Siki Ims Autumn/Winter 2011 collection in classes.

When working across cultural lines, the overriding call to action is to evaluate how this pedagogic case study could enhance the teaching of pattern-cutting in global fashion education. We hope instructors are inspired by the results and see them as a catalyst to develop further exciting projects that encourage new thinking and shifts in power, resulting in exciting ways to create patterns. We hope the minimal reference point will have international relevance because it can be accessible to all countries and cultures. This approach should also prompt educational faculties to look at their wider curricula and examine different approaches to cultural misuse in fashion design activities such as research, design development, marketing and promotion, as well as in other design disciplines such as textiles or illustration. The case study results have allowed us to document these initiatives; therefore, we have established an important reference point for new thinking in pattern-cutting that transcends cultural appropriation and bias and is globally significant. Overall, it should encourage students and professionals in the fashion studio to pick up fabric and start pattern-cutting as an approach to design without referencing visual artefacts related to other civilizations and their populations, subconsciously or physically.

## REFERENCES

Aldrich, Winifred (2002), *Pattern Cutting for Women's Tailored Jackets*, Oxford: Blackwell Publishing.

Aldrich, Winifred (2008), *Pattern Cutting for Women's Wear*, Oxford: Blackwell Publishing.

Almond, Kevin (2010), 'Insufficient allure: The luxurious art and cost of creative pattern cutting', *International Journal of Fashion Design, Technology & Education*, 3:1, pp. 15–24.

Almond, Kevin (2013), *The First International Symposium for Creative Pattern Cutting*, University of Huddersfield, Huddersfield, 6–7 February.

Almond, Kevin (2016), 'The status of pattern cutting', *Fashion Practice: The Journal of Design, Creative Process & the Fashion Industry*, 8:1, pp. 168–80.

Almond, Kevin and Climer, Greg (2019), Student Interviews, San Francisco: Kevin Almond and Greg Climer.

Almond, Kevin and Power, Jess (2016), *The Second International Conference for Creative Pattern Cutting Abstracts*, Huddersfield: University of Huddersfield Repository, https://eprints.hud.ac.uk/id/eprint/28014/23Almondconference%20book-edited.pdf. Accessed 21 March 2023.

Almond, Kevin and Power, Jess (2018), 'Breaking the rules in pattern cutting: An interdisciplinary approach to promote creativity in pedagogy', *Art, Design & Communication in Higher Education*, 17:1, pp. 33–50.

Armstrong, Lisa (2015), 'Riccardo Tisci seduces with Victorian-inspired clothes at Givenchy', *The Telegraph*, 9 March, http://fashion.telegraph.co.uk/article/TMG11458539/Givenchy-autumnwinter-2015-collection-at-Paris-Fashion-Week.html. Accessed 30 August 2020.

Bray, Natalie (1986), *Dress Pattern Designing*, Oxford: Blackwell Publishing.

Burham, Dorothy, K. (1973), *Cut My Cote*, Toronto: The Royal Ontario Museum.

Carr, Elizabeth, Ohrn-McDaniel, Linda and Mehta, Archana (2016), 'Changing perspectives in the patternmaking and draping classroom', in K. Almond and J. Power (eds), *The Second International Conference for Creative Pattern Cutting Abstracts*, Huddersfield: University of Huddersfield Repository, https://eprints.hud.ac.uk/id/eprint/28014/23Almondconference%20book-edited.pdf. Accessed 21 March 2023.

Climer, Greg (2013), 'The cranial cut: Creating a pattern for the human head', *The International Journal of Fashion Design, Technology and Education*, 6:2, pp. 99–103.

Climer, Greg (2016), 'Parsons new curriculum', in K. Almond and J. Power (eds), The Second International Conference for Creative Pattern Cutting Abstracts, Huddersfield: University of

Huddersfield Repository, https://eprints.hud.ac.uk/id/eprint/28014/23Almondconference%20 book-edited.pdf. Accessed 21 March 2023.

Cultural Survival (2007), 'UN Declaration on the rights of Indigenous peoples', 13 September, https://www.culturalsurvival.org/undrip. Accessed 30 August 2020.

Denzin, Norman K., and Lincoln, Yvonna S. (2005), *The Sage Handbook of Qualitative Research*, 3rd ed., Thousand Oaks: Sage.

Designers Party (2011), 'Siki Im Fall/Winter 2011', 1 January, http://www.designersparty.com/entry/Siki-Im. Accessed 30 August 2020.

Fang, Jing-Jing (2003) '3D collar design creation,' *International Journal of Clothing Science & Technology*, 15:2, pp. 88–106.

Fenton, Steve (1999), *Ethnicity, Racism, Class and Culture*, London: Macmillan.

Fischer, Anette (2009), *Basics Fashion Design: Construction*, Lausanne: Ava.

Fox, Shelley and Sissons, Juliana (2016), 'Cutter – designer – cutter: Cutting as design', in K. Almond and J. Power (eds), *The Second International Conference for Creative Pattern Cutting Abstracts*, Huddersfield: University of Huddersfield Repository, https://eprints.hud.ac.uk/id/eprint/28014/23Almondconference%20book-edited.pdf. Accessed 21 March 2023.

Gharib, Malaka (2018), 'When is it ok to wear the clothing of another culture', *Goats and Soda*, 26 October, https://www.npr.org/sections/goatsandsoda/2018/10/26/658924715/when-is-it-ok-to-wear-the-clothing-of-another-culture. Accessed 20 August 2020.

Gorrie, Nayuka (2017), 'Chanel needs to understand Indigenous anger. There's nothing 'luxury' about it', *The Guardian*, 17 May, https://www.theguardian.com/commentisfree/2017/may/17/chanel-needs-to-understand-indigenous-anger-theres-nothing-luxury-about-it. Accessed 30 August 2020.

Green, Denise Nicole and Kaiser, Susan B. (2017), 'Fashion and appropriation', *Fashion, Style & Popular Culture*, 4:2, pp. 145–50.

Hall, Stuart (1997), *Representation: Cultural Representations and Signifying Practices*, Thousand Oaks: Sage Publications.

Hardaker, Caroline and Fozzard, Gary (1998), 'Towards the virtual garment', *International Journal of Clothing Science & Technology*, 10:2, pp. 114–27.

Harding, Lee (2016), 'Abstract approaches to creative cutting', in K. Almond and J. Power (eds), *The Second International Conference for Creative Pattern Cutting,* Huddersfield: University of Huddersfield, pp. 21–22.

Hardingham, Laura (2016), 'How can a box become a garment', in K. Almond and J. Power (eds), *The Second International Conference for Creative Pattern Cutting Abstracts*, Huddersfield: University of Huddersfield Repository, https://eprints.hud.ac.uk/id/eprint/28014/23Almondconference%20book-edited.pdf. Accessed 21 March 2023.

Jefferson, Aileen M., Power, Jess and Rowe, Helen (2012), 'Enhancing the employability of fashion students through the use of 3D CAD', *Journal of Conference Proceedings: Fashion Beyond Borders 14th Annual Conference for the International Foundation of Fashion Technology Institutes (IFFTI)*, 14, pp. 1–15.

Joseph-Armstrong, Helen (1999), *Pattern Making for Fashion Design*, New York: Pearson Education.

Joseph-Armstrong, Helen (2008), *Draping for Apparel Design*, New York: Fairchild Publications.

Kawamura, Yuniya (2005), *Fashion-ology: An Introduction to Fashion Studies*, Oxford: Berg.

Kawamura, Yuniya (2011), *Doing Research in Fashion and Dress*, Oxford: Berg.

Kiisel, Karolyn (2013), *Draping: The Complete Course*, London: Laurence King.

Kim, Alexandra and Mida, Ingrid (2015), *The Dress Detective: A Guide to Object Based Research in Fashion*, London: Bloomsbury Academic.

Knox, Kristin (2011), *Culture to Catwalk: How World Cultures Influence Fashion*, London: A. & C. Black.

Lindqvist, Rickard (2016), 'On the relationship between the shear forces in human skin and the grain direction of woven fabric', in K. Almond and J. Power (eds), *The Second International Conference for Creative Pattern Cutting Abstracts*. Huddersfield: University of Huddersfield Repository, https://eprints.hud.ac.uk/id/eprint/28014/23Almondconference%20book-edited.pdf. Accessed 21 March 2023.

Manning, Charles (2013), 'Karl Lagerfeld "plays" with controversial Native American imagery', *Cosmopolitan*, 11 December https://www.cosmopolitan.com/style-beauty/fashion/advice/a17015/chanel-native-american-inspired-collection/. Accessed 30 August 2020.

McQuillan, Holly (2016), 'Print as encoded way finding a system for the creation of garment form', in K. Almond and J. Power (eds), *The Second International Conference for Creative Pattern Cutting Abstracts*. Huddersfield: University of Huddersfield Repository, https://eprints.hud.ac.uk/id/eprint/28014/23Almondconference%20book-edited.pdf. Accessed 21 March 2023.

McQuillan, Holly, Rissanen, Timo and Roberts, Julian (2013), 'The cutting circle: How to make challenging designs', *Research Journal of Textile & Apparel*, 17:1, pp. 39–49.

Nakamichi, Tomoko (2010), *Pattern Magic*, London: Laurence King Publishing Ltd.

Nakamichi, Tomoko (2011), *Pattern Magic 2*, London: Laurence King Publishing Ltd.

Naughton, Rebecca (2019), 'Appropriation or appreciation? The ethics of cultural appropriation in high end and couture western fashion', *Undergraduate Dissertation*, Leeds: University of Leeds.

Oxford English Dictionary (2018), 'Cultural appropriation', *Oxford English Dictionary*, 9 November, http://www.oed.com.wam.leeds.ac.uk/view/Entry/45742?redirectedFrom=cultural+appropriation#eid1223654010. Accessed 30 August 2020.

Page, Arena (2013), 'Creative pattern technology', *The International Journal of Fashion Design, Technology & Education*, 6:2, pp. 89–99.

Pham, Minh-Ha T. (2014), 'Fashion's cultural-appropriation debate: Pointless', *The Atlantic*, 15 May, http://www.theatlantic.com/entertainment/archive/2014/05/cultural-appropriation-in-fashion-stop-talkingabout-it/370826/. Accessed 4 September 2020.

Picardi, Phillip (2015), 'The underlying issue with that epic Givenchy show', *Celebrity Beauty*, 9 March, https://www.refinery29.com/en-us/2015/03/83536/givenchy-fall-2015-runway-chola-inspiration. Accessed 30 August 2020.

Plummer, Brianna (2016), 'Scaffolding creative pattern cutting throughout the traditional patternmaking curriculum', in K. Almond and J. Power (eds), *The Second International Conference for Creative Pattern Cutting Abstracts*. Huddersfield: University of Huddersfield Repository, https://eprints.hud.ac.uk/id/eprint/28014/23Almondconference%20book-edited.pdf. Accessed 21 March 2023.

Polan, Brenda (2019), e-mail to authors, 5 May.

Power, Jess, Apeagyei, Phoebe and Jefferson, Aileen (2011), 'Integrating 3D scanning data & textile parameters into virtual clothing', *2nd International Conference on 3D Body Scanning Technologies*, Lugano, Switzerland, 25–26 October.

Sato, Shingo (2014), *Transformational Reconstruction*, New York: Antiquity Press.

Shea, Marilyn (2018), 'Community reviews – pattern magic', Goodreads, 21 October, https://www.goodreads.com/book/show/9047345-pattern-magic. Accessed 30 August 2023.

Sul, In Hwan and Jin Kang, Tae (2006), 'Interactive garment pattern design using virtual scissoring method', *International Journal of Clothing Science and Technology*, 18:1, pp. 31–42.

Taylor, Lou (2002), *The Study of Dress History: Studies in Design and Material Culture*, Manchester: Manchester University Press.

Thompson, Alice (2019), 'Cultural appropriation craze is a new ghetto: Trend of criticising people who borrow from other cultures risks taking us back to a time of ignorance and prejudice', *The Times*, 5 June, https://www.thetimes.co.uk/article/cultural-appropriation-craze-is-a-new-ghetto-lngzkj787. Accessed 20 March 2023.

Tilke, Max (1974), *Costume Patterns and Designs: A Survey of Costume Patterns and Designs of all Periods and Nations from Antiquity to Modern Times*, Winter Park, USA: Hastings House.

Vasalou, Asimina, Rilla Khaled, Gooch, Daniel and Benton, Laura (2014), 'Problematizing cultural appropriation', *Proceedings of the First ACM SIGCHI Annual Symposium on Computer-Human Interaction in Play*, pp. 267–76.

Waugh, Natalie (1968), *The Cut of Women's Clothes*, London: Faber and Faber.

# 7

# Diversity in Fashion Illustration:
# An Oxymoron, Don't You Think?

*Colleen Schindler-Lynch*

In this essay, I will discuss some of my observations, strategies and goals for including different representations of beauty in a traditional studio classroom setting. I have taught fashion illustration (analogue and digital) at Toronto Metropolitan University – formerly Ryerson – (TMU-FR) in Toronto for twenty years, instructing students in all years and areas of our programme. Over that time, I have prioritized discussion and the implementation of inclusive bodies, colours, ages and genders in significant ways in my classes. Before I talk about the initiatives I have taken, I first have to frame the subject as I do for my students. I believe the key to establishing thoughtful representation across the many categories of diversity is found in education. Giving pause to dissect, analyse and assess images without making snap judgements and assumptions, and in turn, reinforce the enabling and careful crafting of current visual culture through an informed eye and mind. On a personal note, I teach in an area where I do not see myself reflected in the images I encounter. As a middle-aged, plus-sized, petite woman, I do not exactly fit the image of what the industry submits as fashionable. Oh, I have style! Don't get me wrong, but I do not fit the stereotypical elongated, youthful beauty model preferred today. So I set out to incorporate images and meaningful discussions of inclusion and diversity in my classes. I endeavoured to make changes in small ways that would instil core values in my students, and they, in turn, would hopefully embark on their careers and subscribe to a broader lens for the industry over a long period. In the essay, I touch on topics such as the historical function of illustrated fashion, representing zeitgeist, student's preconceived ideas, the bombardment of images, algorithmic confinement, the power and potential of contemporary fashion illustration, reading images through a drawing-lens, the different perceptions between photography and illustration, and above all individual empowerment.

When you think of fashion illustration, depictions of elongated, stylized women probably come to mind. Fashion illustration is a defined niche in an industry abundant with visual communication; intrinsically embedded in all stages of the design process. Historically, it has parlayed information and visually commented on topics such as advice on dress, activities and etiquette (Mackrell 1997: 135). It has also revealed serious issues, such as the working conditions of labourers in the fashion industry, drawing attention to social realism (McNeil 2005: n.pag.). It has even comically satirized the nature of some fashion fads, yet, overall, it is largely mute on issues of body, colour and age. Some in the fashion industry have taken steps toward more diversified representations on runways, in the pages of magazines, on social media posts and in fashion education. For example, beginning in 2013, the Fashion at the Creative School at TMU-FR formally implemented a more diversified direction in the design curriculum. However, apart from body diversity, we do not see much else when looking at illustration representations of fashion. You have to sift to find strong, powerful, positive images of women and men of different ethnicities that are not culturally insensitive or rooted in stereotypes.

The types of images that we encounter representing fashion in the western world are an amalgamation of knowledge and distilled stylistic preferences. Creating a sinuous body by lengthening the spine, neck, or legs has been a historical hallmark of idealized beauty in many cultures over the centuries. The use of this artistic device contemporarily in illustration did not manifest spontaneously, and you can see the traces of this convention repeatedly throughout history. In the artwork of Mannerist painters of the Late Renaissance, such as Parmigianino, whose *Madonna and Child with Angels*, painted between 1534 and 1540, is also affectionately known as *Madonna of the Long Neck*. Not confined to European painting, elongation is also a recognizable stylistic trait noted in Japanese Bijin-ga woodblock prints such as Utamaro's depictions of beautiful women in the Ukiyo-e, for example (Duong 2019: n.pag.).

When discussing the birth of fashion communication, you need to look further into art history to understand the invention of *beauty*. The definition of beauty has always been intrinsically linked to fashion, whereby fashion is not just about the material draped on the body but about the type of body itself (Baudelaire 1995: 14). 'What poet, in sitting down to paint the pleasure caused by the sight of a beautiful woman, would venture to separate her from her costume?' (Baudelaire 1995: 31). For centuries, artists have had liberal interpretations of body affectations and reflected the zeitgeist of their eras (Danielson 1989: 36). The particular visual definition of beauty found in the stretched proportions of the body is now part of our everyday expectations because it has been a recurring affectation for more than four hundred years. Contemporary fashion illustrators who utilize this characteristic speak a visual language that spans centuries. Drawing attention to potential historical links for this affectation creates awareness – and awareness from understanding the origins, purpose and inherent characteristics of an image, object or topic is a crucial component in education that helps prevent students from merely jumping to conclusions.

Understanding some of the reasons behind the favoured body preferences is necessary. It is also imperative to recognize assumptions and biases that lead to that mental image. The viewer thinks they know what a fashion illustration is 'supposed' to look like, and therein lies a problem. The public is bombarded with images that might make us savvy to some extent – with regard to the category, such as style and aesthetic recognition – but it does not truly make us fluent in visual communication (Schroeder 2004: 235–37). Easy searching through keywords on Google or social media reveals the extent of sameness served to us. The volume of visual material we are exposed to daily and how those images impress us have been researched and studied. Jonathan Schroeder wrote about the savvy consumer; 'Visual consumption often involves mere looking without comprehension, gazing without knowledge, and watching without engagement' (Schroeder 2005: 11). Further stating that 'The overwhelming number, variety, and presence of images interfere with the ability to scrutinize and reflect upon individual images carefully, and lulls viewers into believing that seeing is understanding' (Schroeder 2005: 12). The assumption that all fashion illustrations are elongated or stylized is a misconception of current illustrated fashion imagery.

More is out there; we are not seeing it or being exposed to it because of an algorithmic bubble based on the relevance assigned to us through ranking code search results. In her article, 'You are now remotely controlled', for nytimes. com, Shoshana Zuboff comments, 'We thought that we search Google, but now we understand that Google searches us. We assumed that we use social media to connect, but we learned that connection is how social media uses us' (2020: n.pag.). The more we and others search for a subject, such as fashion illustration, through keywords and hashtags, the more promoted that topic becomes, the higher a search result appears in the list, and the more likely it is to be clicked on again. 'When the top ten results are similar, other different results – that have lower relevance scores based on the query [...] are hidden' (Martie and Van der Hoek 2015: 76). 'Search' reveals similarity based on our previous search history as well as the collective search topics of others. At different times, you are not necessarily searching but consuming, so your actions, likes and follows contribute to what you will be served. Seeking difference requires deliberate action to expand the algorithmic bubble defined by the creators and data miners of social media platforms, websites and online advertising. However, I would like to note that simply changing what and how you search is not a complete solution, in that deliberately seeking difference reinforces the concept of 'Other' (Ehlebracht 2019: 14), which is antithetical to my goal of helping create lasting, meaningful, diverse and inclusive representations through my classroom.

Therefore, I begin each year by setting a framework to dismantle student assumptions and help them understand one of the reasons why they might not see much diversity. I engage the students with a discussion about preconceived notions they might have about fashion illustration and start with a lecture on diversity. We discuss the power and potential of fashion illustration, examining what diversity means and challenging what the students think they know about fashion representation. In my lecture, I talk about reading images through a drawing lens – why and how an illustrator implements the choices they have made and that every decision, mark and element is purposeful and meant to communicate information about current or near-future fashions. All of the elements of an image work in concert to move the viewer around the composition, draw attention to details and provide an overall informative fashionable image. The viewer is directed throughout a composition by the drawing conventions employed by the illustrator. I discuss historical and contemporary definitions of ideal beauty and look at the underpinnings for the affectations one typically associates with fashion illustration. Presenting emotionally and psychologically positive and aspirational images regardless of age, race or size are identified as primary goals when drawing for fashion. These topics are reinforced with a wide range of diversified visual examples used in my presentations. The visual examples ensure that by the end of my lectures, students understand that they do not need to follow formulas or conventions. I empower them to conclude that each of them holds the potential to create lasting change in the industry as they move forward with their careers in fashion. Since I began delivering this lecture in week one, every year, there are a handful of students who come to speak with me afterwards, introduce themselves and thank me for showing how much more is out there.

People consume news and media very differently than even ten years ago. In 2016, for the *Digital Innovators' Summit*, Tim Ewington, co-founder and strategy director of ShortList Media, responded, 'What do you think is the biggest challenge for publishers in the next ten years?' He identified 'The ever-increasing dominance of Facebook and Google as they dominate consumer knowledge and interaction and take the vast majority of digital advertising dollars as a result' (Ewington 2016). Breaking through algorithmic confinement is essential to seeing more diversity in your daily consumption of visual stimuli. Altering your search patterns is something within your direct control; however, the content of what is published on blogs and websites, for example, is not. The public should not be MADE to seek out images of different bodies, ages or colours; they should already be prevalent, evident and accessible. The audience needs to demand more art directors and publications, content creators and influencers to hire and show more diversity online and on their pages. And so, opportunity, access and availability must be provided for more inclusive and representative depictions in published messaging. As consumers of visual culture, we should acknowledge the assumptions we make based on the select material we are served. Whether printed or posted, visibility needs to be equitable. It is not enough for illustrators to just draw more persons of colour; those images need to be commissioned and published for visibility and access.

Formal education in fashion illustration has utilized various textbooks over the years. Textbooks formalize and compartmentalize drawing knowledge for novice illustrators, creating blueprints of standardization with easy-to-follow rules. They only present one side of drawing education, so a textbook or online form of instruction represents conformity and systemization.

For example, one instructional method of figure drawing typically relates the body to basic geometric shapes. Another method presents a formula for achieving realistic height proportion that uses the length of a human head as its standard of measurement. Your head grows very little over the course of your life, compared to your legs, for example, and so it is used as the standard for measurement when drawing the body. I begin teaching foundational figure drawing classes using this traditional eight-head high grid system approach. This system dissects the body into eight equal parts and helps locate where elements of the body are likely to occur.

Both instructional drawing methods successfully assist novice students in visualizing and understanding the proportion of a figure; however, in my classes, students are quickly encouraged to abandon formulas in favour of observation. The formula will only get you so far and does not consider divergent body types. Identity and diversity will only be found through careful observation.

Drawing trends come and go just like the styles of fashion garments. The illustration is an area that reveals the zeitgeist and cements preferences of a particular era. Over the years, I have used three academic textbooks specific to rendering fashion in my classes at TMU-FR for the last fifteen years – *Fashion Sketchbook*, sixth ed. by Bina Abling (2012), *Fashion Drawing, Illustration Techniques for Fashion Designers* second ed. by Michele Wesen Bryant (2016), and *Illustrating Fashion: Concept to Creation*, third ed. by Stephen Stipleman (2011). I reviewed multiple editions of all three textbooks to further understand the disparity in fashion illustration education. These books contain excellent information about drawing straight-sized bodies, garments, patterns and accessories, and as new books and editions became available, older texts were replaced. Most current texts contain various images rendered by various artists, but no one includes complete instruction on all body types, colours, ages and genders. Aside from some examples of diverse representations of colour, there remains little instructional information about rendering the various categories of inclusivity. I discovered a significant gap in the knowledge presented. What limited content pertaining to differing body sizes and skin colours is available, consists of very few pages throughout an entire publication and appears as tokenism rather than a commitment to impart drawing knowledge of divergent bodies. Only the Abling (2012: 30–31) textbook had two out of four hundred and seventy-seven pages about rendering plus-sized figures. There is only one plus-sized figure drawing with a few demarcation lines and four subsequent illustrations to support the topic. Still, not a single illustration example is included throughout the rest of the book. The brief mention of drawing fat bodies presents virtually no instruction other than 70 words,

> This growing venue in the industry needs its own separate figure illustration, as it should not be drawn in the usual elongated manner, because the fuller figure is often considered an extension of the petite market sizing. This figure, which should have as much fashion flair, attitude, and style as any other fashion illustration, is drawn more realistically as eight heads tall or less with a slightly thicker, shorter body.
>
> (Abling 2012: 30)

Michele Wesen Bryant's (2016) textbook did not contain drawing instructions for fat bodies, although it had a broader spectrum of figure categories, such as youth. Similarly, the Stipleman (2011) text contained no drawing instructions for proportion models outside the stereotypically stretched fashion figure. A search online revealed no books about drawing or rendering plus-sized bodies. There are, however, ready-made plus-size croquis templates created for designer use. Fashionary recently published a boxed set of *Poses for Fashion Illustration, 100 Essential figure template cards for designers, Women's Edition* (Fashionary and Lim 2019: 81–84) – but again, similar to the textbooks, only four poses represent plus-sized bodies, and these are on the small side. However, there are some encouraging tutorials, such as those offered on the website *FashionIllustrationTribe.com* by Laura Volpintesta (2020: n.pag.), where she promotes '[…]tak[ing] the tools and customiz[ing] the rules for ANY BODY TYPE!'. There is a deficit in the educational material available beyond tokenism in a few texts and tools. I was at a loss; there was a complete lack of resources and supplemental instruction to refer to my students.

At TMU-FR, the representation of differing bodies was a priority in the illustration curriculum. I developed a set of plus and petite croquis for students to use when designing garments. When teaching proportion and the plus-sized body, there were no pedagogical resources available either to me or to my students. The fashion curriculum was changing, and our illustration courses needed to support students' success. Although resources for plus-sized templates are now more readily available and accessible online, I have yet to find examples, let alone discussions and instructions for plus-sized teens or plus-sized male bodies of any age. The fashion industry still has work to do.

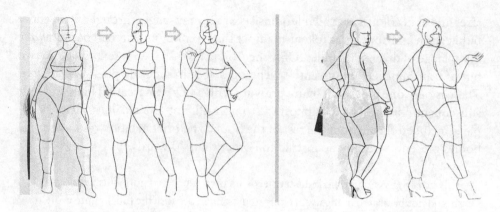

FIGURE 7.1: Colleen Schindler-Lynch, Digital croquis drawn over images from the internet, 2020. Computer-Aided Design (Pinterest 2020; Reynolds 2015; Schindler-Lynch, Colleen 2020).

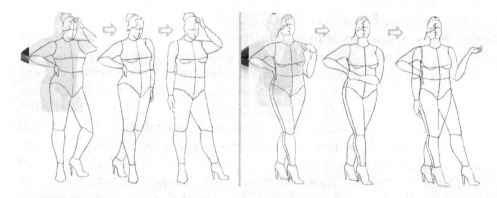

FIGURE 7.2: Colleen Schindler-Lynch, Digital croquis drawn over images from the internet, 2020. Computer-Aided Design (Pinterest 2020; Reynolds 2015; Schindler-Lynch, Colleen 2020).

I discussed the proportion with instructors in other areas of our programme so that my croquis would be in keeping with the Judy sizes ordered by the School of Fashion, thereby offering a beneficial tool for the students to use in their classes as well as moving forward in future years of the programme. Students were excited about the opportunity to design for different bodies. I created an array of croquis in various poses, each rendered in plus, straight and petite sizing. I also developed a selection of disabled croquis in seated poses as an additional category lacking visual support.

I looked for images of plus-sized figures that subscribe to the visual language of fashion in poses akin to those found in straight-sized figures. They needed to be logical, easy, open poses where the vantage point is located midway on the body so that perspective does not shift. The postures should have interest and be active but not action-based. There are a lot of fashion editorial and catalogue images that are not conducive to designing garments. Poses such as jumping and walking were overlooked in favour of static poses, leaning or gesturing. I looked for a shift in the core of the pose – a curved centre line, tilted shoulders and hips, and the potential to add or alter the appendages. The figures needed to be free from shapewear which would alter their proportion. Representations of the front, side and back views were needed to understand a garment in the round. Using a photograph of an appropriate pose is an easy way to get an unaffected, realistically proportioned body to reference. So, I sourced host images online and in magazines (Madden 2015; Reynolds 2015; Whelan 2016; Sorrell 2016; Pinterest 2016; Pinterest 2020). I was careful to use images that were not considerably edited in Adobe Photoshop.

However, it is impossible to tell sometimes if minor adjustments have been made to retouch, correct or supposedly improve the body in the picture. The host photo is used at the beginning of the process – as a starting point, but I ensure that departure from the original occurs. I continue developing the croquis series by maintaining the pose's core but changing the figure's elements or adding alternate appendages. Once I have adjusted the croquis in these significant ways, the

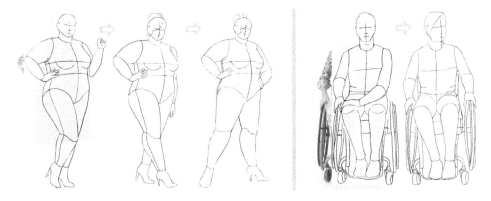

FIGURE 7.3: Colleen Schindler-Lynch, Digital croquis drawn over images from the internet, 2020. Computer-Aided Design (Pinterest 2020; Reynolds 2015; Schindler-Lynch, Colleen 2020).

drawing is ready to be digitally cleaned in Adobe Photoshop and then Image Traced in Adobe Illustrator.

While I identify a lack of diversity in the available pedagogical tools, flaws in published resources, and some potential reasons for a narrow experience with diversified fashion imagery, including assumptions and biases, I would like to address the consistent use of elongation as the preferred fashion affectation. I am a proponent of affecting the body in fashion illustration, but please bear with me. The purpose of fashion illustration in the twenty-first century is very different from its use in the eighteenth and nineteenth centuries. For example, the role of fashion illustration has historically been to communicate in-depth visual knowledge about a garment. Cally Blackman, in her book *100 Years of Fashion Illustration*, states 'Many women employed a dressmaker or made their own clothes: the formulaic and highly detailed fashion illustrations of the time enabled domestic and profes- sional dressmakers to copy the latest designs' (2007: 8). She further states,

> These images were common, publicly accessible and had a strictly prescribed purpose. Their function was reportage: to record and disseminate current or near-future infor- mation about fashion. They recorded exact details in order for the fabrics, trims and garments to be recreated with high specificity.
>
> (Blackman 2007: 8)

Teaching a formula for body mapping proportion is helpful in the early part of education, but it is the act of observation that allows an illustrator to 'see'. Once a basic understanding of rendering the body is grasped, the empowerment of obtain- ing skill and manipulation of the basic rules can occur. Empowerment gives voice to the careful and purposeful crafting of current visual culture through an informed eye and mind. The prevalent use of elongation as a model of affectation is some- thing we have been conditioned to; however, it is also something we recognize as a law of nature. When you pull on something like an elastic for example, it gets longer and thinner. It is an inherent understanding of the properties of physics – perhaps something we do not consciously think about, but it is something we recognize when we see it. Students must understand that elongation is the easiest of the affectations to represent and control. The other side of that coin is if you push instead of pull, an object's mass is compressed, making it shorter and wider. This is a more difficult proportion model for us to understand and master. (This analogy also insinuates that there can only be two possible solutions, which is limiting in and of itself.) A glaring flaw is revealed if we use the same eight-head high body mapping formula to aid us in understanding the height proportion of the human body for a shorter, compressed model. When you are born, your head is a larger proportion of your overall length. For example, a toddler might measure five-heads high, and mature adults are approximately eight-heads tall. Therefore, if we use this formulaic model to determine the realistic proportions and render fashion figures as only five or six heads high, we naturally perceive and understand the proportion model as that identifying as a child – as someone who is not fully grown.

Shortening the body's height in illustration requires an additional affectation applied to another element to remove connotations of characteristics we typically associate with the figure of a child. An illustrator might significantly increase the size of the head, for example, making it disproportionately large so that there can be no misunderstanding of intention or purpose. The artist has to go over-the-top to ensure that an adult's attributes are not personified in a child-sized figure. A multitude of exaggerations and affectations are available for the illustrator to use. In recognizing this potential pitfall, illustration offers creativity and empowerment over other fashion media methods, such as photography. However, education that relies heavily on formulaic texts has some culpability in fostering a hegemonic view.

I try to distinguish the various media used to communicate fashion for my students. Indeed, one cannot deny that if only an edited, narrow kind of visual information is conveyed, the influence of that information would be skewed – this is an important point. I contend that the confusion around body image and definitions of beauty does not lie with an illustration. Throughout history, artists have depicted the figure, and the public has understood that a painting is a translation of its subject. In the last decade of the twentieth century, something curious began to happen. The use of technology in the form of photo editing software unleashed a digital nip-and-tuck assault on photographic fashion images (Brändlin 2015: n.pag.). With the advent of programmes like Photoshop in 1987, perceived flaws were erased rather than simply hidden under heavy makeup. Later, with the introduction of layers in Photoshop 3, a proliferation of editing in post-production could easily wipe away any sign of perceived imperfection, morphing and customizing a body to conform to the beauty standards of the time. Photoshop could remove slices of bodies, and no one would know. In the book, *Spoken Image: Photography and Language*, author Clive Scott (1999: 19) speaks of photographic reality and the importance of being visually fluent – understanding that what is portrayed in a photograph is inherently different from the object in front of the camera. Photography has the potential to capture the tableau in front of the lens, and production has the potential to alter that moment. The viewer reads and understands a photo as a frozen moment – a preserved memory, so we buy into its supposed authenticity. The distinction is that there is a fundamental difference in the perception and intent of the medium and subsequent resultant images. Photography sells an affected image to the visual consumer as authentic (Brändlin 2015: n.pag.).

Currently, body dysmorphia continues with the 'Instagram aesthetic' and its insistence on perfection. Apps like *Facetune* and *Adobe Photoshop Fix* feed the non-professional's need to modify images by having the ability to quickly remove imperfections and liquify and distort body proportions to make someone's photographs publishable or Instagram-worthy. Journalist and content creator, Danae Mercer, was interviewed for Insider.com. As a somewhat controversial influencer on Instagram and the former Editor-in-Chief of *Women's & Men's Health Middle East*, she has a significant following. Mercer says 'The danger with social media is we feel like it's more "real-life" than what we now see in magazines and on TV [...] But it isn't, not really. It's incredibly filtered' (Mercer 2020: n.pag.). Is it the same in illustration? In April 2013, a campaign designed to show the effect distorted figures in fashion illustration have on the public was undertaken and published in the Star Models, 'You are not a sketch' campaign. It was designed to draw awareness to the issue of anorexia (Krupnick 2013: n.pag.).

It presented a sketch of a figure with the proportions of a typical fashion illustration and translated it into a photo representation of a body. The results were strikingly disturbing. When translated into photographs, the affectations on the drawings left the models woefully emaciated and drew our attention to these distasteful and distorted representations. Here, you can see that photography is being presented as 'reality'. The viewer should note that the pictures do not truly represent the figures in the illustrations. Images are doctored, and the models have more emphasis across their front rib cages; their joints are more bulbous, and the shading is darker, giving them a sick look. These are interpretations purported to reflect reality, and therein lies the problem. Illustration and photography are not on equal footing: we should not lump them into the same category because it is not a fair or accurate comparison. Photography and illustration (digital or analogue) are perceived differently. 'The versatility, accessibility and, above all, familiarity of computer images in this age of visual overload have enabled a new relationship between viewer and the drawn image, locating them [computer illustrations] as intermediaries between photography and art' (Blackman 2007: 260). For centuries, artists have taken liberties with body proportions, and people understood the notion of expression as separate and distinct from reality.

In my classes, I make a critical distinction about the preference for stretched bodies in fashion illustration. I try to keep the language I use in mind when speaking with students and make sure to present multiple avenues for affecting body proportion so that the students do not think there is only one solution. Note that earlier in the article, I used the word 'affected' rather than 'elongated'. I have already established that there is a considerable history of body affectation on which to look back and reflect on its origins. However, elongation is merely one method of affectation. I am not advocating for the presumed canonization of lengthening the figure without purpose. Stylization is not the problem – in fact, it is welcomed. Viewed as a way for students to put their personal stamp on their work, stylization helps create distinct expressions and individualization. The problem is when an image is thoughtlessly stylized, when a lack of criticality is evident or merely following a formula just because that is 'how it has always been', is where we run into trouble. It is a mistake to think that all fashion illustrations should represent figures of accurate body proportions, and that solves the problem. Fashion illustration also expressively communicates emotion and ephemera, like the sound taffeta makes when in movement or the scratchy texture of tweed. The garment and body relationship is symbiotic, with elements inextricably bound together – a rapport that is not always balanced. Today the body as the subject is a growing debate in fashion, but at times, the clothes were the subject, and the body, person, or identity was subordinate. In talking about the purpose of early fashion plates, Valerie Steele states, 'Every element in the fashion plate is subordinate to the goal of showing off the latest fashionable clothes to the best advantage on generically attractive female figures' (Steele 2017: 101).

Whereas, in the late twentieth and early twenty-first centuries, Cally Blackman talks about the shift in the subjects depicted in fashion illustrations, 'The representation of fashion during the last half of the twentieth century has relied heavily on photography, which has increasingly prioritized image over content. Fashion editorial spreads […] seldom show clothes in any detail' (Blackman 2007: 261). For so much attention to the current body discussion, I would like to point out that a current trend in fashion illustration is a hyper-real, almost photographic depiction of detail along with an incomplete or nearly non-existent body. Illustrators such as Richard Kilroy and Antonio Soares, whose drawing styles are similar to Coles Phillips 'fadeaway girl' illustrations of the early 1900s (Felten 2019: n.pag.), create powerfully drawn images that are both graphic and realistic. In their artwork, fashion itself, the clothes are missing or barely there. The viewer is left to decode the intangibles of fashion – lifestyle, attitude and current body preferences as its subject. In thinking back to the expressionist figure drawings of illustrators from the 1980s, like Isao Yajima, where the body is almost wiped off the page, current illustrators like Kilroy and Soares speak volumes and begs the question – what does it say about the importance, the validity or perceptions of the body if it is not even depicted?

We are exposed to hundreds of images every day. Not in church, or at museums – but all around us in advertising, on the Internet, on television, in newspapers, on billboards, magazines, buildings, radio, cable, t-shirts, credit cards, shopping carts, and cash register receipts. We live in a visual information culture. In no other time in history has there been such an explosion of visual images. And yet we seem to pay little attention to them, we do not always 'understand' them, and most of us are largely unaware of the power they have in our lives, in society, and how they function to provide most of our information about the world.

(Schroeder 2005: 3)

Years ago, my inner saboteur concluded I would not change the world. I was not capable of affecting the widespread change that is necessary. Instead, I tried to reorient the direction of my lens. I may not be in a position to have a prominent voice in the global fashion industry, but what is within my scope of influence is my classroom. I can make sure we have necessary discussions, that my classroom would be a creative outlet for my students and that it would be a safe, diverse and inclusive space for all. In centring my efforts to implement change through my class, I have, in effect, helped slowly affect the industry from the ground up. I reframed all of my projects to include representations of different ethnicities. Whether drawn in watercolour or pastel, for fashion illustrations or children's books, inclusivity is identified as a priority. I am encouraged by what my students have created. One of my first-year fashion design students, Iris Kowalewski, painted inclusive figures in the language of traditional fashion illustration emphasizing garment structure and the portrayal of the pattern.

FIGURE 7.4 & 7.5: Iris Kowalewski, *Inclusive Traditional Figures Emphasizing Garment Structure and Pattern*, 2019. Watercolour on substrate. Courtesy of Iris Kowalewski.

FIGURE 7.6: Lauren Barless, *Children of Multiple Ethnicities, Varying Skin Tones, Different Models of Body Proportion and a Little Humour and Whimsy*, 2007, Watercolour on substrate. Courtesy of Lauren Barless.

FIGURE 7.7: Lucy Weissflog, *Children With Appropriately Proportioned Bodies For Their Ages*, 2014, Watercolour on substrate. Courtesy of Lucy Weissflog.

In a second-year communication illustration course, the students read a children's story about positivity and communicating emotions. Then, the students divided the narrative and designed characters for the story while relating fashion through the patterns and textures in the garments and surroundings. Lauren Barless submitted fun watercolour illustrations that conveyed children of multiple ethnicities, varying skin tones, different models of body proportion and a little humour and whimsy. Lucy Weissflog portrayed sensitivity and emotion in her depiction of children with appropriately proportioned bodies for their ages. Both students rendered inclusive, positive and endearingly human depictions of children.

A fourth-year communication student, Helena Antunes, researched and created a book on diversity and fashion illustration for her undergraduate thesis. She represented different bodies, persons of colour, disabled, aged and non-binary fashion figures. Using differing figure perspectives metaphorically challenges what is perceived as normal or ideal. In using drawing conventions, Helena could communicate intent and meaning beyond what was drawn.

Fashion illustration began as a way to impart information about garments and dresses and captured the zeitgeist of the era. One can see a vast and complex field in this area of fashion communication. As the title of this essay implies, there are biased assumptions about the look and purpose of fashion illustration. I have been very proactive in consciously implementing diversity in the pedagogy of my classes at TMU-FR. Throughout this chapter, I have reflected on experiences in my classroom, presented plausible reasons why we do not see much diversity when we experience fashion communication and spoken about my goals and pedagogical methodologies. Academia is my 'industry', and fashion is the 'stakeholder'. As such, high standards, progressive thoughts and actions must be advocated for and upheld to form the strong foundation necessary for change. If there is something I hope my students take away from their experience in my classes, it is the ability to confront bias in fashion images. I hope they give pause and take time to dissect, analyse and assess images without making snap judgements. Visual education through an informed eye and mind is the key to lasting, meaningful change.

Asking the students to question, demand, require and understand that change can happen, change IS happening – little-by-little, semester-by-semester, year-to-year – is a process, but fashion messaging is changing. We certainly need to demand more of the industry. Still, the more immediate goal, for me, at least, is to help educate and instil positive practices and methodologies that will make lasting changes in a broad sense for future generations of industry leaders and contributors. To be sure, there are substantial obstacles to more inclusive pedagogy – challenges such as finding and booking diverse models for students to draw, ensuring there are garments for models that fit larger AND smaller bodies and finding examples to include in lectures providing equitable representation. These represent minor obstacles but not barriers to making inclusivity and diversity priorities in a classroom. Diversity is worthy of focused study and effort; anything else would be a sampling, a cursory examination or tokenism. I have stopped using textbooks because sections on inclusivity are too small to truly count. If textbooks are to continue as valuable resources, then publishers need to adapt and respond to the current push for equitable content in the drawing instruction of fat, people of colour, aged and differing models of proportion not currently represented in their products.

As I stated earlier, I recognize that my sphere of influence may seem small – a tiny fish in a very vast industry. I singularly cannot change the direction of fashion or my department, but I can contribute in incremental ways. I can affect change in my classes by centring discussions of diversity in every class, by developing design tools when I have identified a gap in fashion pedagogy and recently, I proposed a course devoted to illustration and diversity to ensure equity is addressed in the curriculum. In this course, representing colour, body size, gender and age will be the focus. Fashion illustration needs to acknowledge and accept its role in providing images for art directors that are far too narrow in their representation; likewise, clients and art directors need to broaden their scope. Although I advocate for expressive affectation, it should be executed with purpose and intent. Careful crafting of current visual culture ensures a departure from the stereotypical images of elongated, stylized women. The potential for fashion illustration to act as a vehicle for critical commentary and social change has historical precedent. One of its superpowers is that it offers a voice distinguishable from photography to propose vibrant, expressive, imaginative and inclusive works for anyone and everyone. I try to empower my students because empowerment gives voice, and voice brings change.

# REFERENCES

Abling, Bina (2012), *Fashion Sketchbook*. Sixth ed. Fairchild Books: Bloomsbury.

Baudelaire, Charles (1995), *The Painter of Modern Life and Other Essays*, (ed. and trans. J. Mayne) Second ed. Phaidon Press.

Blackman, Cally (2007), *100 Years of Fashion Illustration*. Laurence King.

Brändlin, Anne-Sophie (2015), 'The impact of Photoshop', DW, 27 February, https://www. dw.com/en/how-25-years-of-photoshop-changed-our-perception-of-reality/a-18284410. Accessed 19 July 2020.

Danielson, Donna R (1989), 'The changing figure ideal in fashion illustration', *Clothing and Textiles Research Journal*, 8:1, pp. 35–48.

Duong, Leeanne (2019), 'Objects of beauty: Women in Ukiyo-e prints', Medium.com, https:// medium.com/make-it-red/objects-of-beauty-women-in-ukiyo-e-prints-2edbb430580b, Accessed 19 July 2020.

Ehlebracht, Mark (2019) 'Social media and othering: Philosophy, algorithms, and the essence of being human', *Consensus*, 40:1.

Ewington, Tim (2016), 'How has the media changed in the past 10 years? We ask the experts. Interviewed *DIS'*, 21 August, https://www.innovators-summit.com/news/detail/ article/how-has-the-media-changed-in-the-past-10-years-we-ask-the-experts/. Accessed 9 July 2020.

Fashionary and Lim, Connie (2019), *Poses for Fashion Illustration: 100 essential figure template cards for designers*. Hong Kong: Fashionary International Limited.

Felten, Eric (2019), 'Stealing Time With My Fadeaway Girl', *The weekly standard (New York, N.Y.), [Online]*, (vol. 25(12).

Krupnick, Ellie (2013), 'Anti-anorexia ads stun with tagline 'You Are Not A Sketch'. Huffing-tonpost, 13 April, https://www.huffingtonpost.ca/entry/anti-anorexia-ads-photos_n_3110649, Accessed July 9, 2020

McNeil, Peter (2005), 'Caricature and Fashion.' *The Berg Fashion Library*.

Mackrell, Alice (1997), *An Illustrated History of Fashion: 500 Years of Fashion Illustration*, Costume & Fashion Press, Batsford.

Madden, Aemilia (2015), 'Lane Bryant's #PlusIsEqual campaign will make every woman feel beau-tiful', *Popsugar*, 12 September, https://www.popsugar.com/fashion/photo-gallery/38211715/ image/38355995/Lane-Bryant-PlusIsEqual-Campaign. Accessed 8 November 2020.

Martie, Lee and Van der Hoek, Andre (2015), 'Sameness: an experiment in code search', In *2015 IEEE/ACM 12th Working Conference on Mining Software Repositories*, Florence, Italy, 16-17 May, IEEE Press, Accessed on July 9. 2020, pp. 76-87.

Mazzola, Francesco [Parmigianino], *Madonna with Child and Angels* (1534-1540), Florence: Uffizi Gallery, https://www.uffizi.it/en/artworks/parmigianino-madonna-long-neck, Accessed July 9, 2020.

Mercer, Danae, (2020), Interview by Hosie, Rachel, 'A journalist is exposing the ridiculous ways influencers contort their bodies to completely change how they look in Instagram photos', *Insider.com*, 10 April, https://www.insider.com/danae-mercer-influencer-exposing-truth-about-instagram-bodies-reality-tricks-2020-4, Accessed July 16, 2020.

Pinterest (2016), 'TWO #35', issuu, 3 June, https://www.pinterest.ca/pin/149604018851483276/. Accessed 8 November 2020.

Pinterest (2020), 'Plus size clothing Women's plus size clothing UK', *prettylittlething.com,* https://www.pinterest.ca/pin/451556300138087843/. Accessed 8 November 2020.

Reynolds, Sam (2015), 'Size 22 model', *Mirror*, 13 May, https://www.mirror.co.uk/news/gallery/size-22-model-5689017. Accessed 8 November 2020.

Schroeder, Jonathan E. (2004), 'Visual Consumption in the Image Economy.' *Elusive consumption*, pp. 229–244.

Schroeder, Jonathan E. (2005), 'Visual Consumption', *Visual consumption*. (Vol. 4). Psychology Press.

Scott, Clive (1999), *The Spoken Image: Photography and Language,* Reaktion.

Schindler-Lynch, Colleen (2020), *Digital croquis drawn over images from the internet*, CAD, courtesy of Colleen Schindler-Lynch.

Sorrell, Charlie (2016), 'Wheelchair users now have a clothing line that fits their needs', *Fast Company*, 25 February, https://www.fastcompany.com/3057044/wheelchair-users-now-have-a-clothing-line-that-fits-their-needs?. Accessed 8 November 2020.

Steele, Valerie (2017), *Paris Fashion: A Cultural History*. Revis ed. Bloomsbury Publishing USA.

Stipelman, Stephen (2011), *Illustrating fashion: concept to creation*. Third ed. Fairchild Books: Bloomsbury Publishing USA.

Volpintesta, Laura (2020), 'Plus Size Fashion Model Drawing Tools for Fashion Designers.' FashionIllustrationTRIBE, August 29, 2020. https://www.fashionillustrationtribe.com/plussize-fashion-model-drawing-tools/.

Wesen Bryant, Michele (2016), *Fashion drawing: Illustration techniques for fashion designers*. Second ed. Laurence King Publishing.

Whelan, Nora (2016), 'Tess Holliday's new plus-size clothing line is for the bad girls', *BuzzFeed*, 10 March, https://www.buzzfeed.com/norawhelan/tess-holliday-penningtons-clothing-line. Accessed 8 November 2020.

Zuboff, Shoshana (2020), 'You are now remotely controlled', *New York Times*. 24 January, https://www.nytimes.com/2020/01/24/opinion/sunday/surveillance-capitalism.html?fbclid=IwAR0srdDVSgTGmrObQgM5afy_S7miJrPknTelH3j8Nbs8V6VuULTkmkEBs_I, Accessed July 20, 2020.

# 8

# Fashion Pedagogy and Disability: Co-Designing Wearables with Disabled People

*Grace Jun*

While inclusivity is undeniably essential, implementing inclusive design is more complex than simply designing with disabled people in mind. It often fails to treat disabled people as equals, sometimes disempowering them to have real agency on products and processes. This is most apparent in fashion. If disabled people are included in the design process, it is an afterthought. Fashion design processes need to become more equitable because disabled people are not a monolith. As an educator exploring designs that are inclusive of disability, such as adaptive clothing, it is urgent to have more design courses that truly include disabled people as collaborators and creative makers. My approach to teaching inclusive design is not the only framework for courses but does offer the challenges I have faced in fashion design collaboration and becoming more aware of negotiating disability agencies in a design process. More so, my approach to teaching and design is ultimately influenced by my personal experiences with disability.

One such experience was an event connecting fashion with disability rights called the *Disability and Assistive Technology Summit,* held in 2016. During the event, speakers discussed the use of inclusive design to 'make products with disabled people for everyone' (McFarland 2016: para. 10). I was invited to attend the summit at the White House to recognize a t-shirt designed by a girl with autism, Eliza, at Open Style Lab (OSL). OSL is a National Design Award winning nonprofit organisation launched at the Massachusetts Institute of Technology (MIT) in 2015 with the mission to make style accessible to all people regardless of cognitive or physical disability. The organisation provides educational programmes that team interdisciplinary groups of disabled people to co-design wearable solutions. Leading OSL's programmes and community activities shaped my creative practice and teaching, yet posed several challenges in developing educational programmes that aimed to be interdisciplinary yet also respectful of each discipline's strength. For example, OSL's ten-week unique summer programme teamed engineers, designers and therapists with disabled people to co-design wearable solutions (Miller 2016). I was excited, yet overwhelmed, by working with the complexities of diverse participants each summer. Selecting approaches that are unique to engineering or fashion design was challenging. Designing clothes for disabled people would benefit from perspectives and skills found in material sciences or occupational therapy. A broad perspective and selecting appropriate tools were essential to making adaptive clothing. So, to further my teaching experiences, I began providing guest lectures for the *Principles and Practice of Assistive Technology* course at MIT. Soon after, I accepted my first full-time position in academia as an assistant professor of Fashion at Parsons School of Design. This started my teaching and research career in designing with disability.

My personal experiences of temporary disability, first and foremost, influence my passion for adaptive design research. From an accident that left me with injuries to losing my voice for a year, I drew on these experiences to inquire about the physical challenges related to the body and its relationship with clothing. As a designer, I re-evaluated what design meant to me when I recognized that the environment and objects surrounding me were not designed for one-hand use or voiceless interaction. I remember being unable to get dressed on time for a job interview and consequently missed that opportunity. That experience made me appreciate the power of independent dressing. More so, I began to explore the spectrum of disabilities, the stigmas associated with them, and the designs created to facilitate greater independence.

My research focuses on the transformative potential of clothing. Clothing becomes an extension of the body and becomes the interface between the self and the environment, where the external and personal space meet (Loschek 2009: 17). In doing so, fashion can be interpreted with meanings implied through materials, such as physical materials that act to protect or conceal culture. Cultural functions (including social and psychological) are communication, individualistic expression, social or economic status and political or religious affiliation (Barnard 2002: 49–71). I was fascinated with the complexity of fashion and its presentation, which social, psychological and physical functions can inform. This became an opportunity to investigate the transformative powers of fashion for people facing disempowering circumstances. Yet, I am not alone in finding connections between clothing and disability. Discussions among scholars, activists and designers, such as the *Fashion and Physique Symposium* in 2018, are evidence of the momentum to bring adaptive clothing design to address diversity gaps within the current retail industry. The *Fashion and Physique Symposium* was organized by the Museum at FIT (MFIT) that included lectures and panels on topics such as the emergence of the plus-size fashion industry in the early twentieth century and fashion accessibility for disabled people in the technological age. With this symposium and the exhibition *The Body: Fashion and Physique*, MFIT provided a dialogue about how the fashion industry has contributed to the marginalization of certain body types and shed new light on the work of designers, models, and activists who challenge what constitutes the 'ideal' fashion body (The Museum at FIT 2017). As one of the speakers for this symposium, among Olympian Aimee Mullins and Fashion Designer Becca McCharen Tran, I discussed this opportunity about a wearable garment I created for women who need to track movement for physical therapy. While working with the SHARE Cancer Support organization and watching my mother post tendonitis surgery, I explored solutions that utilized construction techniques for a blazer with the affordances of stretch, motion and ease of wear. For women experiencing paralysis after breast cancer surgery, I developed a wearable garment with gyro sensors that detect arm movement. The sensors were connected through a microchip and copper fabric circuit sewn onto a jacket design. The signals were then translated to a prototype mobile application to demonstrate how high or low a wearer raised an arm (Uys 2017). It was the first design I created that integrated all my expertise: mobile user experience, fashion design, and a passion for exploring creative solutions with disability. This wearable garment is now part of MFIT's permanent collection and has informed much of my teaching when integrating technology into adaptive clothing (Figure 8.1).

Currently, at the University of Georgia, I am examining the narratives between adaptive fashion and Disability Studies. My research practice explores dressing experiences and how design can be an agency for self-expression. I accomplish this by continuously interacting with disabled people, conducting qualitative research on current adaptive design solutions with my team at OSL, and consulting companies on the benefits of inclusive design. I have discovered common wearability factors based on my engagement with disabled people over the last seven years. Research from other scholarly work and my own experience have made me realize there is tension between *customized bespoke designs* and *universal solutions*. How can we be inclusive of as many disabilities and produce significant quantities to include all people? This question constantly informs my teaching, where I aim to understand the various needs of disabled people better so I can help improve their quality of life through design. As my research informs my teaching, my teaching also allows me to share and learn from the students who are also exploring Disability Studies and fashion design.

My teaching includes current design research and examining past examples and publications with related information. For example, I showed students a

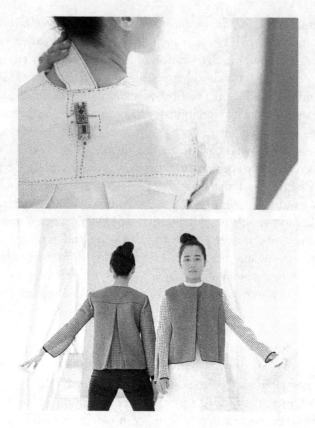

FIGURE 8.1: Grace Jun jacket design collaboration SHARE Cancer Support, 2016 (Tosti 2016).

healthcare informational booklet that included Wagman's early research on functional clothing for user-specific situations. (Wagman 1977). I also keep up to date with scholars and disability activists asking similar questions about disability and fashion design. Yet, I know there are many opportunities to include adaptive and functional clothing for disabled people in Fashion Studies, especially portraying disabled people as co-designers or authors of solutions.

Early research that intersects with fashion is valuable, such as disability and gender, critical race theories, and production manufacturing needs to create custom garments (e.g., Hall and Lobo 2017; Carroll and Gross 2010; Thorén 1996). For example, Tameka Ellington states that to empower disabled people, future research on beauty and disability must consider understanding the stigma surrounding disability (Ellington and Lim 2017). Therefore, all people, especially non-disabled people, can understand the critical need for environments and clothing designed with inclusion. Her insight reflects disability and gender theories like Gerschick's research, which informs the social perception of bodies and identities (2020).

Some brands have created fashionable pieces by using these insights and the understanding that clothing for disabled people needs to be functional and empowering. From early pioneers like Rebirth Garments to new adaptive fashion lines by Tommy Hilfiger, adaptive apparel now includes a larger spectrum of gender, size and ability. Yet, there needs to be more adaptive brands and education on inclusive fashion design. 'By having fashionable garments, assistive devices, and prostheses, the person's style and personality are at the forefront – not the disability' (Ellington and Lim 2017). Focusing on the designers' collaborative processes informs my approach toward Disability Studies and fashion.

I accomplish this by teaching and engaging with various disability groups and healthcare industries in the community. Much of my research work is influenced by a curriculum I developed for the nonprofit organization, OSL. I designed this curriculum to encourage co-designing functional yet stylish designs. It includes applying universal design or inclusive design theory, creative problem-solving, and human-centred design to discover solutions (Brown 2008). Creating a collaborative design experience for multidisciplinary groups allows me to observe, learn about and guide solutions that could improve the quality of life for disabled people through outcomes such as adaptive clothing, wearable technologies and other designs related to the body. In doing so, I have gained insight into merging other disciplines with fashion design, influencing how I teach higher education courses.

I think my greatest strength in teaching is my ability to develop connections and identify design needs with disability organizations and rehabilitation groups. It is not often that either crosses paths with a leading design school. More so, there are few design frameworks educators can use when designing with and for disabled people. Because designing with and for disabled people asks educators to incorporate one main ingredient – trusting relationships. Without them, a disability and design class would simply lack the fundamental connection necessary to facilitate the process for students (Figure 8.2).

Undergraduate fashion courses are an exciting and collaborative opportunity for disabled people to influence the future of fashion design. Furthermore, educators can provide the next generation with a diverse lens to see the world that is not only collaborative with disabled people but essential. Few topics are as urgent as design and disability since they impact us all. At some point in our lives, we may face age-related physical impairment, which is rarely considered in academic programmes. Over five years, I focused on creating opportunities for students to directly engage with disabled people and collaborate on wearable designs in the School of Fashion at Parsons, The New School. This manifested in two courses related to the core curriculum: (1) an elective course open to all undergraduate and graduate students who are teamed

FIGURE 8.2: BFA Fashion Design programme (Systems & Society pathway) thesis class in collaboration with AARP and Open Style Lab, 2020 at The New School (Ma 2020a).

with other design students across The New School; and (2) a core BFA fashion thesis course for fourth-year undergraduate students. Because the elective allowed 'students with diverse skill sets', the course produced many unique outcomes that combined art, design, sculpture, technology and architecture (Sgambati III 2021). This was particularly exciting because I could incorporate my professional background and practice in user experience design for wearable devices. By not limiting students to apparel outcomes, the student and disability collaborator could create any wearable design. A flexible goal for the course allowed me to share fashion techniques (draping, pattern-making, construction) and design methods that integrate spatial theories and technologies that enhance accessibility. In doing so, students were introduced to new technologies like Clo3D or smart materials that react to heat, which helped further explore functional capabilities in clothing design (Carter 2018). For example, reactive materials may be useful for those with sensory nerve damage, as seen in people with spinal cord injuries. Heat-reactive textiles could help prevent burns from spills when applied to clothing (Jun and Tan 2018).

Aside from introducing new technologies to create adaptive clothing, there are other challenges when designing for disabled people. For example, understanding the sociocultural implications of fashion and its ability to translate people's styles. Accessible clothing must combine design and inclusive perspectives within fashion education. Due to limited resources and a lack of time to accommodate in-depth research into one semester, most fashion syllabi do not incorporate accessibility research, such as sociopolitical research on disability rights or information about the Americans with Disabilities Act (ADA).

A year-long fashion course allows some flexibility to integrate Disability and Gender Studies. Students enrolled in the year-long fashion thesis have time to focus on the details of garment design, construction, pattern making and draping and the time to read, discuss and apply various Disability Studies research. Unlike the elective, longer courses allow students to inquire deeply about accessibility and inclusion topics in conjunction with fashion techniques and material finishes.

Regardless of the types of students in the course and semester period, the theory of accessible design and inclusion manifests when theories and ideas are applied. Fashion must connect to human needs. To accomplish this, I integrated two weeks into the syllabi for students to connect with disabled people. Both classes I taught share not only similar scheduling but also design processes. For example, I introduce design exercises that assist students in interpreting a disabled person's needs into tangible outcomes such as clothing. This exercise helps students critically apply observations of human behaviour to understand the best materials and designs. During this exercise, there is a constant feedback loop between all participants, collaborators and students when developing a design with disabled people. *Friction* between design perspectives and the needs of disabled people manifests in functional needs and personal tastes. The first challenge in developing adaptive clothing is the disconnect between the design process and the perceived needs of end-users. The second challenge concerns integrating materials and production processes that contribute to the user's physical and functional needs (Jun and Tan 2018). My personal strength lies in guiding this friction between function and aesthetics, like in the design exercise method portrayed in Figure 8.3.

By working with a disabled person, this exercise helps students gather ethnographic observations, analyse them and turn them into design prototypes. I support the synthesis of a student's insight with a disability collaborator by analysing the observations collected in the form of quotes, pictures and voice recordings. These observations have successfully guided students to contextualize the process. Like a mood board process, students connect observational words and images into phrases they can later interpret in clothing design. During an observation exercise like this, I situate myself outside the student's work process. I try to observe what data and insight the student brings to the class and provide a discussion where this exercise can help frame their ideas.

Teaching methods like this combine universal design and co-design, allowing me to understand what to focus on when designing with disability. Historically, universal design is a process that enables and empowers a diverse population by improving human performance, health and wellness, and social participation (Steinfeld and Maisel 2012). Since then, this concept has been more broadly described as the 'Design for All' philosophy by the European Institute for Design and Disability (EIDD 2004). In my syllabi, I create assignments where this theory

FIGURE 8.3: Grace Jun teaching inclusive design for the BFA Fashion Design programme (Systems & Society pathway) thesis class in collaboration with AARP and Open Style Lab, 2020 (Ma 2020b).

can be applied and practised. After each assignment, I utilize it to assist students in prioritizing what to create for upcoming assignments, which builds onto future exercises as a design process.

Methods from occupational therapy and dress fitting were merged to create designs that explored the function and aesthetics of clothing. Concurrently, observations and questions about the body, mobility, desired activity, full range and limited range of motion lead to experiential design problems and, ultimately, a process to engineer garments for high performativity. One example is donning and doffing, the practice of getting in and out of clothing. It requires a synthesis of behaviour observation studies and material exploration (e.g., creating different buttons, creating unique fabric manipulations, or transformative silhouette forms) focusing on the user's desired activity. Some design solutions include accessible hooks and accessories that allow optimal performance to achieve the desired activity. For example, catheter pockets were also considered variables when constructing garments to maintain easy access to use the restroom quickly. Meeting the criteria of functionality and aesthetics allows students to consciously consider the possibilities of how design problems creatively manifest into tangible solutions. The process naturally addresses under-represented body types and opens a dialogue for inclusivity that improves products and attitudes concerning the body. Students begin to identify how accessible design can redistribute the value of inclusivity.

The teaching methods I use are intrinsically tied to my experiences working with more than 60 disabled people and, therefore, are more instinctually guided. This is why I am writing a book on each story and design process. Part of the design process is interpretation, and my design teaching practice has been influenced by seeing so many real-life examples. Without my specific background, there are many guidelines that will support educators in adding disability frameworks to their courses. Below are the key frameworks and methods I have created and used when approaching disability with fashion design education:

## The wearer

At the crux of all design for disabled people, courses are the idea of agency. Designing with disability investigates the following opportunities that examine the role of the wearer as not only a consumer but a co-designer or leader in making fashion accessible:

- Empowering and providing opportunities for disabled people to participate and co-create in the design process.
- Employing disabled people as class mentors through faculty funds and grants. This also provides opportunities for disabled people to develop leadership skills critical for social engagement and disability awareness campaigns.
- Reframe outsourcing and labour to help train disabled people who may not have skills in sewing or construction.

## The space

To develop an accessible classroom environment, learning materials and classroom structures must be approached in different ways. I design each course to invite disability advocates, therapists and disabled people as collaborators in the fashion design process. The curriculum addresses the following methods when approaching accessibility:

- Students and collaborators discuss and agree on inclusive vocabulary.
- Developing a process that constantly embraces prototyping and failures in design as part of the holistic process, the importance of communicating with accessible tools such as subtitles or other technologies.
- Challenging the definition of clothing, dress, and wearable space when exploring the relationship between body and designed piece.

Having the right clothing or lack of clothing can include or exclude people from communities, opportunities and participation in important life experiences, which affects their well-being (Adam and Galinsky 2012). Scholars like Goering notes the long history of how medical models devalue disabled people, yet fashion has the power to transform perspectives on value (Goering 2015). Fashion's role, responsibility, perspective and future should be continuously challenged. Inclusive education is an essential part of the fashion learning experience. As educators, we directly influence students' creative process. We must strive to create learning structures that directly engage with communities because, more than ever, we must make designs that empower people. Design collaborations through class, community engagement, and my work at OSL have allowed me to build stronger bridges between people who studied fashion design with specific disability groups, therefore, steering away many products that look less medicalized. Collaboration is essential for this change to occur. The more faculty cross-collaborate and combine research practices, the greater the chance to look for differences that help diversify the learning experience. Adaptive fashion is a growing field that needs prominence in all stages of design education. For example, faculty collaborations could include educators researching or teaching disability politics, anthropology or robotics. Together, there is an opportunity to create workshops, writing and frameworks that can be applied to a variety of class situations when designing with disabled people.

I believe education can challenge fashion exclusivity in size, gender and ability. There is a lack of understanding of the needs of disabled people, as well as a space to question perspectives on disability where design can make an impact. Therefore, visual examples of adaptive clothing and stories told by disabled people regarding fashion are needed. Fashion has the power to create transformative experiences for the human body and one's identity (Freeman et al. 1985). Like a second skin, it projects a type of persona, image and style that a wearer chooses through a combination of colour, material and form.

The landscape and demands of the fashion industry are constantly evolving. Designers are challenged to negotiate new problems and parameters, such as the lack of mass sustainability of materials and the effects of mass production on the environment. This requires new methods and critical thinking from a broader range of disciplines, and inclusive pedagogy is paramount to survival.

Inclusive practices are desirable, and brands are desperately trying to prove that their products have a social impact. The rising influence of body diversity and size is evident in the fashion industry. With brands like Chromat and Lane Bryant, the once-standardized ready-to-wear sizes, influenced by the Second World War industrial boom, were challenged to be more inclusive. While the inclusion of plus-sizes and people of colour has established a space for body diversity, the diversity of ability is just beginning to carve out its own space in the fashion industry (Petrova and Ashdown

148

2012). From Tommy Hilfiger's adaptive clothing campaign to Nike's FlyEase accessible trainer shoe, there is a growing number of advertisements and messaging around disability (Jackson 2019). The conversation between disability and fashion is changing the course of the industry. More so, it demonstrates the urgent need for products to reflect the evolving changes of a consumer whose body may change over time.

Nonetheless, there are ways disabled people can be included in making and creating fashion. There is a need for collaboration where the representation of disabled people is authentic. The obvious need for authentic representation is a sensitive topic for an already marginalized group whose healthcare rights and living standards have been fought for since the ADA. Furthermore, opportunities to engage with disabled people can be complex and often in siloed disability organizations, medical fields, activist groups and personal experiences. This only exacerbates the barriers when designing for and with disabled people.

Where there is a lack, there is an opportunity for fashion education to change. Designing with disabled people fosters inclusive thinking, builds empathy and has the potential to develop meaningful relationships. Nevertheless, there are numerous challenges when designing with disability, which I have faced when teaching a fashion class. From the process of how to create adaptive clothing to initiating a collaborative experience between students and disabled people, the following challenges below exemplify my insights in the classroom:

### Integrating historical research, interdisciplinary relationships and disability contexts with design

Even with the ADA, clothing remains a barrier for disabled people (injury, birth or ageing) due to design. From policy to health, designing for disabled people draws on expertise from several disciplines. It is challenging to create a design curriculum that provides a rich exploration of topics such as dexterity, range of motion and sensorial factors for the body.

### Building trust and relationships with disability groups to collaborate in the classroom

Building trust and relationships with disability activist groups are essential for collaboration in the classroom; it is joyous and laborious. I reach out to disabled people each semester to participate in our classroom. Facilitating and supporting collaboration where disabled people have agency in the design process is a constantly evolving process.

## Identifying usability needs

From fitting to draping, there is an array of techniques fashion students learn throughout their undergraduate programme. In particular, patternmaking is a difficult yet essential skill for creating new silhouettes that are functional, beautiful and adaptive. I have found it challenging to navigate the line between students making a garment for disabled people while also encouraging them to make it attractive for non-disabled people. More so, the creative process is not prescriptive. No single model can work for fashion students to create an adaptive design. The design process, not just in fashion, relies on the curriculum structure and the individual learning process for each student. I am constantly learning what specific skills are necessary to create a balanced and aesthetically functional design for disabled people.

## Accessibility

There is a need to document the collaborative design process in an accessible format, such as a video with subtitling and closed-captions. Without proper documentation, these learning examples are not accessible for future courses. Other than digital constraints, I also face physical barriers while developing learning experiences for the class. For example, there are limited rooms and buildings accessible for disabled people. From the height of fashion tables to heavy doors with narrow corners, it can be complicated to assist disabled people in the classroom.

These are the recurring challenges I have faced when teaching a fashion class about designing with and for disabled people. As educators, we have the opportunity to advocate for disabled people who are discriminated against, especially in higher education. Disability communities rarely cross paths with design schools. The considerations and management of people actively participating heavily rely on the faculty to create the framework and syllabi. It demands faculty to go beyond their teaching and service requirements to create a class structure like this.

Nevertheless, as educators, we have the chance to create engagement opportunities for students that fully integrate the voices of disabled people into the educational process and especially in the classroom. Students will no longer presume what disabled people need or want. Instead, we can offer a truly collaborative, human-centred design process. With nearly 40 million people in the United States identifying as having a disability, we can no longer design for just one size or body shape (Safronova 2017). Fashion's unsustainable practices and lack of body representation can be challenged by questioning the very people who are working, designing, making and wearing such garments or accessories. While 'an inefficient design process and sometimes an inappropriate design, may be accessible to disabled people but in practice unusable' (Newell et al. 2011). Designing *for* people is giving way to the idea of designing *with* people. Moreover, that attitude drives a conversation on what design education could look like tomorrow. There is even greater urgency for inclusive design today, evident with COVID-19. Fashion designers and educators are the foremost creative thinkers that have the chance to bring change in moments of crisis. In a time when fashion has the power to protect and remove stigma, the call for educational change is now.

## REFERENCES

Adam, Hajo and Galinsky, Adam D. (2012), 'Enclothed cognition', *Journal of Experimental Social Psychology*, 48:4, pp. 918–25, https://doi.org/10.1016/j.jesp.2012.02.008.

Barnard, Malcom (2002), *Fashion as Communication*, London and New York: Routledge.

Brown, T. (2008,), 'Design thinking', *Harvard Business Review*, 86:6, pp. 84–92.

Carroll, Katherine and Gross, Kevin (2010), 'An examination of clothing issues and physical limitations in the product development process', *Family & Consumer Sciences Research Journal*, 39, pp. 2–17, https://doi.org/10.1111/j.1552-3934.2010.02041.x.

Carter, Paul (2018), 'The tech making fashion accessible for disabled people', BBC News, BBC Click, 7 February, https://www.bbc.com/news/av/technology-42896720. Accessed 2 January 2022.

European Institute for Design and Disability (2004), 'Home page', https://dfaeurope.eu/what-is-dfa/dfa-documents/the-eidd-stockholm-declaration-2004/. Accessed 16 January 2023.

Ellington, Tameka N. and Lim, Stacey (2017), 'Rendered powerless: Disability versus Westernized beauty standards', *QED: A Journal of GLBTQ Worldmaking*, 4:3, pp. 170–76.

Freeman, Carla M., Kaiser, Susan. B. and Wingate, Stacy. B. (1985), 'Perceptions of functional clothing by persons with physical disabilities: A social-cognitive framework', *Clothing & Textiles Research Journal*, 4:1, pp. 46–52, https://doi.org/10.1177/0887302x8500400107.

Gerschick, Thomas J. (2000), *Toward a Theory of Disability & Gender*, Vol. 25, Chicago: The University of Chicago Press, pp. 1263–68.

Goering, Sara (2015), 'Rethinking disability: The social model of disability and chronic disease', *Current Reviews in Musculoskeletal Medicine*, 8:2, pp. 134–38, https://10.1007/s12178-015-9273-z. Accessed 10 July 2020.

Hall, Martha L. and Lobo, Michele A. (2017), 'Design and development of the first exoskeletal garment to enhance arm mobility for children with movement impairments', *Assistive Technology*, 30:5, pp. 251–58.

Jackson, Lottie, (2019), 'Why 2019 was a landmark year for disabled fashion', *The Guardian*, 30 December, https://www.theguardian.com/fashion/2019/dec/30/why-2019-was-a-landmark-year-for-disabled-fashion. Accessed 10 July 2020.

Jun, Grace and Tan, Jeanne (2018), *Universal Materiality*, Hong Kong: The Hong Kong Polytechnic University.

Loschek, Ingrid (2009), *When Clothes Become Fashion: Design & Innovation Systems*, London: Bloomsbury.

Ma, Yiqin (2020a), *BFA fashion systems Å~ society pathway thesis class in collaboration with AARP and Open Style Lab*, New York: The New School.

Ma, Yiqin (2020b), *Grace Jun teaching inclusive design for the BFA Fashion Systems Å~ Society Pathway thesis class in collaboration with AARP and Open Style Lab*, New York City: The New School.

Mace, Ron (1985), 'Universal design: barrier free environments for everyone', *Design. West*, 33, pp. 147–52.

McFarland, Fiona (2016), 'White house disability and inclusive technology summit, American Association of People with Disabilities', *AAPD,* https://www.aapd.com/white-house-disability-inclusive-technology-summit/. Accessed 27 February 2023.

Miller, Meg (2016), 'The MIT Lab that's quietly pioneering fashion for everyone', Fast Company, Innovation by Design, 15 August, https://www.fastcompany.com/3062726/the-mit-lab-thats-quietly-pioneering-fashion-for-everyone. Accessed 2 January 2022.

Newell, Alan F., Gregor, Peter, Morgan, Maggie, Pullin, Graham and Macaulay, Catriona (2011), 'User-sensitive inclusive design', *Universal Access in the Information Society*, 10, pp. 235–43, https://doi.org/10.1007/s10209-010-0203-y.

The Museum at FIT (2017), 'The body: Fashion and physique', Fashion & Textile History Gallery, 5 December, https://www.fitnyc.edu/museum/exhibitions/the-body-fashion-physique.php. Accessed 22 December 2021.

Petrova, Adriana and Ashdown, Susan P. (2012), 'Comparison of garment sizing systems', *Clothing & Textiles Research Journal*, 30:4, pp. 315–29.

Safronova, Valeriya (2017), 'Designing for all abilities', *The New York Times*, 9 May, https://www.nytimes.com/2017/05/09/fashion/parsons-design-disability.html. Accessed 12 September 2020.

Sgambati III, Joseph P. (2021), 'Open style lab, in collaboration with parsons school of design, helps prove accessibility is fashion forward', *Metropolis Magazine*, 23 May, https://metropolismag.com/profiles/open-style-lab-2019/. Accessed 22 December 2021.

Steinfeld, Edward and Maisel, Jordana L. (2012), *Universal Design Creating Inclusive Environments*, Hoboken: John Wiley & Sons, Inc.

Thorén, Marianne (1996), 'Systems approach to clothing for disabled users. Why is it difficult for disabled users to find suitable clothing', *Applied Ergonomics*, 27:6, pp, 389–96, https://doi.org/10.1016/S0003-6870(96)00029-4.

Tosti, Alex (2016), *Adaptive Clothing*, New York City: SHARE Cancer Support.

Uys, Emile (2017), 'Designing for an inclusive & considered future with Grace Jun', *Design Indaba*, 28 July, https://www.designindaba.com/videos/conference-talks/designing-inclusive-considered-future-grace-jun. Accessed 22 December 2022.

Wagman, Judi (1977), 'Review of the book Clothing for the handicapped: Fashion adaptations for adults and children, by M. T. Boward', *Canadian Journal of Occupational Therapy*, 44:3, p. 147.

# 9

# Decolonizing the Mannequin

*Tanveer Ahmed*

'What is fashion?' is a question I often pose to undergraduate fashion students at the beginning of classes; a simple question which, surprisingly, perplexes them and often renders an uncomfortable silence in the classroom. As a prompt, I then show students two images of busy streets in London and ask them to consider which street is more fashionable: Bond Street in Central London, synonymous with many designer label shops such as Burberry and Chanel; and Ealing Road in Wembley, North-West London, a road housing many South East Asian and Indian diaspora fashion design shops, such as Variety Silk House. At this stage, a lively debate ensues, resulting in more confusion and uncertainty, but with the addition of understanding the assignment: 'Why are some fashions included in the classroom and why are some fashions excluded?'

This chapter explores fashion design pedagogy using a decolonial feminist[1] methodology to examine this question further. Inspired by decolonial feminists of colour, who have critiqued how education systems reinforce inequalities (hooks 1994; Mohanty 2003), this approach to fashion design exposes how fashion design knowledge is presented as neutral in undergraduate fashion design. Therefore, drawing on women of colour feminist scholarship helps to emphasize how encouraging students to value the role of everyday life and ordinary experiences can potentially disrupt hegemonic thinking.

This class was carried out as a workshop with first and second-year undergraduate fashion design students in higher education to help them to develop more open and reflective approaches to fashion design. The workshop asks undergraduate fashion design students to design for someone they know, rather than an artificial standardized fashion industry-sized body. This approach aims to expose and challenge how fashion tools, such as the mannequin, might problematically reproduce heteronormative ideas that encourage racist and capitalist design practices. The workshop outcomes showed fashion designs on various body types, including, for example, elderly and disabled people. The fashion design students welcomed these designs; however, the workshop raised problematic questions around assessment and degree classifications (for example: 'Were these designs menswear or womenswear?'). Above all, it showed the continued need to disrupt the fashion design process and expose how mannequins, and other forms of fashion knowledge, legitimize and reproduce societal and cultural differences.

## Which 'fashion' am I teaching? Which 'fashion' am I not teaching?

*It is the summer of 2003, and I am interviewing for a fashion lecturer post in London. I'm nervous about my interview and have bought a skirt I can't afford. I don't own skirts as I was brought up as a Muslim, and when I visit my parent's home, I still can't wear a skirt. During the interview, I am asked how I propose teaching pattern-cutting in fashion. I reply with the suggestion of multicultural fashion workshops on how to make non-western garments such as the shalwar kameez. After the interview, I was taken aside by the course head and told 'not to bother with that multicultural fashion'. I was left feeling that looking at garment construction from the Indian subcontinent in contemporary fashion practices in the United Kingdom is not just unfashionable but also irrelevant in fashion curricula.*

This incident is significant to me because it highlights how systems of cultural hierarchies operate in fashion and the dissonance between ordinary forms of fashion and forms of fashion that fashion design education values. Since I began teaching fashion design, countless students, many of them people of colour, have told me that they already know how to pattern-cut because their family has taught them that skill. I also understand what they mean because I identify as a British Muslim cisgender female of South Asian Indian heritage and I have been taught similar things at home too; I know how to measure with my handspan, how to copy a pattern from another garment, cut straight into cloth and avoid unnecessary waste of fabric. Many of the students want to use each other's bodies to drape fabric and make garments for themselves. While such an approach is encouraged in the community evening classes in dressmaking that I also teach, in undergraduate fashion design, the emphasis is to work on the mannequin. My response to students' requests to use each others' bodies is to refer them to the curricula and the fashion industry, where standardized body sizing and United Kingdom mannequins sized eight or ten are used. However, this answer leaves me uncomfortable because this approach erases different forms of fashion knowledge resulting in a false division and hierarchy of knowledge.

## What is 'fashion' for me?

Despite these varied displays of alternative knowledges and skills in the class-room, as an educator, I recognize the complexities of incorporating students' fashion knowledges – along with various non-western and global south knowl-edges. We exclude that knowledge in undergraduate fashion design curricula because it is not considered a source of fashion knowledge. This distinction results in non-western fashion systems used as design inspiration, a source for various forms of othering representations, such as exotic and oriental representa-tions (Craik 1993; Gaugele and Titton 2019); and western systems of fashion as the dominant discourse in undergraduate fashion, associated with being avant-garde and cutting edge.

This distinction has also been my experience of fashion. My relationship with fashion, dress and clothing has caused me many dilemmas due to the different, and often conflicting, ways my family has taught me to dress — compared to how it was taught to me in different educational contexts in the United Kingdom. In contrast to how I was taught fashion, my parents, relatives and Asian community members taught me that dress and clothing are carri-ers of important religious and cultural values. Therefore, my home life was defined through adherence to rules about what can and cannot be worn. Since immigrating to the United Kingdom, my mother has continued to wear Indian forms of clothing and has always worn a sari. Many first-generation female immigrants from the Indian subcontinent that came to the United Kingdom have followed similar dress patterns with limited assimilation of western cloth-ing styles, even in the workplace. This contrasts with most immigrant men who had already assimilated into the norms of western clothing since colonial rule in India.

Growing up in London, I developed a taste for multiple styles of fashion and clothing, influenced by varied western street styles along with Asian styles too. Trips to heavily populated Asian areas in London, such as Southall and Wembley, to see the Indian clothing and fashion shops were as frequent as visiting London's Camden Market and Oxford Street. Growing up in a Muslim family would also involve visits to the mosque and to extended family in the Middle East and India, both of which required wearing a *hijab* ('a head cover-ing worn in public by some Muslim women') or *shalwar kameez* ('a traditional dress of South Asia'). So, when I first began studying fashion as a teenager, I was aware that these formative experiences contributed to my thinking about fash-ion design in more pluralistic and diverse ways than my predominantly white peer group. And now that I am teaching fashion design, those feelings have not disappeared.

## The tools of fashion design education

This lack of various fashion knowledges in undergraduate fashion is reflected in the unsustainable way the fashion industry operates: short-term collections, standardized body sizes and retail stores that look the same (Fletcher 2019). While an increasing number of fashion sites are raising concerns about hegemonic heteronormative and standardized values embedded in fashion design, such as through modest fashion YouTube makers (Torkia 2020) and fashion exhibitions including *Body Beautiful: Diversity on the Catwalk*, The National Museum of Scotland (2019), less attention has been given to the area of fashion design education. How can such counter-narratives become translated into fashion design pedagogies to nurture and respect different peoples irrespective of their body size, race, gender, class, abilities and sexualities? How can we create a design process that imagines inclusive ways of designing beyond the exclusion, appropriation and exploitation of marginalized peoples and knowledges?

To address these concerns, I have been examining the fashion design process by reviewing the different resources used to teach fashion design, such as library collections, sketchbooks and the tools used in the fashion design process, such as the mannequin and pattern-cutting blocks. During the past twenty years that I have been teaching fashion design – in various educational contexts, from university and colleges to community settings – I have noticed that practice-based teaching has changed very little, except for the addition of some computer-aided technologies. Most significantly, the fashion studios look the same as they did when I was a design student. A quick internet search of fashion design colleges will show images of students with measuring tapes around their necks, tentatively pinning paper or calico amid a fashion studio strewn with fashion detritus, rolls of fabric, sewing machines and large pattern-cutting tables covered in dot and cross paper, shears and brown card pattern-cutting blocks.

In all these images, one fashion tool remains commonplace, essential and unquestioned: the ubiquitous fashion industry mannequin sized eight or ten that is part of the fashion design process. Unlike the 'judy' or 'dressmaker's dummy', which are generally adjustable figures, most fashion colleges predominantly use standardized body forms with a few adjustable or plus-sized mannequins. Today in most classrooms, the mannequin may have a head shape, but more often is a disembodied torso-shape, disconnected from its limbs and mounted onto a stand to which legs and arms can be attached. Mannequins represent an abstracted human form, seemingly universal and neutral; a blank canvas for students to experiment with their paper patterns and make toiles (the prototypes made from cheap calico fabric). Usually made from polystyrene, mannequins are often covered in light beige stretch fabric on either a female or a male gender form.

This attempt at giving flesh tones to the lifeless mannequin by mimicking light-coloured white skin characteristics reinforces racial hierarchies and white supremacist thinking to privilege white bodies. This dominance of 'white bodies', in the shape of mannequins in the fashion classroom, normalizes whiteness to make non-white bodies feel 'out of place' (Puwar 2004). How different might the classroom look with mannequins covered in fabric of various hues and tones of brown through to black? Furthermore, the mannequins are always presented as male/female binary non-disabled bodied forms preventing any exploration of gender or ableism as part of the design process.

There have, however, been attempts to change standard mannequin sizes, both in the fashion industry and in fashion design education, although this has resulted in mixed responses. For example, a student-led petition in 2016 at Parsons School of Art, New York, asked for more than four plus-sized mannequins in the design studios for one thousand students. The successful petition resulted in Parsons School of Art gaining eleven plus-size mannequins up to size 26, although, while students got the equipment to design for plus-size they were not provided with educational support to use the dress forms. Furthermore, to my knowledge, there is yet an entire plus-sized fashion design course in any higher education setting. Consequently, small tokenistic gestures by the fashion industry continue to gain unfavourable publicity; for example, when a group of plus-size mannequins were used by sports brand Nike in their London stores in 2019, the public response included countless fat-shaming comments on social media.

These concerns should make fashion design educators wary of how mannequins cement heteronormative values as universal in the fashion design process. How might fashion concepts constructed onto mannequins reinforce this tool's central role in reproducing classifications about the human body based on simplistic binary oppositional thinking: male/female, non-disabled/disabled, and plus-size/standard-size? These binaries underpin the fashion industry's hierarchical categorisation of bodies as white, heteronormative, non-disabled and male or female. How might fashion design education provide the space to expose the invisible norms shaping fashion design practices? It is only by deconstructing how fashion design shapes sexism, ableism, racism, xenophobia, class exploitation, homophobia and transphobia that alternative, inclusive – decolonial feminist – forms of fashion design can be imagined; and, racialized and gendered hierarchies in fashion design education can be resisted.

### The de-humanized fashion design process

For many years, the ways in which I have taught fashion design stemmed from my position – my identity, histories and memories – as a way to initiate questions to deconstruct how colonial power structures create hierarchies in the fashion design process (menswear vs. womenswear and high fashion tailoring vs. low fashion street style and so on). This approach echoes that of decolonial feminist thinking, which addresses how knowledge construction is rooted in decolonial theories and women of colour feminism. Those engaged in decolonization projects aim to deconstruct and de-link from ongoing colonial thinking that continues to support hierarchical forms of knowledge, which result in the domination of western knowledge, while excluding and erasing knowledge from the global south and beyond (Lugones 2007; de Sousa Santos 2014; Patel 2016). Similarly, women of colour feminists have argued for the need to re-centre ontological knowledges that values emotions, positionality and the historicity of female bodies by exposing how patriarchal knowledge dominates through multiple axes of oppression, known as intersectionality (Collins and Bilge 2016).

Both decolonial and women of colour feminist theories share an understanding of how the patriarchal and colonial matrix of power (Quijano 2000) manifests itself through sexist and racist forms of knowledge. Problematically, these knowledges – or epistemologies – contribute to how disciplinary canons are built on hierarchies of knowledge embedded with objective and Eurocentric universalist values. The project to decolonize design attempts to unpick the social relations of difference in the design process and make explicit the links between sexism, racism, heterosexism, capitalism and Eurocentrism and key concepts of patriarchy, racism and colonialism (Schultz et al. 2018).

Therefore, for many decolonial feminists, pedagogy and learning have become a key site of struggle where 're-writing and re-righting' colonial and patriarchal epistemologies are explored in the classroom (Smith 2012). Many of these attempts focus on resisting normative values embedded through top-down educational structures; and, instead recognizing the values of difference as a way to build alternative knowledges that have been excluded and erased from pedagogies (Icaza and Vazquez 2018). Many decolonial feminist writings on education argue that higher education has become a key site through which colonialism has, for hundreds of years, reinforced power structures that naturalize and reproduce capitalist and racist thinking (Mohanty 2003; Bhambra et al. 2018). This is echoed by feminist authors Sara Carpenter and Shahrzad Mojab, who use a feminist Marxist analysis to show how the education process has become an abstraction: a de-politicized and commodified space, disconnected from human existence and replaced with neo-liberal concepts around competition, marketization and individualism (Carpenter and Mojab 2017). Carpenter and Mojab's analysis has helped me critically question how disconnected the fashion design process is from all kinds of social realities, including humans, from those who manufacture clothing to those who wear them.

I have observed how students design for an imaginary universal body type when using a mannequin as part of the fashion design process. The mannequin, therefore, physically symbolizes an abstraction: a body disconnected from its head and limbs that cannot speak, express emotions or walk and has no historical or cultural context of what a body is or does. Even the standardized bodies that walk on a fashion catwalk can move, yet here in the fashion classroom students are encouraged to work with a lifeless form. Therefore, fashion design students are designing on a static, dehumanized form that has little to do with a living, moving, and breathing person, even though such people will wear the final outcomes that the fashion student designs. Could using a mannequin in the fashion design process be a clear example of abstraction in fashion design education?

Carpenter and Mojab elaborate on the abstraction process, asserting that the 'challenge for revolutionary feminist educators is the task of contending with the complexity of abstraction in which we live' (Carpenter and Mojab 2017). Responding to this challenge, how might fashion design educators alter their approaches and encourage new forms of fashion designing that revalue and re-centre human beings, their feelings and relationships into the design process? Carpenter and Mojab offer two fundamental approaches for critical educators: first, the need to recognize the material conditions in which we live, and second, to identify the forms of thought that separate us from our social realities and the natural world (Carpenter and Mojab 2017).

Therefore, these two approaches stress the vital job of reconceptualizing educational content and teaching methods for critical educators. For fashion design pedagogies, this would mean re-thinking how the fashion design ideation process functions to elevate the status of design – and designers – and disconnecting fashion from its users and wider manufacturing and production processes. It also requires developing strategies that enable educators and students to engage with broader political, ethical, historical and cultural knowledge and practices. This is exemplified in work undertaken by scholar Françoise Vergès who writes on processes of decolonial feminism and proposes a methodology centred on teaching issues around colonial history through a material-led approach that centres the products of enslaved people (Vergès 2018)[2]. Vergès cites her use of a banana to open discussions on the history of enslaved people, cultural rituals, mythology, clothing and music, dance and so forth in relation to issues about the global North/South division, race, gender, imperialism, geography and history (Vergès 2018).

A material-led approach can, however, give rise to essentialist notions of cultural identity if it is undertaken without stressing the importance of historical and social contexts. Academic Chandra Talpade Mohanty further elaborates on this point in the seminal book *Feminism without Borders*; she warns that the decontextualization of identity politics in education through notions of individualization depoliticizes pedagogies. This approach can then result in tokenistic pedagogies around pluralism and diversity (Mohanty 2003). This point is especially salient in fashion design contexts where identity is often appropriated as design inspiration rather than a source of knowledge.

Therefore, for Mohanty, political identity is not simply a topic for classroom discussion or curricula content; it is, moreover, a process that gives agency to students and educators to participate in a 'politics of engagement' (Mohanty 2003). This important distinction has helped me to think about how students – and myself as an educator – could interact with each other in the classroom to embed values around social relations and practices into fashion design practices. Addressing these concerns has helped me develop an ongoing project that centres my personal histories with those of students to collectively disrupt the fashion design ideation process.

### Re-embodying the fashion design process

To address these concerns in the context of fashion design education, I have been inspired by the list of ten items in the 'Killjoy Survival Kit' assembled by feminist author Sara Ahmed in the important and inspiring book, *Living a Feminist Life* (Ahmed 2017). Ahmed describes this kit as a strategy, and item ten in this kit describes the importance of bodies, 'Bodies speak to us. Your body might tell you it is not coping with what you are asking, and you need to listen. You need to listen to your body. If it screams, stop. If it moans, slow down. Listen' (Ahmed 2017: 247).

Have you ever produced fashion designs for people you know? Why are you mostly designing for an imaginary female sized eight or ten? Inspired by Sara Ahmed's ideas about what bodies do, I have used these two questions in classes as a starting point for my Ph.D. research with college-level fashion design students in the United Kingdom. This research aims to re-centre and reconnect fashion design students with the social reality of human bodies, experiences and values; and, expose the artificial hierarchical categories at play when mannequins are used as part of the fashion design process.

Echoing the material-led approach of Françoise Vergès outlined earlier; one class has focused explicitly on the role that mannequins play in the fashion design process. This class has been carried out as a workshop with first- and second-year undergraduate fashion design students in higher education to help them develop more open and reflective approaches to fashion design. The institution proposed the workshop as a stand-alone class outside of any formal assessment to offer students a space for testing alternative fashion ideas in contrast to technique-led and formally assessed classes.

I began the workshop class by sharing personal photographs of my family and friends dressed in various fashions, some for different occasions, paying close attention to their social and historical contexts. These examples are of living and breathing ordinary people with whom I have a relationship, and I include photographs of myself too. As my family originates from the global south and its diasporas, the photographs include examples of non-European dress forms: myself wearing my full black hijab on a religious occasion (Figure 9.1); my plus-size mother wearing her work wear, a patterned polyester sari, my elderly grandfather at home in a *lunghi* ('a type of sarong worn around the waist originating from the Indian Subcontinent') and my brother on a religious pilgrimage to Mecca, Saudi Arabia wearing the *ihram* ('two pieces of white towelling cloth').

I also include photographs of friends, including a pregnant friend in maternity wear, my friend's baby in a grow suit and my children in dungarees. I highlight the garments' details to show historical contexts and stress how such styles are constantly changing. Therefore, I am showing a selection of photographs that capture living and breathing diverse bodies: the elderly, children, infants,

FIGURE 9.1: My mother and I wearing the hijab, 1990s. Photograph courtesy of Tanveer Ahmed.

Muslim women, plus-sized women and non-western men; these capture a variety of fashions, such as genderless fashions and religious fashions, and, furthermore, do not subscribe to western heteronormative ideas of fashion culture. Therefore, this display of cultural difference helps to raise more comprehensive pedagogical questions about what is and is not a fashionable body.

The second part of the workshop then connects to students' sociocultural contexts by asking them two questions: first, to think about five people they know and have a relationship with; sometimes, I ask them about five people that they love to help them focus on people with whom they have an especially strong bond (Ahmed 2018); and, second, if they have ever designed clothes for these people as part of their undergraduate fashion education. Some students reply that while they have designed garments for friends and family, it has never been a part of a class project. This pedagogical approach encourages undergraduate fashion students to think critically about what types of bodies they design for and what type of bodies they do not design for; and what the distinction is between fashion designing at university and fashion designing outside the university. Each time I taught this class, students have replied that, so far, their fashion classes have only focused on designing and illustrating for standard sized female or male bodies, perhaps with an occasional one-off project that looks at another type of body, such as a disabled person. Most students design their final collections for thin male or female markets, and a small number of students might design a genderless or plus-size collection. However, very few, if any, will design for children or babies, the elderly, pregnant bodies or clothing associated with religious beliefs.

The second part of the class then requires students to design a garment or fashion concept for one of their friends or family members they had listed, by adapting a mannequin – by changing its physique by adding padding to make the figure fuller, for example – or working on each other's bodies. Returning to Mohanty's call for an engaged pedagogical process, this part of the project is deliberately collaborative to encourage students to discuss the various types of bodies they might be working on. The focus for this fashion design ideation process is on living, breathing bodies connected to contexts and this forces students to discuss criteria such as comfort, durability and respect.

During these workshops, I have heard groups of students discuss: the multiple ways that bodies change throughout life, from a crawling baby to a walking toddler, from a teenager to a fully grown adult and during pregnancy, how skin will begin to sag and develop bumps and lumps; and, why disabled people remain absent from fashion curricula. In this way, working on each other's bodies remains a powerful approach to fashion design, especially given how those students who only undertook adaptations on the mannequin remained confined to the hierarchies of gender and body ableism (Figure 9.2).

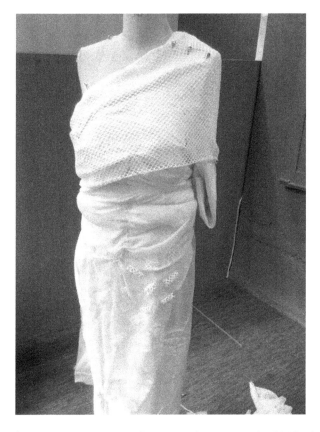

FIGURE 9.2: Student experimentation with 'ageing' the mannequin, 2019. Photograph courtesy of Tanveer Ahmed.

Overall, this approach to using bodies or adapting the mannequin as the first part of the design ideation process can also create unexpected outcomes because students can make connections between bodies and cloth without needing to test out ideas through two-dimensional illustrations or two-dimensional paper patterns. Furthermore, using cardboard pattern-cutting blocks becomes a redundant element of the fashion ideation process, and instead, it is refreshing to see students move around the classroom in fabric. Textiles become a more central part of the design process, and experimental draping and pleating methods can provide an alternative to tightly structured and sewn garments which dominate many forms of western garment construction.

By working collectively and sharing ideas about different body shapes, the students are disrupting the conventional linear fashion design process that usually begins with taking sources of inspiration and building a fashion design concept around a standardized body. Instead, the fashion design process here takes a different starting point – the body – and, in this way, centres the user. This design approach is more commonly used in other design disciplines, such as product or furniture design. However, this new and alternative fashion ideation process goes further because it situates the user in a set of social relations so that they draw on and connect to a wider set of design criteria, such as the user's age and religious beliefs.

This alternative set of design criteria contrasts sharply with the usual criteria in fashion design which prioritizes aesthetics, presentation and technical skills; instead, these become replaced with criteria that value sociocultural and ontological factors and relations. During experimentation, the workshop will be full of enthusiasm and energy; however, towards the end of the class, as we begin to think about packing up, some students will question how they can technically record the final outcome without the use of a pattern to duplicate the fashion design; other students will also question authorship and how they can receive a fair assessment from collaborative work. These questions prompt more questions about capitalist practices and the relationship between standardized bodies and capitalist modes of production that require manufacturing multiple garments in standard sizing. Indeed, the institution that piloted this project discontinued it because of problems related to group work, assessment and issues of implementation – or lack of technical skills. Further questions were raised about the aesthetics of the final outcomes and how some designs 'looked' shabby.

## Reflections and conclusion

My intent in this chapter was not to suggest that fashion educators abolish the mannequin in fashion design classes or even that mannequins should be adapted or changed; neither was the intent to encourage fashion students to access more plus-size or adjustable mannequins. Instead, my fashion classes have been an attempt to give students collective agency to engage – with guidance – in exposing the neutrality of the fashion design process. Helping students think critically about their position in relation to what they are taught can help them disrupt and transform the fashion design process by situating people and sociocultural factors more centrally in fashion design.

This approach, therefore, points to the need for fashion design educators to engage with their students as a collective to co-create spaces where cultural differences are valued. A workshop class format was used here; however, without formal assessment or inclusion in the entire curriculum, there is no clear understanding of whether students did or did not build on their learning in subsequent classes.

For this reason, more creative ideas around participatory forms of fashion design pedagogy are needed to encourage shared learning. The hope is that dominant fashion knowledges is challenged; otherwise, it will continue to perpetuate universal assumptions and reproduce capitalist and racist fashion design practices. While this chapter discusses how the mannequin represents a form of abstraction, it also points to many other sites and tools in fashion design education that also, arguably, present forms of abstraction and therefore require further challenging; from pattern-cutting blocks to the library collections that differentiate and categorize between non-western forms of clothing and European fashions.

Re-connecting fashion design pedagogies with historical and sociocultural contexts between educators/students and students/students, offers possibilities for collective struggle and resistance against ongoing colonial thinking in fashion design. However, it is important to stress how such a process must be carefully planned and worked through; simple duplication or a one size fits all approach would not work. My personal background enabled this specific decolonial feminist approach; however, another fashion design educator may not be in the same position to raise similar issues.

While decolonization is an ongoing project, in the context of this research, it might enable fashion educators and students to see that how we design in undergraduate fashion is never politically neutral, and worse, can cause harm by contributing to racist, patriarchal and capitalist fashion design systems. While this is not an easy path for educators or students, and presents what could be described as, 'a pedagogy of discomfort' (Boler and Zembylas 2003), as a fashion design community, we all need to recognize and centre our discomfort with current fashion design pedagogies and acknowledge how cultural and racial bias is constructed in the fashion design process. If we can do this, fashion design education can be transformed into a radical space to reconceive fashion for future inclusive and sustainable forms of fashion design.

## Call to action

### Rewriting and re-righting mannequin resources

This call to action asks fashion design educators and students to undertake an audit of mannequins in their fashion design department. This activity aims to expose how classification systems are hierarchically categorized in fashion design and, therefore, present a key approach for any fashion educator aiming to decolonize fashion design education. To expose how colonial thinking is maintained through heteronormative body classification, this pedagogical approach asks students to undertake the following:

*Step one:* Take an audit of mannequins in your school's fashion department by counting how many mannequins are in the department. Next, classify them according to the following body types: child, baby, man, woman, transgender, plus-size, petite, colour, disabled and so forth. Which categories dominate? Which categories are absent?

*Step two:* What were the findings? How will you address the imbalance? Will students take the findings to their equality and diversity committee at their institution and demand an investigation? Or could students start a political campaign, such as a petition for a wider variety of mannequins or the need to abolish them altogether? Could students adapt mannequins for developing toiles, or are there other creative methods that could be developed?

## Anti-racist mannequins

To address the use of light-coloured flesh-tone fabrics that cover mannequins and normalize white supremacy in fashion design, this project centres an anti-racist approach to design. Together educators and students can research or make their own mannequin covers in different hues and tones representing the diversity of skin.

## Fashioning dis-comfort

To further explore and expose colonial thinking in the fashion classroom, these are a set of guiding principles to help centre cultural differences in the fashion design process and encourage discussion that are purposefully both *uncomfortable* and produce feelings of *discomfort*. Fashion educators and students are asked to share their lived experience of fashion – successes and failures – to support a richer conversation and dialogue around what bodies are included and excluded in fashion; and why this may be the case. In this way, fashion is not about simply getting students to make clothes for each other. Instead, the aim is to find ways to incorporate different bodies into the fashion design process.

## NOTES

1.  I have avoided using the problematic term Black Asian and Minority Ethnic (BAME) which is typically used in the United Kingdom or the acronym BIPOC commonly used in the United States which has limited usage in the United Kingdom context. Therefore, I have used the term women of colour or people of colour throughout to include Black, First Nations, Indigenous and people of colour, even though I am aware that these terms are contested.

2.   Vergès Françoise (2018), 'Decolonial feminist teaching and learning: What is the space of decolonial feminist teaching?', in J. de Sara, I. Rosalba and R.U. Olivia, *Decolonization and Feminisms in Global Teaching and Learning*, London: Routledge, pp. 91–102.

## REFERENCES

Ahmed, Sara (2017), *Living a Feminist Life*, Raleigh: Duke University Press.

Ahmed, Tanveer (2018), '"All about Love": How would bell hooks teach fashion design?', in C. Storni, K. Leahy, M. McMahon, P. Lloyd and E. Bohemia (eds.), *Design as a Catalyst for Change – DRS International Conference*, Limerick, Ireland, 25–28 June, New York: Design Research Society, pp. 542–55, https://doi.org/10.21606/drs.2018.665.

Bhambra, Gurminder K., Dalia, Gebrial and Nişancıoğlu, Kerem (2018), 'Decolonising the university in 2020', *Identities*, 27:4, pp. 509–16.

Body Beautiful: Diversity on the Catwalk (2019), https://www.nms.ac.uk/bodybeautiful. Accessed 3 July 2020.

Boler, Megan and Zembylas, Michalinos (2003), 'Discomforting truths: The emotional terrain of understanding difference', in T. P. Peter (eds), *Pedagogies of Difference: Rethinking Education for Social Change*, East Sussex: Psychology Press, pp. 110–36.

Carpenter, Sara and Mojab, Shahrzad (2017), *Revolutionary Learning, Marxism, Feminism and Knowledge*, London: Pluto Press.

Collins, Patricia Hill and Bilge, Sirma (2016), *Intersectionality*, London: Polity Press.

Craik, Jennifer (1993), *The Face of Fashion: Cultural Studies in Fashion*, London: Routledge.

de Sousa Santos, Boaventura, (2014), *Epistemologies of the South: Justice against Epistemicide*, 1st ed., Abington: Routledge, https://doi.org/10.4324/9781315634876.

Fletcher, Kate (2019), 'Clothes that connect', in E. Resnick (ed.), *The Social Design Reader*, London: Bloomsbury Publishing, pp. 229–40.

Gaugele, Elke and Titton, Monica (eds) (2019), *Fashion and Postcolonial Critique*, Berlin: Sternberg Press.

hooks, bell (1994), *Teaching to Transgress: Education as the Practice of Freedom*, New York: Routledge.

Icaza Garza, Rosalba and Vázquez, Rolondo (2018), 'Diversity or decolonization? Researching diversity at the University of Amsterdam', in B. Gurminder, G. Dalia and N. Kerem (eds), *Decolonising the University*, London: Pluto Press, pp. 108–28.

Lugones, Maria (2007), 'Heterosexualism and the colonial/modern gender system', *Hypatia*, 22:1, pp. 186–209.

Mohanty, Chandra Talpade (2003), 'Feminism without borders', *Feminism without Borders*, Raleigh: Duke University Press, https://doi.org/10.1515/9780822384649.

Puwar, Nirmal (2004), 'Thinking about making a difference', *The British Journal of Politics and International Relations*, 6:1, pp. 65–80.

Patel, Leigh (2015), *Decolonizing Educational Research, from Ownership to Answerability*, London: Routledge.

Quijano, Anibal (2000), 'Coloniality of power, Eurocentrism and Latin America', *Nepantla*, 1:3, pp. 533–80.

Schultz, Tristan, Abdulla, Danah, Ansari, Ahmed, Canlı, Ece, Keshavarz, Mahmoud, Kiem, Matthew, Prado de O. Martins, Luiza and Vieira de Oliveira, Pedro J.S. (2018), 'What is at stake with decolonizing design? A roundtable', *Design and Culture*,10:1, pp. 81–101.

Smith, Linda Tuhiwai (2021), *Decolonizing Methodologies: Research and Indigenous Peoples*, London: Bloomsbury Publishing.

Torkia, Dina Dinatokio (2020), 'Fashion family & funniness', YouTube, https://www.youtube.com/c/dinatokio. Accessed 10 July 2020.

Vergès, Françoise (2019), 'Decolonial feminist teaching and learning: What is the space of decolonial feminist teaching?', in Jong de Sara, Icaza Rosalba and Rutazibwa U. Olivia (eds), *Decolonization and Feminisms in Global Teaching and Learning*, London: Routledge, pp. 91–102.

# 10

# A Starting Point for Fat Fashion Education

*Deborah A. Christel*

'It's happening to me too', my mother said incredulously as she wrestled with a pair of yoga pants in a lululemon dressing room. Excited to start a new yoga class with her friends, she had gone shopping for cute yoga clothes. Not able to find any size fourteen on the sales floor, she asked for help. The sales associate unenthusiastically pulled two size fourteen items from the stockroom – lululemon's largest at the time – but even that would not fit. Her excitement to work out with her friends turned into discouragement and concern. She calls me, her daughter who is studying athletic apparel design, to get advice about where to buy yoga pants. After a few hours of scouring the internet, I found that no major brands offered yoga pants for average-size women. As a thin privileged woman myself, a swarm of questions swirled in my head as I listened to her experience: Size fourteen isn't big, and you're not fat, so why doesn't it fit? Why are there only two items? Is that the largest size? Wait, what about the millions of fat people? Where do fat people shop for athletic clothing – or everyday clothing? How are they treated in stores? Furthermore, how do fat men and people who sit at the intersections of overlapping systems of discrimination (such as race, gender, sexuality, class, nationality and disability, among others) clothe themselves, and how do they deal with the greater emotional and physical harm caused by exclusion from what should be a simple act of buying clothing? Is this a systemic problem? Furthermore, why haven't I been taught about plus-size design?

These questions set the stage for my journey in developing fat fashion education. Millions of people can relate to this experience, as more than 70 per cent of women in the United States wear plus-size clothing. That is, greater than two-thirds of American women wear size sixteen, and the average American woman wears between size sixteen and eighteen (Christel and Dunn 2017). Yet, this population is painfully excluded from access to affordable, comfortable and fashionable clothing. Considering my undergraduate fashion courses were void of plus-size design or social justice, and I suspect my experience parallels most students in collegiate fashion programmes, How can we expect a fashion designer to both consider and be able to design for fat bodies? As fashion education has remained relatively unchanged in its heteronormative, Eurocentric, thin-centric, skill-centred pedagogy, it is clear that ignorance is inherent in the curriculum and must change. To address the need for change, I draw on my twelve years of experience as a fashion design educator, plus-size designer, size-inclusive fashion business owner and fat advocate. This chapter sets forth Fat Studies concepts, the interweaving of Fat Studies and fashion, and my experience teaching a plus-size swimwear course. I further reflect on navigating the political structures in higher education, the challenges encountered and the potential ways we can be agents of change.

## Unfolding fat

To ground this chapter, I will define weight bias, weight stigma, fat, plus-size, fatmisia, fatphobia and thin privilege. According to Washington, 'Weight bias can be defined as the inclination to form unreasonable judgments based on a person's weight, and weight stigma is the social sign that it is carried by a person who is a victim of prejudice and weight bias' (2011: A94). I use the word 'fat' to describe bodies outside the socially acceptable thin body. I retain the word "obese" when citing literature or quotes using it, placing it in scare quotes to denote what Fat studies scholars consider medicalizing terminology (Wann 2009: xiii). In fashion, the term 'plus-size' is inescapable and refers to women's clothing sizes fourteen and above (Plunkett 2015). Plus-size, like gendered clothing sections, are a cultural construct, an identity and a merchandising label that helps locate sizes (Peters 2014). Plus-size also has gendered implications and is assumed to be exclusively feminine. The perceived-male equivalent is 'Big and Tall', which has problematic assumptions of its own. 'Fatmisia' (also called Fatphobia or Sizeism) is a systematized discrimination or antagonism directed against fat bodies/people based on the belief that thinness is superior' (Simmons University Library n.d.: n.pag.). 'Fatphobia' has been popularized because it is easily interpreted as a fear of fat and fat people. It falls into our understanding of other phobia-suffixes to define oppressive attitudes; homophobia, transphobia and xenophobia. Mental health advocates have been clear that phobias are real mental illnesses, and conflating them with oppressive attitudes and behaviours invites a more significant misunderstanding of mental illnesses and the people who have them. Describing bigotry as a phobia can increase the stigma that people with mental illnesses face. Avoiding the term fatphobia is about refusing to pit marginalized communities against one another and prioritizing harm reduction. Last, 'thin privilege, similar to male privilege, white privilege, heterosexual privilege and ability privilege, among others, 'refers to the unearned advantages awarded to thinner people, and while it is often invisible, thin privilege is an embedded system through which fat oppression is maintained' (Bacon[1] et al. 2016: 42).

Unaware of weight bias, thin privilege or Fat Studies until graduate school, I was able to find language for my mom's and millions of others' shopping experiences. In Fat Studies, similar to Women's Studies, we are taught how to draw on feminist and interdisciplinary methods to place fat people at the centre of inquiry while examining social and cultural constructs, systems of privilege and oppression, and the relationship between power and the body (Watkins 2016: 161). During this course, I understood how my implicit bias towards fat people inhibited me from being an inclusive designer and educator. In lacking awareness of my thin privilege, I perpetuated weight bias. In essence, I was part of the problem. During graduate school, which would be the beginning of my fat fashion pedagogy development, I conducted a study with Dr Kelly Reddy-Best (Christel and Reddy-Best 2012). Our hypothesis was that fashion students have bias and believe that fat people are to blame for being fat. We asked undergraduate students from a variety of majors, including fashion design and merchandising, to complete the Beliefs About "Obese" People (BAOP) survey (Allison et al. 1991). The survey assessed their beliefs about weight being within a person's control. The results revealed that undergraduate fashion and merchandising students have strong negative beliefs about fat people (Christel and Reddy-Best 2012). Similar results were found with a larger sample size two years later (Christel 2014). With our hypothesis proving true, the next step was to investigate why weight bias exists and how we can reduce it within fashion education and industry.

First, to understand why weight bias exists, I drew upon social conduct theory, which explores how people socially respond to personal responsibility (Weiner 1995). Since fat people are considered at fault or *guilty* for their fatness, they are treated with contempt, blame and social rejection. Conversely, if a person is viewed as not responsible or *innocent* for a negative outcome (i.e., a car accident), they are treated with empathy and compassion. Weight bias stems from inaccurate perceptions and dangerous ideologies, including the beliefs that fat people are lazy, lack willpower, lack moral character, have bad hygiene, have low levels of intelligence and are unattractive. Negative beliefs and ideologies lead to stigmatizing acts and policies that manifest in various ways. For example, fat people are subject to negative verbal comments, teasing, physical assault, and subtle behavioural slights such as eye-rolling and avoiding physical proximity (Brownell et al. 2005).

Stigmatizing acts and policies are well documented within the fashion industry. A comprehensive review of systemic discrimination towards fat people within the fashion industry deserves a book of its own; here are a few examples where weight bias prevails. For decades, studies have shown that frustration and dissatisfaction during shopping are everyday experiences for plus-size women (Rosen et al. 1991: 32). Furthermore, fat women report that shopping spaces are too small to accommodate their bodies (Colls 2004; Bickle et al. 2015), they have fewer options compared to smaller sizes (Christel 2012; Romeo and Lee 2015), clothing fits poorly (Boorady 2014), customer service is poor (Matthews and Romeo 2018), plus-size customers are charged more for the same fashions (Money 2017: 1), plus-size clothing sections are segregated, and the shopping experience can be stressful (Tiggeman and Lacey 2009). Plus-size shoppers are left to feel as if they have little control over what they wear, and many cope with these limitations by either avoiding the shopping experience or wearing men's clothing (Rosen et al. 1991; Christel et al. 2016). Although limited, a growing body of research demonstrates that fat men also experience discrimination when shopping (Barry 2019; Ruggs et al. 2015: 1483).

The stigmatizing acts and policies shared above exemplify how thin privilege is maintained. You most likely benefit from thin privilege if you have never experienced the above. Those of us who fall within culturally acceptable body sizes can make responsible use of our privilege and work to destabilize hegemonic, fatmisic beliefs. The methods used in Fat Studies were integral in changing my beliefs about fat people, and I knew I had to create a similar transformative experience for future fashion creatives.

How can we reduce weight bias? We can reduce weight bias through educational interventions. Weight bias interventions have proven to shift weight biased attitudes among fashion students (Christel 2016a, 2016b; Pearl 2018). Weight bias interventions are common practice in other disciplines, such as students in dietetics (Lynn Finbow 2019), medical students (Fitterman-Harris 2019), pre-service health professionals (Werkhoven 2020) and clinical psychology trainees (Brochu 2020).

Additionally, weight bias reduction interventions are commonly conducted among faculty in higher education, for example, in medical school (Berman and Hegel 2017: 605), chiropractic doctoral programmes (Kadar and Thompson 2019) and among health professional educators (Werkhoven 2017). To my knowledge, no fashion faculty has agreed to participate in an intervention regarding their beliefs about fat people. Despite suggestions (Christel 2014) and personal efforts to anonymously survey weight bias among fashion faculty, the recommendation for faculty assessment was rejected. Generally, faculty do not consider fat people when developing best practices, even though most women in the United States wear plus-sizes (Christel and Dunn 2017). As the Fat Studies field grows and plus-size market demands increase, fashion educators would do well to inform themselves – as potential perpetrators – about the field's purpose and relevance.

### Plus-size swimwear course

My opportunity to fully implement fat fashion began with a new assistant professor position wherein my start-up package included teaching a one-time, sixteen-week special topics class about plus-size swimwear design. The course I developed and taught took place at a land-grant university in the United States Pacific Northwest. Land-grant universities with fashion curricula historically stem from home economics and provide students with one semester or a quarter of skill-based foundational courses (e.g., patternmaking, sketching, draping, construction, tailoring, technical design, product development, etc.), with little room in the curriculum to allow for in-depth theoretical or social justice education. I was met with my first challenge even before the course was listed on the registry; the name of the class. I wanted the class to be called *Fat Fashion Design*. However, other faculty thought using the word fat would offend fat people. I informed them that courses grounded in fat pedagogy and social justice seek to challenge weight-based oppression (Watkins 2016). Since size-related topics rarely surface on syllabi outside of Women's Studies and Fat Studies, it was unrealistic to expect a fashion department to include the word 'fat' in a course name. As a new assistant professor and at the advice of senior faculty, I acquiesced, and the class was called *Special Topics: Plus-Size Swimwear Design*.

The course was sponsored by Speedo USA and combined a fashion design component and a weight bias intervention (Christel 2016b). The course's design component centred on designing swimwear with fat women instead of the traditional design process of designing for them. The eleven students in the elective class consisted of fashion design and merchandising juniors and seniors. In teams of two or three students, the goal was to design a plus-size swimsuit that fit their target market needs and Speedo's brand image. To complete the design components, students conducted in-depth market research, held focus groups with fat women swimmers and analysed their bathing suit concerns and needs. Next, students were provided with a variety of fat croquis and created sketches (Figure 10.1), technical designs, points of measure and a bill of materials; sewed sample swimsuits; and developed line sheets and merchandising floor plans.

Using fabric provided by Speedo USA, the students fit their prototype suits on fat models and conducted a photo shoot for their final design. As seen in Figure 10.2 (Plut and Seleibier 2014b), the photographs served as a sample

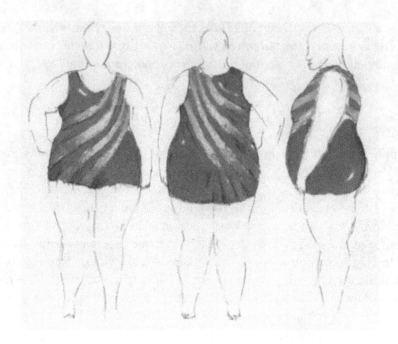

FIGURE 10.1: Student swimwear sketch using a fat croqui in three angles. Courtesy of Guilianna Plut and Trevor Seleibier (Plut and Seleibier 2014a).

FIGURE 10.2: Student team 1, Plurimi Swimwear Ad, 2014. Washington. Photograph courtesy of Guilianna Plut and Trevor Seleibier (Plut and Seleibier 2014b).

magazine advertisement for their project. Lastly, the students presented the final designs to Speedo's executive board, which selected a winner.

## Tenants of weight bias education

In conjunction with the design component, I designed the class following tenants of weight bias education. The following section will go through how I applied each tenant to the course and how this approach effectively reduced students' bias towards fat people (Christel 2018).

The key tenants of weight bias education include the following:

- addressing implicit beliefs about fat people
- reading and critical reflection
- engaging with fat people
- fat activism.

## Addressing implicit beliefs about fat people

It is not wrong to be thin or fat because it is a natural part of human difference. Still, thin individuals are freely awarded privileges, and most tend to remain unaware of their privileged status. The $76.2 billion weight loss industry reflects the fervent desire and efforts of people who want to acquire or retain thin privileges (Market Data 2022). For thin people, regardless of where a person's thinness originates, acknowledging privilege is a prerequisite for changing the systemic oppression and advantages that harm fat people and benefit thin people (Bacon et al. 2016). Reducing weight bias for students first includes objectively seeing their own perspectives of fat people. This was accomplished through the BAOP survey that assessed the students' beliefs about weight being within a person's control (Allison et al. 1991).

However, bringing awareness to privileges can cause students to feel anxiety, guilt and embarrassment (Boatright-Horowitz et al. 2012: 899). It would be complicit not to address my privileges. As a white, cis-presenting, thin-bodied person, I have experienced very little hostility or discrimination from students. While fat faculty (May and Tenzek 2018, Cameron 2014), faculty of colour (Kelly et al. 2017), queer (Anderson and Kanner 2011, Bacon 2006) and disabled faculty (Abram 2003) experience stigmatization from students (May and Tenzek 2018), I benefit. Some educators with a privileged body might shy away from teaching fat fashion or other disciplines because the subject of discussion is a microaggression they may not have experienced (Kannen 2016). Conversely, Dr Bacon observed that Fat Studies education from a thin professor was met with less resistance than a fat professor (Bacon 2009). Dr Bacon said, 'discussion of fat acceptance that I am exposing to students could be more palatable as it may not be received as my personal agenda'.

To mitigate the potential of hostility, before distributing the BAOP survey, I shared how my beliefs about fat people changed. Learning is maximized when students can see the context for learning in other people's real-life situations in which the material will be applied (Brownell et al. 2005). I believe this vulnerability gave these students a sense of security, knowing I had gone through the same process and would not judge them because doing so would be hypocritical. Students took the survey and scored their results, and then I explained what their scores meant. A higher score was associated with fewer negative beliefs about fat people, and a lower score indicated a higher weight bias level. I recommended that students keep their scores private because the process of examining beliefs is personal, and they would not benefit from social comparison. People who make frequent social comparisons are more likely to experience feelings of envy, regret, guilt and defensiveness (Suls et al. 2002). To provide anonymity and trust with the class, I asked the students to seal their surveys in an opaque envelope and identify the envelope with only their student numbers. At the end of the course, students were asked to retake the survey, assess possible tangible growth, and compare it with their original score. I suggest having students score their own surveys. Studies have found that when students are involved in tracking their assessments, they take more ownership of their learning, increasing their intrinsic motivation (McMillan and Hearn 2008: 45).

## Reading and critical reflection

Second, I used a stigma reduction approach that combines reading empirical research about weight bias, followed by reading personal narratives of individuals who have experienced weight bias. Each week, the course focused on a topic and, through critical reflection, asked students to consider myths about weight and health, their beliefs about the content and how it personally and professionally related to them. The topics included the historical and social construction of fatness, health, medicine, weightism in popular culture, weightism in fashion, ethical and moral issues, fatness as social inequality, embodying and embracing fatness, and reading personal narratives[2]. Each topic further included participation in small activities, then again using critical reflection to reframe their perspectives. For example, activities included watching popular television shows, investigating websites and talking about Fat Studies with people outside the class.

Reflective writing helps us make sense of our experiences and creates a coherent narrative. Creating a cohesive narrative and connecting the dots between cause and effect is essential in critical pedagogy. The weight bias education process assigned reading and reflections at the beginning of each week and was due by mid-week before students engaged in course activities. The readings supplemented the activities, allowing students more time to process the information and critically reflect. Students turned in assignments through our online university course portal. I read each submission promptly and gave individual comments regularly throughout the semester. Learning from critical reflection is most effective when assignments occur regularly and the instructor provides feedback for students to analyse further and develop the capacity to engage in deeper and broader reflection (Rich and Parker 1995). It was understood that I would not bring up their writing or comments during class, and our only correspondence about weight bias would be through our online portal or during one-on-one meetings.

I reminded students that they might find some deep-seated beliefs challenged and, in that I am not a therapist, I suggested some one-on-one work with a gifted counsellor to be helpful. In my own experience, a counsellor was beneficial to unpack my internalized weight bias – the condition wherein a person has adopted the stereotypes and beliefs associated with their body as truth (Purton et al. 2019). Many psychologists believe that the extent to which we judge others reflects how much we judge ourselves (Henriques 2017). Needing to unpack decades of fatmisic beliefs was challenging but necessary to create fat fashion pedagogy and design for fat bodies without prejudice.

## Engaging with fat people

Third, weight bias was reduced through direct and active engagement with fat people by including them in the design process. In his research review, Taylor (2007) found that one of the most powerful ways to foster transformative learning is by offering direct experiences meaningful to learners. For example, in our class, students met with fat women, measured their bodies and listened to their stories.

I recruited plus-size women for the focus groups through a call on the university's faculty newsletter and a water aerobics class I was taking at the time. At first, I was surprised that 30 women replied and attended the focus groups. However, after reflecting, I think the response was high because fat women are rarely asked about their clothing needs and opinions. Based on market research, students created questions for the focus group and focus group meetings lasted 30 minutes to an hour. At the end of each meeting, students invited the participants to continue the class project by serving as models. Model requirements included weekday availability to visit the studio for measuring, fit testing and photography. While the constraints limited our pool of participants, five women agreed.

One student reflected on how surprised they were to see fat fit-models as happy and friendly as thin models. Based on students' bias and exposure to perpetual negative media representations of fat people, one assumed that fat people were cantankerous and angry. Yet, through direct and active experiences with fat people, students had the opportunity to shift their thinking about fat from a pathologized perspective to a form of human difference.

One student reflected on the focus group and wrote:

I think people should use discourse to get to know one another. I would say that our country focuses more on appearance, especially when choosing who we want to interact with or how we want to treat them, which is very sad. I learned a lot by asking questions to plus-size women, and don't know that I would have ever had the chance to do that in another class.

Another student wrote:

I do not think it is fair to criticize someone over how they look because you do not know them or their story, let alone their history, or anything about them, and it is completely unfair to make a design decision about someone you don't know based on appearances alone. Fat people deserve the same rights as everyone else – the same opportunities as everyone else – because they are people just like you and me, and there is no excuse to deny someone's livelihood based on personal biases.

## Fat activism

Finally, fat activism is defined by Cooper (n.d.) as

a broad and eclectic definition of activism, which I take to mean intentional actions that seek to bring about change. I also consider fat activism to be an evolving entity, or, rather, a series of entities that are sometimes interwoven and sometimes estranged from each other.

(n.pag.)

Furthermore, Cooper writes:

My fat activism comes from queer feminist sensibilities, intersectionality, and absurd spectacle. I am interested in co-creating life-affirming experiences. Through activism, I want to expand ideas about fat identity and culture. I have argued that most fat activism takes place in small, personal, and understated ways in the everyday. I am no different, and surely activism is embedded in pretty much everything, but sometimes I go all out! [...]. I think my fat activism here looks a lot like live art; these interventions are like happenings.

(n.pag.)

Another Fat Studies scholar explains fat activism as queering fatness (Pausé 2014). Queering fatness challenges assumptions about fat people by defying and rejecting norms, creating art, photography, fashion and other forms of media that do not align with the ideals of power structures. Cooper's and Pausé's sentiments of fat and queer activism align with the approach we used; by listening to and implementing fat women's needs, we co-created life-affirming experiences. Many focus group participants were grateful for the experience to be heard and the models were happily surprised to see their bodies represented in the sketching process. The photo shoot experience was empowering for fat women, and while perhaps understated, they presented a picture of fatness that deviates from the norm and provided an alternative narrative to the fat model, the students, and the executive board at Speedo USA.

After the photo shoot, a student wrote in their reflection:

Society tells me that I need to be thin [...], but I am not. American women are exposed from a young age to the idealized 'perfect body.' Society tells me that my health doesn't matter, but my size does. I work out four days a week and exercise just like our models. I play field hockey; I have a lot of muscle. I eat healthy and get enough sleep, yet I am judged on my size. One study that we read talked about how women of all sizes feel better about themselves when they see plus-size models. Why do we rarely see them? Is it the thin models' fault? Not really; it is the people who constantly choose these thin models.

At the beginning of the course, one student fervently questioned Fat Studies, 'I have no idea why we are being forced to learn about "obesity." It has nothing to do with fashion'.

At the end of the course, the same student reflected:

I used to think that 'obese' people deserved their size because they ate too much, and when you eat too much you gain weight. But, I now know there are factors that make people 'obese' and everyone's body is different. I definitely do not believe that overweight people should be discriminated against. It is wrong in every way.

## Course conclusion

Bottom line, every student improved; quantitatively in their BAOP scores and qualitatively as seen in their critical reflections.

By the end of the class, third and fourth-year students not enrolled in this one-time special topics plus-size design class became excited by, wanted and expected plus-size education. When students shared this with other faculty members and questioned the department chair about future plus-size classes and education, the enthusiasm was met with agitated opposition. At that time, the tenured faculty, the majority, were unable to change or consider including fat fashion in their courses. A plus-size colleague vocally disapproved of my teaching fat fashion or teaching plus-size fashion design techniques, such as interviewing fat people, using larger mannequins and employing fat individuals as fit models. Her justification was that's not how the industry does it. The industry standard is to use a size eight fit model. As the youngest assistant professor, it was discouraging to find most tenured faculty either agreed with her or passively disengaged. I reminded her of the millions of plus-size people desiring fashion, and still, she refused.

Change takes time. This particular faculty member concluded her industry experience in the 1980s after ten years at a major fashion company. Her rejection of advancing fashion design through the inclusion of fat bodies was perhaps a reflection of her inability to teach the topic (Guthman 2009), her fatmisic beliefs and her own internalised weight bias. Furthermore, tenured faculty have no incentive to advance or modernize their courses or curriculum; not doing so would be of no consequence to their secured positions. When professors and educators fail to critically engage the structural forces that shape fat people's lives, they forfeit the opportunity to challenge the discourses used to justify fat hatred.

Students were hungry to learn; I was ready to teach, and the challenge moving forward was how to incorporate fat fashion into every fashion course I taught without causing upset to other faculty. Regrettably, after a year of teaching, students voiced that my fat fashion methods clashed with other design faculty, which posed several problems. When students asked other faculty about including plus-sizes in patternmaking, illustration and construction courses, they were told it was unnecessary. The illustration course justified exclusion by saying that illustrations are artistic and not intended for realistic interpretations. Other classes, such as patternmaking and draping, were said to be traditional practices that did not change.

With the understanding that structural change can be difficult, and that is what I was ultimately asking for, it may also have been viewed as a threat because it challenged the current teaching ability and individuals' self-efficacy (Ryan and Deci 2000). Teaching fat fashion has been challenging as well as rewarding. Paralleling a fat design project with an educational intervention allowed students to see weight bias independently. While perhaps overwhelming to consider the workload associated with a weight bias intervention and an intense design project, educational initiatives using numerous tactics to reduce weight prejudice have been shown to be the most promising (Tracy et al. 2014). One student reflected on the amount of coursework by saying,

> The course load became very overwhelming at times. Also, sometimes it was hard to meet the page requirement. Other than the volume of the papers, this was an amazing class and an excellent professor who showed mastery of the subject.

In a perfect world, weight bias education would be a foundational course during the first two years of the fashion curriculum, and higher-level courses would teach plus-size design techniques in conjunction with other skill-based courses. Incorporating plus-size fashion would require full faculty participation and willingness to learn. Faculty must learn about weight bias to independently see the systemic exclusion and discrimination of fat bodies in their curricula. Faculty must learn before teaching; how they are privileged, then how to design, sketch, drape and construct garments for fat people. If educators cannot independently see weight bias, their ability to teach will be gravely flawed.

One of the most rewarding aspects of teaching fat fashion is seeing students independently identify oppression systems in their internships and future careers, as this ability will shift the fashion industry. Most rewarding, students who have taken this and other fat fashion classes have vowed to conduct their careers in ways that counteract weight bias and discrimination toward fat people in the fashion industry. In the course evaluations, one student shared the following:

> I have found myself deeply motivated to continue to research the topic of plus-size discrimination after this course. Because of this class, I am going on to graduate school to learn more about how to make changes in fashion.

Here is one encouraging comment from a student who has gone on to work for a major fashion company:

> Going into the class, I expected to learn about plus-sized design. What I didn't expect was to learn about my own internal weight bias. Dr. Deb gave us prompts, articles, and projects that helped students reflect on how we had seen, contributed, and been a part of weight bias. Finally, she gave us a test at the beginning of the semester and then again at the end to see where our biases were and if they changed. I didn't think mine had, but slowly over the course of the semester I had made major improvements. Before the class, I didn't notice weight bias, and I didn't see how it affected everyday life. This class brought it front and center and allowed me to try to be an ally. However, the most disappointing thing to me is that weight discrimination isn't

qualified as a legal form of discrimination [so] it is really hard to maintain progress and even fight for it. I appreciated that I had the opportunity to be a part of this class, that I can take my learnings with me, and that I have amazing friends and mentors who call me out when I slip into bad habits or show bias.

## Call to action

I hope my experience illustrates that rigour, insightful reflection and commitment to growth can be an entry point into a larger, empowering and transformative world of inclusion. While some of my experiences have been heart-wrenching, being a part of creating inclusion has been worth it. Every student in our swimwear class decreased their levels of weight bias and left with more positive attitudes toward fat people (Christel 2016b). New information and a new perspective can permanently change our consciousness, and, as a result, the way we see the world will never be the same. I will leave you with this question, Who's ready to make some waves!?

## NOTES

1. Previously published as Dr Linda Bacon, Dr Bacon is now named Lindo Bacon.
2. Further specifics and detail of the course content are published in the Journal of Fat Studies: An Interdisciplinary Journal of Body Weight and Society. Christel, D.A. (2018), 'Fat fashion: Fattening pedagogy in apparel design', *Fat Studies*, 7:1, pp. 44–55.

## REFERENCES

Abram, Suzanne (2003), 'The Americans with disabilities act in higher education: The plight of disabled faculty', *Journal of Law & Education*, 32:1, pp. 1–19.

Allison, David B., Basile, Vincent C. and Yuker, Harold (1991), 'The measurement of attitudes towards and beliefs about obese persons', *International Journal of Eating Disorders*, 10:5, pp. 599–607.

Anderson, Kristin J. and Kanner, Melinda (2011), 'Inventing a gay agenda: Students' perceptions of lesbian and gay professors', *Journal of Applied Social Psychology*, 41:6, pp. 1538–64.

Bacon, Jen (2006), 'Teaching queer theory at a normal school', *Journal of Homosexuality*, 52:1–2, pp. 257–83.

Bacon, Linda (2009), 'Reflections on fat acceptance: Lessons learned from privilege', Linda Bacon, https://lindobacon.com/wp-content/uploads/Bacon_ReflectionsOnThinPrivilege_NAAFA.pdf. Accessed 3 July 2020.

Bacon, Linda, O'Reilly, Caitlin and Aphramor, Lucy (2016), 'Reflections on thin privilege and responsibility', in E. Cameron and C. Russel (eds), *The Fat Pedagogy Reader: Challenging*

*Weight-Based Oppression Through Critical Education*, New York: Peter Lang Publishing, pp. 41–50.

Barry, Ben (2019), 'Fabulous masculinities: Refashioning the fat and disabled male body', *Fashion Theory*, 23:2, pp. 275–307.

Berman, Margit and Hegel, Mark (2017), 'Weight bias education for medical school faculty: Workshop and assessment', *Journal of Nutrition Education & Behavior*, 49:7, pp. 605–06.

Bickle, Marianne C., Burnsed, Katherine E. and Edwards, Karen L. (2015), 'Are US plus-size women satisfied with retail clothing store environments?', *Journal of Consumer Satisfaction, Dissatisfaction and Complaining Behavior*, 28, pp. 45–60.

Bishop, Katelynn, Gruys, Kjerstin and Evans, Maddie (2018), 'Sized out: Women, clothing size, and inequality', *Gender & Society*, 32:2, pp. 180–203.

Boatright-Horowitz, Su L., Marraccini, Marisa and Harps-Logan, Yvette (2012), 'Teaching antiracism: College students' emotional and cognitive reactions to learning about white privilege', *Journal of Black Studies*, 43:8, pp. 893–911.

Boorady, Lynn (2014), 'Overweight and obese consumers: Shape and sizing to design apparel that fits this specific market', in *Designing Apparel for Consumers*, Sawston: Woodhead Publishing, pp. 153–68.

Brochu, Paula (2020), 'Testing the effectiveness of a weight bias educational intervention among clinical psychology trainees', *Journal of Applied Social Psychology*, 51:5, https://onlinelibrary.wiley.com/doi/abs/10.1111/jasp.12653. Accessed 10 October 2020.

Brownell, Kelly, Puhl, Rebecca, Schwartz, Marlene and Rudd, Leslie (2005), *Weight Bias: Nature, Consequences, and Remedies*, New York: The Guilford Press.

Cameron, Erin (2014), 'Throwing their weight around: a critical examination of faculty experiences with challenging dominant obesity discourse in post-secondary education', Ph.D. dissertation, Thunder Bay: Lakehead University.

Christel, Deborah (2012), 'Physically active adult women's experiences with plus-size athletic apparel', Ph.D. dissertation, Corvallis: Oregon State University.

Christel, Deborah (2014), 'It's your fault you're fat: Judgements of responsibility and social conduct in the fashion industry', *Clothing Cultures*, 1:3, pp. 303–20.

Christel, Deborah (2016a), 'Obesity education as an intervention to reduce weight bias in fashion students', *Journal of Education & Learning*, 5:2, pp. 170–79.

Christel, Deborah (2016b), 'The efficacy of problem-based learning of plus-size design in the fashion curriculum', *International Journal of Fashion Design, Technology & Education*, 9:1, pp. 1–8.

Christel, Deborah and Dunn, Susan (2017), 'Average American women's clothing size: Comparing national health and nutritional examination surveys (1988–2010) to ASTM international misses & Women's plus-size clothing', *International Journal of Fashion Design, Technology & Education*, 10:2, pp. 129–36.

Christel, Deborah (2018), 'Fat fashion: Fattening pedagogy in apparel design', *Fat Studies*, 7:1, pp. 44–55.

Christel, Deborah, O'Donnell, Nicole H. and Bradley, Linda A. (2016), 'Coping by crossdressing: An exploration of exercise clothing for obese heterosexual women', *Fashion & Textiles*, 3:1, pp. 1–19.

Christel, Deborah and Reddy-Best, Kelly L. (2012), 'Bias towards obese persons among undergraduate apparel design and merchandising management students: Grounds for dissatisfaction among overweight Americans', in Proceedings of the *69th International Textile and Apparel Association Annual Conference*, November 14–17, Honolulu, HI.

Colls, Rachel (2004), 'Looking alright, feeling alright: Emotions, sizing and the geographies of women's experiences of clothing consumption', *Social & Cultural Geography*, 5:4, pp. 583–96.

Cooper, Charlotte (n.d.), 'Fat Activism', http://charlottecooper.net/culture/performance/fat-activism/. Accessed 27 January 2021.

Fitterman-Harris, Hannah F. (2019), 'Weight bias reduction among first-year medical students: A randomized, controlled trial', Ph.D. dissertation, Saint Louis: Saint Louis University.

Guthman, Julie (2009), 'Teaching the politics of obesity: Insights into neoliberal embodiment and contemporary biopolitics', *Antipode*, 41:5, pp. 1110–33.

Henriques, Gregg R. (2017), 'Character adaptation systems theory: A new big five for personality and psychotherapy', *Review of General Psychology*, 21, pp. 9–22.

Kadar, Gena E. and Thompson, Garrett (2019), 'Obesity bias among preclinical and clinical chiropractic students and faculty at an integrative health care institution: A cross-sectional study', *Journal of Chiropractic Education*, 33:1, pp. 8–15, https://www.journalchiroed.com/doi/pdf/10.7899/JCE-17-15. Accessed 27 January 2021.

Kannen, Victoria (2016), '"How can you be teaching this?": Tears, fears, and fat', *Counterpoints*, 467, pp. 31–39, http://www.jstor.org/stable/45157127. Accessed 17 January 2021.

Kelly, Bridget Turner, Gayles, Joy Gaston and Williams, Cobretti D. (2017), 'Recruitment without retention: A critical case of Black faculty unrest', *The Journal of Negro Education*, 86:3, pp. 305–17.

Lynn Finbow, Terri (2019), 'The student body project: Evaluating a multi-strategy weight bias reduction intervention with food and nutrition students in Nova Scotia, Canada', Ph.D. dissertation, Halifax: Mount Saint Vincent University.

Matthews, Delisia and Romeo, Laurel (2018), 'A qualitative exploration of perceptions, shopping motivations, and demands of plus-size women: An ethnic approach', *Journal of Textile and Apparel, Technology and Management*, 10:4, pp. 1–14.

Market Data LLC (2022), 'The U.S. weight loss market: 2022 status report & forecast', https://www.researchandmarkets.com/reports/5556414/the-u-s-weight-loss-market-2022-status-report. Accessed May 5 2022.

May, Amy and Tenzek, Kelly (2018), 'Bullying in the academy: Understanding the student bully and the targeted "stupid, fat, mother fucker" professor', *Teaching in Higher Education*, 23:3, pp. 275–90.

McMillan, James and Hearn, Jessica (2008), 'Student self-assessment: The key to stronger student motivation and higher achievement', *Educational Horizons*, 87:1, pp. 40–49.

Money, Crystal (2017), 'Do the clothes make the (fat) woman: The good and bad of the plus-sized clothing industry', *Siegel Institute Ethics Research Scholars*, 1:1, https://digitalcommons.kennesaw.edu/cgi/viewcontent.cgi?article=1004&context=siers. Accessed 10 January 2021.

Pausé, Cat (2014), 'Causing a commotion: Queering fat in cyberspace', in C. Pausé, J. Wykes and S. Murray (eds), *Queering Fat Embodiment*, Surrey: Ashgate Publishing, Ltd., pp. 45–71.

Pearl, Rebecca L. (2018), 'Weight bias and stigma: Public health implications and structural solutions', *Social Issues & Policy Review*, 12:1, pp. 146–82, https://spssi.onlinelibrary.wiley.com/doi/10.1111/sipr.12043. Accessed 17 January 2021.

Peters, Lauren Downing (2014), 'You are what you wear: How plus-size fashion figures in fat identity formation', *Fashion Theory*, 18:1, pp. 45–71.

Plunkett, Jack W. (2015), *Plunkett's Apparel & Textiles Industry Almanac*, Houston: Plunkett Research, https://www.hookedlansing.com/book/9781628315677. Accessed 17 January 2021.

Plut, Guilianna and Seleibier, Trevor (2014a), Plurimi Swimwear Ad, Pullman: Special Topics: Plus - Size Swimwear Design.

Plut, Guilianna and Seleibier, Trevor (2014b), Plurimi Sketch, Pullman: Special Topics: Plus – Size Swimwear Design.

Purton, Terry, Mond, Jonathan, Cicero, David, Wagner, Allison, Stefano, Emily, Rand-Giovannetti, Devin and Latner, Janet (2019), 'Body dissatisfaction, internalized weight bias and quality of life in young men and women', *Quality of Life Research*, 28:7, pp. 1825–33.

Rich, Ann and Parker, David L. (1995), 'Reflection and critical incident analysis: Ethical and moral implications of their use within nursing and midwifery education', *Journal of Advanced Nursing*, 22:6, pp. 1050–57.

Romeo, Laurel Dawn and Lee, Young-A (2015), 'Exploring apparel purchase issues with plus-size female teens', *Journal of Fashion Marketing & Management*, 19:2, pp. 120–35.

Rosen, James C., Srebnik, Debra, Saltzberg, Elayne and Wendt, Sally (1991), 'Development of a body image avoidance questionnaire', *Psychological Assessment: A Journal of Consulting & Clinical Psychology*, 3:1, p. 32.

Ruggs, Enrica N., Hebl, Michelle R. and Williams, Amber (2015), 'Weight isn't selling: The insidious effects of weight stigmatization in retail settings', *Journal of Applied Psychology*, 100:5, p. 1483.

Ryan, Richard M. and Deci, Edward L. (2000), 'Intrinsic and extrinsic motivations: Classic definitions and new directions', *Contemporary Educational Psychology*, 25:1, pp. 54–67. https://www.sciencedirect.com/science/article/abs/pii/S0361476X20300254. Accessed 22 January 2020.

Simmons University Library (n.d.), 'Anti-Oppression: Anti-Fatmisia', Simmons University Library, https://simmons.libguides.com/anti-oppression/anti-fatmisia. Accessed 27 January 2021.

Suls, Jerry, Martin, René and Wheeler, Ladd (2002), 'Social comparison: Why, with whom, and with what effect?', *Current Directions in Psychological Science*, 11:5, pp. 159–63.

Taylor, Edward W. (2007), 'An update of transformative learning theory: A critical review of the empirical research (1999–2005)', *International Journal of Lifelong Education*, 26:2, pp. 173–91.

Tiggemann, Marika and Lacey, Catherine (2009), 'Shopping for clothes: Body satisfaction, appearance investment, and functions of clothing among female shoppers', *Body Image*, 6:4, pp. 285–91. https://www.sciencedirect.com/science/article/abs/pii/S1740144509000643. Accessed 22 January 2021.

Tylka Tracy, L., Annunziato, Rachel A., Burgard, Deb, Daníelsdóttir, Sigrún, Shuman, Ellen, Davis, Chad and Calogero, Rachel M. (2014), 'The weight-inclusive versus weight-normative approach to health: Evaluating the evidence for prioritizing well-being over weight loss', *Journal of Obesity*, 2014, pp. 1–18, https://www.hindawi.com/journals/jobe/2014/983495/. Accessed 17 January 2021.

Wann, Marilyn (2009), 'Foreword', in Rothblum, S. Esther and S. Solovay (eds), *The Fat Studies Reader*, New York: New York University Press, p. xiii.

Washington, Reginald L. (2011), 'Peer reviewed: Childhood obesity: Issues of weight bias', *Preventing Chronic Disease*, 8:5, p. A94, https://www.ncbi.nlm.nih.gov/pmc/articles/PMC3181194/. Accessed 15 January 2021.

Watkins, Patti Lou (2016), 'Sixteen: Inclusion of fat studies in a difference, power, and discrimination curriculum', *Counterpoints*, 467, pp. 161–69, https://www.jstor.org/stable/45157140?seq=1. Accessed 12 January 2021.

Weiner, Bernard (1995), 'Inferences of responsibility and social motivation', *Advances in Experimental Social Psychology*, 27, pp. 1–47, https://www.academia.edu/download/39471762/Inferences_Of_Responsibility_And_Social_20151027-9086-j8ypvh.pdf. Accessed 17 January 2021.

Werkhoven, Eleftheria Thea (2017), 'The use of a higher education intervention to modify the level of nutrition knowledge, Degree of weight bias and general obesity awareness among pre-service professionals', MA thesis, Sydney: The University of Sydney, https://ses.library.usyd.edu.au/handle/2123/17606.

Werkhoven, Thea (2020), 'Designing, implementing and evaluating an educational intervention targeting weight bias and fat stereotyping', *Journal of Health Psychology*, 26:12, pp. 2084–97.

# 11

# Black Lives Matter:
# Fashion Liberation and the
# Fight for Freedom

*Brandon Spencer and Kelly L. Reddy-Best*

The purpose of this chapter is to outline the counter-story (Delgado and Stefancic 2017) of one Black male undergraduate fashion student, Brandon Spencer, who is the co-author of this chapter, and his vision for the future that rejects white supremacy in fashion education. We tell the story of Brandon's experience as a student in the Apparel, Merchandising and Design (AMD) programme at Iowa State University (ISU) and his experience working with Kelly Reddy-Best, an associate professor in the programme who is also a co-author on this chapter. We explore how Brandon's leadership ignited a highly successful, activist faculty/student co-developed course entitled *Black Lives Matter: Fashion, Liberation and the Fight for Freedom*, which can serve as an elective or a required history option in place of the typical western fashion history. We first provide the background as to how the course came about before offering details about course execution and the student learning outcomes, which are centred around the tenets of critical race theory (Delgado and Stefancic 2017). We also both discuss our experiences throughout the process of co-developing the course and then teaching (Kelly) or taking the course (Brandon). We provide insight into the process of putting a course with the phrase 'Black Lives Matter' in the title through the curriculum system in a predominantly white institution in the middle of the farmland in the United States. Last, we discuss how white faculty can navigate teaching a course centring on people of colour with heightened attention to the related power dynamics and how disrupting those dynamics can lead to meaningful educational experiences for both students of colour and non-students of colour. We end our chapter with several calls to action for faculty, students, staff, administrators and others invested in the future of an anti-racist (Kendi 2019) educational system.

Overall, this new course is a space where students learn to reject and question past hierarchies of white supremacy in the fashion curriculum and also learn the importance of moving their knowledge beyond the walls of the academy and into the surrounding community. All students who complete the course arguably develop a sense of their activist identity as they learn about power, privilege, oppression and empowerment as related to fashioning the body. We challenge and encourage our readers to imagine a future where we are not viewed as change agents for simply telling the histories of historically marginalized communities. Can we imagine a world where this type of course is not embedded in a Black Studies programme but is at the core of fashion programs that for *too long* have perpetuated unrealistic beauty ideals, ableist design practices and enabled white supremacy in our history-telling? We specifically mention 'core' courses here because, often, courses focusing on marginalized communities are offered as options or electives, further pushing these communities to the sidelines. We believe this course and others like it are the start of the revolution in fashion education toward eradicating everyday racist behaviours, whereby we can all work towards engaging in what Kendi (Kendi 2019) refers to as anti-racist behaviours. Next, we focus on Brandon's experience and leadership in this course with his brief reflection on his experience in the AMD programme and how the course came about.

### *Brandon's reflection on the course co-development and being a Black male in a predominantly White fashion programme*

In the fall of 2016, I started my college career eager to gain new experiences that would not only shape my worldview but also promote unprecedented growth within myself. However, that growth came at the price of often feeling like I did not belong in my major and that I was simply not equal to my white classmates, which is a common experience for many Black males in higher education (Allen 1992; Harper 2012). Determination kept me going; the will to fight and not stop pushed me past the discrimination I felt on a day-to-day basis. During my first semester, while attending ISU, I enrolled in *AMD 165 Dress, Appearance and Diversity in Society*, where I met Dr Kelly Reddy-Best. Dr Kelly became an extremely helpful resource for me as I would bring situations to her attention about my experience in the course while working with other students, and she took the time to actually listen to what I had to say. Before the fall semester was over, I had already officially changed my major to AMD because her course showed me that fashion was one of my true passions.

Once the spring semester came, I took the core AMD classes to learn how to design and sew. The AMD programme has very few males, let alone Black males. So there would be times when an instructor would simply look for the dark spot in the room instead of calling my name for attendance. During class, I would raise my hand and eventually just put it down because my arm had gotten too tired from being ignored. I barely felt supported within my programme and often struggled more than I should have because of it. I had to repeat classes and ultimately suffered a low-grade point average. However, I did not let it stop me, and I continued to prevail against the odds placed in front of me.

During some of these very difficult and rather lonely times, Dr Kelly was still there to hear what I had to say and to be of any help to me that she could. Our interactions with one another quickly blossomed into a working relationship once she explained to me that I should apply for the Louis Rosenfeld Undergraduate Research Internship. When it came time to apply for the internship, I had to present my research topic. This was actually quite simple, given it was an idea I previously had for a story I wanted to write when working for the *Iowa State Daily* (the school newspaper) in my first year of college. However, my editor at the time denied my story on the Black Lives Matter movement, so I took this as my opportunity to publicize it. The passion that fuelled me to research such a heavy topic was that I wanted my voice to be heard as a Black man who navigates white spaces every day, as well as to give voice to an entire movement of people who share those same feelings and struggles. After numerous discussions, Dr Kelly and I came up with the idea to offer a 400-level senior seminar course on Black identity, politics, resistance movements and fashion.

All in all, the experience has been life-changing and something that I am beyond grateful for. I am thankful for the guidance and support of Dr Kelly and her always being there when I felt like nobody would listen to what I had to say. I was able to bring more attention to a movement that is not properly respected in mainstream American media and culture while defending its importance to Black men and women across the country. The course is important not just to me but to all Black people.

## Context for and developing of the course: Rural Iowa, Whiteness, and curriculum embedded in supporting the status quo

In this section, we outline a brief context of the space where the course was developed and offered and how the process unfolded to get the course into the curriculum. ISU is a large land-grant institution located in Ames, Iowa, and, according to its registrar page in 2020, it had about 33,000 students enrolled.

Much of Iowa is covered in farmland, and the population is majority white. Des Moines, the largest city in Iowa, is about 37 miles or 59 kilometres south of Ames and, according to the most recent United States census data, had a population of about 216,000. Ames is a small college town with a total population of about 65,000. To give readers a feel for the town, there is a small downtown area with a single main street where one can find a local hobby shop, tea shop and a few coffee shops, businesses and restaurants. There are small family-owned businesses and large big-box stores throughout the town. Almost all amenities are available in Ames; however, because of the majority white population, there are limited resources for people of colour, such as a Black hair salon. People outside of Iowa, particularly those from a coastal region, might view it as a 'flyover state'; they do not see it as a destination but only as a space that they rarely think about and only pass over in an aeroplane. There is a joke frequently told by Iowans, 'Iowa, not Ohio', suggesting that these states in the Midwest are often interchangeable, owing to their lack of perceived distinctness. Yet within Iowa is a thriving land-grant institution, ISU, which is home to one of the first fashion programmes in the country, originally called Home Economics and since renamed Apparel, Merchandising and Design.

Similar to Iowa, ISU also has limited diversity and is categorized as a predominantly White institution. According to the most recent race and ethnicity report at ISU, about 15 per cent of the domestic students are students of colour or Indigenous students. Within the AMD programme, there are few people of colour, yet those specific statistics are unavailable. The twenty faculty and advisers in AMD as of 2020 are dominated by White women, yet there are a few international faculty members of Asian descent, and the department is led by a Black woman. Of note is that since the university opened in 1858, Eulanda Sanders is the first Black woman in the history of the university to hold this title and position, beginning in 2017.

In AMD, the courses and programmes are robust, with over 40 unique classes offered. Students take an integrated core and then focus on creative and technical design, product development or merchandising. Currently, there are two *History of Western Dress* courses that students take, in addition to one entitled *Cultural Perspectives on Dress*, which has an international perspective and lacks a social justice lens. One of the core courses is *AMD 165, Dress, Appearance and Diversity in Society*, which has an entirely social justice lens and provides a foundational unit on meanings and interpretations of social justice with implications for fashion, dress and identity. All of this is to say that, introducing a course such as *Black Lives Matter: Fashion, Liberation and the Fight for Freedom* is *far* from the norm in this programme. None of the other 40+ classes centre on, or mildly consider historically marginalized populations, despite the significant opportunity given the numerous courses we offer.

To create a new course in the curriculum, a faculty member creates a course syllabus outline, which is then presented and discussed in one faculty meeting. The faculty receive the materials at least one week prior to this meeting. Then, in the next faculty meeting, typically four weeks later, we put up a motion to vote on the course. Three people voted no to put the course in the official curriculum catalogue. At the same time, our course was up for a vote; another generic marketing course passed unanimously. It is disheartening that 15 per cent of the faculty members felt strongly enough against the course to vote no. In our faculty, we do an anonymous digital vote, and during the open discussion of the new course, faculty members voiced no opposition. How and why did these members not see the value of this course? Why are they interested in upholding the status quo? We will never really know. Overall, the course was voted into the curriculum and is currently offered every other even spring semester.

## Course overview

The goal of *Black Lives Matter: Fashion, Liberation and the Fight for Freedom* is for students to use historical and cultural methods to examine the history of the Black Lives Matter movement and its relationship to past resistance/ activist movements and fashion and appearance. The students also summarize and evaluate the literature on Black activism and Black identity. Last, they plan and develop a public exhibition and opening event. After completing this upper-level, seminar-style course, students will be able to:

- describe the Black Lives Matter movement and other past Black activist/resistance movements;
- examine the relationship of Black activist movements to fashion and appearance;
- describe Black identity as related to fashion and appearance;
- examine how scholars use historic and cultural research methods to explore the history of the Black Lives Matter movement and its relationship to fashion and appearance;
- summarize and analyse literature (scholarly, popular press, or film) on Black activism, Black identity and dress, and Black resistance movements;
- conduct original research using cultural and historic methods;
- identify the basics of developing a public exhibition based on original research;
- plan and execute an opening event for a research exhibition; and
- plan and develop a public research exhibition.

In the course outcomes, for two reasons, we planned an exhibition and an opening event. First, AMD is housed in the Apparel, Events, and Hospitality Management department. Therefore, our department chair advised us to make the course attractive across the departments. Second, because part of ISU's land-grant institution mission is to move knowledge beyond the campus borders, an exhibition and opening event embodies that vision.

## Modules

We built the course around eight modules, including (1) Introduction to the Black Lives Matter Movement; (2) Scholarly vs. Non-Scholarly and Historic Research Methods; (3) Black Identity and Dress; (4) Politics, Activism and Dress; (5) Racial Profiling and Police Brutality; (6) Black Activism Movements; (7) Black Lives Matter, Fashion, Appearance and the Body; and (8) Cultural Appropriation vs. Appreciation. In the course, we primarily focus on the United States, yet we do not ignore some of the more significant global connections relating to the African diaspora. In the appendix, we outline the course topics, associated readings, films and course materials that students engage with throughout the semester.

## Course materials

No single textbook or set of films is available for the course; therefore, we compiled the course materials to best meet the learning outcomes. When possible, we aimed for literary or visual materials created by Black people or people of colour, yet this was not always possible given the dearth of materials written on these topics. We start the course by watching short films about the Black Lives Matter movement in addition to reading the *Herstory* of the movement as told by the founders on the movement's website. The students also read a popular press article from the perspective of a journalist on the ground during some initial protests. The students are introduced to historic and cultural research methods, and then they have one unit to ground them in the basics of Black identity, dress and fashioning the body. Then, we discuss the intersection of politics, activism and dress, followed by a unit on the pervasiveness of police brutality and racial profiling of Black people in the United States. Next, we engage with an overview of the history of the various Black activist movements, from enslavement in the United States to the Black Power movement and the development of the Black Panther Party to the modern-day Black Lives Matter movement. The course concludes by examining the intersection of the Black Lives Matter movement with fashion and appearance and discussions about cultural appropriation vs. appreciation because numerous fashion designers have used the movement as inspiration in their design process. These final units tie the course back to the apparel major, where critical conversations can happen surrounding inspiration from the histories.

## Course assessments

In the discussion-based course, students complete a scholarly critique of each reading in addition to other smaller assignments used to asses their learning outcomes. For the final project, students conduct original research using a cultural or historical methodological approach that would contribute to a public exhibition. Each student develops a research question that fits the exhibition's overall theme, identifies materials to analyse and then writes a short essay. Each semester, the purpose of the exhibition is to educate the public about the history of the Black Lives Matter movement and its relationship to politics, activism, fashion and appearance. The students are allowed to interpret this broadly to fit their interests as well as organizing the logistics of a one-semester undergraduate student research project that is completed within two months. Past students' final projects included topics such as a brief history of the Black Lives Matter movement; Black identity and hair; Black males and appearance stereotypes; celebrities' use of appearance and dress practices as activism; and critical analyses of Black Lives Matter merchandise sales.

For the public exhibition, students condense their essays to fit onto a 36 by 48-inch poster and make it accessible by writing at an eighth-grade level. Writing at an eighth-grade level is a standard museum practice to ensure that individuals from most educational backgrounds can enjoy and understand the exhibition, increasing access and equity of the content. The public exhibitions are displayed for two weeks in the Ames Public Library (see Figures 11.1 and 11.2). In the exhibition, we include a poster with many, but not all, of the names of unarmed Black people killed by police violence since the Black Lives Matter movement began because the students felt it was necessary to honour and focus on those individuals and remember their names during this exhibition and event.

At the opening event, the students first have open-exhibition engagement time and stand with their posters where the attendees can engage more closely with them and their research. This time allows for in-depth conversations about their research with the public (Figure 11.3). During this time, the students can have conversations about the class, why it exists and the experiences it has given them, in addition to discussing their research findings. In past exhibition openings, people packed the space, in addition to curious individuals who were at the library and saw the crowd of onlookers.

FIGURE 11.1: Image of the public exhibition at Ames Public Library. Photograph courtesy of authors.

FIGURE 11.2: Student presenters Dyese Matthews and Katrine Cadman engaging with exhibition opening attendees. Photograph courtesy of authors.

Then, all students complete a five-minute presentation of their research for attendees, including university and community members. Because the library put the opening event on its public calendar (Figure 11.4), the event is full of engaged and interested community members who ask numerous questions during the question-and-answer session. One of the past audience members related to the concept of Black identity and hair and stated that she also had experienced

FIGURE 11.3: Brandon Spencer presenting his final research project at the Ames Public Library auditorium. Photograph courtesy of authors.

microaggressions related to people asking about or touching her hair as a Black woman in a predominantly white environment.

### Brandon's reflections on taking the course

Being part of the development of such an amazing course taught me so much about the power of research. Through the time spent reading and finding publications showcasing the importance of the Black Lives Matter movement from a historical perspective of dress as a form of protest, our project was far bigger than I originally imagined. This then led to the development of the course, which surprisingly I was allowed to take regardless of my hand in its creation. Being in the class gave me even more reason to continue my research. The experience was like no other

FIGURE 11.4: Audience members during the student presentations at the Ames Public Library. Photograph courtesy of authors.

because the work being done within the class was not just to earn a grade but to push the mark further from where we started in the class creation.

Taking a class such as this on a predominantly white campus, without a doubt, was a stepping stone towards pushing a curriculum of diversity. It was a chance for many students of colour within the AMD department to have a course that represented them and their own experiences. While, for the white cohort of the department, it gave them a chance to learn the relevance of these experiences and how Black men and women are treated simply on their appearance. I am thankful for the non-students of colour who took the class and produced their own research that further helped push the message of why the Black Lives Matter movement is indeed needed. Because when they entered the course, chances were that their knowledge of the matter was slim-to-none. But in the end, they could deliver a whole presentation on their findings, validating the fact that this course offered something for everyone to learn. It was simply a shared experience like no other.

### Kelly's reflections on teaching the course as a White faculty member

My reflection for this course centres around encouraging white faculty members to think critically about how their own positionality influences their course content in their online and physical class spaces. Also, I encourage faculty to think that it is never too late to start engaging in critical self-reflection and the lifelong process toward understanding and implementing social justice in their pedagogical practices.

As a white cisgender woman working in a fashion department who has a great deal of privilege, I have mostly felt comfortable in my work environment. That is, I do not regularly encounter everyday experiences of microaggressions, I am rarely talked over in meetings, and I see other successful faculty members in my department who 'look like me'. That said, I identify as queer and am in an interracial marriage with a Black cisgender man. I grew up in a white family surrounded by mostly white people, and when I married my husband almost eleven years ago, my entire perspective on race changed. I never spoke about race growing up; in fact, when my family and I drove from New Jersey to Philadelphia for special dinner occasions, I distinctly remember them locking the doors when we drove through Black neighbourhoods.

The moment that arguably changed my perspective was when my husband and I moved apartments in our marriage's first year. It was getting darker, we were carrying a few more items, and I asked my husband to carry the TV. He looked at me and said, 'Black people don't carry TVs at night'. I live and breathe next to a Black person for whom I care deeply and have seen most kinds of microaggression and overt discrimination, from white people trying to touch his hair to white people handing me the bill at a restaurant, or more disturbingly, a group of white police officers aggressively surrounding and interrogating my husband for 'trespassing' on a construction site next to our house because he 'fit the description'. I have also seen him fired or intensely interrogated by human resources for being 'aggressive'. What got me to the point of centring social justice in my teaching philosophy, and arguably my life philosophy was (1) the continued oppression I saw my husband face day after day and (2) continually engaging in every possible professional development dedicated to developing empathy toward marginalized communities. If you plan to engage in critical pedagogies as a person in the dominant group (e.g., white, heterosexual, able-bodied), then it is critical to examine your own life experiences and privileges and how they inform your teaching practices. If you are committed to being an anti-racist, ask yourself: 'how can you de-centre whiteness from your class?' I have learned from my own positionality that engaging in social justice teaching takes time and energy. If you are in it for the long haul, you will have to do an enormous amount of labour to convince other faculty members of its worth. But in the end, combating white supremacy through higher education is just one piece of this massive puzzle, and until police brutality against Black people stops, there is still so much work to be done. From my perspective, there is no other way to approach the curriculum, and it is our duty as white people to use our power to combat these issues.

## The future and a call to action

In this course, we create space for students to learn about Black identity, dress, politics and activism in a predominantly white institution. Critical race theory is a lens through which to think about race, racism, social power and inequity. It is a way to centre Black voices and Black experiences (Delgado and Jean 2017). In this course, all of the readings, assignments and discussions about appearance, identity and the body are focused on Black identities, giving much-needed space in the apparel curriculum to these topics. Fashion courses have for too long left out marginalized populations, including Black people and other communities such as the queer community and fat people. There is significant interest among universities in considering diversity and inclusion; this course can be a model for considering these topics in the apparel curriculum, with a focus on expanding teaching beyond the classroom and, in this case, the public library. It also exemplifies how student-led initiatives by marginalized students can bring richness to an apparel programme that desperately needs to diversify its curriculum. Although we provide these calls to action, we want to clarify that setting out this type of laundry list does not guarantee educators will engage in meaningful social justice lens practices. We offer these as considerations for starting or continuing your lifelong journey toward rejecting white supremacy in fashion education. In solidarity, we offer you these starting points:

- Educate yourself on white supremacy and intersectionality. This is a starting point and by no means is enough. It is the basic necessity for the crucial work leading to structural change.
- Commit to continued education on ending white supremacy.
- Share with other members of the faculty and new students what you have learned and how you were taught and upheld white supremacy, then share how you plan to move forward with the new information learned. Then, further acknowledge mistakes that will happen in the future and accept your past and future mistakes. Take responsibility for ways you might have upheld white supremacy in your class, yet move forward with this new and informed knowledge. Part of the reparations process is to publicly apologize for past mistakes.
- Make structural changes. Without structural change, there can be no real significant impact across your unit. Therefore, you need to re-write your unit's missions and policies with a social justice lens. Without these structural changes, you will not be able to convince resistant faculty members of the changes that are needed, and the changes may not be sustained. Look at the structural levels, including programme learning outcomes, curriculum requirements, course content, course materials (books, design materials such as marker colours, etc.), classroom digital and physical spaces, student

extracurricular activities and department programming (guest lecturers, etc.). Policies to consider at each level can include:

- Create a programme-wide goal where all classes in the curriculum have at least 50 per cent of the course content, if not more, taught with a social justice lens.
  - o Require all mandatory core classes to focus on or consider a social justice lens in at least 50 per cent of the content. For example, a case study assignment in a fashion business course can focus on a fashion brand owned by a person of colour– such as Stuzo Clothing, a company owned by two Black queer women in Los Angeles. Are you offering the history of western dress because 'That's how it has always been taught?' Ask yourself why?
  - o All instructors must include at least one course material authored by a person of colour. Or, for design materials, instructors need to consider multiple identities in the tools such as the colour choice of markers on the supply list. Another possibility is that lecture slides utilize diverse identities in at least 50 per cent of the slides, if not more.
  - o The unit can have standard syllabus language, which states that faculty members are committed to rejecting white supremacy in digital and physical spaces and will hold themselves and the students accountable.
  - o Student organizations associated with the unit need to engage in activities that centre on people of colour or other marginalized communities. For example, we have a fashion magazine called *Trend*.
  - o Many units also support programming that includes guest lectures, panels, or industry members engaging with the unit. The unit can consider implementing a policy where guests or panel topics must centre a social justice lens at least 50 per cent of the time, which might mean working with fashion brands owned by people of colour.
- Be open to criticism because if you engage in social justice work, you will experience criticism. Therefore, be open to what others have to say, especially people of colour and people from other historically marginalized communities.
- Encourage other faculty, especially resistant faculty members, to participate in the change. One place to start on this difficult task is to ask the department chair if the multicultural liaison for your unit can present the student diversity statistics to the members of the faculty and, if available, the results of a recent campus climate survey. This happened in our department, and it would be a great lead into considering why diverse perspectives are important for the students in our own classrooms. Additionally, you could ask for assigned service time to develop presentation materials on social justice in the curriculum for a faculty meeting. Showing faculty members how to consider social justice initiatives is vital because many folks want to do this but do not feel

equipped to do so. Yet, there will still be faculty, like some we encountered, who do not care or see the need. It is an ongoing conversation and a continual battle leading to our last point.

- Never give up. This advocacy takes continuous labour and energy that cannot stop until Black people stop dying from police brutality. Keep asking the hard questions and challenging practices rooted in white supremacy and oppression in faculty meetings, and demonstrate your belief in the continued importance of justice and equity in fashion education. Continue advocating for the structural changes needed in your unit's mission and policies.

## APPENDIX

These materials are in the order they were read or viewed in the course, not in the typical alphabetical order.

### Module 1: Brief introduction to the Black Lives Matter movement

Black Lives Matter (n.d.), 'Herstory', https://blacklivesmatter.com/about/herstory/. Accessed 16 March 2020.

Lowery, Wesley (2017), 'Black lives matter: Birth of a movement', *The Guardian*, 17 January, https://www.theguardian.com/us-news/2017/jan/17/black-lives-matter-birth-of-amovement. Accessed 16 March 2020.

Grant, Laurens (2017), 'Stay woke: The Black lives matter movement', Video, 38:57, https://www.youtube.com/watch?v=eIoYtKOqxeU. Accessed 16 March 2020.

blklivesmatter (n.d.), 'BLM 5th anniversary teaser', Video, 3:21, https://blacklivesmatter.com/pressroom/black-lives-matter-global-network-releases-video-to-commerate-our-5th-anniversary/.Accessed 16 March 2020.

The Real News Network (2015), 'A short history of Black lives matter', Video, 10:56, https://www.youtube.com/watch?v=Zp-RswgpjD8. Accessed 16 March 2020.

### Module 2: Scholarly vs. non-scholarly and historic research methods

University of Washington, Tacoma (2020), 'History: Primary & Secondary Sources', https://guides.lib.uw.edu/c.php?g=344285&p=2580599. Accessed 4 February 2020.

William Madison Randall Library (2017), 'Primary Sources for Historical Research', https://library.uncw.edu/guides/finding_primary_sources. Accessed 16 June 2017.

Newton Gresham Library, Sam Houston State University (2019), 'The History Research Process', https://shsulibraryguides.org/c.php?g=86883&p=637482. Accessed 31 October 2019.

### Module 3: Black identity and dress

Kaiser, Susan B (2012), *Fashion & Cultural Studies*, New York: Bloomsbury (Chapter 4: Ethnicities and "Racial" Rearticulations).

## Module 4: Politics, activism and dress

Ford, Tanisha C. (2015), *Liberated Threads: Black Women, Style, and the Global Politics of Soul*, North Carolina: University of North Carolina Press.

Yi, David (2015), 'Black armor: Some Black American men are dressing up to deflect negative attention, as a conscious means of survival' https://mashable.com/2015/08/08/black-men-dressing-up-police/#SEFkm7w14Gqm. Accessed 8 August 2015.

## Module 5: Racial profiling and police brutality

Hall, Alison V., Erika, V. Hall and Jamie, L. Perry (2016), 'Black and blue: Exploring racial bias and law enforcement in the killings of unarmed Black Male civilians', *American Psychology*, 71:3, pp. 175–86.

Seabrook, Renita and Heather Wyatt-Nichol (2016), 'The ugly side of America: Institutional oppression and race', *Journal of Public Management & Social Policy*, 23:1, pp. 20–46, http://hdl.handle.net/11603/3677

Carbado, Devon (2017), 'From stopping Black people to killing black people: The fourth amendment pathway to police violence', *California Law Review*, 105:1, pp. 125–64, 10.15779/Z38GK24

Lopez, German (2018), 'Police shootings and brutality in the US: 9 Things you should know', Vox, 14 November 2018, https://www.vox.com/cards/police-brutality-shootings-us/us-police-shootings-statistics. Accessed 8 November 2022.

Mapping Police Violence (2017), '2017 mapping police violence report', https://policeviolencereport.org/. Accessed 16 March 2020.

## Module 6: Black activist movements

PBS (2012), 'Slavery by another name', Video, 90, https://www.pbs.org/video/slavery-another-name-slavery-video/. Accessed 16 March 2020.

Jennings, James (2000), *The Politics of Black Empowerment: The Transformation of Black Activism in Urban America*, Michigan: Wayne State University Press.

Taylor, Keeanga-Yamahtta (2016), *From #BlackLivesMatter to Black Liberation*, Illinois: Haymarket Books.

Khan-Cullors, Patrisse and Asha Bandele (2018), *When They Call You a Terrorist: A Black Lives Matter Memoir*, New York: St. Martin's Press.

## Module 7: Black lives matter, fashion, appearance, and the body

Nguyen, Mimi T. (2015), 'The Hoodie as sign, screen, expectation, and force', *Signs: Journal of Women in Culture and Society*, 40:4, pp. 791–816, https://doi.org/10.1086/680326.

## Module 8: Cultural appropriation vs. appreciation

Hill, Selena (2017), 'High fashion brand unapologetically appropriates #BlackLivesMatter', *Black Enterprise*, http://www.blackenterprise.com/brand-appropriates-blacklivesmatter/. Accessed 23 June 2017.

Byrd, Rikki (2015), 'This designer stopped everyone in their tracks with a fashion show about police brutality', *Mic*, https://mic.com/articles/125193/this-designer-stopped-every-onein-their-tracks-with-a-fashion-show-about-police-brutality#.g2H3kaO7l. Accessed 11 September 2015.

## REFERENCES

Allen, Walter R. (1992), 'The color of success: African-American college student outcomes at predominantly white and historically Black public colleges and universities', *Harvard Educational Review*, 62, pp. 26–44.

Delgado, Richard and Stefancic, Jean (2017), *Critical Race Theory: An Introduction*, New York: New York University Press.

Harper, Shaun R. (2012), 'Black male student success in higher education', in *A Report from the National Black Male College Achievement Study*, Pennsylvania: University of Pennsylvania: Center for the Study of Race and Equity in Education, https://web-app.usc.edu/web/rossier/publications/231/Harper%20(2012)%20Black%20Male%20Success.pdf. Accessed 27 February 2023.

Kendi, Ibram S. (2019), *How to Be an Antiracist*, New York: One World.

# 12

## Designing for Drag

*Sang Thai*

This chapter is imagined as a podcast interview.

**INTERVIEWER:** Today we have Sang Thai who is a lecturer in the School of Fashion and Textiles at the Royal Melbourne Institute of Technology (RMIT). Sang has an interest in the intersectionality of fashion, particularly in race and sexuality, and how fashion might be designed for activism within this space. We are going to talk about a project he ran supporting students to create costumes for a drag performance featured as part of a drag festival in Broken Hill in regional Australia in 2018 and 2019.

Hi Sang, thanks for joining us.

**SANG:** Thanks for having me.

**INTERVIEWER:** It sounds like an exciting project, so how did you get involved?

**SANG:** The project came through our university Office of Indigenous Engagement. I am fortunate to work in an institution with a strong track record in LGBTIQ+ and inclusion spaces. RMIT University has been awarded Employer of the Year in the Australian Workplace Equality Index – LGBTIQ Inclusion Awards in 2019 and 2020 (Phelan 2020). The Office of Indigenous Engagement was led by Professor and Deputy Vice-Chancellor (Indigenous Education and Engagement) Mark McMillan, an Indigenous Wiradjuri man. I should note that Indigenous people in Australia are also referred to as First Nations People.

It came to me through an informal discussion with my programme manager, who suggested it be of interest given my research. I had just started my master's degree, which has since become a Ph.D. Prior to that, I had been teaching primarily in the branding and commercial enterprise space in the degree programme based on my previous experience as a designer in the Australian fashion industry.

**INTERVIEWER:** Did you say Indigenous engagement? Was there a connection there?

**SANG:** Yes, the project looked to work with some emerging Indigenous drag queens and performers. We work with Felicia Foxx and Jojo Zaho. Felicia had just recently competed in the Miss First Nation drag competition. Local drag queen Philmah Bocks mentored the performers. Philmah is also co-director of the *Broken Heel Festival* based in regional Australia or what is known colloquially as the 'Outback' – the desert heart of much of Australia. The project was an excellent opportunity to embed a 'cultural appropriation' workshop centred on our relationship with Indigenous people in Australia, which has historically been quite fraught.

**INTERVIEWER:** Ok – so much to unpack there.

**SANG:** [Laughs] yes ...

**INTERVIEWER:** Let's start with the *Broken Heel Festival*.

**SANG:** Yes, Broken 'Heel' – as in the shoe heel, obviously a pun on the place name as well. The *Broken Heel Festival* takes place in Broken Hill annually. The festival runs over three days, a weekend that celebrates all things drag. The festival is inspired by the iconic 1994 Australian movie, *The Adventures of Priscilla Queen of the Desert* (Elliott 1994). It is based in the Palace Hotel in Broken Hill, featured in the film. They filmed in Broken Hill as a substitute for Coober Pedy, another small outback Australian town. The whole festival is quite amazing – thousands of tourists from the LGBTIQ+ community descend on the town every year – in 2018, it was in its fifth incarnation. The shop fronts on the main street are decorated to celebrate the festival, and there are drag performances across three stages each night, with a street parade during the daytime on Saturday. It's quite a subversion of the conservatism and discrimination that you would expect in a small remote country town.

**INTERVIEWER:** So the whole town gets involved?

SANG: Well, there are still pockets that clearly are not as 'into it' or not that interested in participating – not that we faced any overt discrimination when we were there.

INTERVIEWER: We? Do you mean the students?

SANG: Yes, in the first year, some students stumbled into another pub on the main street and pretty much walked straight out after they received some strange looks – quote, 'it was not for them'.

INTERVIEWER: So the students went to Broken Hill as well?

SANG: Yes, the project involved the students designing outfits for a group of drag queens in a feature segment. We ran the design studio project in 2018 and 2019, and in its first incarnation, we worked with Art Simone, Karen from Finance, the two Indigenous queens as previously mentioned – Felicia Foxx and Jojo Zaho, Philmah – the festival director and Christina Knees-up who was a drag queen local to Broken Hill.

INTERVIEWER: Karen and Art are pretty high-profile names.

SANG: We were very lucky to have the students work with them. The students worked in groups conceiving designs that reimagined an Australian 'ought Coutu'ah' or 'haute couture' in a very heavy Australian accent. The tongue-in-cheek brief called on them to consider ideas about identity and 'Australian-ness'. These are strong recurring themes in the original *Priscilla* film. For those who don't know, the film's basic premise is that three drag queen performers travel from Sydney on a bus christened *Priscilla* and make their way into central Australia, where they have been booked to perform. The complete film title is *The Adventures of Priscilla, Queen of the Desert* – I guess it is a […] comedy, and I think these things talk to interesting ideas of an Australian identity but also how they intersect with drag and queer culture.

The costumes in the movie include outfits that resemble, and are inspired by, Australian flora and fauna – like the frilled neck lizard – and other para-phernalia like the iconic dress made from 'thongs' or flip flops. The students were asked to respond to and also capture the unique personas of the drag performer they were designing for. They included a costume 'reveal' or transformation as part of their designs.

INTERVIEWER: Wow. Ok – that seems like a lot of things to juggle.

**SANG:** [Laughs] [...] thinking about it, yes, I guess so, but they were supported through the development and production of their designs.

**INTERVIEWER:** So, what kinds of things did you do with them?

**SANG:** We had quite a few workshops that looked at methods for transforming a man's body to create what is essentially a gender illusion of a stereotypical 'woman's' silhouette. This included a padding workshop that looked at working with foam and wadding to alter the men's forms to a more hourglass shape. Anyone familiar with drag would be familiar with hip pads that drag queens commonly use to bulk up their thighs and backside (Figure 12.1). We basically used the same principles to transform a dressmaking dummy, or form, to match the performer's 'padded' dimensions.

Corsets and cinchers are a typical way for drag performers to create more hourglass and feminine shapes. We were lucky to have Laure Weir, a costumier from France, lead the students through a lot of the technical making – particularly related to corsets. There was also a millinery workshop to

FIGURE 12.1: A padded body in the foreground with students in the background, 2018. Photograph courtesy of Sarah Adams, RMIT University.

support headwear development – and a workshop about stretch fabrics which is essential for draping around extreme proportions.

**INTERVIEWER:** It sounds very busy.

**SANG:** It was!

**INTERVIEWER:** Did you know much about drag before this?

**SANG:** Only what I had seen on *RuPaul's Drag Race* and the acts at the local bars. I had some idea about what it entailed, but really it was limited. The documentary *Paris is Burning* is the most immediate popular culture reference (Livingston 1990). The film documents the 1990s Harlem Ballroom Scene if you haven't seen it. The Ballroom scene also inspired Madonna's song 'Vogue' of the same year. It captures some of the roots for many tropes and drag lexicon that have become mainstream. Terms such as 'Shade', 'Tea' and 'Realness' are now ubiquitous in queer and LGBITQ+ culture and, to some extent, broader popular culture. These are important concepts and ideas relevant to how we create in queer culture.

In drag, for example, the tradition of 'realness' talks to a way of 'passing'. Scholars have talked about 'passing' as a way to avoid the discrimination of stigmatized identities and identifications (Renfrow 2004). We have laws in Australia that legislate against discrimination of LGBTIQ+ individuals at federal and state levels[1]. In *Paris is Burning*, the contestants dress in drag and compete in categories of 'realness' like 'executive realness' or 'daytime realness', transforming themselves into presentations of the community that they are specifically excluded from (hooks 2012: 275). Often these are representations of white women against the stigmatized identities of Black and non-traditional gender or non-heteronormative.

I think drag is an excellent starting point to consider notions of gender, and *Paris is Burning* is a good place to really feel the complexities of intersectional identities expanded from Kimberle Crenshaw's seminal paper about Black women and discrimination (Crenshaw 1989).

**INTERVIEWER:** Yes, ok. Drag is a subversion of gender, right?

**SANG:** Well, not necessarily. There may have been something subversive about a cisgendered man dressing up as a woman, but this is based on the traditional binary notions of male and female. Often also, the gender representations in drag, perhaps, reinforce specific notions of femininity or female gender representations. The signifiers of womanhood are often exaggerated with comic effects – hourglass figures, makeup, and big hairstyles – the tools for gender performance. My understanding of notions of gender has shifted through the work of Judith Butler, and the students I have encountered recently have already vastly expanded their understanding of the non-binary notions of gender. Gender performativity as understood by Judith Butler speaks to gender as something that is performed not with an innate identity but rather through a reflexive process of repeated stylized actions (Butler 2006: 34). Ultimately, it speaks to the agency of individuals to construct their own gender identities[2].

According to Butler, the distinction in drag between the biological body and gendered expression can help to illustrate 'the presence of three contingent dimensions of significant corporeality: anatomical sex, gender identity, and gender performance' through the disruption of the unity of these in 'normal' gender constructs (Butler 2006: 197). The students in this project designed costumes initially as a team and then took their discoveries of gender to expand on them in their own individual projects in the second half of the semester.

**INTERVIEWER:** It sounds very complicated logistically. How did you manage the structure – I mean, do students even 'like' working in groups?

**SANG:** [Laughs] Group work can be problematic sometimes, but I guess I find it always works best when the students have some control over who they choose to work with. The funny thing is that in fashion we always work collaboratively and rarely is it produced in isolation, yet we perpetually celebrate individual creatives!

It's probably good to give a little context for how it sat within our degree programme to really understand how it was structured. The students were Bachelor of Design with Honours in the second semester of their third year of a four-year degree. In this particular semester, we run a twelve-week design studio course that comprises 50 per cent of their overall study load. A range of design studio briefs is released before the start of the semester where the students select from a broad range of contexts and specializations that align with their interests. By this stage, the students have developed a foundation of knowledge and skills in making – materials as well as contextual studies – history, theory and industry practice. This studio course broadly aimed to develop the student's design and communication capability through applying and extending their skills and knowledge through research, conceptual thinking, making and communication in a particular fashion specialisation.

The project was conceived as two halves. The first phase was very much centred on producing outcomes for the *Broken Heel Festival* performance and working in the existing drag context. From my experience, it's always a hard balance to work with students to produce real-world outcomes with very strict limitations and deadlines while ensuring scope and freedom for a more critical and expanded approach. Having the freedom to consider more expanded notions in the second half helped the students accept the limitations of the performance brief for the *Broken Heel Festival*. I am always keen to position the students in the role of designer and creative, working collaboratively with any partner and managing and supporting the students through the collaborative process.

In the first iteration, eighteen students formed their own groups of three and were assigned a drag queen based on the preferences submitted via an online form. There was an initial 'meet the queens' session that set up the brief and allowed the students to engage directly with their allocated queen. Before the session, they were prompted to research each drag persona. In this session, Philmah presented the production concept, including the performance music as possible points of inspiration. The queens 'padded-up' and students recorded their before and after body measurements (Figure 12.2). This transformation is always very stark and a real eye-opener.

FIGURE 12.2: Students measuring the padded body, 2018. Photograph courtesy of Sarah Adams, RMIT University.

After this initial session, the students met twice weekly during scheduled class time to further research and develop their costume concepts. The brief called on them to develop at least three costume concepts that they would present several weeks later to festival director Philmah for review and feedback and ultimately developed into a final costume.

The overall brief asked them to consider not only an outfit that was suitable, and sufficiently comfortable and appropriate, for a drag performance context but also:

- Include a 'costume reveal' in the context of drag,
- Be informed or responsive to high-end luxury fashion perspectives,
- Include a separate fashion headpiece that coordinates with the outfit,
- Respond to the theme: 'ought Coutu'ah Australiana' and performance theme 'The Nature of Fashion',
- Reflect and respond to the drag queen's persona, and also consider sovereignty and designing for Indigenous peoples near you.

**INTERVIEWER:** So, the students responded to an 'Australian-ness' through *Priscilla*?

**SANG:** The film has a particular Australianness about it. Not only are there references in the costumes to indigenous flora and fauna, but what is really interesting is the references to the imagery of the iconic Australian outback. The reality is that most Australians live in major metropolitan cities. So they don't really have a deep connection with the desert, but it's an integral part of our iconography. Uluru (formerly known as Ayers Rock) is one of the most recognizable landmarks of Australia in the 'red centre' – a reference to the iron-rich dirt in the desert.

Thinking through drag is quite liberating when applied to national iconography. Often the legitimacy of fashion, particularly within an academic environment, is a somewhat serious endeavour, and I think traditionally, these are linked with couture or European fashion systems. Drag is 'fun' and subversive and is able to 'not take itself seriously'.

There is a synergy here with Australians' conception of ourselves and our 'laid-back' sensibility and the ability to 'laugh at ourselves'. Drag has a strong tradition of comedy – with a whole genre of 'comedy queens'. According to Butler, a parody or pastiche of gender can engender laughter through the 'loss of the sense of "normal" [...] especially when "the normal", "the original" is revealed to be copied, and an inevitably failed one, an idea that no one can embody. In this sense, laughter

210

emerges in realization that all along the original was derived' (Butler 2006: 189).

I would argue that all Australian drag queens are comedy queens. I don't know; perhaps the ability to 'laugh at oneself' or to 'not take oneself seriously' is born of marginalization? I wonder how much of this use of comedy is about making stigmatized identities accessible to the mainstream. There is a strong western tradition of the court jester or 'the fool' telling truths through the guise of comedy or self-deprecation.

In Australia, we famously had a prime minister accused of referring to Australia as the 'arse-end of the world' in a private conversation with a counterpart[3]. Hannah Gadsby, an Australian comedian, also brilliantly captures how self-ridicule through comedy has contributed to her own mental decline in a stand-up comedy show titled *Nanette* (Gadsby 2008). This piece is also a great illustration of the conditions experienced by marginalized LGBITIQ+ communities and identities.

But yes, sorry, Australianness. In drag and costume – I find that 'costume' is a term that is often derided …

**INTERVIEWER:** Is it? By who?

**SANG:** I guess by the general populace who will often describe extravagant outfits on the runway as 'costume' as a differentiator to what they would wear on the street. Usually, this is about dismissing it as not 'fashion'. In my experience, 'costume' has also historically been used not as a positive descriptor for student work. Nonetheless, this sense of costume and drag can give students the impetus to appropriate and replicate. Just as the Ballroom Culture looked to recreate existing dress, particularly of the European luxury houses of the 1980s, as evidenced through the naming of troupes or groups as houses, an ode to couture 'houses' – modern drag has reference to iconic fashion designs. McQueen, for example, is a designer that is often referenced. Embedded in drag culture is also a tradition of resourcefulness.

Captured through 'challenges' in *RuPaul's Drag Race* such as 'Drag on a Dime' or any other 'unconventional materials' challenge – borrowing terminology from another reality competition. Not having the 'expenses' to buy actual custom-made costumes, as aptly put by the late drag queen Chi Chi DeVayne ('New Wave Queens!' 2016, MTV). Aside from 'mopping' or stealing, the ability to transform or elevate ordinary materials to make them look more 'expensive' speaks to a lot of certain conditions. Often discrimination and stigmatization limit access to employment opportunities and the ability to pay for expensive 'couture' – the term used here as a sarcastic catch-all for desirable fashion rather than that specifically of Parisian origin[4]. As students who are studying, limitations around the ability to 'afford' expensive materials are an interesting and often lived parallel. Fortunately, for this project, partial funding for the student material was supported through the RMIT Office of Indigenous Education and Engagement. There were some students who supplemented this bursary with their own funds.

**INTERVIEWER:** Sure – you said earlier something about maybe more freedom in design as I understood it?

**SANG:** Sorry, yes! So basically, I meant to say that the creation of drag allows you to engage in parody and make literal translations into outfits – of animals or other things.

**INTERVIEWER:** Like a Koala or a sexy Koala?

**SANG:** Yes! You know, a costume can be cosplay or replication, or interpretation of an existing character from another form. In fashion terms, it could also be lo-fi configurations of high-end fashion. The rules around comfort and materiality are also challenged. Hot glue, papercraft, stapling – all become acceptable ways of making. Although for this specific project, one criterion was to make the outfits constructed to a quality that allowed for comfort and multiple wearings.

**INTERVIEWER:** And was there a sexy Koala?

**SANG:** [Laughs] no, but we had one that might have constituted a sexy cockatoo. Having said that out loud – that sounds like a punt! [laughs]. Well, it started more covered up or a caped cockatoo that revealed itself into a revealing beaded corset featuring cockatoos and other Australian flora.

**INTERVIEWER:** That's right, you said there was a 'reveal'?

**SANG:** The costumes did 'reveal'. This was through the request of the producer Philmah Bocks. Reveals are always a bit of a complicated thing to engineer into a costume. The reveal is a definite trope of modern drag – it is a stage and fashion 'moment'.

**INTERVIEWER:** Everyone loves a reveal!

**SANG:** They certainly do! There's probably something there around a metamorphosis that is particularly attractive to the LGBITQ+ community. Stories of psychological transformations accompanied by physical transformations are typical of narratives of oppression – overcoming stigma and shame to celebrate a sense of identity[5]. 'Coming out', from darkness to light [...] The transformation of the dull caterpillar into a beautiful butterfly offers an attractive metaphor to translate in costume through colour, shape and other visual expressions. For the *Broken Heel Festival* performance, a change of tempo and style in the music signalled the transformation.

**INTERVIEWER:** I wish we could see them.

**SANG:** You can actually – the show from the festival is featured on the Australian Broadcasting Network (ABC 2018), the Broken Hill Facebook page (ABC Broken Hill 2018) and RMIT also has a small YouTube showreel (Figure 12.3) (RMIT University 2018).

**INTERVIEWER:** Great! We'll check it out. So, the students went to Broken Hill?

**SANG:** They did; we got on a chartered bus that took us there in about nine hours. We stayed for two nights out in a caravan park just on the outskirts of town.

FIGURE 12.3: Philmah Bocks in Saturday Night Shindig performance at the *Broken Heel Festival,* 2018. Photograph courtesy of 'Broken Hill' media and Rebecca Small, RMIT University.

**INTERVIEWER:** And what did they think?

**SANG:** It was a great experience for them. Obviously, it was a little stressful since there were real-life outcomes, but I think being present for the festival with their peers and having the satisfaction of their outfits performing live is really transformative. I am a real believer in experiential learning. I have taken students to Vietnam on a study tour before, and we've visited workers and factories. Still, it is not until you stand in a hot and humid factory with the sounds and activity around that you understand the conditions – the students all write about this in their reflective journals.

   The brief for both halves of the project asked the students to document their research, experiences and reflections in a portfolio journal which was submitted to support their final garment artefacts. This was a fluid process that asked them to document their participation in making and theory workshops and articulate their ongoing discoveries in relation to the key themes presented in this design studio through a mixture of annotated images and text. The portfolio was also used to present their progress for feedback during class sessions.

**INTERVIEWER:** So what happened in the second half?

**SANG:** In the second half, the students were asked to develop new fashion propositions that responded to their experience and understanding of gender and performance. The brief asked the students to individually use their learnings from part one to explore expanded notions of drag and its place within contemporary performative gender discourse to develop and inform fashion outcomes. They were asked to conceive and develop outfits suitable for a performance that engaged and drew from the techniques and ideas developed in the first half. I haven't mentioned that in the first part of the project, we were invited to present a preview performance at a central shopping mall as part of Vogue's Fashion Night activation. It became an opportunity for a few of our students who volunteered to drag-up as part of the cast alongside some more established drag queens. The students had also decided that I should join the drag performers!

**INTERVIEWER:** Amazing! Was that your first time?

**SANG:** Well, I had participated in what my friends describe as 'lazy drag', which for me means to put on a dress, a bob wig and some lipstick, usually with stubble because I refuse to shave. So it was quite a different experience to shave my face, wax my arms, and have my face professionally painted or 'beaten'! I think back, and it would have been great to have all the students participate more – although they were a part of the performance, it would have been great to have allowed more time for them to experience being 'in' drag. I originally planned a makeup workshop, but it had been cut since the schedule was already too full.

The public 'happening' was produced in collaboration with Melbourne Central Shopping Centre, led by colleague Dr Adele Varcoe and was supported in attendance by members of the faculty as well as the dean of the RMIT School of Fashion and Textiles – all of whom had been strong supporters from the very outset. The project was recognized with a school teaching award at the end of the year. This experience clearly had a lasting impact on the students who appeared in drag for the event, which was evident in their final project.

**INTERVIEWER:** Final projects?

**SANG:** Yes, there were varied outcomes for students final individual projects – many thinking through their own personal lived experiences to relate to broader ideas of gender and performance. One student continued to explore their Catholic upbringing manifest through the creation of their own drag persona – a seemingly cathartic exercise to challenge stigma and discrimination.

Another student drew inspiration from their own cultural heritage – that of Beijing Opera, which, like in western Shakespearean tradition, had men play the women's roles. It was aptly titled *Spilling the Tea*, presenting a modern hybrid of contemporary East Meets West within modern conceptions of drag presented with gender fluid expressions. Another student conceived of a performance for the *Rainbow Serpent Festival* – a *bush doof*, ('music dance festival in Australia'). The performance looked to 'free the nipple', an ode to perceived double standards present through social media platforms that would censor the nipples of women and not men. The costumes drew from the tropes of 'festival' wear, using the iconic Arnott's Shapes biscuits as a motif.

**INTERVIEWER:** And how did you get to those outcomes?

**SANG:** We first started unpacking some of the themes and ideas related to drag. The first stage was really about working within the existing model for developing fashion for drag. In the second stage, we considered the implications of gender and performance, some of which I have already spoken to.

Early in the project, we also had a visiting historian Professor Peter McNeil deliver a lecture on his recent contribution to the exhibition and catalogue *Reigning Men Fashion in Menswear, 1715–2015* to share some of his insights into drag (Takada et al. 2016). The school arranged this serendipitous event.

Thinking through fashion, we started with the very fundamental and accessible ideas in fashion, such as colour. Why, for example, is pink for girls and blue for boys? Exploring historian Jo Paoletti's study of this phenomenon in American history opened up a dialogue about other hegemonic conceptions of gender in relation to fashion[6].

What is also really interesting is if we go back to *Paris is Burning*, our modern conception of drag is squarely rooted in Black history. RuPaul is a Black drag queen who presides over her drag 'family'. A lot of what is made into a commercial piece of reality television is rooted in the Ballroom Scene and Culture. I think this makes for some interesting perspectives in relation to race and drag – and although we don't necessarily have the same type of racial tensions here in Australia that are present in the United States, it does open up conversations with students about our own relationship with our Indigenous communities in Australia.

This is also particularly important around discussions of appropriation and who benefits when the culture is transformed for mass consumption. bell hooks talks about this in *Reel to Reel* and how the original documentary is made through the eyes and gaze of a white cisgendered woman (hooks 2012: 275). Though the filmmaker identifies as lesbian and, therefore, a part of the broader queer or LGBITQ+ community, the film is also made for consumption by a broadly white audience. There is a tension between this and notions of 'representation' – which, for me personally, is important because often there is the need for allyship for those with more privilege to bring these more marginalized representations into the mainstream. Unless I don't know, is there another way?

If you watch *Werq the World*, a documentary series spin-off from the *Drag Race* franchise, Kennedy Davenport also mentioned that it is much harder as a Black drag queen (Rischen 2019). They generally have fewer fans, often evidenced during the meet-and-greet sessions, which I assume translates to a smaller audience, less desirability and, therefore, a smaller capacity to book shows and earn income. Anecdotally, it's interesting to see how these race relations play out on *Drag Race*. I mean, who can forget scenes where The Vixen rises against the narrative of being the 'angry Black woman' prompted by Aquaria ('Diva Worship' 2019, VH1).

**INTERVIEWER:** Is there a parallel here in Australia?

**SANG:** Yes, I mean we have a very, in quotation marks, 'complicated' relationship with our Indigenous community, which is shifting. I recently went to New Zealand, and the Maori culture is so much better acknowledged across all their public service and governance – they have a treaty. There's still a lot of resistance here in Australia to making formal gestures, such as changing the date of Australian Day commemorating White settler colonization in Australia. The counter-narrative that has been adopted widely is 'Invasion Day'.

Working with the two First Nations drag queens came out of the work that the University is doing toward reconciliation. At one point, I did ask one of them if or how their indigeneity affected how they 'did' drag. Interestingly they talked more about how they were not yet a 'polished' drag queen but were not a total beginner as well, and that they have a lot to learn from Philmah about drag. I guess their indigeneity didn't necessarily seem to be expressed in their drag aspirations. Obviously, this surprised me somewhat, given the scope of the project. One of them wore a sequined dress of the First Nations Peoples' flag, which is quite a political statement.

I am really interested in how their intersectional identities play out here. By doing drag, I guess, do you need to adhere to the pre-existing 'ways' to do it? I am also fascinated by what this means, particularly for LGBTIQ+ communities. How much do you need to maybe leave behind your other cultural identifications to become gay or lesbian? Is there a preference for a western model because we are in Australia? Or because western democracies are more liberal in relation to LGBTIQ+ rights?

For me, I guess the interesting thing is that their indigeneity is what made them stand out, and I wonder when they would discover how this might more broadly inform their drag. This also raises the question of who decides the markers of indigeneity and the implications for the expression of intersectional identities.

**INTERVIEWER:** Did the students' designs respond to this?

**SANG:** Well, actually, yes. An opportunity to engage with this was embedded into the curriculum. We had a guest lecturer from the School of Media and Communications deliver a workshop on appropriation, more specifically as it relates to our First Nations People. I mean, appropriation always requires a nuanced understanding and discussion and our expectation around what is best practice, like anything, is evolving and changing. I know personally, there is always a fear of doing or saying the wrong thing, but ultimately, Professor Mark McMillan talks about this idea of approaching it with a 'learning mindset', which opens the way for more open and respectful dialogue (Cranney 2018: n.pag.).

The students were presented with various real-life examples and scenarios to discuss. Ultimately, who's knowledge and how it is used, shared, and consumed is important but really needs to be understood within the bigger picture. Those student groups who chose to design for the Indigenous drag queens engaged with ideas of indigeneity in different ways, some choosing to use colours that referenced the First Nations Peoples' flag – another group collaborated with an Indigenous textiles artist to create prints that were further embellished with more contemporary beads and sequins.

**INTERVIEWER:** What do you mean by the bigger picture in this case?

**SANG:** At the time, I had just finished Reni Eddo-Lodge's book *Why I am No Longer Talking to White People about Race* (2017), and it made me think more broadly about ideas of structural racism and intersectionality. This was before concepts of systemic racism had become more mainstream and readily understood through the Black Lives Matter movement has had a notable crescendo in 2020. What really resonated with me was an understanding of racism that I have experienced in Australia as a first-generation migrant of Chinese Cambodian descent, and rather than just thinking about individual instances of racism but more broadly, the sum effect of discrimination overall.

In my lifetime, people of Anglo-Saxon descent have always countered that they have been excluded or discriminated against by other ethnic minorities and that racism works 'both ways'. However, ultimately structural racism acknowledges that though there may be instances of discrimination on both sides, there is still an imbalance whereby a community of people may experience it more. The structures also reinforce this. We are all guided by unconscious associations that lead to unconscious bias in a range of circumstances. Cordelia Fine discusses this bias in her book *Delusions of Gender* (2011). In studies where study groups were asked if women belonged in a range of high-profile professions which have historically been the domain of men, most answered in the affirmative. However, in tests measuring the reaction times for associating those professions, people overwhelmingly drew connections to men faster than women.

**INTERVIEWER:** Ok, but what does this mean?

**SANG:** I guess what I am trying to say is that discrimination can clearly be a result of unconscious bias that we all share collectively through our lived experiences. While we might think we are liberal and do not discriminate, we are always complicit to it within the greater social ecology. So, questions of appropriation need to be addressed through an understanding of who is being systematically oppressed and marginalized. Of course, there are also overt forms of discrimination, including racism.

This has real implications in relation to our Indigenous communities in Australia and how we might now engage their knowledge and cultural and creative practices. It brings to question the appropriateness of a dot painting on a boomerang, mass-produced in China and sold as a souvenir. I guess this can be thought through in fashion as well. What are ways that the fashion 'system' oppresses and marginalize? And what of the intersectional identities in fashion?

**INTERVIEWER:** What significant impact do you think it has had on you?

**SANG:** It obviously made me aware of my own intersectional identity and really made me understand the impact and conditions that I have experienced in my life. I mean, these biases can easily be self-directed – in my case, internalised racism or internalised homophobia[7]. I grew up in Australia and have a real interest in ideas of Australian-ness with my feet straddling my Asian culture at home and Australia more broadly.

On reflection, I spent much of my professional career before teaching as a designer designing for the 'other'. In my most recent role, I led the design team that developed clothing for a very typical suburban Australian male consumer. We referred to him affectionately as 'Barry BBQ'. I remember when I first started, I introduced a range of pink and aqua shirts into the range which prompted some unrest from the general manager at the time. Were they too 'gay'? It always made me wonder if I had been a heterosexual white Australian man if he would have had the same misgivings.

It's made me interested in considering how my own intersectional identity might inform a unique fashion practice that might challenge existing subjectivities in fashion in relation to race and queerness. I am interested in ways that we can do this in the mainstream that is accessible, so we can bring people on the journey. How do we work within the existing system and achieve this? Perhaps this is also a consequence of my cultural upbringing. We were migrants and always understood our place in this country was conditional on 'fitting in'. Doing well despite the marginalization, I guess, contributes to what has been described in America as the 'Model Minority Myth' (Chou and Feagin 2016).

It has also challenged me to reconsider how we teach and assess.

**INTERVIEWER:** What do you mean by this?

**SANG:** To think more inclusively, I think we need to be open to how the value systems or subjectivities are a sum of our lived experiences, and this is also true of the students. I guess thinking about those things that locate us in our 'habitus', it is important to think about what is valued and privileged in how we assess and grade. What is an inclusive assessment, and what values or subjectivities are important? How might preparing the students for the 'real world' or to be 'job ready' be perpetuating certain inequalities and privileges that exist already in the broader fashion system? How can the existing fashion system be shared while framing the possibilities to do better?

I had a student remark once that the university only had pattern blocks in standard commercial retail sample sizing – in our case, an Australian size twelve – they wanted larger sizes. One of my colleagues suggested that the student could grade up the pattern or draft their own block to their desired measurements. The student countered that they didn't think they should be disadvantaged by having to spend more time drafting or adapting a suitable block when their peers did not need to. At the time, I remember thinking they were right!

The effect of COVID-19 and remote learning has also really pushed us to accommodate the individual learning circumstances of students and engage more personally with their lived conditions in ways we never did before. This has included consideration of their access to technology, equipment and materials and how this might translate into their final outcomes. I am sure this is something that will continue to inform how we teach and assess.

**INTERVIEWER:** You make it sound like it was a very smooth and easy project.

**SANG:** No! There were many challenges! [Laughs] I think mainly for myself personally – prior to the project, the thought of even bringing in a travel mug with pride rainbow to the university filled me with trepidation and required a great deal of consideration. The emotional labour needed to carry through 2017 as debate raged in Australia over same-sex marriage already felt immense. Of course, since the project was initiated through the higher levels of the university, the support was clearly there.

We had students with various cultural backgrounds, and these sensitivities played out from the beginning. There was a student who opted out, stating religious concerns, and I just wasn't sure how the students would respond to a man dressed in drag. I can only think of my own first exposure to a drag queen – an overwhelming and confusing spectacle. I could barely keep up with the plot the first few times I watched *RuPaul's Drag Race*, so overwhelmed by the colour, lights, personalities and dual personas in and out of drag.

The themes explored were also very sensitive and required a great deal of maturity. While there were opportunities to make fun (as drag does of everything), we were careful to reinforce the need for professionalism among the students, which Philmah reciprocated with the drag queens. However, there were still missed plane flights for fittings and the usual things that can go awry with productions, including wardrobe malfunctions.

So much of the project was also about leading the students to find authentic ways to design that looked to work collaboratively. Whenever a student looked to be appropriating from communities that were not part of their own lived experiences, we would suggest relating it back to their own stories and seeking contact with individual people as primary sources.

This project would not have been possible without the university funding, including partially funding the student's travel expenses to Broken Hill – the nine-hour coach ride each way from Melbourne. However, we could easily achieve the same learnings with more local performers and smaller productions. Incorporation into local pride events would also possibly provide scope for external funding.

**INTERVIEWER:** What would you say to others interested in drag or incorporating it into the curriculum?

**SANG:** It has been an incredible learning experience for myself and the students. Drag can help to frame ideas around performance and performativity in relation to gender. Its roots in African American culture also offer space to reflect on whiteness and implications for appropriation. Black feminist theory has helped me to understand and consider my place in perpetuating inequities in fashion but, more importantly, as a designer and teacher to designers, to empower ourselves to contribute to greater diversity through a more inclusive fashion practice. This project has also helped demonstrate how we can work authentically with more marginalized communities through thoughtful collaboration with a learning mindset. So much of this is about generosity in creating a shared future and empowering students through 'doing'.

**INTERVIEWER:** Lots of things to think about! If people wanted to get in touch, is there a way to do that?

**SANG:** Absolutely; you can e-mail me at sang.thai@rmit.edu.au.

**INTERVIEWER:** Thank you, Sang, for joining us today for this discussion.

**SANG:** Thanks for having me!


## NOTES

1. In Australia, the Sex Discrimination Act 1984 (SDA) makes it unlawful to discriminate against a person because of their sex, gender identity, intersex status and sexual orientation. Further protections include the 'Australian Government Guidelines on the Recognition of Sex and Gender' and the 'Equal Opportunity Act 2010' in Victoria. However, Australia only recently endured a lengthy debate over marriage rights, including a country-wide Marriage Law Postal Survey of 2017 that resulted in the Marriage Amendment (Definition and Religious Freedoms) Act 2017 and same-sex marriage legalisation. The current conservative and right-leaning government has, however, sought to erode protections through its Religious Freedoms Bill that LGBTIQ+ advocates had argued would legislate the right for religions to discriminate against persons of the community effectively. At the time of writing, the bill was undergoing community consultation for the second draft of the legislation.
2. Elizabeth Wissinger reads through Butler that the iterative process of gender actions allows for 'slippage outside accepted norms' (Wissinger 2016: 289).
3. This claim was made in a 1994 autobiography by a then former Prime Minister Bob Hawke of his successor Paul Keating who was sitting Prime Minister of Australia at the time. The allegation caused a public stir (Milliken 1994).
4. The pay gap for diverse sexes and sexualities is well documented. The conversation reported in 2020 on a study by the Melbourne Institute of Applied Economics and Social Research found that gay men and lesbians earned 20 per cent and 30 per cent less than their heterosexual counterparts. It also reported that a study conducted in the United States found that transgender individuals were '11 percentage points less likely to be working compared to nontransgender or cisgender people' (Carpenter and Gonzales 2020: n.pag.).
5. An example is Alan Down's seminal book *The Velvet Range: Overcoming the Pain of Growing Up Gay in a Straight Man's World* (Downs 2012).

6.  There is a great starter video published by Public Broadcasting Service (PBS) of America in their Origins of Everything that simply outlines Jo Paoletti's research. PBS, 'Why was Pink for Boys and Blue for Girls?' (2018).
7.  Internalized racism and homophobia are forms of internalised oppression where individuals have oppressive views of their own groups.

## REFERENCES

ABC (Australian Broadcasting Corporation) Broken Hill (2018), 'Some of colour from last night's fashion parade and drag show collaboration between the Broken Hill's Broken Heel Festival and RMIT', Facebook, 9 September, http://www.facebook.com/watch/?v=299637260830664. Accessed 27 February 2023.

Australian Government (2013), *Australian Government Guidelines on the Recognition of Sex and Gender*, Canberra: Australian Government.

Butler, Judith (2006), *Gender Trouble: Feminism and the Subversion of Identity*, New York: Routledge.

Carpenter, Christopher and Gonzales, Gilbert (2020), 'What the supreme court on lgbt employment discrimination will mean for transgender Americans', *The Conversation*, 17 June, http://theconversation.com/what-the-supreme-courts-decision-on-lgbt-employment-discrimination-will-mean-for-transgender-americans-140878. Accessed 27 February 2023.

Chou, Rosalind S. and Feagin, Joe R. (2016), *The Myth of the Model Minority: Asian Americans Facing Racism*, New York: Routledge.

Cranney, Rhys (2018), 'Broken Heel meets Broken Hill and the school of fashion', *RMIT University*, 2 August, http://www.rmit.edu.au/news/all-news/2018/aug/broken-heel-meets-broken-hill. Accessed 27 February 2023.

Crenshaw, Kimberle (1989), 'Demarginalizing the intersection of race and sex: A Black feminist critique of antidiscrimination doctrine, feminist theory and antiracist politics', in *University of Chicago Legal Forum*, 1:8, pp. 139–67.

'Diva Worship' (2019), N. Murray (dir.), *RuPaul's Drag Race Untucked*, Season 10, Episode 3 (14 March, USA: VH1).

Downs, Alan (2012), *The Velvet Rage: Overcoming the Pain of Growing Up Gay in a Straight Man's World*, Boston: Da Capo Press.

Eddo-Lodge, Reni (2017), *Why I Am no Longer Talking to White People About Race*, London: Bloomsbury Circus.

Elliott, Stephan (1994), *The Adventures of Priscilla Queen of the Desert*, Universal City: Gramercy Pictures.

Fine, Cordelia (2011), *Delusions of Gender: The Real Science Behind Sex Differences*, London: Icon Books.

Gadsby, Hannah (2018), *Nanette*, Sydney: Netflix.

hooks, bell (2012), 'Is Paris Burning?', *Reel to Real: Race, Class and Sex at the Movies*. New York: Routledge, pp. 275–90.

Legislation.gov.au (2018), *Sex Discrimination Act 1984*, Amendment registered 14 December, http://www.legislation.gov.au/Series/C2004A02868. Accessed 27 February 2023.

Legislation.vic.gov.au (2015), *Equal Opportunity Act 2010*, Amended 1 September, http://www.legislation.vic.gov.au/in-force/acts/equal-opportunity-act-2010/020. Accessed 27 February 2023.

Livingston, Jennie (1990), *Paris is Burning*, UK: Second Sight Films.

Marriage Amendment (Definition and Religious Freedoms) Act 2017, http://www.legislation.gov.au/Details/C2017A00129. Accessed 27 February 2023.

Milliken, Robert (1994), 'Keating's rear view of the lucky country causes storm: Careless remarks have damaged the PM's nationalist stance', *The Independent*, 26 June, http://www.independent.co.uk/news/world/keating-s-rear-view-of-the-lucky-country-causes-storm-careless-remarkshave-damaged-the-pm-s-nationalist-stance-writes-robert-milliken-in-sydney-1-425378.html. Accessed 27 February 2023.

'New Wave Queens!' (2016), N. Murray (dir.), *RuPaul's Drag Race*, Season 8, Episode 4, (28 March, USA: MTV).

Paoletti, Jo Barraclough (2012), *Pink and Blue Telling the Boys from the Girls in America*, Bloomington: Indiana University Press.

PBS (Public Broadcasting Service) (2018), 'Why was Pink for Boys and Blue for Girls?', YouTube, 31 January, http://youtu.be/ohwbtkMXJJ0. Accessed 27 February 2023.

Phelan, Karen (2020), 'Employer of the Year', June 11, http://www.rmit.edu.au/news/all-news/2020/jun/inclusion-awards. Accessed 27 February 2023.

Renfrow, Daniel G. (2004), 'A cartography of passing in everyday life', *Symbolic Interaction*, 27:4, pp. 485–506.

Rischen, Jasper (2019), 'Werq the world: Kennedy Davenport', Werq the World, Season 1, Episode 7, World of Wonder Productions.

RMIT University (2018), 'Broken Hill festival', 2 October, http://www.rmit.edu.au/media-objects/multimedia/video/staff-site/broken-heel-festival. Accessed 27 February 2023.

Takeda, Sharon Sadako, Spilker, Kaye Durland, Esguerra, Clarissa M., Blanks, Tim, McNeil, Peter and Los Angeles County Museum of Art, Host Institution (2016), *Issuing Body. Reigning Men: Fashion in Menswear, 1715–2015,* Los Angeles: DelMonico Books, Prestel.

Wissinger, Elizabeth (2016), 'Judith Butler: Fashion and performativity', in A. Rocamora and A. Smelik (eds), *Thinking through Fashion: A Guide To Key Theorists*, London: I.B.Tauris, pp. 285–99.

# 13

# Curating Empowerment: Negotiating Challenges in Pedagogy, Feminism and Activism in Fashion Exhibitions

*Jenny Leigh Du Puis, Rachel Rose Getman,*
*Denise Nicole Green, Chris Hesselbein,*
*Victoria Pietsch and Lynda Xepoleas*

Exhibitions have the potential to transform and inform the public understanding of fashion. For activism to work and have a broader impact, it must be visible; therefore, the fashion exhibition is an ideal public stage for activist interventions. From the perspective of one faculty member and five students, we critically reflect upon the process of curating the 2018–19 fashion exhibition, *WOMEN EMPOWERED: Fashions from the Frontline* (WE).1 WE began as a class project, developed by the faculty member and became an internationally recognized exhibition curated by students. We discuss the pedagogical intentions behind the exhibition, theoretical and conceptual background, curatorial challenges, research process, logistical challenges, media coverage and our hopes for the future of fashion exhibitions. WE challenged both students and the public to rethink terms like 'women', 'empowerment', 'fashion' and 'frontline' and to consider fashion's potential to create, enhance, facilitate and represent positive social change. Collaboratively curating a fashion exhibition is, by necessity, a process of critical self-reflection. In this chapter, we discuss these successes and failures and argue that the public display and interpretation of fashion items is a form of activist outreach and public engagement.

## Background and pedagogical intentions

### Denise Nicole Green, faculty member

The inspiration for *WE* came to me in January 2017 after I had travelled to Washington, DC to participate in the Women's March. I witnessed (and was a participant in) a sea of pussy hats, which used design elements of colour and form to create a powerful visual message (Figure 13.1); however, I felt ambivalent. While I was encouraged by the collective action of making, wearing and marching with a shared aesthetic, I was also disturbed by the exclusionary and essentialist 'pussy' discourse. The aesthetic was not necessarily shared by all but predominantly by white cisgender feminists like myself. As we know in Fashion Studies, ambivalence is a powerful emotion that catalyses change (Davis 1992; Kaiser 2012; Kaiser et al. 1995). I began to think about other ways that women have used fashion individually and collectively to make statements, demand rights and draw attention to injustices. As the list grew in my mind, a common thread surfaced: in most cases, women used *fashion in public* and sometimes dangerous spaces *where they faced some sort of opposition.* I found this process of brainstorming intellectually stimulating and ever-expansive. In each example, I learned something about fashion's

FIGURE 13.1: Pussy hats on display in *WE* that were made for various Women's Marches held across the United States in 2017. Photograph courtesy of Grace Anderson.

role in activism and promulgating productive social change. From a pedagogical perspective, I knew that this prompt would not only elicit ideas from students but also inspire them to conduct further research and find ways to tell the stories they uncovered. I applied for a grant from the Cornell Council for the Arts Biennial to fund an exhibition titled *WOMEN EMPOWERED: Fashions from the Frontline*, under the premise that the exhibit's content were curated by students and ultimately displayed in the Cornell Fashion + Textile Collection (CF+TC).

Students in the class were split into four teams: (1) curatorial, (2) research, (3) graphics and (4) administration (e.g., budget, logistics, etc.). The process began with a discussion of the title of the exhibition, critical definition of terms, self-reflection and brainstorming. Throughout the course, students were challenged to reflect critically about their positionality – that is, how their own intersectional subject positions shape the way they see and are seen in the world. From these conversations and further work on their own, the curatorial team presented the class with a range of possibilities for the conceptual and physical organization of the exhibition. From there, the research team delved into the archives and followed-up on a 'wish list' of pieces they might borrow from individuals or other institutional collections. The research team presented the class with an array of possibilities sourced from collections on Cornell's campus as well as options from private collections, in addition to pieces I had previously secured (e.g., Justice Ruth Bader Ginsburg's judicial collars, the skirt suit worn by Cecile Richards when testifying before Congress, etc.). The class voted on the items based on their thematic placement and the corresponding dimensions of the exhibition case, which limited the number of garments and accessories that we could display.

Throughout the process, students faced numerous challenges that could have undermined the activist intentions of the exhibition. For example, representing diversity through display was a tremendous problem because the mannequins available to us were mostly thin, hyper-feminine (in posture and appearance), and appeared white (mostly) and non-disabled. Our budget did not allow for the purchase of new mannequins; therefore, students incorporated the use of dress forms (which could be padded out and manipulated more easily and do not include faces or physical postures) and manipulated existing mannequins and head forms with paint and nylon coverings. In addition, student curators chose to highlight accessories, like shoes, which could be displayed without the use of a body simulation.

Ultimately, students focused on women's strategic use of the fashioned body in spaces where they faced challenges to overcome. To interpret the clothing and accessories as actors in women's work on the frontline, the graphics team created an exhibition guidebook for visitors to take home. The guidebook provided additional images, historical context and critical interpretation of the displayed pieces.

For example, a suffragette ensemble from 1916 was lauded and critiqued as a frontline fashion that made a public and visible statement, but one that was part of an exclusionary movement that served privileged, wealthy white women. This theme was revisited in the contemporary display of pink pussy hats (Figure 13.1). Each student contributed two short interpretive essays about the women and their fashions featured in the show. The 45-page exhibition guidebook enabled visitors to engage with critical interpretations of the pieces within context, and the guidebook and exhibit have since evolved into a website[1] (https://exhibits.library. cornell.edu/women-empowered).

I hoped to foster criticism, debate and discussion in the classroom by providing students with an open-ended and somewhat vague exhibition title. We ultimately brought these critical reflections to the public through the exhibition's focus on fashion and its potential to create and reflect change and social in-justice. The failures and shortcomings of the exhibition, and the limitations of the curatorial display space, also prompted critical self-reflection among visitors and student curators.

### *Theoretical and conceptual background: Defining women and empowerment*

**Chris Hesselbein, Ph.D. student**

Our first meeting as the curatorial team was one of those moments when everything that seemed straightforward the day before was suddenly up in the air. Who do we include under the label of 'women?' What do we mean by 'empowerment?' Where might we find the 'frontline?' As finished products go – be they garments, articles or exhibits – such initial debates tend to be ironed out and become invisible by the time a consumer, reader or visitor encounters the final outcome. This chapter is a welcome opportunity to return to the messy and fraught beginnings that underpin *WE* and highlight how even the best intentions might lead to imperfect outcomes. Focusing on the conception, process and outcome of the exhibit, I recount how we as curators struggled to define what empowerment means in relation to women's fashion, how we decided to represent our interpretation of this concept throughout the exhibit visually, and last, how our choices, despite all our deliberations, nevertheless implicated us in some of the problems we wished to avoid.

The title of *WE* affirms the claim that clothing can empower women, but our initial curatorial discussions quickly made it clear that there was no consensus on how this might be the case. We were worried that tying 'fashion' to 'women' would contribute to the common misconception of fashion as an exclusively feminine practice and thus perpetuate the invisibility of women's achievements in other professional domains. We eventually decided to situate the 'frontline' of 'empowerment' in the public spaces where women visibly exert their agency, choice and voice, which seemed like a promising means for highlighting women's collective action against oppressive power structures and towards achieving positive change. Another concern was that emphasizing the obvious connection between body and clothing would reproduce stereotypical notions of women's agency as being attributed primarily to bodily appearances rather than to their intellectual or political achievements but also result in the exclusion of trans and non-binary bodies. We attempted to navigate the tension between contrasting bodily discourses – without ignoring important arguments that might resist or rely on certain conceptualizations of the body – by including the (in)famous 'pussy hat' (Figure 13.1) as well as the boots worn by a local trans musician Biannica Dominguez/Black Widow (Figure 13.2). We had the good fortune that Dominguez could attend the exhibition's opening reception and contribute to discussions among attendees in person. Our curatorial choice to focus on public spaces swiftly resulted, unsurprisingly, in a list of highly prominent women – suffragettes, state representatives, governors, supreme justices, magazine editors – but also in a list of (perhaps less prominent but

FIGURE 13.2: Biannica Dominguez/Black Widow's boots on display in 'The Stage' exhibition case. The boots are labelled with 'R' and located between two mannequins on the right side of the case, 2018. Photograph courtesy of Daniel Chamberlain.

nevertheless public) performers, athletes, activists, academics and designers. All of the items eventually included in the exhibit belonged to people who were directly or indirectly involved in pushing the boundaries of what women are, what they (can) do, who or what they might be attracted to and what they have a right to.

However, our curatorial focus on agency resulted in many important drawbacks that, although raised in reflective discussions throughout the process, we never fully managed to overcome. The amplification of one person's voice frequently comes at the expense of other voices and sometimes even in perpetuating intersecting and equally problematic power structures. A prime example of this problem is the many suffragettes who, in fighting for women's rights in the nineteenth and early twentieth century, either failed to include perspectives of persons of colour or actively silenced them. Although the exhibit's guidebook allowed us to critically reflect on our curatorial choices and highlighted such issues for the visitors, we should have provided an equally critical counterbalance to some of the more recent and contemporary items included in the exhibit. This is a deceptively obvious yet crucial point because criticizing the mistakes of others is easy in hindsight; however, seeing one's own missteps in the present is a lot harder and perhaps more important.

A similarly problematic consequence of our emphasis on the actions of relatively prominent women and the spaces and institutions in which they operate is that we failed to include those who live in the shadow of the public frontline, but are active on everyday frontlines – namely the many women whose menial and emotional labour in jobs, homes, families and communities across the world remains invisible and undervalued. The implicit hierarchy that actively obscures such forms of labour is an obdurate cultural dynamic that we (academics, curators, creators and citizens) must resist to show how things can be seen and otherwise appreciated. Once overcome, this hopefully provides a starting point for creating exhibits that include everyday items and spotlight the less visible or glamorous yet equally important aspects of our lives.

## Curatorial considerations

### Jenny Leigh Du Puis, Ph.D. student

Our collective, and at times divergent, conceptualizations of empowerment impacted the overall organization and execution of the exhibition. Everything from the layout of the objects inside the cases, the colour of the logo, the selection or omission of specific items and our promotion plan was influenced by formative and critically self-reflective conversations that sent the *WE* exhibit off on its initial journey. We knew that clarity of our conceptual intentions and motivations would be critical to the success of this curatorial project. Fashion exhibitions that showcase activism in some way can be revelatory and disruptive to our paradigmatic perspectives (Kuldova 2014); therefore, it was imperative to maintain an openness to objects and stories both within and beyond our own personal experiences as students, curators and citizens of the world. WE, therefore, sought to showcase garments and accessories that told stories of empowerment from an array of voices, backgrounds and perspectives.

The curatorial team was charged with developing a range of organizational options for the exhibition, and, as a class, we debated these ideas and collectively decided to explore the place-based, physical spaces where fashion plays a role in the empowerment of women. These spaces included: The Stage, The Arena, The Academy, The Government, The Street and The Everyday and were delineated within the exhibition by separate glass display cases. We aspired to show that fashioned empowerment manifests in ways that are diverse and, at times, divergent; there are many types and forms of empowerment, and that which reads as empowering for some may not resonate with others. Indeed, while our decision to include everyday items was intended to showcase voices and experiences encompassing worldviews not represented by more prominent or public aspects of the exhibition, we could not demonstrate an exhaustive display due to limitations of time, access and the failings of our own biases. In Buckley and Clark's (2016) discussion of everyday fashion in the museum, particular attention is given to looking beyond unique examples or those of an ascribed higher status to ensure that broader voices and perspectives are depicted and heard in museum fashion exhibitions. In WE, the curatorial perspective of representing a multitude of everyday voices was demonstrated through the handmade pussy hat display and a collection of T-shirts exemplifying a range of garments from commercially sourced items to homemade protest shirts and representing causes from women's empowerment to Black Lives Matter, from body positivity to commemoration of the Stonewall Riots, and more (Figure 13.3).

Just as Buckley and Clark (2016) described the influence of external practices on the development of a museum collection, my professional experiences and practices also informed my approach to my position on the curatorial team. Drawing upon my prior career in live entertainment, I framed the exhibition as though putting on a show: set a theme, find appropriate objects, design the aesthetic, maintain open communication, meet deadlines and open on time. For the class as a team, everything from designing the look of the cases, arranging mannequins and staying on top of the production schedule was important to develop the end result in a way that would not only satisfy the requirements of the class project but would also reach and impact as many people as possible.

FIGURE 13.3: The T-shirt case, 2018. Photograph courtesy of Grace Anderson.

During the week of exhibit installation, I set up a station in the middle of the action to act as a point person as the frenzy of activity reached its peak. Personally, my empowerment came through overseeing the literal and figurative structure of the exhibition while being involved and helping out wherever needed. Sometimes it was contacting women whose garments would be featured, dressing manne-quins for photography or late-night meetings and e-mails to update the team on the day's progress and the next day's action items.

I was particularly attached to The Stage case which featured (an array of public performance pieces from various fields) some items from circus performers, giving voice to stories of embracing grief and loss, owning the power of a strong character in a show, using a touchstone to help one through a life-changing time. Additionally, I designed the Rainbow Raver costume for a professional performer in Las Vegas as a freelance costume designer before returning to academia. Although I did not request specific items for the show, the owner-model of the ensemble was quick to submit it for consideration. We conducted many tours for the public and groups such as high school students, nursing home residents and Girl Scouts. The Rainbow Raver ensemble featured at the end of the tour quickly became a crowd favourite – from the bright colours and texture of the garment to the message of empowerment behind it, this piece helped us to end the exhibition tours on a colourful and uplifting note.

## Research process

### Lynda Xepoleas, Ph.D. Student

After the curatorial team decided on a theme, I was in charge of sources that reflect how diverse women have strategically used fashion to empower and uplift themselves as well as others. After countless hours of scanning items housed within fashion and costume collections on and off campus, I realized that most collections tend to emphasize the glamorous accounts of work produced by couturières or high-end retailers. Therefore, the dearth of diversity in fashion and costume collections challenged the rest of the research team and me to look at other archives, especially those with missions to document and preserve histories of diverse and often marginalized communities and individuals.

On Cornell's campus, we are fortunate to have access to the Human Sexuality Collection, which includes primary sources related to the social construction of diverse sexualities, and the Kheel Center for Labor Management-Documentation Archives, which documents the experiences of the working-class and labour struggles. At first, we were surprised to learn that these collections, housed in the Cornell University Library, included dress- and textile-related items. For instance, I came across a box of ephemera within Cornell's Human Sexuality Collection that contained several fashionable items worn by women who competed in the 1994 Gay Games, including the ID badge of martial arts competitor Terri Cvetan. After additional research, I learned that this was the first time women were allowed to compete in this particular event. My discovery of Terri Cvetan's ID badge led us to display her ephemera (Figure 13.4) alongside other articles of clothing worn by Olympic and collegiate athletes, thereby showcasing the athletic achievements of diverse women. By engaging with archives with an activist-inspired mission and documenting everyday individuals and organizations, we were able to unearth many other stories related to fashion and female empowerment not typically represented or acknowledged within fashion and costume collections.

We also chose to apply qualitative research methods and interview some women featured in WE. This approach was critical for us to identify how less prominent figures like designers, athletes, academics, etc., have used fashion to carry out different types and forms of empowerment. For example, my conversations with Penny Mapes, a member of Cornell's first women's ice hockey team, revealed that she had to don and doff her equipment in public restrooms before and after every practice, and she also had to repurpose men's athletic wear because there was not enough money in the budget to buy new equipment.

Understanding how extant objects embody 'a complex interplay of cultural beliefs, identity, memory, and body imprints' can be a difficult process (Mida

FIGURE 13.4: 'The Arena' display case included Gay Games ephemera from Cornell's Human Sexuality Collection and a martial arts gi and belt that were worn and loaned by Terri Cvetan, 2018. Photograph courtesy of Grace Anderson.

2015: 37). This is because, by the time an article of clothing reaches the archive, information about how it was once worn or used by a living person has either been lost or removed. By making the curatorial process participatory, we could speak directly with women and understand how they used everyday items like athletic equipment to overcome obstacles, become visible and make statements.

Overall, our decision to speak with women featured in WE and access archives that reflect an array of voices, backgrounds and perspectives allowed us to display more inclusive stories related to fashion and empowerment. We didn't just want to highlight fashions worn by prominent political or social figures; rather, we recognized the importance of consulting additional resources on and off Cornell's campus that in the end, enhanced the activist mission of WE and revealed forgotten, ignored or invisible stories of fashioned empowerment.

## Logistical challenges

### Victoria Pietsch, undergraduate student

Several logistical challenges arose across the ideation, curation, loan acquisition and installation processes of WE. As we reflected upon and brought awareness to how women's fashions are viewed and interpreted, each of these roadblocks provided its own irony and a sense of urgency that reinforced our curatorial intent.

The lack of access – to people, information and items under consideration for display – was a frequent frustration. Sometimes, a lack of response to our inquiries prevented us from telling interesting and important stories. Despite our considerable privilege as an elite academic institution, we often lacked the clout and credibility to convince others to lend us an item from their collection. In other instances, access to communities played a role. Both the curatorial and the administrative teams strove for diversity, which meant including items and stories from communities they may not be part of without being predatory, extractive or essentializing. The challenge in telling other peoples' stories is finding methods to do so and communicating those stories in a non-exploitative way that maintains the exhibition's mission: to share stories of fashion and empowerment.

Miscommunications also limited and informed what garments and paraphernalia were displayed. For example, Cornell University's e-mail service rerouted messages containing the word 'pussy' into junk folders. This prevented us from including numerous community members' pussy hats simply because we did not see their e-mails. Likewise, our service filtered our e-mail correspondence with Deborah Sundahl into our e-mail junk folders. Deborah Sundahl is a pioneer of sex-positive feminism and sex education, and she was featured in our exhibition. Her book's title, *Female Ejaculation and the G-Spot*, had been in her e-mail signature when she responded to our requests for interviews and invitations to the opening event. The censorship of our communications limited our exhibition's scope, an irony that presented as a logistical limitation and challenged our goal of generating awareness. Female curators, donors and activists attempted to bring to light stories of female empowerment by leveraging the tools and infrastructures that are typically conducive to this progressive dialogue. In doing so, they were prohibited – or protected – because of the words used to speak about their bodies and stories.

The operational setbacks largely informed the process of acquiring items for display. Attempts to borrow and display items from our university collections were refused due to security measures and environmental control concerns. In one scenario, we were not allowed to borrow a suffragette ensemble but we persevered by borrowing a suffragette ensemble from another institution. In a different instance, our attempts to highlight garments related to Martha Van Rensselaer's war relief work in Belgium were challenged despite her role as a co-founder of our own College of Human Ecology. In our attempt to celebrate, reflect upon and critique the varied stories of female empowerment, we found ourselves turning to the permissions of our own institution with similar scrutiny. These logistical parameters, established for the garments' preservation and security, circumvented our mutual goals for awareness and education.

Additionally, the installation process for *WE* was not exempt from logistical frustrations. For example, the Rainbow Raver ensemble was too tall and voluminous to be housed in the provided exhibition space (Figure 13.5). The outfit,

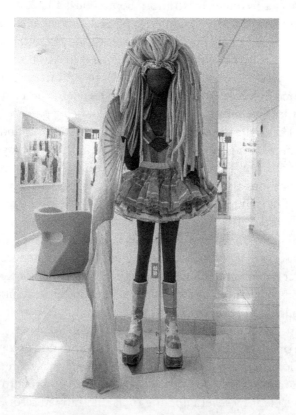

FIGURE 13.5: Rainbow Raver ensemble worn by Nickole Muse and designed by Jenny Leigh Du Puis, 2018. Photograph courtesy of Mark Vorreuter.

typically worn and intended to be portrayed on stilts, could not accommodate the limited space available within the glass vitrines. We responded to these foundational constraints by creating a new space for the Rainbow Raver, representing how it commands attention in daily life. Backed by an infrastructural pillar of the exhibition space, the Rainbow Raver's position, protected publicly by velvet ropes, tempted the same interactivity it would experience in active use. Intentionally or not, its location at the end of the exhibition confronted the administrative setbacks we'd encountered throughout the conception of *WE*. Understanding that empowerment and exposure were not born from a lack of opposition and suppression, *WE* and the Rainbow Raver overcame logistical setbacks by working past them to share stories of empowerment unapologetically.

## *Media coverage, digital exhibit and iterative design process*

### Rachel Getman, Master of Arts student

The media and popular press played an unexpected role in the iterative design process of *WE* while propelling us into the public eye. Although our first press release went out in early November, only after an Instagram post mentioned the inclusion of Representative Alexandria Ocasio-Cortez's campaign shoes (Figure 13.6) and Justice Ginsburg's dissent collars that the exhibit caught the attention of the media (Figure 13.7).

After Representative Ocasio-Cortez's election to Congress, media coverage intensified throughout all aspects of her life; from her age to her appearance, nothing was off-limits to criticize, and including her in our university's exhibit was no exception. Our exhibit became entangled in the public criticism surrounding Representative Ocasio-Cortez's clothing and appearance, exemplifying the ways in which clothing can be used to disempower and detract from women's public image. For example, Fox News criticised and focused on Representative Ocasio-Cortez's shoes instead of a major climate report released from The White House that weekend (Kwong 2018). Some media outlets criticized our exhibit for its liberal leanings, although we featured women outside the government, including athletes, performers, activists and educators. Over 45 popular national and international press articles mentioned *WE*, including CNN, Fox News, Breitbart, Teen Vogue, The Hollywood Reporter and Broadly Vice. Online media coverage increased weeks before the exhibit opened, and journalists contacted us requesting print and radio interviews.

Although the exhibit received praise, this coverage added new vulnerabilities and exposure. Both liberal and conservative media outlets discussed our exhibit

FIGURE 13.6: US Representative Ocasio-Cortez's campaigning shoes displayed alongside the lipstick colour ('Beso' by Stila) she wore during the 17 June 2018 televised congressional debate, 2018. Photograph courtesy of Daniel Chamberlain.

from various perspectives and different agendas. The press led viewers to our public Cornell Fashion + Textile Collection Instagram, allowing people to comment and interact with us in the final weeks between the press release and exhibit opening. We received feedback, including compliments, encouragement, constructive criticism, aggressive and negative messaging and hateful threats. Some commenters discussed our lack of conservative representation, criticizing our reference to the military frontline without including women from the military, while others bullied. Given this response, we saw an opportunity to re-examine the scope of our exhibit and widen the inclusivity of the women featured.

The dialogue initiated by the media between our class and the public allowed for the exhibit to evolve into a form of public collaboration, moving our exhibit beyond the classroom and into the public domain. We realized that our primarily

FIGURE 13.7: 'The Government' and 'The Street' display case featured US Representative Ocasio-Cortez's campaign shoes (centre) and Justice Ginsburg's judicial collars (far left), 2018. Photograph courtesy of Daniel Chamberlain.

liberal perspective had possibly limited the scope of our exhibit. We agreed with some of the criticism we received, specifically the lack of military and conservative representation. We listened and responded by including Maj. Kate Hopwood Kinnee Payne's Second World War US Navy reserves WAVES blue uniform. Her duties included managing 'degaussing' projects – de-magnification of Navy ships to reduce the effectiveness of enemy radar. Later, Maj. Payne founded a library and meditation centre in Ithaca, New York (Payne 2008).

Media attention and public interaction through social media not only propelled our class into the public as activists ourselves – hyper-aware of our own positionality and vulnerability – but allowed for public dialogue and awareness of accessibility. With accessibility in mind, we created a website for the exhibit compliant with the Americans with Disabilities Act (ADA ) that features a documentary of the exhibition process, photos of the exhibit's opening and each garment on display, thus making a digital exhibit accessible to the public. Intentional or not, digital documentation of the cases, press and process, became an archive of its own, tracking and mapping the development and outcomes of the exhibit. The website allows viewers to move through each exhibit case, view individual items with metadata and watch videos to virtually experience the exhibition. With the help of the media and virtual exhibit, *WE* traversed beyond its physical location in the university's display space and onto the digital frontline.

## Call to action

Based on the organization and curatorial experiences described above and the challenges encountered along the way; we propose two major calls to action about fashion exhibitions. First is disrupting prevalent academic norms around scholarly output, which currently do not formally, or at best only partially, recognize curatorial labour as a form of scholarship that concretely contributes to academic practice and/or theory. We call upon our colleagues, fellow students and other interested parties to recognize the impact of well-researched fashion exhibitions and to support one another by exchanging ideas, sharing resources, facilitating loan requests, attending exhibitions and writing reviews. For example, to facilitate the production of fashion exhibitions, we call on institutions – e.g., university collections, historical archives and museums – to reassess their policies for loans and display. These institutions, which strive to educate and inform, may undermine their outreach missions through restrictive loan and display policies. Elsewhere, we ask our academic colleagues to develop and implement a peer review process for evaluating curatorial scholarship (Green et al. 2019).

The second call to action is the role of fashion exhibits beyond academia, namely in challenging, transgressing and transforming existing understandings of fashion across broader swathes of society. Doing so exposes the latent and often problematic social norms that inform the relationship to our clothes and those worn by people who are different than us. For example, as notions of gender are continually contemplated and reinterpreted, we call on researchers, curators, educators, institutions and activists to critically reflect upon the perspectives and communities included in identity-based exhibitions. As curators of *WE*, we considered how our definitions and examples of empowerment may have differed from others' perspectives, which informed the tone and reach of the exhibition. After interactions with the public on social media following international media coverage of the exhibit, we were challenged to consider women from ideologically dissimilar backgrounds to our own. Therefore, we call upon curators to reflect critically upon their positionalities and biases and consider potential oversights and exclusion. We encourage curators to seek out archives and collections that strive to document and preserve diverse histories. We recommend using qualitative research methods, including interviews and oral histories, to unearth past and present fashion histories that are often absent from fashion and costume collections.

For fashion exhibitions to disrupt, inspire and educate, they must be physically and digitally accessible. Installing an exhibition requires access to an exhibition space, artefacts and funding. Even with all of these privileges, the exhibition itself is ephemeral. Creating an open-access digital exhibition that chronicles the physical installation is an opportunity to document and share the exhibit with the wider public. Furthermore, digital platforms enable the inclusion of materials that otherwise may not be displayed; for example artefacts with conservation issues, items that could not fit into the display space, loans that could not be secured, etc. Digital exhibitions do not necessarily need a physical analogue; therefore, we see the digital fashion exhibit as an opportunity for curators to create and display public scholarship in Fashion Studies.

Both calls to action spotlight the invisible and underappreciated labour in curatorial scholarship and activism and acknowledge the complexity of fashion as an aesthetic, social and material form. The hegemonic power of social norms under capitalism informs exclusionary practices that are often materialized in and through fashion; however, fashion also has the potential to acknowledge, transform and celebrate such social differences. The fashion exhibition is an important site of public education and engagement that should challenge visitors to critically reflect by thinking more expansively about fashion's role in social change.

## NOTE

1.  https://exhibits.library.cornell.edu/women-empowered.

## REFERENCES

Buckley, Cheryl and Clark, Hazel (2016), 'In search of the everyday: Museums, collections, and representations of fashion in London and New York', in H. Jenss (ed.), *Fashion Studies: Research Methods, Sites and Practices*, London: Bloomsbury, pp. 25–41.

Davis, Fred (1992), *Fashion, Culture, and Identity*, Chicago: Chicago University Press.

Green, Denise Nicole, Du Puis, Jenny Leigh, Xepoleas, Lynda May, Hesselbein, Chris, Greder, Katherine, Pietsch, Victoria, Getman, Rachel and Estrada, Jessica Guadalupe (2019), 'Fashion exhibitions as scholarship: Evaluation criteria for peer review', 39:1, pp. 71–86, *Clothing and Textiles Research Journal*, https://doi.org/10.1177/0887302X19888018.

Kaiser, Susan B. (2012), *Fashion and Cultural Studies*, London: Berg.

Kaiser, Susan B., Nagasawa, Richard H. and Hutton, Sandra S, (1995), 'Construction of an SI theory of fashion: Part 1. Ambivalence and change', *Clothing and Textiles Research Journal*, 13:3, pp. 172–83.

Kuldova, Tereza (2014), 'Fashion exhibition as a critique of contemporary museum exhibitions: The case of "Fashioning India: Spectacular Capitalism"', *Critical Studies in Fashion & Beauty*, 5:2, pp. 313–36.

Kwong, Jessica (2018), 'Fox news cares more about Alexandria Ocasio-Cortez's shoes than a devastating climate change report, CNN host says', Newsweek, 26 November, https://www.newsweek.com/fox-news-alexandria-ocasio-cortez-shoes-cnn-1231762. Accessed 26 November 2018.

Mida, Ingrid (2015), 'Animating the body in museum exhibitions of fashion and dress', *Dress*, 4:1, pp. 37–51.

Payne, Kate Hopwood (2008), 'Obituary', *Ithaca Journal*, 21 May, https://www.legacy.com/obituaries/theithacajournal/obituary.aspx?n=kate-hopwood-payne&pid=113654828. Accessed 27 February 2023.

# 14

# Beauty to Be Recognized:
# Making the Fashion Show Accessible

*Ben Barry, Avalon Acaso, Robin Chantree, Johnathan Clancy,*
*Bianca Garcia and Anna Pollice*

Fashion shows are not designed for accessibility. As a disabled fashion professor with low vision, my experience attending fashion shows has become alienating as my vision has changed. I can only make out the clothes in full detail, embellishment and movement if I sit in the front row and the model is directly in front of me. Disability fashion activist Sinéad Burke has explained that – at three feet and five inches tall – most fashion show seats are too high for her to get onto. When she does sit down, her feet dangle and cause her to experience pins and needles (Blanks 2018). When disabled model Aaron Rose Philip signed with Elite Models, the agency received enthusiasm from designers to book her for New York Fashion Week. However, the agency was unable to confirm any runway bookings because Aaron uses a wheelchair, and there was no wheelchair access to the runway at the shows (Tsao 2018).

The experiences of Sinéad, Aaron and myself illuminate that, across disability embodiments, fashion shows assume that only non-disabled bodies attend these events as guests and move down the runway as models. The lack of access results from the worldviews and skills of fashion show producers who design these events based on the frameworks they were taught in fashion school, the fashion industry and society. As designer Mike Monteiro (2019) suggests, 'Either by action or inaction, through fault or ignorance, we have designed the world to behave exactly as it's behaving right now' (10). The fashion industry is rooted in ableism because, in part, dominant understandings position fashion and disability in opposition. Fashion is associated with desirability and status, while disability is considered deviant, tragic and undesirable (Barry 2019; Kafer 2013). It is no wonder that Aaron Rose Philip observed, 'the image of a disabled person and their body in high fashion is almost nonexistent' (Fox-Suliaman 2020).

243

This chapter – and the course that we will share – is an intervention into the ableism of the fashion industry and the fashion show specifically. We will explore how students in two fashion courses collaborated to design a fashion show grounded in Critical Disability Studies and crip theory. Following disability justice activists, we deliberately use the word 'crip' as a reclamation of the pejorative 'cripple'. Crip, as a noun, refers to a cultural identity for disabled people. As a verb, it means to open up with desire for the ways that disability generates understandings and practices that disrupt normativity (Chandler 2014; Kafer 2013). Our fashion show – called *Beauty to Be Recognized: A Crip Fashion Show* – aimed to crip the production of a normative fashion show by demonstrating how disability generates new possibilities for fashion and beauty beyond the worldviews and aesthetics of compulsory able-bodiedness (McRue 2006). First, our chapter will describe the impetus and structure of the course. Then it will analyse the successes and challenges of designing the fashion show, and it will conclude by providing advice for fashion educators who want to mobilize Critical Disability Studies in fashion event planning courses. Imagining and creating a fashion industry grounded in access is crucial because, as Rice et al. (2019) argue, 'nothing less than people's access to the category of human is at stake' (216).

Our chapter is co-written by one instructor and five graduate students who designed the fashion show. Our objective for this collaboration is two-fold. First, we hope to provide readers with diverse perspectives on the course based on our experiences and positionalities. Second, we aim to follow the crip principle of interdependence over the compulsory non-disabled valorization of independence. Mia Mingus (2017) explains that independence is both the idea and the high value placed on the belief that people should be able to do everything themselves. Instead, interdependence 'is working in coalition and collaboration' by recognizing that people have different contributions to offer and, subsequently, can mutually support each other (Mingus 2010). Through interdependent writing, we have brought our different experiences, skills and support for each other to the development of this chapter.

## Course philosophy and design

For the 2019 Fall Semester, I was assigned to teach *Diversity in Fashion* in my department's MA fashion programme. I proposed this course in my first year at Toronto Metropolitan University (TMU), but this would be my first time teaching it. The course description in the university's calendar explained that the class analyses identity, marginalization and systemic change in and through fashion:

This course challenges us to reflect on how identity and the body are constructed, negotiated and disrupted through the production and consumption of fashion. We explore interdisciplinary frameworks about diversity and fashion and critically examine how fashion intersects with marginalized positionalities and embodied differences. With this knowledge, we develop radical ways of understanding, designing, marketing and engaging with fashion in order to ignite systemic social transformation.

My current research focuses on disability and fashion, and I had intended to include a module on disability in this course. However, I decided to centre disability after a chance meeting at *Cripping the Arts* in Toronto, a symposium exploring disability arts and activism. During a coffee break, my former student – who was working at the symposium – introduced me to the Arts Manager at the British Council, the United Kingdom's international organization that fosters cultural relations and educational opportunities. The British Council was partnering with local universities to introduce *relaxed performance* into performance-based courses, such as choral music and theatre performances. Relaxed performance is an approach that makes theatre-going accessible to everyone – including, but not executively, disabled people – by 'letting bodies be bodies' (LaMarre et al. 2019: 7). The method introduces modifications to the environment and performance to break down physical, attitudinal, sensory and other barriers, such as inviting people to move and vocalize freely in the theatre space. The approach began in the United Kingdom in the 1990s, and the British Council has been working to share the method with Canadian theatres (LaMarre et al. 2019). The British Council were interested in exploring how relaxed performance could be applied to performance courses more broadly, beyond theatre. The chance meeting led to a partnership with my department in which, with support from the British Council, we would incorporate relaxed performance into the fashion event planning curriculum.

The partnership brought together my graduate course with the *Fashion Promotions* course in our BDes Fashion Communications programme, which Daniel Drak taught, to produce the fashion show.[1] While students in *Fashion Promotions* produce a large-scale fashion show as their core learning outcome, the course had not yet incorporated accessibility into its content. Including relaxed performance would, therefore, extend student learning by developing approaches to ground access in fashion show production. In bringing these two courses together, we also aimed to recognize the number of students and the variety of skills required to produce this fashion show. We divided the workload between the courses: The graduate students would develop Critical Disability Studies expertise and translate this knowledge into event design, while the undergraduate students would develop skills in producing accessible fashion shows.

The two courses were simultaneously scheduled for students to meet for common lectures and group work. However, the courses started the semester separately. The graduate students took the first three weeks to learn about intersectionality, the representation of disability in fashion media, the models of disability (i.e., individual/medical, social and political/relational models) and crip theory. The undergraduates were introduced to the frameworks of disability and crip theory, and they focused on learning about contemporary fashion show approaches and debates. The courses were brought together in week four to learn about relaxed performance and accessible design. With funding from the British Council, two professionals specializing in relaxed performance, disability arts and accessible design – Cara Eastcott and Kristina McMullin – attended the class to deliver guest lectures. They also visited the class on three other occasions to advise students on the development of the fashion show. The two courses stayed together after week four, for the remainder of the semester, to allow the students time to collaboratively develop and execute their plans.

Based on the activities required to design and produce the show, the students were divided into six committees, including art direction, promotions, casting, styling, production and access. A graduate student led each group; these students met weekly before class to update each other on their group's progress and keep track of shared goals and timelines. The first course project asked each committee to draw upon theories from the readings and lectures to develop a concept proposal for their role; for example, casting would create a strategy for recruiting models, while promotions would develop a communications plan. Then, they presented their proposal to the class and guest experts for feedback. The final project asked students to individually write a paper reflecting on their experience producing the fashion show. They had to describe their work on the fashion show, evaluate the successes and challenges of applying theories to practice and explore what they would do differently in the future.

## Beauty to Be Recognized: A Crip Fashion Show

On 3 December 2019, the students produced *Beauty to Be Recognized: A Crip Fashion Show* in the Centre for Urban Innovation at TMU. The show's design was grounded in concepts from Critical Disability Studies, followed the tenets of relaxed performance and included an audio description and American Sign Language (ASL) interpretation for the models and audience. The fashion show featured 29 disability-identified people as models. An audience of 250 people attended the show – including fashion professionals, friends and families of the models, members of faculty, students and members of the public (Figures 14.1–14.5).

Rather than elevated and narrow, the runway was on the same level as the audience; it was an exaggerated t-shape to allow ample room for the models to move. Models did not move in a uniform style or have complementary choreography but instead moved in ways that were most natural and comfortable for their bodies. Furthermore, we did not use spotlights or keep the audience in the dark; instead, we kept all the lights on.

The models wore their favourite outfits that they had selected from their wardrobes. As each model made their way onto the runway, they were introduced by two students in the MA fashion course – Christine Ramkeesoon and Sonali Prasad – who read an audio description of who they are and why they selected their outfits. By wearing clothing from their closets and being introduced with a description, the show challenged the objectification of disability by centring the individuality and agency of each model. Both models and patrons were encouraged to vocalize freely and move about during the show.

While relaxed performance provided an entry into considering access in fashion shows, the inclusion of Critical Disability Studies and crip theory in the course radically expanded how the students conceptualized access and event design. As discussed in the introduction, relaxed performance encourages students to modify the existing fashion show space and the fashion show itself to make it

FIGURE 14.1: Painter and photographer Cx models in *Beauty to Be Recognized*, 2019. Photography by Steve Nguyen.

FIGURE 14.2: Deaflympics track and field athlete Courage models in *Beauty to Be Recognized*, 2019. Photography by Steve Nguyen.

FIGURE 14.3: Fashion design student Heba models in *Beauty to Be Recognized*, 2019. Photography by Steve Nguyen.

FIGURE 14.4: Basketball fan Victor models in *Beauty to Be Recognized*, 2019. Photography by Steve Nguyen.

FIGURE 14.5: A group of models at the finale of *Beauty to Be Recognized*. Models Sage, Akio, Alana and Darien are pictured in the foreground from left to right, 2019. Photography by Steve Nguyen.

more welcoming for disabled people (LaMarre et al. 2019). In contrast, crip theory centres the disability experience to expose how non-disabled bodies have been constructed as unmarked – the natural order of things – whereas disabled people have been constructed as abject subjects who deviate from the norm (Kafer 2013). When applying crip theory to relaxed performance, it urged students to question the assumptions implicit in modifying a fashion show designed initially for non-disabled people. It illuminated how relaxed performance can assume non-disabled people are the standard body from which the design of fashion shows should be adapted to accommodate disabled people. The premise here is that non-disabled people are the norm; disabled people deviate from this norm, and, subsequently, fashion shows should be modified. Instead, crip theory encouraged students to create a fashion show where access for disabled people was the genesis of their event design.

In the following sections, five graduate students in the course describe how they designed a fashion show grounded in radical access for disabled people. They reflect on their work, how they applied theory to practice and the successes and challenges of the class.

## Art direction (Robin)

As a non-disabled individual, my relationship to disability has always been as an outsider – perhaps 'ally', if one were being charitable. For me, I was taking this course to learn about event planning that actively moves theory into practice rather than sequestering important concepts behind the too often closed doors of academia. As a trans and queer artist, I was familiar with the potential for creative expression to build community and the uplifting effect these cultural events can have on marginalized people. Having spaces to celebrate everything you love about your community, qualities that an oppressive social order actively tries to suppress, is the kind of healing experience that remains too rare. While I did not bring a personal disability perspective, I believed that mobilizing academic resources to support disabled people could be meaningful, so long as we took the means to centre disability perspectives.

I was one of two graduate students on the art direction team. We were tasked with the branding and graphic design for *Beauty to Be Recognized*. My role as a graduate student, not the team lead, was to help centre Critical Disability Studies theories for our undergraduate peers and guide their creative decisions. We chose the name *Beauty to Be Recognized* to pay homage to the disability justice performance project *Sins Invalid*, referencing their often stated phrase 'beauty always, always recognizes itself' (Kafai 2018: 232). We saw this name encapsulating three aspects of the show: how fashion shows play a role in the discourse around beauty, the position of this show as disability representation, and honouring the work of disability activists and artists who came before us. In this way, the name *Beauty to Be Recognized* transforms the dominant narrative of disability from invisible and undesirable to visible and desirable, and it recognizes the activism of disabled artists who have long told their stories through their work.

The visual direction of the show utilized a pixel motif inspired by Jasbir Puar's (2017) use of assemblage theory. Puar posits that assemblage reimagines queerness as 'temporally and spatially contingent' rather than as perpetually fixed or oppositional (205). Puar's concept challenges how other formulations of identity, specifically intersectionality, can be taken up as a way to quantify identity, pinning it down to specific instances of self rather than allowing subjectivities to exist in a state of flux informed by time and place. Similar to the relationality of identity, raster images require our eyes to make sense of various coloured squares to recognize an image. One must accept the relationships between the disparate squares and acknowledge them as a whole to recognize the picture, similar to how one must accept the multitudinous components of an individual's identity to recognize them fully.

A major challenge was our limited timeline for the show. We worried we would not be able to consult with disabled people to create a theme or brand for the show within the twelve-week course. Additionally, decisions around the show's brand identity had to be solidified well in advance because these decisions would inform the aesthetic of the entire event, including advertising for models. Considering our team was mostly non-disabled students, we had about two weeks to make decisions on behalf of a community we were not part of, based on theories many of us were just learning. Thankfully, our consultants and instructors gave us feedback on our ideas and helped guide us to the ideas that were working. As a result of these discussions, we found that using abstract imagery was the most effective because it left open space for individual interpretations. We were also introduced to colour, scale and other visual considerations necessary to create accessible graphic designs. These learnings equipped us with the knowledge that helped us create more accessible work and strengthened our graphic design skills.

The efforts of the art direction committee paid off; the show's graphic design was well received by the attendees. This is not to imply I was anticipating it would not be; certainly, the undergraduate students on our team were well-versed in the Adobe Creative Suite, but there was a substantial amount of praise for how 'professional' the show materials looked. 'Professional' can mean many things, but in this instance, I was left with the impression that two things were being praised: the amount of care being invested into the show and the aesthetics of the show mirroring those typically seen in an industry context. As such, the show's professionalism asserted the desirability of disability in fashion, challenging the ableist assumptions of who is fashionable and beautiful.

## Promotions (Bianca)

My relationship to disability began in the classroom when I learned from feminist disability scholars like Alison Kafer and queer disabled fashion designers like Sky Cubacub of Rebirth Garments. As a non-disabled person, I came into this radical fashion show with the privilege of learning about disability rather than living it. Since being a part of *Beauty to Be Recognized*, my relationship with disability has confronted and disrupted the ableist assumptions deeply embedded within fashion productions, myself and those around me.

As the promotions committee leader, I worked with my team to share the narrative of disability as desirable and beautiful to promote the show and attract patrons. We created social media posts that aimed to centre the interests of disabled people as well as public education about disability. Our posts shared images that disrupted stereotypical narratives of disability, educational resources about Critical Disability Studies and details of how we would make the fashion show accessible. Each post was created with image descriptions and alt text. The art direction team created graphic illustrations of the models, and we paired these graphics with captions written by the models about themselves and their outfits. Our educational posts offered definitions of relaxed performance, ableism and crip theory, and our event accessibility posts included disability access symbols. We also created an audio and written invitation to ensure people could engage with the information in a way that was accessible to them.

To support access, our team also co-wrote drafts to convey information clearly and concisely without confusing jargon or lengthy sentences. We used respectful language rather than words that rely on a degrading image of disability. For example, we wrote 'disability-identified individuals' instead of 'handicapped people'. On the day of the show, we considered how disability creates a 'reorientation to time' by documenting the event through recorded video and Instagram livestream as viable ways to experience the show (Kafer 2013: 26). We created and played a slideshow about crip theory with accessible design elements for legibility, including large size font and high contrast between text and background colour, and accompanied with verbal descriptions. After the show, we shared photographs of the event on social media.

Our work was certainly not perfect, but our social media platform was a successful act of disruption. It was created through collaborative ideation and a messy process of brainstorming ideas together through honest, critical and constructive disagreement. These disagreements and confrontations were necessary and generative because dialogue and debate 'push us to recognize and acknowledge our own assumptions and the boundaries we draw around our own work' (Kafer 2013: 150). For weeks, the art direction and promotions teams had constant back-and-forth exchanges about ideas for the model's graphic illustrations. This disagreement cultivated collaborative brainstorming and forced us to re-examine our positions, intentions and impact as organizers of this show. Whenever a team member from art direction questioned non-disabled assumptions inherent in some of our ideas, I confronted my feelings of shame, guilt and disappointment. Then, I implemented their feedback, gradually feeling reassured that we were generating more accessible and inclusive content.

I entered this class with the mindset that promotional work is more or less about spreading the word about an event or getting as many people as possible to attend. As I continued to learn and apply the theories we learned to practice, I realized that promotional work requires – perhaps above all – care and thoughtfulness in the narrative put forth. To transform the dominant narrative that objectifies disabled people through stereotypes, we portrayed disability as a beautiful life and shared information about Critical Disability Studies. These promotional practices were fundamental in exposing and disrupting the fashion industry that operates under the assumption that only non-disabled people's lives are worth celebrating.

## Casting (Anna)

Before this course, the partial inclusion of larger-sized bodies on the runway represented a step in the direction of inclusion. Our crip fashion show, however, did more than evoke a sense of inclusion by prioritizing disabled bodies; it reversed the circumstances by normalizing disability and having non-disabled people adapt to a disabled way of being and doing. As a non-disabled person, I have not had the opportunity to engage with disabled people intimately, nor the experience to question accessibility. My perspective has now shifted. Our environment is not designed with disability at the fore but as an afterthought. The lack of consideration unjustly excludes a significant number of people from the fashion industry.

I was the team leader for casting and coordinated the recruitment and selection of models for the fashion show. As our show prioritized disabled people, we drew upon intersectionality, crip theory and crip time to inform the entire casting process – from designing the model criteria to model recruitment to model engagement. Our model criteria were broad to welcome a diverse group of disabled people as models, particularly those who identify as trans, non-binary and genderqueer and/or Black, Indigenous and People of Colour. The casting invitation introduced our relaxed performance fashion show and explicitly asked for 'disability-identified individuals who want to model in the show to help advocate for an accessible, inclusive fashion industry'. Modelling experience was not required,

> only your excitement to participate in a relaxed fashion show where you will celebrate your beauty as you are and as you wish. You choose what to wear. You choose to have your hair done. You choose to have make-up applied.

Moreover, crip time challenges normative measures of time grounded in non-disabled norms and it allows for flexibility in expectations around time, including deadlines, start/stop times and last-minute changes (Kafer 2013). We followed crip time by, for example, making the casting call deadline flexible and welcoming new models to join throughout the casting process. Any scheduled meetings with models were organized within a broad time frame, allowing models to drop in when they could join and still fully participate.

In addition to recruiting models, the casting team communicated with the models to ensure their needs were centred during the fashion show. After recruitment, our team developed a questionnaire to gather the models' information, including their access needs, biographies, personal photos, descriptions of their outfits and a release form with consent to share their information on our social media before, during and after the performance. Additionally, it was essential for all the teams to understand the models' access needs to ensure they could fully participate in the fashion show and enjoy the experience. Through the questionnaire and follow-up e-mails, the casting team learned about models' access needs, including preferred ASL interpreters, dietary restrictions and physical access needs. We also learned about each model's individual needs around timing; for example, some models did not have the capacity to arrive several hours before the show because of their energy levels and others needed to arrive early for their bodies to feel comfortable in the space. We shared this information with the other teams as we developed our plans for the fashion show.

One week before the show, the casting committee held a meet-and-greet with models. The purpose was for the models and students to meet in person, get to know one another and discuss any questions or concerns. The casting committee shared the entrance points, elevator information and other access details for the meet-and-greet with the models. On the night of the meet-and-greet, members of the casting team were at the main entrance of the building to welcome models and guide them to the event space by way of stairs or elevators. The meet-and-greet developed personal connections and an understanding of each model's needs. It was an important exercise in learning how to communicate in person. The course consultants introduced appropriate ways to physically communicate with disabled people by respecting specific boundaries. For example, we learned to ask before helping and never to assume we know what is needed; speak directly to the person and not their support person; and ensure not to touch a person's mobility aid. These practices, and others, became very real at this event.

Weeks before the show, there were countless e-mails, many phone calls and the sharing of personal information – both ways, which created a safe space to simply be. Within this space, I experienced crossing over from prioritizing my needs to adapting to the needs of others, confronting my ways of doing and being. In a sense, I was 'cripped' into a disability-centred world. Learning a new language with which to communicate and implementing a degree of flexibility within scheduling cripped the entire casting committee. This fashion show was not intended to inspire people through disability but rather to bring disability and fashion together to create new narratives. I hope that what was learned from this fashion show will make its way into all our future productions.

## Access (Johnathan)

I came into the course as someone who grew up with glasses, learning disabilities and a history of mental illness with symptoms of attention-deficit/hyperactivity disorder (ADHD) – with which I was later diagnosed. I also have a background in theatre production work, specifically stage management and design. These two histories informed my decision to take the course and become part of the access committee. As the leader of the access committee, my group was responsible for developing the access guide – a document to inform patrons in advance of an event about its access features, including images, descriptions and dimensions of the event venue and routes to the event space. We also coordinated access elements for the show and the front-of-house. My background with disability made me feel confident that I could contribute a perspective that might otherwise not be present. Meanwhile, my experience as a stage manager – a role that involves liaising with contractors and working with the front-of-house – seemed like a great fit for this contribution.

Working with the ASL interpreters and audio describers was one of the most significant successes for our team because it centred collaboration between ourselves, community activists, disability professionals and models. For the ASL interpreters, the head of the organization we hired from was one of our models – and a friend to several others – and so our discussions about how to arrange for an appropriate number of interpreters allowed the models themselves to have agency. The four interpreters we hired for the event ensured that the audience and models had support throughout the event. Similarly, working with the audio describer allowed models to collaborate in their representation. Models sent responses through the casting committee about how they would like to be described ahead of time or had the opportunity to fill out a cue card of their descriptions on the day of the show. Whatever information was included in the description was their choice. Even with the best intentions, audio descriptions can be fraught with challenges. Descriptions can bias specific details of one's appearance by unnecessarily focusing on certain body characteristics, and by using language that the individual being described might not use to describe themselves. Giving the models agency over their descriptions meant they could control what was said about them and how it was said.

The access committee also worked with the production team to set up the space for the event. Several key practices made our arrangement of the fashion show space a success. First, we used the measurements from our audit checklist – a report we created to gauge accessibility features and obstacles, including measurements of doorways, halls and the event space – to create a runway that wheelchair users could easily navigate. Second, the position of the runway led to the room's door, which allowed models and patrons to quickly enter or leave if they needed to take a break at our Chill Zone. The Chill Zone was a space away from the main fashion show and designed to reduce stimulation, provide breaks for patrons and livestream the event. Finally, we had seats for models to use after their runway performance in the wings of the stage, should they need to rest. This allowed them to see each other perform, rest and transition into the final phase of the event, where models and patrons could engage with each other.

The joy of seeing the event come to life created an empowering resolution to the course that I was not able to appreciate at the time because there had been so much to do. The fashion show provided an outlet for going beyond discursive learning about disability and fashion by creating an intervention that would celebrate difference in a context where it is often absent, marginalized and fetishized. Working with the community in this way reminded me of my own agency in being able to interrupt discourse and support new futures in fashion.

### Access committee (Avalon)

When I first saw that *Diversity in Fashion* was being offered, I didn't know then how much I needed this class. Disability was not something new to me. I have lived with 'invisible' psychiatric disabilities since I was young. Growing up in a low socio-economic environment – with our early years in a family shelter – I can say that most of our neighbours and friends all identified as disabled. Whether it was invisible or visible, I was exposed at an early age that not everyone had the same life. However, I never thought about disability and fashion until this course. Fashion to me was always the same image: a tall woman walking fast-paced down a runway. This course taught me that something bigger was happening: what makes someone disabled is not their disability but enforced social injustices.

I was on the access team for the show and was mainly involved with two tasks: assisting with the access audit and creating the access guide. Using the PISSAR Checklist (People in Search of Safe and Accessible Restrooms) (Kafer 2013), the access team inspected the event space to take note of any physical barriers that may limit access for models and patrons. I took photos of the area, including restrooms, elevators, entrance doors and signage. I used these photographs for the access guide, which was described in the section above.

On the day of the fashion show, I was an usher at the building's entrance. I followed the concept of crip time, where we acknowledge flexibility and reorientation to time when it comes to everyone's pacing (Kafer 2013). Our job consisted of greeting and escorting patrons to the elevators or stairs. We also pointed out the location of the bathroom and the Chill Zone areas. By applying crip time, each patron was supported based on their pace and needs. Reflecting upon my experience, I now realize the differences between ushering for a relaxed performance event versus a more traditional performance. Unlike a traditional event in which ushers follow a standard procedure, we acknowledged each patron who came through the door for our show as an individual with their own needs – taking time, care and effort for each person.

The fashion show was also personal for me because my sister was one of the models, and because of this, I saw our event through her experience. Being very anxious before the event, she was worried that she would not be allowed to bring her 'support' items (i.e., food, water, fan) or do her 'safe' routine (i.e., taking walks, talking to me when needed). However, she felt more relaxed after going through the access guide and meeting the casting committee members. The team assured her that she could bring her support items to the show and do her 'safe' routine before it. This showed me how effective our event was in acknowledging each person's needs.

## Calls to action

While *Beauty to Be Recognized* created a framework for how fashion event planning courses can be grounded in access, it was also our first experience doing so. As such, we faced challenges alongside successes. While we aimed to honour crip time in our fashion show production, we were restricted by time limitations and the quick pace of a twelve-week course. Task deadlines were very close together, and each committee relied upon the work of the others to move the process forward. For example, the access guide content needed to be completed and edited within one week in order to send it to art direction for graphic design. This rapid schedule meant fewer opportunities to adjust deadlines if students' schedules conflicted and support students who worked at a slower pace. As a result, students with flexible schedules or who worked faster were disproportionately called upon, while others felt like they had fewer opportunities to contribute. This experience highlighted how the rapid speed of both the fashion industry and the university disadvantages people who need more flexible time and pace. Additionally, the ASL interpreters and the audio describer require at least a month's notice to prepare for public events. Without this lead time, they had to rush their typical process to support our show. We recommend that future courses engage these professionals at least two months before the event.

For students to create a fashion show grounded in access, it was necessary to devote time to theories from Critical Disability Studies. Most students who enrolled in the course had little to no knowledge about disability. This class was their first time questioning ableism and considering physical and cultural barriers for disabled people. To provide sufficient time to produce the fashion show within a twelve-week course, the introduction to disability theories and activism was front-loaded and limited to the first four weeks. Not surprisingly, the knowledge gap left some students feeling insecure about making decisions for the fashion show.

For example, selecting a name for the fashion show was challenging. While students actively tried to position the name – *Beauty to Be Recognized* – as a homage, a consultant pointed out the phrasing was 'insider language' and perhaps inappropriate when used by non-disabled people. The class addressed this feedback by crediting Sins Invalid and sharing the reasons for using the phrase on social media and promotional materials. Still, it may have been more appropriate to ideate a new name entirely. Fashion educators who wish to design a similar class might cross-list the course with their university's Disability Studies programme. They might also offer a full-year or two consecutive courses (with the first serving as a prerequisite for the second) to offer students the time and space to learn about Critical Disability Studies.

Future classes should also devote considerable and ongoing space for students to consider their relationship with disability, internalized ableist assumptions, and the origins of these understandings. Including individual and roundtable reflection exercises at the beginning and throughout the course can help build community amongst the class, as well as help students navigate feelings of shame and fears of judgement that may result from their current understanding of disability. *Beauty to Be Recognized* was activist work, but like any activist work, it must be rooted in radical honesty and self-inquiry, especially when not all organizers are part of the group they are advocating. Instructors and students must practise ongoing reflexivity in the classroom to help transform the dominant narrative of disability and create spaces that support disabled people's access to, authorship of and representation in fashion shows.

Another challenge was the budget for the fashion show. The original budget was CAD 3000 with an extra CAD 600 for contingencies, partially supported through our partnership with the British Council of Canada. To ensure access – the very premise of the fashion show – we needed ASL interpreters to be available for several occasions: when models arrived for the rehearsal, for hair and make-up, when models were backstage, when the audience arrived and during the show. As interpreters work in pairs to allow for breaks, we hired two pairs of interpreters. We had one pair with the models backstage and the other with patrons in the event space. Each interpreter cost CAD 500 for a total of CAD 2000. Additionally, we hired an audio describer to provide access for blind people and people with low vision during the event. The cost was CAD 1000 for their time and equipment. There were the additional expenses of make-up artists, hair stylists, staging, audio/visual equipment, model honoraria, printing and refreshments. Fortunately, one of the course instructors was the Chair of the School of Fashion, and, as such, they were able to access additional university funding. However, other instructors, especially part-time lecturers, might not have this access. For those interested in producing an accessible show, we recommend budgeting at least CAD 5000 or otherwise narrowing the scale.

## From adapting to cripping fashion pedagogy

To truly ground access in fashion pedagogy, we need to move beyond adapting course content and crip the structure of courses themselves. How can we holistically centre crip time to allow students, instructors and community participants to contribute at paces that work for them? How can we ensure our course content and delivery methods are designed to be as accessible as our crip fashion projects? How can we reimagine departmental budget planning to include access costs for all courses as a standard practice rather than one-off requests? How can we structurally benefit disabled community members who contribute to a course? For example, can we share fashion knowledge or offer complementary enrolment to university certificate programmes?

We do not have answers to these questions *yet*, but we leave it to you (and us) to address them in future course iterations. By recognizing the wisdom and creativity generated by the disability experience in both course content and course structure, we can transform fashion education and the fashion industry. We will not only help students develop worldviews and practices that honour disabled people, but we will create fashion educational cultures that support disabled people to study according to their own needs and, ultimately, become the instructors and creatives needed to help transform the narrow systems of fashion.

## NOTE

1. Daniel Drak was previously an instructor in Fashion and Creative Industries at Toronto Metropolitan University and is currently an assistant professor in Strategic Design and Fashion Management at Parsons School of Design. He co-developed and co-taught the curriculum for *Beauty to Be Recognized*.

## REFERENCES

Barry, Ben (2019), 'Fabulous masculinities: Refashioning the fat and disabled male body', *Fashion Theory*, 23:2, pp. 275–307.

Blanks, Tim (2018), 'Sinéad Burke versus the bell curve', Business of Fashion, https://www.businessoffashion.com/articles/people/sinead-burke-versus-the-bell-curve. Accessed 15 July 2021.

Chandler, Eliza (2014), 'Disability and the desire for community', Ph.D. thesis, Sociology Justice Education, University of Toronto.

Fox-Suliaman, Jasmine (2020), '6 models on ableism, visibility, and personal style, Who What Wear', https://www.whowhatwear.com/disabled-fashion-models. Accessed 2 July 2021.

Kafai, Shayda (2018), 'Reclaiming and honoring: Sins Invalid's cultivation of Crip beauty', *Women's Studies Quarterly*, 46:1/2, pp. 231–36.

Kafer, Alison (2013), *Feminist Queer Crip*, Bloomington: Indiana University Press.

LaMarre, Andrea, Rice, Carla and Kayla, Besse (2019), *Relaxed Performance: Exploring Accessibility in the Canadian Theatre Landscape*, Ontario: British Council Canada.

McRue, Robert (2006), *Crip Theory: Cultural Signs of Queerness and Disability*, New York: NYU Press.

Mingus, Mia (2010), 'Interdependence (excerpts from several talks), *Leaving Evidence*', https://leavingevidence.wordpress.com/2010/01/22/interdependency-exerpts-from-several-talks/. Accessed 15 July 2021.

Mingus, Mia (2017), 'Access intimacy, interdependence and disability justice', *Leaving Evidence*, https://leavingevidence.wordpress.com/2017/04/12/access-intimacy-interdependence-and-disability-justice/. Accessed 3 July 2021.

Monteiro, Mike (2019), *Ruined by Design: How Designers Destroyed the World. And What We Can Do to Fix It*, San Francisco: Mule Books.

Puar, Jasbir (2017), *Terrorist Assemblages: Homonationalism in Queer Times*, 2nd ed., Durham: Duke University Press.

Rice, Carla, Harrison, Elizabeth and Friedman, May (2019), 'Doing justice to intersectionality in research', *Cultural Studies Critical Methodologies*, 19:6, pp. 1–12.

Tsao, Tommy (2018), '21 under 21: Aaron Philip was shut out of NYFW, but she's just getting started', *Teen People*, https://www.teenvogue.com/story/aaron-philip-21-under-21-20. Accessed 3 July 2021.

# 15

# A Diversity Network:
# Industry and Community Collaboration
# for Inclusive Fashion Design Education

*Mal Burkinshaw*

I have always looked at the world through a lens of empathy and human rights. As a child, I certainly recall feeling sensitivity to any observed prejudice and injustice regarding human differences. Undoubtedly, this perspective was influenced by my queer identity and being an identical twin, where one's identity, differences and appearance is constantly observed, judged and compared. Despite the personal privileges through my lived experiences as a cisgender white man, I have always felt a certain affinity with those who are not treated equally and marginalized by supposed societal norms.

As I write this in 2022, we are navigating and addressing important global issues relating to equality on an unprecedented scale. The need to embrace inclusivity, respect and understanding of the lived experiences of ourselves and others to improve our society is more important than ever. I am now in an esteemed position as the Head of Design at Edinburgh College of Art (ECA), the University of Edinburgh, in Scotland, with the goal to activate positive changes in design education, informed by my work on equalities and diversity as the Programme Director of Fashion between 2010 and 2020.

Despite a lengthy career in education, foregrounded by a desire to challenge the typical ways to teach fashion design, I still vividly recall my first day of study at The Royal College of Art for my postgraduate degree in 1997. During London Fashion Week, I stood at a vending machine while a statuesque and voluptuous model grabbed a drink, turned, and walked past me to be featured in a fashion show. I am, to this day, quite certain that this was Sophie Dahl, one of the first curvaceous models to be accepted and celebrated in the United Kingdom at the time. At this point in my studies, this appeared to my peers and me to be rather revolutionary and, certainly in the fashion industry, quite a radical move. In fact, I recall often feeling quite angry as a young designer to only ever see Dahl's name in press articles linked to observations and comments referencing her size and weight. To an extent, this remains a theme for models today who do not fit the illogical standard size. 'Plus-size' (a term that I personally do not use in teaching) and curvy models are written about and certainly celebrated. However, models representing diversity are still othered. For what we call a *fast* industry, any progress towards acceptance of models outside of the norm beauty standards has been strikingly *slow*.

Perhaps similar to other educators, my fashion training did not consider any diversity of body shapes, sizes, colours, disabilities or non-binary genders in the design process. In my undergraduate degree, however, I relished the experience of attending weekly life-drawing classes that included nude models of many sizes, shapes and ages. It was here that we celebrated the diversity of human body types.

In Fashion Studies, in somewhat stark contrast to the celebration of all ages and sizes in life drawing, there seemed to be an unwritten rule that fashion illustration was a realm inhabited by fantasy depictions of humans, even, one might argue, interstellar! Perhaps informed by examples of renowned illustrators and designers, I certainly fell victim to designing through the drawing of what I might term *super aliens*, with legs twice the size of torsos, waists the width of ankles, necks the length of forearms and lips the size of feet. From the perspective of a burgeoning fashion designer, designing for a human body was certainly quite a confusing experience!

On reflection, it now seems a rather abstract notion that we could so naturally celebrate the diverse human body through life drawing. Still, these skills were not connected to the process and depiction of human beauty through fashion design. Even at this stage in my studies, I felt a certain disconnection, superficiality and emptiness in my design capabilities. For example, once I had manufactured an outfit and showcased it on a model in a catwalk show, it was a world away (quite literally!) from the proportions and fit that I had designed on paper.

At the Royal College of Art, I began to change my approach to fashion sketch and illustration to depict more realistic human proportions. As opposed to my previous depictions of the body through abstract and elongated sketches, proportional sketching helped me to understand and plan the best silhouette and fit for my design work, and there were no surprises when the final work was viewed on a real, live body. In the 1990s (although still the case at many institutions today), fashion teaching did not include consideration of body diversity through illustrative means. It is still quite unusual to see student fashion portfolios or sketchbooks that depict broad diversity.

In terms of embedded knowledge and skills relating to designing for diversity, I cannot say that my experience working in the fashion industry was different from my experience as a student. After graduating from ECA and The Royal College of Art in London, I worked for a very high-profile fashion brand in Europe, whose main marketing images depicted and celebrated diversity. Yet, the representation of diversity within the design studio or the design process was very limited at that time. I felt there was a disconnection between the advertising campaigns that represented global diversity, yet as designers, we were not equipped or encouraged to consider diversity in any stage of our research or design processes. While the campaigns were beautiful, I felt it was somewhat dishonest and lacked genuine representation of the models and their identities.

My experience in the fashion industry highlighted that having limited formative educational practice or discourse about human diversity was quite problematic. I felt that we were perhaps not the well-rounded designers or visionaries that we once thought we were on graduation day. Surely we would have been fully rounded and prepared to address broader global fashion markets if only an educational language had been implemented that challenged us, as students, to consider the full scope and reality of who our work was really for. Would my experience designing for an industry brand have felt more meaningful if the importance of embedded knowledge, respect and celebration for all bodies and beauty had been at the heart of the design process rather than solely through the imagery created to promote the final outcome?

Whilst there have been great improvements in recent years, diversity representation within fashion education is *still* more typically displayed through the final context of student work – on catwalks, photography, fashion illustration and their portfolio. While this communication of more diverse human representation is undoubtedly positive, it is unclear how any consideration to designing for diversity may have been intrinsic or embedded within the designers' ethos, within their research or design processes, and crucially, as core to their training.

Retrospectively, although I value every teaching contribution that led to my evolution as a designer and academic, I now see that everything in my educational career challenges the pedagogy I studied under. I began my part-time teaching career in 2001 while continuing to work as a freelance designer and managing a fledgling design company. I particularly relished this shift back into education, which became my main career focus and passion. By 2008, and with good lecturing experience under my belt, my mission as an educator and leader really began to flourish. I realized I could provide students with a framework that could normalize inclusivity for marginalized people within research, design processes and final outcomes. It was here, moving into unexplored educational territories, that the challenges really emerged, and I wondered how to navigate this change without established educational examples. However, it was clear that this required our educators to jump on board and challenge their own established and more traditionally entrenched teaching practices.

Today, and having spent almost twelve years navigating this education space without an institutional vision or directive that sets diversity and equality as a mandatory part of fashion curricula, the reliance on teaching such important subjects still falls too heavily on individual educators who are passionate about diversity and equality. Instead, there should be far greater alignment between institutions to establish clear mandatory pedagogical principles, frameworks, learning outcomes and objectives that set a higher standard and in turn, attract passionate educators, deterring those unwilling to personally advance. As educators, we must now take the responsibility to ask ourselves if we are simply following prescriptive and outdated teaching methodologies. Do we encourage students to identify superficial concepts? Do we require students to consider the feelings of the end-wearer at any point in the design process? Do our fashion projects require students to define narrow age groups, income brackets, genders, lifestyles and personality types of their proposed markets without considering diverse needs, emotions or personal preferences? Do we lack diversity and equality in our end-of-year catwalk shows? Do our student portfolios generally portray illustrations of tall, thin, elongated, white, binary models? If the answer is yes, it is time to activate a change! It is the responsibility of fashion educators to cumulatively support the future fashion industries by supplying graduates with the embodied skills and knowledge that will help them improve the lives of their customers and audiences. To do this, fashion educators must question their teaching practices and act swiftly. The industry is moving to address positive social change, and there is a high risk that our graduates may not have the emotional awareness needed to step into future careers.

We must nurture our students to understand that fashion must include all bodies and can have a positive and long-lasting impact beyond a catwalk show or portfolio. After all, fashion, as a physical product, image, exhibition or film, rarely disappears and becomes an invaluable visual public archive beyond the season it is designed. Therefore, fashion demonstrates the capacity to improve both present and future societal well-being, reflecting and influencing society, politics, economics and environments in ways other disciplines cannot.

At ECA, to achieve this goal, we established a Diversity Network (DN) to help activate academia to broaden the context for student design work, explore emotionally impactful and considerate design solutions and generate purposeful and socially conscious design outcomes.

## Building a diversity network

The Edinburgh College of Art Diversity Network (ECA-DN) was established in 2010 with the award-winning charity *All Walks Beyond the Catwalk* and with support from the UK Government Equalities Minister Lynne Featherstone's Body Confidence initiative. *All Walks Beyond the Catwalk* was founded by Caryn Franklin, Debra Bourne and Erin O'Connor to challenge the fashion industry's dependence on unachievable and limited body and beauty ideals by respecting diversity. It was the first charity for body image and diversity activism in the United Kingdom, seeking to ameliorate how the industry represented narrow portrayals of diversity through high-impact campaigning. They emphasized on their website,

> We believe that diversity in front of the lens and behind it – mindset and physical representation – is crucial for emotionally considerate practice. Fundamentally: Fashion can be a powerful carrier of messages towards shaping personal identity and self-esteem. Respecting customer difference and individual need is evermore important in this global economy [sic].
>
> (www.allwalks.org 2012)

Equalities Minister Lynne Featherstone spearheaded the world's-first United Nations (UN) event about body image and how women were portrayed in the media (GOV. UK 2012a). The 2010 body image event was one of a series during the UN Commission on the Status of Women where Lynne spoke out about the need for governments, private sectors, and civil society, to address how the unrealistic idealized media images bombarded upon youth contribute to eating disorders and the increase in mental health issues among youth in the United Kingdom (GOV. UK 2012b).

With support from *All Walks Beyond the Catwalk* and research funding, the ECA-DN soon became a critical educational space for discourse and knowledge exchange led by fashion academics, helping pioneer new ways to educate our future designers about their responsibilities to improve consumer well-being. Through research, new pedagogy, exhibits, runway shows, symposiums and forums, our DN connects academics across the United Kingdom to share best practices on the theme of Diversity. We promote the responsibility of fashion educators to teach our future fashion designers the importance of emotionally considerate design and pioneer projects that encourage students to engage with the needs and feelings of the end-user (All Walks 2012).

When the ECA-DN was formed in 2010, we were unaware of any similar pedagogical approaches to diversity in fashion education, specifically where it could be embedded as an essential design tool. There was simply little way for a student designer to know how to take accountability for their research and design outcomes regarding social and psychological impact. The ECA-DN became a critical educational platform to allow discourse and knowledge exchange led by fashion academics, in turn helping to pioneer new ways to educate future designers about their responsibilities to improve fashion consumer well-being.

The ECA-DN helped us establish clearer department standards of practice and incorporate emotionally considerate approaches to design in our curriculum. Furthermore, we collaborated with museums to create accessible exhibits, hosted symposiums with industry professionals and showcased student work through annual catwalk shows. In the following section, I will outline some of the ECA-DN processes, the outcomes and student experiences.

## Creating standards of practice

Whereas clear educational frameworks are essential to teaching practices, simply expecting students to 'go through the motions' of perceived and firmly entrenched learning methods cannot be progressive or particularly exciting to deliver as an educator. It cannot make sense that our students' incredible talents and capacity to improve the lives of global audiences may be limited by narrow educational practices that rarely allow or encourage us, the educators, the freedom to challenge the traditions of our discipline.

Our department standards of practice have included a range of new projects and teaching methods, guided by a manifesto abolishing normative codes in teaching students about their supposed customer markets. In devising the ECA-DN, I acknowledged the notion that, as designers, we work with and address human bodies constantly. Yet, there was little awareness or critical reflection on how we talked about and represented diversity through our words. Therefore, I realized that emotionally informed language must be placed at the heart of diversity teaching and addressed through collaborative student and staff engagement.

The following exercise is one I encourage fashion educators to try at the start of initiating Diversity Studies into student learning. I found this to be a highly effective platform for re-shaping preconditioned narrow language relating to beauty ideals and the consumer. It is important to note here that the language that works and makes sense for our programme and geographic region might not have the same cultural meanings to others worldwide.

### Language Labs

As a teaching team, we introduced a series of language labs between fashion student groups and programme staff, first to explore how fashion designers refer to different types of bodies and second to explore if our language was limited, celebratory, acceptable, respectful and representative. We asked first-year students to brainstorm and write as many descriptive and celebratory words about diverse body types and beauty representation. The students considered how the individual they represented might interpret the words and how the words might affect self-esteem. Following this session, we exhibited the words on the walls of our department for reflection, viewing and debate. After discussing the words, the surprising results revealed that most of these words were not celebratory and, if directed to the beholder, could detrimentally impact their self-esteem. Adjectives included rotund, sturdy, big, pale, busty, short and stocky. We also noted that there were very few words to express or celebrate the varieties of race, age, gender, facial features and hair, among others.

Working with our lecturers, we divided the students into a series of life-drawing sessions where the models represented the demographics lacking in our language lab. After a few weeks of classes, we repeated the language lab, expecting the results to be a small extension of vocabulary and the same tone as our previous session. However, the majority of words expressed in this second session were more expansive and sensitive to how the beholder could interpret them. Words such as rich, velvet, alabaster, willowy, sumptuous and perfect emerged on the walls of our department. One student even expressed the word *Sonsie* ('an uncommon historical Scottish term to describe a more curvaceous body type'). I consider this to be strong evidence that there was a clear need to explore and encourage creative methods, rather than lecture-based, to enable fashion students to describe diverse bodies as part of their studies. After all, these are the types of bodies that would be wearing their future work. In this experiment, I think traditional life drawing was just as impactful for them as it was for me. Life drawing advances skills beyond improving drawing techniques. It offers a more cerebral, compassionate and thoughtful consideration of the body. Future sketching sessions could invite the models and muses to participate in the language labs, as the words they use for individual identification would enable fashion students to understand how to celebrate with words that are meaningful to the wearer and not just the designer.

## Emotionally considerate design

Before the inception of the ECA-DN, I was frustrated on hearing lecturers and students discuss 'model beauty' as the peak of aspirational physical aesthetics, where fashion garments were seen to be at their optimum appeal only when worn by tall, slim and young models. Sadly, I had also been privy to comments from staff and students at model fittings or backstage at fashion shows, including 'she's too short for that dress' or 'her hips are too wide for those trousers'. During garment fitting sessions, where it is normal practice for fellow students to offer themselves as models to help their peers, they often unintentionally became an object of such open 'body shaming' by staff and students alike. I was vigilant and swift to take action to speak with academics or students who perpetuated this type of problematic discussion, yet it also highlighted the problem of designers not evidencing any emotional consideration for the feelings of those very people whom they seek to celebrate through their work; I felt strongly that this evidenced a form of 'inconsiderate design' within our own pedagogy.

I decided to explore removing conventional teaching constraints and established a new manifesto. As such, we removed references to traditional or commonly expressed *codes of fashion*, including outdated notions of what is and is not supposed to flatter or compliment the wearer. The designer and, therefore, the consumer is often led by a predetermined way of thinking about their style. Meaning designs often perpetuate outdated messages that suggest only certain colours complement specific skin tones or that stripes, prints and hem lengths are only appropriate for certain body types or ages. At ECA, we gave power back to our students to question the purpose of such traditional codes. We asked them to address whether they, the designer, really held the right to dictate what looks good on whom and how *considering the emotional impact* of their work might actually be the most important skill to inform their studies. Essentially, we provoked the idea that designers with prejudice, who lack understanding of socially conscious design approaches, may not be the most effective, employable or meaningful designers for the future world. In 2010, whilst there was a burgeoning and visible recognition of the impact of fashion on the environment, there was little awareness of the impact of fashion on human physical well-being or mental health.

At the inception of the ECA-DN, and supported by Caryn Franklin, I devised the term 'Emotionally Considerate Design' as a foundation for design. This term can be used to overarch all fashion design processes, whereby the designer embeds an ethos of empathy, understanding and celebration of all bodies. From the outset of a project, this inspiring phrase motivated students to holistically consider the wearer as a catalyst and primary influence towards their design work.

We felt that integrating emotionally considerate design into our curriculum needed to be creatively delivered in the first two years of study, allowing our students to critically reflect on their learning and helping them to see the value of instilling principles of diversity into their subsequent practice. I devised a design project for second-year students that sought to implement emotionally considerate design practices focused on designing and pattern-cutting for diverse groups of people who were not well represented through catwalk or fashion marketing at the time. This original design project was called 'Fashion and the Muse' and was initiated in 2012. In 2017, this became one of the first recognized credit-bearing international practice-led fashion design courses in Diversity Studies, now titled *Designing Diversity for the Fashion Industries.*

## Outcomes

### Designing diversity for the fashion industries

This course, running in our second semester, originates from the very simple idea of offering students a platform to think more deeply about who they were designing for and to establish the importance of the emotions and self-esteem of the wearer in the design process.

The course brief requires the students to select their own model, which becomes the ultimate inspiration and catalyst for their research and design work. Here, they are encouraged to work directly with an individual that they find inspirational in terms of their style, appearance, identity and personality. Although each student designs for their model, there is rich peer-to-peer learning through collaborative group discussion and observation within the studio environment. The students work together to cast a diverse group of models, representing a wide demographic of age, race, height, size, gender and ability.

Working together, the student and their model develop mutually collaborative research and design ideas to empower and celebrate the model with design imbued with meaning and depth. Rather than asking students to seek external, abstract or visual research themes to inspire a design, the models were set as the sole research concept. There was no need to run to a library, tear pages from fashion magazines, take photographs of architecture or nature or exploit the pages of Google or Pinterest; the research would be in front of them, and an actual talking, opinionated, breathing, feeling person.

Through this method, the students developed a more empathetic approach to design, including consideration of colour theory, construction, sizing, fit and materials. This course, which still runs successfully, requires students to think far beyond the tailor's dress form; they are tasked with unique design problems or viewpoints from their models that often challenge their personal aesthetic preferences. Equally, the students must understand how to compromise as part of their design process, an essential skill for an industry career largely directed by consumer needs and where the designer is not always in control of their sales. As a result, representation and celebration of diversity become core to every stage of the design process, and all sketch development methods and illustrated outcomes for this course must realistically reflect the muse's appearance. By using this approach, it becomes normal practice for students to not only integrate diversity in the design process but to genuinely demonstrate diversity throughout their fashion portfolios.

This two-way design process becomes a valuable and equal discourse between the designer and the wearer and is instrumental in informing how students approach subsequent work. The close relationships students often build with their models helps instil an emotionally conscious approach to design, where care and empathy become inherently and naturally embedded into the practice. Students continue to develop in-depth design approaches addressing design for diversity, including age, size, race, gender and disability. Following this, all future design briefs encourage students to embed emotionally considerate research and design methods into their creative practice.

This course vision was also introduced as a core part of the curricula at the Shanghai College of Fashion Innovation, Donghua University (a collaborative partnership with ECA), demonstrating its wide-reaching global impact. In addition to our successful pedagogy, the ECA-DN has contributed to public exhibits, catwalk shows, forums and symposiums.

### Forums, symposiums, exhibits and catwalk shows

One of the most fantastic ECA-DN projects included a major exhibition, *Beauty by Design: Fashioning the Renaissance*, featured at the Scottish National Portrait Gallery from 2014 to 2015 (The University of Edinburgh n.d.). The exhibition informed critical public debate relating to diversity in fashion, increasing the accessibility of fashion design to new audiences, including the visual and hearing impaired. It also embedded student learning and new design projects related to the awareness of changing historical perceptions of beauty and image and how this impacted fashion design and style. *Beauty by Design: Fashioning the Renaissance* has since been exhibited at significant international venues, including The International Centre for Lace and Fashion in Calais, France, The Bonnington Gallery in Nottingham, The Shanghai Museum of Textiles and Costume, and recently Palazzo Michiel, Venice, as part of Venice Design 2019.

In 2018, ongoing work culminated in the *Diversity Network Fashion Forum*, funded by the Royal Society of Edinburgh, at the National Museum of Scotland in Edinburgh, a major industry event attracting worldwide leaders to debate diversity and image with a broad public audience. The event included high-profile speakers and guests, including the British Fashion Council, United Kingdom designers Teatum Jones, Linda Mukangoga, designer of Rwandan Fashion brand Haute Basso, stylist Ibrahim Kamara, fashion photographer Campbell Addy, Daphne Selfe – 'the world's oldest supermodel', Lina Plioplyte – Director of Advanced Style, and disabled model and activist Kelly Knox (chenault 2017). Outfits designed by our students as part of their Designing Diversity for the Fashion Industries course in 2019 were also featured in the National Museum of Scotland's 2019 exhibition *Body Beautiful: Diversity on the Catwalk*. The curator, Georgina Ripley noted,

> National Museums Scotland's involvement with Edinburgh College of Art's Diversity Network was a catalyst for our exhibition. As a result of close collaboration with ECA, the exhibition also included displays of student work, their participation in the exhibition film, and their contribution to the exhibition's online content. Body Beautiful is the first museum exhibition in the world to address diversity on the catwalk, reflecting Edinburgh College of Art's position as leaders in education around diversity and emotionally considerate design.
>
> (National Museums Scotland n.d.)

Additionally, the class outcomes are regularly featured in our end-of-year catwalk shows in Edinburgh, where the cast of models are invited to showcase their bespoke outfits to a live audience. The course has involved regular collaboration between DN academic partners, fashion industry sectors, and mental health and well-being charities by actively sharing and exchanging perspectives on diversity awareness. The DN has championed dynamic and creative design projects between hair and make-up students at Solent University in Southampton, led by equality activist Sharon Lloyd, and fashion marketing and management courses at Heriot-Watt University, Robert Gordon University in Aberdeen, and UCA Epsom. Essentially, these collaborations empower students to understand why diversity is vital to their future careers and how diversity informs and enhances the design of meaningful products and marketing messages.

These wide-ranging activities and collaborations have helped inform new teaching practices whereby diversity is pivotal to a student's full design process, from the research stage to sketching, prototyping, collection outcomes and portfolios. As such, I can attest to the benefits and values that the formation of such an initiative can offer to enhance fashion education from multiple perspectives and experiences. We have strong evidence that our approach to diversity nourishes and enriches student's learning and teaching experiences and can ultimately improve the quality of our graduate's design, communication and marketing skills. Pivotally, diversity inclusion equips graduates to face careers in an increasingly challenging and complex world.

## Student's voice

Cumulatively, the voice of future designers is the most important voice to listen to. Three former design students share their opinions and experiences on how the DN influenced their education and what they believe is the real impact of a learning environment that respects, embraces and celebrates diversity. Their willingness to share and reflect on experiences within our programme informs the moment and is a powerful tool for future learning as we work to fill in gaps and improve our teaching methods. I hope that this will encourage educators who have not yet introduced diversity practices to join the force of change and see the power fashion education holds in improving the future.

### Nikita Vora: Edinburgh College of Art 2018–21

When studying fashion at ECA, it was clear that the most valuable lesson academics continuously emphasized was the notion that beauty is not one tone or one aesthetic. They foster a positive environment where students are encouraged to embrace muses and customer profiles, including *all* skin tones, an exciting direction that I believe all institutions should be moving towards. The curriculum inspires students to continuously celebrate diversity as a true reflection of our society.

ECA reflects a refreshing approach in ensuring that our concepts go beyond trend and are capable of covering history, culture, social and philosophical courses. Creating an environment where students continuously educate themselves and others on topics they might not be exposed to has allowed us to gauge a greater understanding of ourselves and others. As a student from an ethnic minority, it is empowering to see students and tutors who want to develop this environment encouraging those within the fashion industry to go beyond the stereotype.

As an Indian woman, the colour of my skin bears thousands of stories and lessons from myself, my family and my ancestors. Searching for role models, especially in the fashion world, is a subconscious fixation that I believe we were all seeking growing up, and to some extent, we always will. This enables us to dream about our future, yet I never saw a prominent figure in the western fashion industry who looked like me. 'Does this world not include people like me?' And 'Am I not beautiful?' often appeared in my mind.

In my graduate year, I worked towards a concept that focused on the racism my community has historically experienced, including personal accounts from my family, friends and myself. My final collection (Figures 15.1 and 15.2) was dedicated to conveying that the South-Asian community must all speak up together. I wanted to educate my community to do better. My collection, therefore, honoured the extensive beauty of Indian people and culture and acts as a positive celebration of those who will speak up.

The BA fashion curriculum at ECA actively encouraged me to embrace topics about my heritage and community, where I am not only educating others but I am

FIGURE 15.1: Nikita Vora, *Example of Illustrative Design Work Expressing Cultural Identity and Heritage*, 2020, CAD. Courtesy of Nikita Vora.

also educating myself about who I am. I hope other institutions and the fashion industry embrace and celebrate diversity to allow young Indian girls like myself to grow up realizing their power and beauty. I am grateful that the BA Fashion curriculum at ECA has helped me grow into a proud Indian woman who loves her heritage, culture and colour.

### Amelia Wang: Alumni, Edinburgh College of Art 2017–20

Going to university is an incredible time to open our minds and take us out of our comfort zones. It acts as a microcosm for the 'real world', placing us in a pool of unfamiliarity and introducing distinctive outlooks which we may or may not align with. This is a critical moment where judgements, opinions and viewpoints are deeply moulded. Thus, this time must be used purposefully to establish a balanced

FIGURE 15.2: Nikita Vora, *Example of Illustrative Design Work Expressing Cultural Identity and Heritage*, 2020, CAD. Courtesy of Nikita Vora.

and informed appreciation for the bigger picture. I enormously value my experience as a mixed-race woman, having grown up in London with a British mother and a Chinese father: I recognize that I was supported in an environment where both of my cultures existed freely and equally. I am grateful to have been taught to love my heritage and feel particularly fortunate to have sisters to whom I can entirely relate.

Outside of the safety of my family, there were times at university when I encountered acts of thoughtlessness and senselessness concerning my race. The BA fashion programme at ECA, however, provided a learning environment focused on sensitivity, responsiveness and space to develop, where we were encouraged to form an 'emotionally considerate' design ethos. Bringing awareness to diversity and celebrating inclusivity is a normalized approach within the department. I have simultaneously been motivated to appreciate, embrace and celebrate my heritage more than ever before.

Fashion has a huge ongoing responsibility to inform how the public receives messages about race, beauty, gender, ability and identity. At ECA, amalgamating my cultural perspectives within my graduate collection (Figures 15.3–15.5), and expressing them outwardly as a final outcome has been a natural process and directly translates and celebrates the connectivity of my two cultures.

I feel strongly that all fashion institutions globally can improve and take responsibility for educating students in new ways that constructively contribute to the fashion industry. As I write this in the year 2020, it is unacceptable that inclusivity is vaguely seen within design curricula worldwide. Additionally, BIPOC recruitment efforts need more money and more support from top levels of the administration; how can courses successfully understand if the university cohorts are not diverse themselves? I have personally experienced the impact of studying in a fashion programme that actively listens and strives to pinpoint what needs to change. I only hope that global fashion education speeds up, spreading the importance of diversity with this same momentum that will eventually elevate the integrity of inclusive design within fashion industries.

FIGURE 15.3: Amelia Wang, *Graduate Collection Inspired by Familial Memories, Cross-Generational Relationships, and the Significance of Growing Up with Multiracial Heritage*, 2020. Courtesy of Amelia Wang.

FIGURE 15.4: Amelia Wang, *Graduate Collection Inspired by Familial Memories, Cross-Generational Relationships, and the Significance of Growing Up with Multiracial Heritage,* 2020. Courtesy of Amelia Wang.

## Rhys McKenna: Alumni, Edinburgh College of Art 2012–18

As a student at ECA, I cannot state more emphatically how important the curriculum focus on diversity helped inform my design ethos. The values of diversity instilled in my courses are exponentially relevant to my ongoing practice. As an alumnus, I am equipped to design with humanity, respect and empathy, and many collaborators, companies and co-creators appreciate this.

I have been empowered by the thematic approach to diversity, where it is standard course practice for students to develop skills in designing for various audiences and tackling and challenging complex questions relating to diversity. At

FIGURE 15.5: Amelia Wang, *Graduate Collection Inspired by Familial Memories, Cross-Generational Relationships, and the Significance of Growing Up with Multiracial Heritage*, 2020. Courtesy of Amelia Wang.

ECA, the enthusiasm and commitment to this initiative ran like electricity in the air throughout the department. We were briefed to develop design skills by working on projects for consumers not commonly represented in the fashion sphere.

We were encouraged to speculate and critique how fashion could incite change for a more diverse and empowered future. I explored how disabled people form (important and often misunderstood) relationships with fashion and style. I devised a project to address disability within fashion and sports (Figure 15.6). My research involved collaboration and mutual discussion, exploring together how physicality affects one's relationship with clothing and self-esteem.

As a result of this formative project, concepts of understanding body ergonomics and well-being became ingrained in my subsequent design practice. Equipped with this developing research knowledge and supported by a curriculum that actively celebrated diversity and design empathy, I was able to wield a new awareness of my work and its place within the wider practice of design.

CELEBRATING DIVERSITY THROUGH
EMPATHETIC DESIGN
**INSPIRED BY RUNNING BLADE**
USERS

FIGURE 15.6: Rhys McKenna, *Second Year Project Exploring Disability, Diversity and Sport*, 2014, CAD. Courtesy of Rhys McKenna.

The critical design skills that I learned at ECA have been of utmost importance to my prosperous career in the fashion industry. I currently work for Adidas, where human-centric design is an everyday practice. It is clear now that emotionally considerate design is not only a desirable quality in design graduates but a necessity.

I now approach design with knowledge of how to consider and address the needs and desires of athletes and consumers in very specific sports and life situations where they must be supported, empowered, protected and celebrated. I have learnt that all people, of all abilities, all bodies and all voices are central to the design process. The ECA curriculum and teaching approach taught me what it means to be a designer with a moral compass. It is so important for fashion graduates to embrace an inclusive attitude toward their consumers; to be eloquent in the language of empathy-led design. I attribute the curriculum as the driving factor that equipped me to be the designer I am today.

## Reflections

Any challenges embedding diversity into our student's learning experience have, wonderfully, been far outweighed by the many positives. Our first challenge was the continuous need to justify the initiative's importance to fashion educators.

While several progressive colleges and institutions also felt this was an important movement, there were occasions when I heard educators say diversity was not critical to their student's learning experience.

Others commented that diversity in fashion had actually existed for a long time, citing supermodel diversity as a justification for their reasoning, and therefore there was little work to do. There was also a perception that the 'job was done' if diverse models were in a catwalk show alone rather than embedded within the underlying educational narrative.

Additionally, I recall hearing academics commenting on how a diversity initiative would benefit their marketing and recruitment drive. Such perspectives are in contrast to our goals, which are grounded in generating better, emotionally engaged designers whose work resonates with fashion audiences in new and healthier ways, in turn influencing positive approaches to design and marketing in our future industries.

Granted that I am proud to share our approach with prospective students, it is not to 'sell the programme' but to ensure the applicants understand the value embedded diversity training will bring to their educational experience and beyond. During the formative years of the Diversity Network activities, narrow thinking around topics of diversity in fashion remained, and it was often treated or dismissed as a fad that would expire. Now, it would be hard-pressed to find an institution that is not urgently striving to bring a diversity manifesto to its organization!

I was also challenged, on more than one occasion after giving a student or public lecture, whether our goal to celebrate body diversity in fact condoned and encouraged obesity. It was felt, by some, that encouraging students to design for larger bodies endorsed obesity and unhealthy lifestyles. I soon learnt to counteract this argument by expressing that, as fashion designers, we are not medical professionals and have absolutely no right to comment on, discuss or make assumptions about the health of anyone other than ourselves. However, we can influence others to accept and widen the celebration of body and beauty differences. We are certainly able to freely express that larger bodies are beautiful.

On one occasion, after giving a lecture on our approach to diversity, the mother of a daughter with anorexia told me she wished the fashion industry and media had depicted healthier approaches to beauty rather than perpetuated the ideal of 'thinness'. She commented that initiatives such as ours provided solace and hope for her family moving forwards.

Navigating diversity and inclusion in fashion education, where there is an established and professionally recognized ideal for using traditional industry-facing catwalk shows and thin models, also presented key challenges. I had become aware of alarming industry perspectives indicating that student catwalk shows depicting 'non-professional' models were viewed as amateur, demonstrating a lack of institutional funds or support. This necessitated more moderated and tentative approaches to showcasing diversity than we would have liked to at the time. Despite featuring amateur catwalk models as part of our second-year course, our primary goal focused less on completely challenging or dismissing the catwalk or traditional model context but on including a more diverse representation.

Clearly, some of our student's future employers would not yet understand the value of a different approach to catwalk contexts, especially if their own brands were not using diverse models. I strongly felt that, due to the highly competitive nature of fashion design careers, we still needed to take responsibility for ensuring the biggest employability reach for our students and, as such, have continued to use thin models in our shows. Whilst this may have appeared to lack some integrity in relation to our strong ethos to include diversity, it is also important that we try to bridge the gap between where the industry is and where it needs to be. Thankfully, in recent years, such perspectives and judgments on what is or is not professional have started to change, and high-end international fashion shows now celebrate more diversity than ever.

Another challenge the ECA-DN has faced in recent years is accessibility and the housing and sharing of information. Furthermore, there are several outlets and platforms to access the projects we have undertaken, such as the *All Walks Beyond the Catwalk* website, the ECA website and the UK government website, the challenges of COVID-19 somewhat curtailed plans for the creation of a repository of information and for a further ECA-DN Education Summit, which was cancelled in 2020. Now, we are more optimistic, and we have found effective ways to navigate and find solutions to design education and research through the pandemic, and it is anticipated that the ECA-DN will begin to reboot its activities.

Our most salient challenge is to normalize diversity as a mandatory aspect within design education, in the same way that sustainability has become a core focus for global fashion pedagogy. To do this in a long-lasting way, courses and learning outcomes need to be firmly named and set within our fashion degrees, and our teaching visions must become clear and visible to all educators. Without designated courses, degrees and key training aids to support our academics, the teaching and embedding of equalities and diversity will be at risk, only being upheld by lecturers interested in the field.

True success can only be measured when we no longer must justify the importance of including diversity awareness in a student's training. On reflection of my own journey and key achievements since 2010, it is clear to me that initiatives such as the DN can demonstrate a way to activate long-term impact for diversity, equality and 'emotionally considerate design' practices to be embedded into fashion design education.

## *Activate the change*

Since establishing diversity as a part of our curriculum; parallels may be drawn to the increased student success that quickly followed. The fashion industry soon noticed our students in a way they had not before. Since 2012 our students have demonstrated an impressive track record of award success in national and international competitions. A key example of this was the British Fashion Council & Burberry Design Competition in 2016, where three ECA students received awards (including Rhys McKenna, featured above). These are the students who, by 2016, had experienced embedded approaches to diversity within all of their study years and design projects. By 2019, this type of success had increased. Our students won five top prizes at Graduate Fashion Week in London, including the Christopher Bailey Gold Award, Conscious Design Award, Hilary Alexander Trailblazer Award and the Womenswear Award.

This prime example demonstrates how student success can increase when fashion education challenges traditional boundaries and introduces new skills to our students' learning. There is little risk in empowering our students to understand that their work's catalyst, intention and impact should not be tied *solely* to seasonal trends, business needs, catwalk shows and narrow beauty and body aesthetics. This is proof that the industry notices and values graduates who understand their power and responsibility to design clothes that acknowledge real social responsibility, empathy and care embedded into their design principles.

In closing, I implore you, as an educator, to look introspectively before teaching and encouraging this complex subject. I recommend you become reflective and highly critical of your privileges, perspectives and possible biases. We must deconstruct and analyse where our standards of beauty originate. Are you simply following the pattern of how you were taught or maybe you have subconsciously accepted beauty standards in fashion and media? Can you, for a moment, accept and understand your power to positively influence your students and incite the change we critically need to bring to this industry?

I call for fellow fashion educators to see value in empowering our students to respect the natural forms of human difference, diversity, inclusion and equality in all areas of their work, from research to the development processes, sketching, illustration and, of course, catwalk and photography. A fashion designer cannot be a designer for the world unless they can celebrate this world in its diversity and express our world in their outcomes. The key to this is simple; make sure your students know that all people matter, themselves, you … us. Ensure they are freed from the boundaries of old-fashioned teaching methodologies. Update your curriculum now before it holds no meaning for the industries it seeks to serve!

# REFERENCES

All Walks (2012), 'Diversity network', http://www.allwalks.org/diversity-network/. Accessed 20 December 2021.

Body Confidence Campaign Progress Report 2013 (2013), https://assets.publishing.service.gov.uk/government/uploads/system/uploads/attachment_data/file/203405/130501_body_confidence_progress_reportv03.pdf. Accessed 27 February 2023.

chenault (2017), 'Diversity network fashion forum 2018 at the National Museum of Scotland. | Diversity Network', *Diversity Network*, https://sites.eca.ed.ac.uk/diversitynetwork/2017/04/10/diversity-network-fashion-forum-2018-at-the-national-museum-of-scotland/. Accessed 5 January 2022.

Department for Education (2016), '2010 to 2015 government policy: Equality', GOV.UK, https://www.gov.uk/government/publications/2010-to-2015-government-policy-equality/2010-to-2015-government-policy-equality#appendix-4-body-confidence-campaign. Accessed 5 January 2022.

Diversity Network (n.d.), 'Diversity network | Edinburgh College of Art and All Walks Beyond the Catwalk', https://sites.eca.ed.ac.uk/diversitynetwork/. Accessed 5 January 2022.

GOV.UK (2012a), 'Body confidence on United Nations agenda', https://www.gov.uk/government/news/body-confidence-on-united-nations-agenda. Accessed 20 December 2021.

GOV.UK (2012b), 'Lynne Featherstone speech on body image', https://www.gov.uk/government/speeches/lynne-featherstone-speech-on-body-image. Accessed 20 December 2021.

National Museums Scotland (n.d.), 'Body beautiful: Diversity on the catwalk', https://www.nms.ac.uk/bodybeautiful. Accessed 5 January 2022.

The University of Edinburgh (n.d.), 'Beauty by design – fashioning the Renaissance | Edinburgh College of Art', https://www.eca.ed.ac.uk/research/beauty-design-fashioning-renaissance. Accessed 20 December 2021.

# 16

## Redesigning Dignity: A Collaborative Approach to the Universal Hospital Gown

*Brittany Dickinson and Lucy Jones*

One size does not fit all – genders, body types, ages, and abilities – but illness, disease and emergencies do not discriminate. This is especially evident in 2020, the year I wrote this chapter, amid the global coronavirus pandemic. Anybody can contract COVID-19, regardless of age, skin colour, class, ethnic background, gender expression, sexual preference or political orientation[1]. This is a story about the magic that happens when students collaborate with people outside the classroom to reimagine a system that affects everyone. Our story takes place in the Spring of 2017 at Parsons School of Design in New York City, where we were invited to co-teach a new School of Fashion elective in partnership with innovative health-wear company Care+Wear. Our task for this semester-long interdisciplinary studio was to redesign the universal patient hospital gown to preserve the wearer's dignity.

'Dignity' is defined as 'the quality or state of being worthy, honoured, or esteemed' (Merriam-Webster 2020). Interestingly, one of the synonyms for 'dignity' is fashion. 'Fashion' may not be a word we associate with 'hospital gown'; instead, the gown more likely conjures up generic images of a shapeless and shameful mess of fabric, or perhaps it brings up memories or fears of when the garment was worn. Seemingly every design choice, from the material, fit and trims, reveals a garment formed purely for function and not for fashion. Personal sentiments like comfort, modesty, style and personality are sanitized from this simplistic design.

The gown discussed in this chapter is a non-disposable multiuse gown donned by patients in hospital systems across the United States. This one-size-fits-all (or one-size-fits-none) garment design maximizes access and economy. Cost savings are evident in its shapeless rectangular pattern pieces, plain-weave cotton-polyester material and natural selvedge edge finishes. The garment is cut with three main access points at the chest, shoulders and back. A slit in the fabric is hidden behind a single chest pocket supporting a telemetry monitor, and rows of flat snaps allow each shoulder to open completely. The central feature of this garment is an open-back design cut to expose the wearer's entire backside, often presenting a Norman door-like confusion of whether the gown is to be worn forward or backwards[2]. Two sets of ties close the neck and waist, but the tyes short length and placement at the back of the body make it difficult to tye a bow.

Within the walls of a hospital, this open-back gown is worn when lives begin and end. The gown accompanies many procedures, from giving birth to cancer treatments and routine visits to the doctor's office. As a result of COVID-19, one might even say that this garment has become as commonly worn as a t-shirt and jeans, and it can significantly impact a person's well-being and psyche at a time when they are at their most vulnerable. Unfortunately, the gown is often a source of embarrassment due to its revealing and drafty open-back. Its design was over-due for an overhaul.

The class began as a fifteen-week competition-based project consisting of three small teams and merged into a collective vision that continued beyond the completion of the semester. The final proposal (Figures 16.1–16.3) resulted in an approachable and even stylish design that met the needs of both the wearer and the caregiver. In a soft Tencel-cotton blend[3], the kimono-inspired silhouette featured intuitive colour-coded tyes and an innovative overlapped back body construction

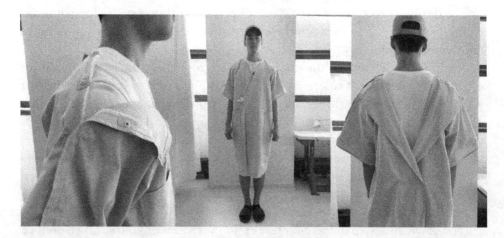

FIGURES 16.1–16.3: Daniel models the final gown design. 2017. New York City. Courtesy of Daniel Lee.

to keep the backside concealed yet accessible, thus preserving the dignity of the wearer. Most importantly, this design received a stamp of approval from not only clinical professionals and individuals who had each spent time in a hospital gown and who regularly visited the classroom to collaborate with the students on the design process.

While the focus of this project was to offer comfort and dignity for the wearer, the success of the gown ultimately hinged on its feasibility in the medical field. Hospital gown re-designs often fail in health settings because they do not pass medical expectations and requirements and are usually not economically viable for hospitals. Combining design and research methodologies (design and systems thinking, people-centric and object-based research strategies) the students collaborated with former and current hospital patients, healthcare industry professionals and supply chain experts throughout the design process – research, sourcing, design, prototyping, testing, production and critique – to reimagine this garment.

## The partnership

There have been several attempts to redesign the universal patient hospital gown. While writing this chapter, we discovered a United States patent from inventor Elizabeth McElroy from Jacksonville, Florida, dated 9 August 1920. McElroy's invention shows a hospital gown with dignity embedded in its concept. The description states that the goal of the design was to 'provide a gown which may be opened at various places, particularly in cases of operation so that any portion of the body may be reached without exposing the entire body' (McElroy 1923: 1).

At the university level, schools such as the College of Design, Architecture, Art and Planning at the University of Cincinnati, Colorado State University's Department of Design and Merchandising, and North Carolina State University's College of Textiles have all sought to reimagine this garment. Attempts have also been made at the designer level, from Ben de Lisi with Kings College Hospital, Diane von Furstenberg with the Cleveland Clinic and, over two decades ago, Cynthia Rowley with Hackensack University Medical Center. As we embarked on our journey at Parsons School of Design, we acknowledged the work of our predecessors and also gained crucial insight and words of wisdom from several readings, particularly 'Designing a New Type of Hospital Gown' (Black and Torlei 2013) and 'A User-centered Approach to the Redesign of the Patient Hospital Gown' (Gordan and Guttman 2013).

The idea for this class was created by Care+Wear Co-Founder and CEO Chaitenya Razdan, Chair of Board of Governors Kay Unger, Dean of Fashion

Burak Cakmak, School of Fashion Director of External Partnerships Shannon Price and Full-Time Faculty Brendan McCarthy. The School of Fashion then invited us to co-develop and teach the course, with Brittany Dickinson as part-time faculty and Lucy Jones as teaching consultant. McCarthy played a critical role in the success of the class by collaborating on course content, managing partnership logistics and providing numerous platforms to showcase the class. The American Association of Retired Persons (now known as AARP) provided funding for the course and prize money for the students, and Zappos provided additional course funding, including sponsoring a summer internship with Care+Wear to finalize the gown for production.

The course was an example of the BFA Fashion Design programme (Systems & Society pathway). Formed in 2015 as one pathway for fashion students to choose, Systems & Society provide the space for students to engage in diverse outcomes beyond the production of new products and to develop new fashion systems that can positively impact our world.

This vision for a new way of approaching fashion design is reflected in the ethos of Care+Wear. Founded in 2014, the company creates innovative and stylish health-wear products to enable positive and effective healing experiences for people who have illnesses or are recovering from them. The company's goal, according to Razdan, is 'to empower every person, whether [...] patient or clinician, to feel their best'. To achieve that, they utilize 'a three-pronged approach that incorporates clinicians, designers, and most importantly, the end user to marry function and design'. Care+Wear's method 'results in products that are not only functional, but also promote dignity, style, and comfort' (Razdan 2020: n.pag.). This approach differs from health-wear companies that have historically focused solely on product functionality.

A special part of our collaboration with Care+Wear included access to a wide network of healthcare professionals and other academics and practitioners working at various points within and related to the hospital system. Razdan and his team invited doctors and nurses to speak to the class and participate in critiques, and they brought in supply chain experts from consultancy firm A.T. Kearney. Care+Wear also set up field trips to local hospitals and an industrial laundering facility so that we could see the gown in its contextual entirety. In addition, being part of The New School granted us access to an extensive network of thinkers and makers, most notably the team at the Healthy Materials Lab, who visited our classroom multiple times throughout the semester to educate and encourage the students to make material choices that are healthier for people and planet[4].

The course was application-based and made available to students across all levels of study at The New School. Applicants submitted a portfolio and 250-word statement of interest to Dickinson, who evaluated and selected our group of nine students: Molly Bonnell, Camila Chiriboga, Chloe Edwards, Yi Chen Ho, Daniel Lee, Irene Lu, Gwyneth Ong, Helena Wang and Terrence Zhou. This cohort represented three seniors, one junior and four sophomores from the BFA Fashion Design programme and one first-year student from the AAS Fashion Marketing and Communication programme. While each student expressed unique motivations to apply for the course, one commonality wove the motives together: a desire to apply their talent and skills to positively impact people's lives.

## The gown

Many theories on the open-back gown's origin make it a fascination for re-design. The universal hospital gown is also sometimes called a 'johnny' or 'johnny gown' (McCormick 2007: n.pag.). This nickname appears to have originated from toilet slang in New England and is widely and confusingly discussed by nurse practitioners as evidenced in online blogs, some writing that the open-back 'johnny' gown refers to its 'easy use of the toilet, or "john," an explanation so simple it's almost guaranteed to be false' (Freeman 2010: n.pag.).

Every detail on the hospital gown serves a crucial function, the chief objective being to maximize access to a person's body for quick and effective treatment. The open back serves several purposes: to allow the caregiver easy access to different body sections, to aid in quick removal of the garment for both the wearer and caregiver, and to remove unnecessary bulk or seams for people needing prolonged times of rest lying down. Speed is of the essence in a hospital setting, and the need for rapid ease of access can be a matter of life or death.

By principle, designers are usually eager to fix, improve upon or critique an object with the assumption that the object will be better once it has been tweaked or redone. However, judging an object or system as an outsider can be easy. In the case of the hospital gown, while it certainly offers much to be critiqued, it is important to note that the gown is the way it is not because it is not considerate of its wearer's dignity. There are so many practical and functional needs that must be met in a medical setting that often, especially in emergencies, patient dignity is simply not the highest priority. Even from a patient's perspective, when one is extremely unwell or experiencing serious pain or discomfort, they can reach a point where their sense of self or personhood becomes blurred compared with the more urgent needs of their body.[5]

The gown often acts as a burden, however, projecting negative thoughts on the wearer and their visitors. According to a 2020 study in the British Journal of Health Psychology, the hospital gown symbolizes illness and, therefore, psychologically impacts the wearer's sense of health and identity. A participant from the study said that before wearing the gown, they were not feeling unwell, but, 'I would say that when the gown comes out there is something somewhere that psychologically goes "this is serious, I'm ill"' (Morton et al. 2020: 8). This sense of losing control of one's personal identity 'permeated participants' responses, as they described the hospital gown as being '"almost prison-like" [...], "a uniform" [...], and symbolic of being "in an institution"' (Morton et al. 2020: 8).

An article published in The Journal of American Medical Association: Internal Medicine, refers to 'post-hospital syndrome', a term coined by Dr Harlan Krumholz, MD, a professor of Medicine and Public Health at Yale School of Medicine, to describe situations when patients are unable to recover from their acute illnesses during a thirty-day period of vulnerability after hospitalized care. This 'trauma of hospitalization' results from the 'depersonalizing and stressful experience of a hospital admission' and is estimated 'to increase the risk of read-mission after discharge' (Rawal et al. 2019: 39).

One resource that was a critical part of our student's research was Lesley Baillie's thesis for London South Bank University entitled 'A Case Study of Patient Dignity in an Acute Setting'. Baillie explores how the hospital patient is stripped of agency and control, such as lack of auditory privacy due to 'staff intrusion behind curtains' (Baillie 2007: 66) or 'mixed-sex' (Baillie 2007: 142) and multi-bed units, as well as the loss of physical control over one's own body due to the use of foreign apparatuses and substances. This is further intensified by the absence of one's familiar dress due to the imposed hospital gown, where bodily exposure appears inevitable (Baillie 2007: 143). Comfort and dignity are critical at times like this when one has little control over so many things.

## The 'impossible' brief

Susan Szenasy writes that objects designed in the twenty-first century should be 'not only beautiful, affordable, enduring, functional, ergonomic, accessible, sustainable, and well made but also emotionally resonant and socially beneficial' (Szenasy [2009] 2014: 281). Addressing these points is no small task.

The students were required to understand not only the physical components of the garment (object-based research) as well as its fit and function (design think-ing) but its psychological and emotional impact on the wearer as well (user-centric research). They also had to understand the entire manufacturing and hospital systems where the gown is used (systems thinking), and they were challenged to address the environmental impact of their designs (sustainability literacy). A constant zoom-in, zoom-out method of identifying both the present and the future, the micro and the macro, shaped the experience of this class. In the first class of the semester, we distributed a gown to each student donated by Care+Wear and asked them to individually conduct a thorough object-based observation and analysis of the garment's function, appearance and construction. We prompted the students with a worksheet of questions based solely upon observation to preserve their beginner's minds. The questions contained personal, emotional and functional objectives. We asked them to scrutinize the gown's details, including fabric, fit, trim, colour and construction. We asked what the design elements evoked – a certain era? A particular gender? A psychological feeling? The students speculated upon the supposed function of each detail and imagined different scenarios and patterns of use. Drawing from knowledge gained in other fashion courses, they pondered the lifecycle of the gown, from raw material sourcing to sewing to laundering and disposal.

As a class, we created a working list of design parameters to be revisited at multiple points throughout the semester. First, we identified the major design criteria for the gown from a wearer's viewpoint. This included dignity, comfort, functionality, psychological impact and ease of use. We then identified the functional requirements from a medical standpoint regarding access, donning and doffing, folding, storage and laundering.

To meet the criteria, the product had to fit a range of needs for a range of bodies. This called for a thorough analysis of commonalities across diverse individuals and situations. Students explored the needs of a breadth of factors, including age, from paediatrics to geriatrics; body size, from infant gowns to extended sizes; and abilities, from people needing prolonged times of rest lying down to disabled and non-disabled people.

We applied systems of thinking to study and critique the entire healthcare system surrounding the gown and to articulate constraints regarding cost, sanitation and materials. We learned that all proposed material, construction, and trim innovations had to be tested for washability, durability and safety, as well as pacemaker and Magnetic Resonance Imaging (MRI) compatibility.

The students formed into teams of three to four people and engaged in various mapping exercises to visualize the gown and its system. Each team conducted a lifecycle analysis of the gown, from sourcing and production to hospital circulation and end of use, and identified key points of design intervention following the framework outlined in Donella Meadows foundational text, 'Leverage Points: Places to Intervene in a System' (1999: 1–19). Each team generated questions about the gown as both object and system to inform the design process, including: Where are the gowns made? Who supplies the fabric? How often do hospitals order new gowns, and how many are typically ordered at a time? What is the average life expectancy of the gown, and how is it determined? What happens to the gown at its end of use, and how is it disposed of? No detail was too small; everything was significant.

In addition to the tasks listed above, we encouraged the students to design the gowns economically with zero-waste cutting techniques, reinforcing the importance of maximizing fabric through innovative patternmaking. This was not only a means to build sustainability literacy but was also a clever way to work around the nearly prohibitive cost restrictions posed by the healthcare system. We examined the impact of toxic additives commonly used for hospital materials and surfaces – like antimicrobial or stain-resistant finishes – and explored in what ways materials might aid or hinder patient recovery. Surface treatments designed to help hospital patients and staff avoid short-term health risks often have adverse long-term health repercussions. Healthy Materials Lab provided an excellent reading to contextualize this discussion, 'The Future of Fabric: Health Care' (Silas et al. 2007: 1–32).

We acknowledge that, especially for an elective that met only three hours per week, this class's design and research requirements were incredibly demanding. At the beginning of the semester, we noted the students became overwhelmed and frustrated, and they initially expressed their worries over being unable to innovate due to the strict design constraints. Additionally, the high-stakes nature of the brief, coupled with the intellectually and emotionally taxing work of systems thinking, were new experiences for most students. But what initially appeared to be limiting became an extraordinary opportunity for innovation and impact. The obstacles drove the creativity; specifically, the project's palpability and urgency brought out the group's dedication. One of our talented senior students, Molly Bonnell, noted that working within this particular set of constraints taught her 'how to be inclusive, how to be sustainable, how to be innovative all within what kind of seemed at the beginning [to be] a really impossible brief' (Bonnell 2020a: n.pag.).

## The personal stories

To draw a stronger connection between dignity and the hospital gown, we wanted each student in the class to intimately experience the garment as an observer and as a wearer. We, therefore, gave them the task of wearing the gown five times during the first week of the semester for at least four consecutive waking hours at a time. They also had to sleep in the gown and wash it. Everyone participated in and rigorously documented this assignment through audio/visual recordings, writing, sketches and other creative interpretations – all methods used throughout the semester.

It is important to recognize the limitations designers experience when embarking upon such empathic design exercises without lived experience. It was understood by this assignment that it could never emulate a real hospital experience since it was conducted in the comfort of one's own living quarters and familiar surroundings. Moreover, it did not carry with it the illness often accompanying a real hospital experience. The students knew they had the privilege and ability to freely disrobe whenever they pleased or to stop the exercise if it was triggering.

As a class, we discussed the psychological impact of wearing such a stigmatized garment. Yi Chen Ho wrote in her journal of the experience, 'I feel more sick while wearing it'. The students shared tales of sleepless nights of twisted fabric tangled around limbs and sheets. They also shared their real-life experiences with hospital gowns, from personal encounters to seeing loved ones wearing them to no experience at all. In 2017, the idea of hospitalization appeared almost abstract to the majority of our young student's minds. Most people in the class did not face the immediate threat or awareness of illness – a stark contrast to today. This, of course, wasn't true for all students. Bonnell shared with the class her intimate history with the gown and what it was like to have cystic fibrosis. Reflecting upon that moment, Bonnell said that in sharing her experience with her peers, 'it helped to break down the assumption that there were only "sick people" and "normal people," and nothing else in between' (Bonnell 2020b: n.pag.).

Breaking down barriers and binaries requires breaking down hierarchies, so it is worth noting that as the class's instructors, we also completed the week-long hospital gown experiment and shared our experiences with the students. As educators, we often feel like we have to be the keepers of information, the authority on a subject. The removal of that expectation acts as motivation for students to step up and become experts. From the beginning, we needed to acknowledge that, despite co-teaching the course, neither of us was an expert on this subject. While we each brought our unique skill sets to the project – seasoned industry experience as a clothing designer with expertise in systems thinking and sustainability (Dickinson) and specialization in designing products with the disability community (Jones) – we were in this together, and there was so much to learn.

### The collaboration

It is essential to note that this investigation was not speculative; rather, students worked closely with the people they aimed to serve. Working closely with people is where the magic happened. Beginning in week five, Care+Wear's network of former and current hospital patients visited the classroom to collaborate with the students. This occurred three times throughout the semester, with three visitors at a time. A total of eight volunteers visited the class over the semester, half of whom visited more than once as both collaborators and guest critics. Working in rounds, they met with each team to try on prototypes and provide feedback on fit, fabric, colour preferences, comfort and modesty. Most importantly, they shared personal stories about their experiences related to dress and body, both in and out of the hospital.

During these collaborative sessions, our students learned how important it was to design a garment that was intuitive for the wearer and not complicated or confusing. Donning and doffing, in particular, had to be seamless and accessible. One of our students, Irene Lu, said that it was valuable to witness people 'try to figure out our prototypes and our final results and see if they could "read" the gown'. She explained that oftentimes when a folded hospital gown is handed to a person, it simply looks like a large piece of cloth with no clear indication of how to put it on, potentially intensifying an already stressful situation (Lu 2020: n.pag.). This prompted the students to build clever folding techniques into the gown's design and to develop innovative trim details such as colour-coded tyes.

Donald A. Norman writes in *The Design of Everyday Things*, 'The designer simply cannot predict the problems people will have, the misinterpretations that will arise, and the errors that will get made. And if the designer cannot anticipate errors, then the design cannot minimize their occurrence or their ramifications' (Norman 1988: 157).

The volunteer sessions helped our students see complications in their designs that they would not have been able to find if working as designers in isolation. We learned about a new obstacle or roadblock with each fitting, critique and site visit. Students presented what they believed to be a near-perfect gown based on significant research and testing, only to discover that some ideas were not feasible, such as a particular trim being unsuitable for industrial laundering or a detail posing a safety risk. For example, we learned that tyes could not exceed a certain length due to the risk of tangling with multiple wires or intravenous therapy (IVs); in addition, the gown's bulk could also interfere, causing trips and falls. One team created a closed-back prototype that was quite conceptual and inspired by Rei Kawakubo's voluminous Comme des Garçons shapes. While aesthetically interesting, it overwhelmed the petite frame of one of our beloved volunteers, Pat, restricting her movement. She quickly explained that this design would never work, mainly because the wearer would not be able to quickly use the bathroom without soiling their gown. This was an 'ah-ha' moment, as up until this point, the much-derided open-back characteristic only appeared to serve the caregiver and not the wearer. This was one of many examples of secondary research connecting to the primary, as we now had a tangible example of the aforementioned 'johnny' nickname.

Devising a one-size-fits-all gown was exceptionally difficult and was noted by many students in interviews for this chapter to be the class's most challenging part. Based on Pat's feedback, the re-designed prototype functioned more like a mini skirt on another very tall and lean volunteer, Diego.

In hindsight, we think the students should have met with our volunteers earlier than week five, given that patient experience was at the heart of the brief. Despite that, our students learned a valuable lesson: that sometimes when one works incredibly hard for something and invests considerable amounts of energy, research and well-intent, it may not always be met with overwhelming praise. This made for an enlightening and humbling learning experience.

## The emotional connection

This course transformed our thinking from designing for to designing with people. Designers often create products for a prospective audience, and clothing designers especially do not spend an intimate or expansive amount of time with the people they wish to serve. In our corporate world, design decisions are usually driven by data, statistics or market evaluations, as opposed to human beings more intuition-based, subjective and personal stories.

The impact of working closely with people from outside the classroom cannot be emphasized enough. 'There were real people involved on the line', Bonnell said, so 'the success of the class was due in large part to the fact that we could put a face to the [wearers] of the hospital gown' and 'not just some anonymous person in a hospital bed' (Bonnell 2020b: n.pag.). As the students became entrenched in the research and emotionally connected to our volunteers and one another, their commitment to the project followed an upward trajectory that appeared to have no stopping point. We could also see how much it meant for our volunteers to be invited to participate in the class. Several of the students noted in interviews for this chapter that the volunteers' positive energy and passion inspired their creativity and solidified their commitment to the project.

The students spoke to volunteers not only about matters of hospital gowns but also about what they liked to wear *outside* of the hospital. The goal was to design a gown that emulated a person's positive feelings in their daily life to maintain a semblance of familiarity, comfort, dignity and identity. We encouraged the students to ask questions such as, 'When do you feel most comforted by your clothes'? Or, 'What type of clothing makes you feel happy'? These interactions further raised the stakes of the class and made the project deeply personal for everyone involved. Camila Chiriboga said that 'just listening to people's actual needs' was incredibly informative. 'Working with someone else and their opinions and their input', she said, 'made me think in ways I would have never thought, and [prompted] ideas that I would have never expected' (Chiriboga 2020: n.pag.). The teams immediately had personal reference points to guide every design decision. We would overhear the students discussing, 'Do you think June would like this'? Or, 'Will this be comfortable for Doug to put on?'

In our class, everyone was a stakeholder, from the students to the volunteers to the medical practitioners involved, so every person's opinion mattered. All feedback was equally important and equally incorporated, which Bonnell said 'added valuable insight to the end product that I just didn't really get from other courses' (Bonnell 2020a: n.pag.).

The design brief in our class was authentic and not contrived; therefore, at no point did any of the students question the project at a fundamental level. Project briefs in fashion schools can often have seemingly arbitrary design constraints motivated by curricular objectives or a professor's ideas about how they can make a project intellectually stimulating. Students are encouraged to dig deep inside their emotional psyche to create highly personal designs, with outcomes that are sometimes merely self-serving. Noël Palomo-Lovinski and Kim Hahn wrote,

> Within many design programs in the USA , the individualized notion of creativity often takes precedence or becomes confused with solving real and pressing issues of function. Creativity for students has become characterized by a romantic notion of initiating ideas or collections devoid of context or rigour.
>
> (Palomo-Lovinski and Hahn 2014: 99)

In comparing this course to others, Yi Chen Ho said, 'Before this class I treated each project as an art project', working 'in a bubble, designing your own thing' (Ho 2020: n.pag.). In a typical fashion design studio, students make prototypes using dress forms provided by the school, the majority of which are size six, and then fit those designs on professional models who mirror those measurements. The live model's function is to provide a standing body for fittings and a moving body for the student to view their design in motion. While interactions with the model are usually respectful and genuine, both know the model might not wear the design in real life.

This exchange is drastically altered when designing a garment someone knows they likely will wear in their life, or may have worn already, and not by choice. Therefore, while working on the gown, the students were constantly forced to face their mortality; this required them to be mentally present 100 per cent of the time. One significant moment was when the students realized that this garment, the product of a design class, might be the last thing a person wears. It might be the last thing loved ones will see someone in. Therefore, it *must* be as comfortable as possible; it *must* preserve the person's dignity, and it *must* not make a bad situation worse; in fact, it *must* be almost *invisible* to the situation.

Irene Lu said of her time in the class that 'designing clothing [...] to serve a purpose, to protect people, to help people' was amazing; in particular, she noted that 'creating garments to be functional, to be actually used, and to be useful immediately to society' was extremely gratifying (Lu 2020: n.pag.). Gwyneth Ong described how this class challenged stereotypes about fashion design as something 'easy' or superficial. She said this class showed that fashion could be about 'caring about other people and working to make lives better' (Ong 2020: n.pag.). Close to the end of the semester, the students approached us as a group and requested that the competition-based project become a collective effort. This demonstration of solidarity to a shared mission showed that our students no longer saw themselves as solo designers. They learned that multiple advocating voices were better than one.

The three teams each presented a final design as originally planned. Rather than one design being deemed the winner, the students combined the most successful elements of each design into one final gown. Working past the semester and into the first few weeks of the summer, they concluded the project by jointly submitting a finalized professional tech pack, prototype and paper pattern. Lu continued working with Care+Wear as a summer intern to prepare the gown for production. And in November 2020, over three years after the completion of the class, another student, Helena Wang, applied for and accepted a full-time design position at Care+Wear. One week before she started her new position, Wang reflected on how she arrived at this point and said with great enthusiasm, 'This class was how I discovered my passion' (Wang 2020: n.pag.). The gown went into production in January 2018, and further design adjustments were made after testing it in hospital networks. At the time of writing this chapter, the gown is currently in use across several hospitals in the United States. As the story of the gown continues to unfold, we look forward to opportunities where we can include the volunteers' voices and experiences more prominently.

## Call to action

Education has been turned on its head due to the global coronavirus pandemic. The end of the 2020 academic year, in particular, was dramatically upended. Students were uprooted from their dorms; international students flew home in a panic, and projects were abandoned or completed without access to equipment. Students petitioned for tuition refunds, and many others took leaves of absence as universities moved to online-only courses. Meanwhile, the fashion system is being dismantled, as the universal uniform of sweats and leggings dominate bodies while *fashion* lies dormant in closets (Aleksander 2020: n.pag. emphasis added). The façade of the industry has long been peeling away to reveal a litany of social and environmental issues; the pandemic has now stripped it completely as we read accounts of severe exploitation of people for commercial gain in global supply chains, and racist CEOs stepping down from their positions at the top of promi-nent clothing brands.[6]

In a morbid twist, the hospital gown now holds the status of an object worthy of design and is arguably one of the most pressing objects for re-design. Personal Protective Equipment (PPE) is now a household acronym and part of the collec-tive vernacular as the Do-It-Yourself (DIY) movement for mask-making and other PPE gained immediate momentum at the onset of the coronavirus pandemic (Petri 2020: n.pag.).[7] This swift creative response is evidence of a widespread thirst for engagement in creative solutions to wicked problems.

Our goal in this chapter is to show through examples the major transformation that can take place in the fashion design classroom when we move beyond the paradigm of teaching students to design clothes based on personal narratives and esoteric references for an anonymous target audience. Too often, students (and professional designers) operate in this vacuum, designing beautiful self-referential products for fictional personas. We believe that this limited approach to fashion design is stale and irrelevant, and that the fundamental tools of design should be applied to facing the realities and problems of the world that directly affect our fellow human beings.

There is enormous potential to create unexpected partnerships between indus-try, academia and the public to develop projects that support the health and well-being of people through fashion design. We would like to see more design institutions collaborate with start-ups, nonprofits and corporations beyond the fashion industry to provide authentic opportunities for students to address the world's most pressing matters. A college education is a privilege, and we should use every possible academic platform to advance meaningful outcomes that rein-force reality.

## NOTES

1. It is important to note that while anyone is susceptible to contracting COVID-19, it dispro-portionately affects people based on a variety of factors, including socioeconomic status. As with the climate crisis, we see the most hard-hit areas in predominantly Black and Brown communities.

2. Donald A. Norman famously wrote, in his book *The Design of Everyday Things*, about poorly designed doors that fail to indicate whether they are to be pushed or pulled.

3. After testing the gown in various hospital systems after the completion of the course, the fabric changed to 100 per cent polyester due to wrinkling and laundering benefits.

4. Healthy Materials Lab is a design research lab at Parsons School of Design focused on raising awareness and creating resources for designers to use materials that are healthy for people and the environment.

5.  Based on the authors' personal experiences.
6.  See: '"Virtually entire" fashion industry complicit in Uighur forced labour, say rights groups' (Kelly 2020: n.pag.), or 'Fashion's racism and classism are finally out of style' (Mull 2020: n.pag.) – to name a couple.
7.  See also the work of Fashion Girls for Humanity, https://www.fashiongirlsforhumanity.org/.

## REFERENCES

Aleksander, Irina (2020), 'Sweatpants forever', *The New York Times*, 6 August, https://www.nytimes.com/interactive/2020/08/06/magazine/fashion-sweatpants.html. Accessed 2 December 2020.

Baillie, Lesley (2007), 'A case study of patient dignity in an acute hospital setting', Ph.D. thesis, London: London South Bank University.

Black, Sandy and Torlei, Karina (2013), 'Designing a new type of hospital gown', *Fashion Practice: The Journal of Design, Creative Process & the Fashion Industry*, 5:1, pp. 153–60.

Bonnell, Molly (2020a), telephone interview with B. Dickinson, 15 January.

Bonnell, Molly (2020b), e-mail B. Dickinson, 31 March.

Chiriboga, Camila (2020), telephone interview with Dickinson, 12 January.

'dignity' (2020), Merriam-Webster, https://www.merriam-webster.com/dictionary/dignity. Accessed 9 August 2020.

Freeman, Jan (2010), 'Oh, johnny', Throw Grammar From the Train, 24 March, http://throwgrammarfromthetrain.blogspot.com/2010/03/oh-johnny.html. Accessed 9 August 2020.

Gordan, Linsey and Guttman, Silvia (2013), 'A user-centered approach to the redesign of the patient hospital gown', *Fashion Practice: The Journal of Design, Creative Process & the Fashion Industry*, 5:1, pp. 137–52.

Ho, Yi Chen (2020), in-person interview with B. Dickinson, New York City, 13 January.

Kelly, Annie (2020), '"Virtually entire" fashion industry complicit in Uighur forced labour, say rights groups', *The Guardian*, 23 July, https://www.theguardian.com/global-development/2020/jul/23/virtually-entire-fashion-industry-complicit-in-uighur-forced-labour-say-rightsgroups-china. Accessed 2 December 2020.

Lu, Irene (2020), telephone interview with B. Dickinson, 12 January.

McCormick, Cynthia (2007), 'Hospital johnny on the spot', *Cape Cod Times*, 13 December, https://www.capecodtimes.com/article/20071213/LIFE/712130301. Accessed 2 December 2020.

McElroy, Elizabeth (1923), 'Hospital gown', US Patent 1,462,515, filed 9 August 1920 and issued 24 July 1923, https://patentimages.storage.googleapis.com/25/3c/2c/b0cc76e758323c/US1462515.pdf. Accessed 9 August 2020.

Meadows, Donella (1999), *Leverage Points: Place to Intervene in a System*, Vermont: The Sustainability Institute.

Morton, Liza, Cogan, Nicola, Kornfält, Susanna, Porter, Zoe and Georgiadis, Emmanouil (2020), 'Baring all: The impact of the hospital gown on patient well-being', *British Journal of Health Psychology*, 25:3, pp. 452–73, https://bpspsychub.onlinelibrary.wiley.com/doi/full/10.1111/bjhp.12416. Accessed 2 December 2020.

Mull, Amanda (2020), 'Fashion's racism and classism are finally out of style', *The Atlantic*, 7 July, https://www.theatlantic.com/health/archive/2020/07/fashions-racism-and-classismare-going-out-style/613906/. Accessed 2 December 2020.

Norman, Donald A. (1988), *The Design of Everyday Things*, New York: Basic Books.

Ong, Gwyneth (2020), telephone interview with B. Dickinson, 12 January.

Palomo-Lovinski, Noël and Hahn, Kim (2014), 'Fashion design industry impressions of current sustainable practices', *Fashion Practice: The Journal of Design, Creative Process & the Fashion Industry*, 6:1, pp. 87–106.

Petri, Alexandra E. (2020), 'D.I.Y. coronavirus solutions are gaining steam', *The New York Times*, 31 March, https://www.nytimes.com/2020/03/31/science/coronavirus-masks-equipment-crowdsource.html. Accessed 2 December 2020.

Rawal, Shail, Kwan, Janice L., Razak, Fahad, Detsky, Allan S., Guo, Yishan, Lapointe-Shaw, Lauren, Tang, Terence, Weinerman, Adina, Laupacis, Andreas, Subramanian, S. V. and Verma, Amol A., (2019), 'Association of the trauma of hospitalization with 30-day Readmission or emergency department visit', *JAMA Internal Medicine*, 179:1, pp. 38–45, https://jamanetwork.com/journals/jamainternalmedicine/fullarticle/2717502. Accessed 9 August 2020.

Razdan, Chaitenya (2020), e-mail to L. Jones, 19 June.

Silas, Julie, Hansen, Jean and Lent, Tom (2007), 'The future of fabric: Health care', *Health Care Without Harm and The Healthy Building Network*, October, pp. 1–32.

Szenasy, Susan ([2009] 2014), 'Reinventing invention', in Ann Hudner and Akiko Busch (eds), *Szenasy, Design Advocate*, New York: Metropolis Books, pp. 279–82.

Wang, Helena (2020), telephone interview with B. *Dickinson*, 25 November.

# 17

# Fashion Exorcism:
# A Journey in Community-Centred Design

*JOFF*

### Neptune

It was Monday, 7 June 1999.

Late afternoon, I was making my way from the subway station to the four-bedroom apartment I used to live in with my parents and my older brother. Eight years earlier, my dad's company had gone bankrupt; we lost everything and had to move in with our grandparents for a year until we moved into this apartment part of a social housing complex. Located in a suburb of Amsterdam called Duivendrecht, each of the closely planted fourteen-story beehive-like buildings was named after a planet in the universe.

Ours was Neptune.

Neptune was the closest to the subway station. Easy to spot from the balcony of my parents' seventh-floor apartment. Whenever I would visit, I'd see my mom waiting on the balcony and watching me as I made it down the path to Neptune. Once close enough, she would use both arms to wave me a rainbow. I moved out of my parents' home earlier that year to live in an anti-squat building smack in the centre of Amsterdam. I started my BA in Fashion Design one and a half years earlier at the Gerrit Rietveld Academy in The Netherlands. I had not been home in a couple of months. I had told my parents that I was too busy with finals for school.

As I dragged my feet down that familiar path, the late afternoon sun cast my body into long shadowy dancing figures. Ahead of me, assigning each tile of the pavement to feelings of either hope or anxiety. As I got closer to the building, afraid to look up, I could feel my mom's concerned eyes piercing down on me. I briefly looked up to acknowledge and comfort her, only to quickly put down my head again. Today was not a day of comfort.

As usual, my mom prepared my favourite dish: Indonesian Rice Table. Dinner was uncomfortably quiet, and I primarily focused on keeping it light by talking

299

about my activities at school. Once we finished, we moved to the living room. Mom sat on our pink and purple floral sofa adjacent to my dad, and I sat on a pair of matching plum and forest green leather armchairs.

DAD: So, how is everything with *you*?

ME: Medium.

MOM: What do you mean, *Medium*?
    I took a deep breath and blurted out, 'I've come to the realization that the religion is too tight a jacket for me, and I've decided to leave it'.

MOM: Have you met a *girl*?

ME: No.

MOM: Have you met a *boy*!?
    Shocked by the question, I stumblingly responded: 'I don't know. I just think that I should be able to love whomever I want to love. All people are beautiful'.

DAD: Let us read some scripture.
    Mom panic-stricken shrieked, 'Can we please leave the Bible out of this, I want to speak with my son!'.

*Mom starts crying*

DAD: sermonized, 'Are you sure about this, knowing the consequences!?'
    I responded calmly with a sentence I had rehearsed days prior, 'If I am created by God, in the image of God – then if this God cannot accept me for who I am, then I cannot accept this God as my God.' Dad sneered, 'Do you understand how this will affect my position within the congregation? I will have to inform the Elderls as this is part of my commitment and responsibility to our God, Jehovah'.

ME: I have already notified them.
    Dad begrudgingly belted, 'Then this will be the last time you will see us'.

ME: But... I love you.

DAD: If you would love us, you wouldn't do this to your family.

Soon after on my way out, they were standing side by side helplessly crying. It was an unbearable sight. I had to stay strong, to not break myself as I knew deep down I made the right decision. Before sharing the news, I imagined the worst-case scenario as a way of convincing myself they would never shun me from their lives – because family love is unconditional, right?

Unfortunately, I was wrong.

## Strawberry Shortcake

I was born into the small universe of a Jehovah's Witnesses family. My grand-parents, aunts, uncles and cousins were in it, and I would rarely see any family member that was not. Jehovah's Witnesses believe that if they abide by the rules of their God, Jehovah, they are granted eternal life. They must spread the word of God and attempt to save humanity from the reckoning of Armageddon. I was spoon-fed to believe that anyone outside of the religion was essentially evil until I converted. I engaged in all of it; Bible School, ringing strangers' doors and, starting at eleven years old, preaching in a suit and tie to a devoted 120-member congregation.

Thanks to my mom, I received an upbringing full of love and care, but it was also extremely isolating and lined with constant conflict. You see, I was not the boy interested in cars, mechanics or soccer. I was interested in ballet, birds, flowers, Strawberry Shortcake and dressing up in my grandmother's nightgowns. My mom, a painter, was the biggest supporter of my creativity. My dad, a car mechanic and a ministerial servant, was entirely disinterested in my creative escapades. My expressions often became topics of arguments between my parents, enlightening the already existing discrepancies within their marriage. Chronically stuck in the middle, I struggled to find a sense of belonging at home; to feel fully supported in who I was meant to become.

Primary school was no different. I was the weird Jehovah's Witnesses kid that did not celebrate any holidays or birthdays and pranced around the schoolyard wearing self-made telephone wire Madonna bracelets singing 'Like a virgin, touched for the very first time …'. Fitting in was not my modus operandi. Wherever I looked in my environment, I was criticized, bullied or gossiped about. I coped by being the family clown. Once puberty hit, the clown in me turned reclusive goth, spending most of the time in my bedroom drawing and listening to my saviour – Prince. My self-expression was such a topic of discontent that I had to hide most of it. Eager to express myself, on the way to high school, I would often switch out my sweatshirt, jeans and Nike's for a glittery lurex turtleneck, apron, clogs and a necklace I made from my mom's empty perfume bottles.

## Birds of paradise

In 1997, I was accepted into the Gerrit Rietveld Academie in Amsterdam, which was contested by the Jehovah's Witnesses congregation but luckily, mom insisted.

Going to art school was everything I had dreamed of. The first day was like walking from a bare concrete room into a saturated, lush jungle. Standing in the middle of the entrance hallway of this glass shoe box-like building, surrounded by bustling students in search of their classrooms, time slowed, my eyes popped and my jaw dropped as it suddenly hit me – I was among the Birds of Paradise: A sparkling multi-colour melting pot of every subcultural movement you could think of, and its cross-pollinated versions expressed by everyone on the gender spectrum. My heart was crying tears of joy.

At 20 years old, I was not bullied, criticized or alienated for the first time in my life. I was considered beautiful and celebrated for who I was. My peers, people I was taught to avoid in life, were the most gorgeous, talented, loving and open-minded people I had ever met. I spent the last twenty years wondering what the hell was wrong with me, now realizing there was nothing wrong with me at all. This realization opened the door to one of my biggest dilemmas: To truly be me, I had to risk losing everything I had known, trusted and loved.

Monday, 7 June, changed my life. I found my community at the Gerrit Rietveld Academie, but I was hesitant. The religious indoctrination left its remnants in the sense that while I knew I made the right decision, I also felt guilt and shame for what I did to my family. Fearful of being judged and an outsider, I was reluctant to share my story with my new peers.

Over the next two years, I tried to call my parents every two to three weeks to no avail. In my final year, I made one more attempt and invited them to the graduation showcase of my thesis collection. Early morning on the day of my thesis examination, I received a postcard from my parents with the message: 'Congratulations on your achievement. Unfortunately, since you have betrayed Jehovah, we will not be able to attend. If the scenario were different, we, of course, would have been proud front-row parents'.

As a further act of liberation, I unofficially rejected my birth name, Joffrey Norman Moolhuizen, and continued under the moniker and acronym JOFF. The acronym allowed me to operate as a collective, duo or solo artist with the intent to create cross-disciplinary collaborations in the context of the image of fashion. With this approach to my practice, I established my own JOFF community with my peers. And while I lacked the much-needed financial, emotional and parental guidance at the time, I succeeded in both my personal and professional life due to the dedicated support and love of my new family. As for my blood family, they have not been part of my life for more than twenty years except for my mom, who eventually divorced my dad and the religion.

While I consider myself a phoenix, having to overcome the segregation inflicted upon me at a young age, I was also lucky, unlike many LGBTQIA+ youths in the world. Statistics from The Trevor Project, a nonprofit suicide prevention organization for LGBTQIA+ youth – paints a stark picture; LGBTQIA+ youth seriously contemplate suicide almost three times more than heterosexual youth, LGBTQIA+ youth are five times more likely to commit suicide and 40 per cent of transgender youth have attempted suicide. LGBTQIA+ youths from highly rejecting families are 8.4 times as likely to attempt suicide compared to LGBTQIA+ youths who come from accepting families (The Trevor Project 2021).

I am sharing my personal story as an introduction because I want you to understand what segregation can look like. And moving forward, how I have used my experience as a catalyst in ushering awareness, inclusivity and responsibility within design education and the next generation of designers.

## *There I am next to me*

In 2015, after a decade-long career in the fashion industry, fulfilling various roles from designer to artistic director, I decided to commit fully to fashion education. I started a new role as associate director of the MFA Fashion Design programme Systems & Society pathway (MFA-FDS) at Parsons School of Design in New York City. One of the first courses Programme Director Shelley Fox invited me to redevelop was *Design Studio 1*, entitled *Personal Identity*. This significant twelve-week design course historically focused on students exploring their identity as an instrument of expression in developing two entirely produced looks and a design portfolio. Classic to the fashion design process, the work started with intensive research and concept development leading to two-dimensional explorations (through collage, drawing, photography, film, etc.) that informed three-dimensional developments that were explored through innovative fabrications, silhouettes and finishings and, finally synthesizing the work into production of looks.

The origins of the new course I developed for *Design Studio 1* go back to my time as an adjunct professor at the Gerrit Rietveld Academie. During this appointment, my long-term collaborator and graphic designer Julia Born and I developed several fashion courses for the Department of Graphic Design. One course, *Prêt-à-Porter*, was a collaborative project with students grouped into *design teams*. During the first day of class, students photographed each item of clothing they wore. The photographs were then further researched and documented from a historical, contemporary and associative perspective leading to a collective Wardrobe Library accessible to all design teams. The design teams used this collaborative research to develop a unique design identity and a collection of looks visualized in a look-book.

In developing the new iteration of *Design Studio 1*, I wanted to challenge the notion of personal identity as an individualized method of expression within design. My professional practice primarily focused on collaboration, so I learned more about my identity in exchange with others than when working alone. Therefore, I implemented the collaborative *Prêt-à-Porter* project framework in the new iteration of *Design Studio 1*. The course was re-titled *There I Am Next To Me*[1] and launched in the fall semester of 2015. Incorporating the Wardrobe Library, the four design teams produced a collection of six to eight outfits.

## Fashion design and society

In April 2017, Rachel Hutt, Arts Coordinator for Youth Offenders at Rikers Island in New York contacted me. Rikers Island is New York City's main jail complex and is only accessible by an unmarked bridge in Queens. The historically violent and horrific complex is known as the world's largest penal colony. It now has schools, clinics, chapels, sports fields, gyms, grocery stores and various shops, a power plant and a bus depot. Rachel Hutt worked with young men and women ages sixteen to 21, organizing art programming in visual art, dance, theatre, music and other out-of-the-box programming for incarcerated youth. Several teenagers had expressed interest in fashion, and Rachel enquired whether there would be any professors and/or graduate students interested in volunteering to conduct a workshop at Rikers Island.

Previously, I volunteered at the Ali Forney Center (AFC), a nonprofit organization that supports and helps homeless and harmed LGBTQIA+ youth. The youth expressed interest in learning about the fashion industry and invited me to share my professional experiences. Knowing their circumstances, I shared my story of facing segregation at a young age. I was hoping to connect with the youth and possibly offer a window of hope, but I realized my example was utopian. Most of the youth were predominantly Black and Brown. Coming from the Netherlands, I had not witnessed racial inequality of this magnitude. It was evident that the American Dream was not for everyone. It was clear I had existed in a privileged bubble, being white, having access to education, healthcare and all the governmental support I required to succeed in life. My success was not contingent on my willpower, strength or resilience. It was contingent on the structures around me that aided my success; to independently have a home, to be able to eat, travel, take risks and to be given the tools to make dreams a reality.

Upon the inception of the MFA-FDS programme in 2010, Shelley emphasized the important relationship between *fashion* and *society* through its programme title. The request from Rikers Island Arts Programming and my experience at the AFC nourished the idea to develop a collaborative course that would further and intentionally underline this societal focus. I proposed to Shelley that we utilize *Design Studio 1, There I Am Next to Me*, for this collaboration and customize the course project to actively centre the voices of marginalized people as part of the design process.

## Wet Wonder Bread

On a blisteringly hot July day, Shelley and I travelled to Rikers Island to meet Rachel Hutt and thirteen incarcerated teenage men at Main 4 Eric M. Taylor Center to gauge their interest. We had never visited a jail in our lives, and to get into the Eric M. Taylor Center from Parsons School of Design took a 30-minute Uber drive, two shuttle bus trips and three security check-ins, which involved two full-body scans, K-9 sniffer dogs and ultraviolet fingerprinting. After passing through several metal gates, the pungent smell of old sweat and wet Wonder Bread greeted us. Walking through the claustrophobic labyrinth-like corridors, the security guards instructed us to keep to the right as inmates passed us on the left. It seemed New York had not updated this place in decades.

Our anxiety raised as we heard muffled reverberating sounds of metal doors opening and closing; people were shouting, moaning and screaming in the distance. The teenager's unit was somewhat of an open cubicle space with several security doors between each section that consisted of a communal shower, bedroom and recreational room – all part concrete and glass. The teenagers were waiting for us in the small recreational room with anchored tables and chairs, a wall-mounted flat-screen TV and a shelf with a couple of books. Walking into the recreational room, I could hear my pumping heart slowly climb into my throat. The teenagers did not look like teenagers; they looked like full-grown adults, most of them over 6 feet tall.

There we were, Shelley in her jade Martin Margiela heeled tabbies, me with my orange bowl cut – with the mission of exciting the men to do a twelve-week fashion project with our new cohort of first-year students. With tension in the air, they largely ignored us. But we took a deep breath and went diligently around the room, introducing ourselves, smiling and shaking their hands in hopes of breaking the ice. Shelley introduced the MFA-FDS programme, and I followed with the proposal for the twelve-week fashion project. Surprisingly, the tension in the air shifted once we finished our introduction. Some put their names on the sign-up sheet, and one grabbed their notepad and asked for our opinion on the drawings they made. An hour later, they were joking with Shelley about her thick British accent and complimenting me for my plump sneakers. Excitement filled the recreational room, and we left with the promise that we would be back later that summer with a more detailed outline of the fashion project.

At the parking lot, Shelley and I looked at each other and questioned; Can we pull this off? The visit that day was emotionally intense. The anxiety of entering Rikers Island, being confronted with the awful conditions, getting a glimpse of the lives and personalities of these beautiful young souls who were being treated like caged animals and witnessing the injustice of systemic racism institutionalized in a place like Rikers Island was overwhelming.

### Future wardrobe

Back at the studio, Shelley and I decided to make a few changes to the organization of the course; we kept the design team set-up of *Design Studio 1* but removed the collective Wardrobe Library component and instead assigned the role of *creative director* to the incarcerated men. The men were in a confining place that silenced their voices. Through this project, we could provide an opportunity for self-expression while collaborating with our students.

The creative director is considered a top position from a hierarchical fashion industry perspective. Whereas the position of the design team is considered subservient to the vision of the creative director. Of course, most students aspire to be in the position of creative director. Nonetheless, by reversing the roles, we aimed to evidence that actively centring marginalized voices within the design process can create meaningful work. Since the men would be released from Rikers in three to six months, I retitled the *Design Studio 1* course *Future Wardrobe*.

The design teams met with their creative director for two hours every other week throughout the twelve-week course for six meetings. During the alternate weeks, the creative director would engage in two-hour speciality workshops that our MFA-FDS faculty members and collaborators delivered. Workshop topics included drawing, music and performance.[2] The creative work developed during the workshops was returned to the design teams at the MFA-FDS studios to be incorporated into the work for their next meeting with their creative directors. All the meetings and speciality workshops at Rikers Island were conducted on a volunteer basis and started at 7p.m. and ended at 9p.m. every Thursday.

The gymnasium at Rikers Island was reserved as a space for us to gather and host the workshops. The first creative director and design team meeting on 14 September was memorable. As we entered the poorly lit gymnasium, we saw the men lined up horizontally, side by side, waiting for us under the gymnasium's basketball hoop. Our students aligned themselves in front of them and introduced themselves. It was a prom-like moment. Then the men and the students sat down at circular primary coloured anti-ligature tables. The first hour was dedicated to getting to know each other. We spent the second hour setting up the creative director and design teams. In line with the hierarchical set-up, the creative directors decided on the collection concept. The design teams were charged with developing the work into a custom-made collection for the creative directors. Every other week, the students would bring their developments on big white foam boards to Rikers to discuss the work and receive direction from the creative directors.

Many of the concepts initiated by the creative directors revolved around their interests, such as music, basketball, childhood memories, their mothers and money. One concept stood out. One of the creative directors wanted to create a collection to support New York City's homeless. His desire to help and support others, considering his situation at the time, was admirable. Design team 2, Hualei Yu, Yong Guo and Moana Mao were tasked to develop this concept into a six-look collection.

Research involved self-initiated primary research by interviewing homeless people on the streets in which they developed a strategy that for each answer given, the students would provide water, food or cash. Through these interviews, they gathered extremely relevant information regarding the dire challenges homeless people face. This involved harsh city regulations around mobile enclosed structures, the necessity of water, the ability to safely store valuable goods and the problems in accessing restrooms, to name a few. The collection *Know Me As A Survivor* showcased a series of highly engineered and transformable garments with built-in water storage, secure pocketing, a tent-like sleeping bag structure that transformed into a coat and even built-in solutions for the discharge of bodily fluids (see Figure 17.1).

The workshops on drawing, music and performance revealed other creative skill sets of the creative directors. During the drawing workshop by Aina and Miguel, some revealed themselves to be extraordinary illustrators. These illustrations were then brought back to the design teams and incorporated into the collection development as either print design or departures for fabrications. The music workshops were one of the highlights of the supplemental workshop series. Henri had set up a mini recording studio in the gymnasium with three microphones, stands and a drum backing track. As soon as Henri hit play, several creative directors jumped behind the mics and poured out their heart and soul through rap. Observing it all, I had a tough time keeping my cheeks dry, as the delivery of

FIGURE 17.1: Design Team 2: Yong Guo, Moana Mao and Hualei Yu, *Future Wardrobe*, 2017. Courtesy of Yong Guo and Hualei Yu.

their poetry was so heartfelt – it was one of those magical moments I will never forget. For the performance workshop, Julia and the creative directors developed a choreography inspired by the memories of gestures they loved outside of Rikers; such as swiping on Tinder, smoking weed, eating good food and dancing, vs. gestures they associated with being inside of Rikers such as feeling trapped, small or contained. The exploration of their emotions through movement was eventually turned into an immersive choreography so joyful that the security guards joined in for a collective dance on the gymnasium floor.

*Future Wardrobe* also came with its challenges. The project was logistically complex as a two-hour visit to Rikers involved an eight-hour commitment. Anything that we wanted to bring to Rikers Island required sign-off weeks in advance. We could not bring anything sharp such as pins, needles, paper clips and pens. Furthermore, in preparation for the project, students, each member of the faculty, and collabora-tors underwent two mandatory pieces of training[3]. Halfway into the project, some men were released, moved to a different unit or opted to work a shift. The horrifying conditions also affected their mental well-being, sometimes leading to mood swings from week to week or a verbal brawl between some men. Security guards were always present to intercept verbal or physical altercations. However, throughout the entire time, the men were always courteous, kind and respectful towards us. In addition to the twelve visits to Rikers, Shelley and I conducted weekly tutorials with each design team, all of which took considerable time, flexibility and dedication.

We gave the men an avenue of expression and a platform for empowerment during a very challenging time in their lives. From their engagement and enthusiasm to connecting and collaborating while purposely building towards a goal provided an opportunity for some men to feel a strong sense of accomplishment. I hope it made their time at Rikers a bit more bearable. We will never really know the extent of the influence, although a couple of men expressed feeling inspired and desired to return to college once they got out. Which, to me, was the biggest compliment we could get.

*Future Wardrobe* was an extremely important course project. It was ambitious as I had no experience working collaboratively with students in a context like Rikers Island. But with the proper preparation, research, guidance and training, the project was a success and a massive learning experience for us as faculty, collaborators and students. It set the stage for the subsequent three *Design Studio 1 projects: The Body Unique, Embodying Universal Bodies* and *The Disability Design Principle.*

## The Body Unique

In the summer of 2018, after several conversations with the Director of Drop-in Support Services at the AFC, Bill Torres, I decided that for the next edition of

*Design Studio 1*, we would collaborate with transgender youth at the Transgender Housing division in Harlem, NY. The course, now titled *The Body Unique*, was co-developed with Senior Director of Transitional Housing Stacey Lewis, Director of Transgender Housing Joanna Rivera and Assistant Director Jamie Louis.

The course project maintained the creative director/design team set-up, but this time teams were grouped into categories representing specific transgender experiences of adversity within society, such as the workplace, public life and nightlife. Before the project began, students researched stereotypes and biases to better understand gender identities and empathize with the experiences of trans youth. In preparation for the collaboration, students and faculty attended a mandatory training session at the AFC.

This time we worked with the transgender youth directly in the MFA-FDS studios. Because the youth was part of governmental programming at the AFC, we were prohibited from monetarily compensating them. In lieu of financial compensation, the AFC advised us to develop weekly incentive packages for these types of volunteering projects, which included MetroCards, gift cards and various sponsored products by collaborators such as Swarovski, Nike and Nars.

The creative directors and the design teams developed garments and a body of work that harnessed a safe space or contrarily increased visibility and re-educated society. Resulting in a much more nuanced perspective on the experiences of the transgender community. At the end of this project, I wondered if these projects would genuinely incite change and if this project supported marginalized communities. Activism often happens in small, understated environments. Even though these projects were one-of-a-kind and not highly publicized, we helped to provide an alternative view of how fashion creation should take place by centring the marginalized. This course reinforced, for the trans community and our students, that marginalized people deserve equitable opportunities to share their wants and needs about personal expression through fashion. The cohort of students involved in *The Body Unique* project has since graduated; and, outside of their own experience, did their final thesis work specifically address marginalized communities? While I do not know the impact of these projects, I have seen a shift in student work that reflects their ability to have greater awareness and social responsibility in their creations.

For example, design team 2 focused on 'Work Power' and comprised three students: Samantha D'Iorio, Karen Heshi and Chi Han ( Figure 17.2). In their own way, each student aimed to address notions of inclusivity. For example, Samantha D'Iorio focused her thesis collection on developing a series of highly engineered garments that were transformable and adaptive to all body sizes. With it, she advocated against everything we have been spoon-fed to believe by the fashion industry.

Karen Heshi's final thesis collection, 'The Performing Suits' (see Figure 17.3), was built around a slicing technique she developed during *The Body Unique*

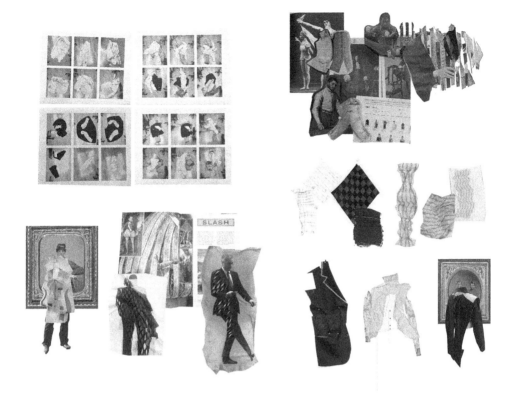

FIGURE 17.2: Design Team 2: Samantha D'Iorio, Chi Han and Karen Heshi, *Work Power, Research and Developments –The Body Unique, 2018.* Courtesy of Chi Han and Karen Heshi.

project. Having grown up in a large family with a working mom, she experienced first-hand the challenges her mom faced in upholding the alternating roles of being a mother and supporting her family financially. Karen's collection centred around the classical men's suit as the epitome of patriarchy. She dismantled the suit by slicing it up through her intricate techniques to represent an image of malleability more indicative of the experience of womanhood.

Chi Han's growth within the programme was more than academic – it was an all-around coming-of-age experience as one of our finest members of the LGBTQIA+ community. *The Body Unique* project was important in his personal development because it provided an avenue to build self-acceptance. His thesis collection focused on a series of auntie dresses he used to dress up in as a kid. With his collection, he addressed notions around femininity and masculinity and opened a dialogue about societal perspectives and stereotypical gender assignments.

FIGURE 17.3: Karen Heshi, *The Performing Suits – Graduate Collection, 2020.* Courtesy of Model Kyle Wo, Make Up Sandy Nicha, Karen Heshi and photographer James Bee.

## Embodying universal bodies

*Future Wardrobe* and *The Body Unique* involved collaborations with compromised identities that were protected for obvious reasons – permitting us to share the work in a limited manner publicly. For *Embodying Universal Bodies*, instead of collaborating with an external organization, design teams were charged to independently recruit their creative directors in the categories of 'People of Advanced Age', 'Transgender/Non-binary', 'Fat' and 'Disability'. This responsibility incited the students to become even more involved in the communities that they were working with. This also allowed the MFA-FDS programme to monetarily compensate the creative directors for their time spent with the design teams. Creative directors included Lyn Slater for People of Advanced Age ( Figure 17.4), Mishka Amethyst and Grace Insogna

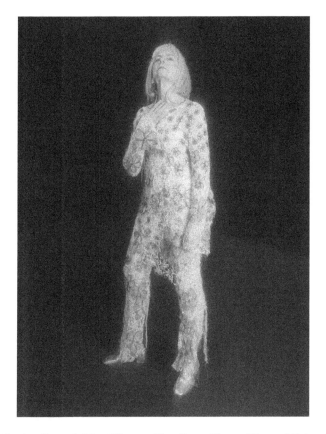

FIGURE 17.4. Design Team 1: Vera Blinova, Ying Feng, Jihoon Kim and Zehua Wu, *People of Advanced Age - Embodying Universal Bodies, 2019*. Courtesy of Creative Director and Model Lynn Slater and photographer Ziyuan Chen.

for Transgender/Non-Binary, Maya S. Adama Finoh for Fat ( Figure 17.5) and Bri Scalesse for Disability ( Figure 17.6). Several lectures supported the course; Lucy Jones, Founder of FFORA – a fashion lifestyle brand centring the needs of those with physical disabilities; Brendan McCarthy, assistant professor of Fashion, who earlier led out on the BFA Parsons x AARP[4] Disrupt Aging in Fashion Project and Huguette Hubard, Former VP of Design at Lane Bryant. The final collections incorporated functional and practical solutions in garment design but, above all, highlighted the emotional and psychological importance of garments. For example, design team 1, working on People of Advanced Age, composed of Vera Blinova, Jihoon Kim, Ying Feng and Zehua Wu struggled the most at the beginning of their project.

The People of Advanced Age category was not easy because ageing is universal and intersectional. Furthermore, ageism is rampant in the fashion industry's perpetual

FIGURE 17.5: Design Team 1: Ariana Patawaran, Zhiqing Zhang, Yoshinori Momiyama & Zisu Tak, *Plus-Size - Embodying Universal Bodies, 2019*. Courtesy of Creative Director and Model Maya S. Adama Finoh, Make Up Mitch Yoshida, Hair Joy Lin and photographer Ziyuan Chen.

idealization of youth. In collaboration with creative director Lyn Slater – who is also a professor of social justice and Instagram influencer – the design team focused the subject of ageing on the experiential and psychological instead of traditional physical solution-based concepts. The collection was based on Lyn Slater's existing wardrobe pieces that held important experiential or nostalgic significance throughout her life. For example, a coat that presented a sense of safety or a floral pantsuit reminiscent of her younger years in the 1960s. The design team then reimagined these pieces through elaborate multi-dimensional textile developments that emphasized the beauty of ageing.

The MFA-FDS final and fourth edition of *Design Studio 1* focused on the 'Disability Community'. Entitled *The Disability Design Principle*, design teams collaborated with their creative directors in the categories of 'Hearing', 'Visual',

FIGURE 17.6: Design Team 4: Madison Hislop, Kyoung Eun Kim, Justin Hsiung, Kenneth Pan and Zoe Whalen, *Disability – Embodying Universal Bodies, 2019*. Courtesy of Creative Director and Model Bri Scalesse and photographer Luke Tew.

'Cognitive' and 'Ambulatory disability'. The course was co-developed and co-taught by Parsons School of Design alumni Lucy Jones. After completion of the course, the project continued into the next and final course of the semester, *Advanced Visual Practicum*. During this course, Faculty and Director Christelle de Castro collaborated with the students in the realization of a documentary entitled *IN:VISIBILITY*, featuring each creative director and the work they developed with their design teams.

## Escapist ideologies

Growing up in a religious cult, fashion was the creative outlet that aided me in exploring my identity and gave me the willpower to stand up for my beliefs.

Ironically, that same fashion industry equally turned out to be the very thing I had stood up against; an escapist ideology that only includes a certain group of people. And when I say the *fashion industry*, it is not something that I point out as an external entity and excuse myself from responsibility. Before my position in academia, I had been part of that industry; I have participated in it fully and regretfully neglected my power positions to advocate for change.

The series of course projects that I have led throughout the years have humbled me, unveiled my own biases and provided me with a greater awareness of the insidious conditioning of the fashion industry. For example, as designers, we often quickly jump to the assumption or belief that we can be the creative solution, the problem solvers and the ones to create change. While I advocate for those in positions of power to use their abilities responsibly, with students, faculty and collaborators, we learned that by collaborating with marginalized communities, it is not always about solving a problem. It is about truly having the ability to listen and include everyone within the dialogue to ensure all voices are part of the fabric of our culture and society. It is actively exercising humanity.

Fashionably late, slowly, change is happening within the fashion industry. We are seeing more beautiful authentic representations of the diverse population in this world. But when this representation is not reflected within its supporting industry structures, such as fashion education, it merely ends up functioning as a façade. If we are lucky, for example, considering its environmental impact alone, the complexities of the fashion industry will take decades to reform. Now, fashion activism is needed more than ever. In fact, it requires an exorcism. For the change to be successful, it must happen collectively within all layers of the fashion industry. The work I have established with all involved, though important, is a drop in the pond considering the magnitude of the issues.

For the reasons above, I will pass on assigning myself the label of *fashion activist*. I choose to situate myself in a position where I am consistently forced to hold myself accountable as JOFF, actively and intentionally placing *love* at the centre of my work.

## NOTES

1. In reference to Alighiero Boetti's 1968 artwork *Gemelli*.
2. Drawing workshops were conducted by faculty and designer Aina Beck and artist Miguel Villalobos; the music workshops were conducted by one of our graduates, music composer Henri Scars Struck and fashion show producer Grace Palmer and the performance workshops were conducted by faculty and performance artist Julia Crockett.
3. One training was organized and conducted by Rachel Hutt and a second by art therapist Kate Pane – who had previously developed and conducted courses at Rikers Island,

Crossroads Juvenile Detention Center, Horizons Juvenile Detention Center and Queens probation.

4.   The American Association of Retired Persons (known as AARP).

## REFERENCE

The Trevor Project (2021), 'Facts about LGBTQ youth suicide', 15 December, https://www.thetrevorproject.org/resources/article/facts-about-lgbtq-youth-suicide/. Accessed 12 June 2022.

# Contributors

AVALON ACASO holds a BFA in Theatre Performance Production and a MA in Fashion from Toronto Metropolitan University. As a person living with invisible disabilities, she is a dedicated advocate for accessibility within the performing arts and creative fields.

\* \* \* \* \*

TANVEER AHMED is a final year Arts and Humanities Research Council (AHRC) funded Ph.D. candidate at The Open University. She is investigating how Eurocentric and racist ideas underpin the design process in fashion education. Tanveer has been recently appointed as a senior lecturer in Fashion and Race at Central Saint Martins, University of the Arts London.

\* \* \* \* \*

KEVIN ALMOND is a lecturer in the School of Design at The University of Leeds. He has a master's from The Royal College of Art and gained a Ph.D. with a thesis entitled, 'Suffering in Fashion'. He has held various posts in academia and the fashion industry.

\* \* \* \* \*

BEN BARRY is dean and an associate professor in the School of Fashion at Parsons School of Design, The New School. Through research, teaching and leadership, he is devoted to designing fashion futures where worldviews and bodies that are currently stigmatized are instead desired. He was previously chair of the School of Fashion at Toronto Metropolitan University.

\* \* \* \* \*

MAL BURKINSHAW studied at Edinburgh College of Art and the Royal College of Art. Following a career in the fashion industry, he became director of the fashion programme at Edinburgh College of Art, the University of Edinburgh, from 2011–2020. He is now the head of Design, overseeing 16 design programmes across undergraduate and postgraduate degrees.

\* \* \* \* \*

JOHNATHAN CLANCY is a Ph.D. candidate in the Gender, Feminist, and Women's Studies at York University and an alumnus of the MA Fashion programme at Toronto Metropolitan University. Johnathan's research examines how fashion objects interact with the performance and production of gendered, classed and racialized hierarchies.

\* \* \* \* \*

ROBIN J. CHANTREE is an interdisciplinary artist and designer residing in Tkaranto/ Toronto but originally from north-eastern British Columbia in Treaty 8 territory, historically the land of the Dane-Zaa people. They hold an MA in Fashion from Toronto Metropolitan University and a BFA from Emily Carr University of Art and Design.

\* \* \* \* \*

DEBORAH A. CHRISTEL is a fat fashion designer, plus-size business consultant and founder of size-inclusive fashion brand, Kade & Vos. Before starting her business, she was an assistant professor of Fashion Design. Her research and activism has been shared in publications including *The New York Times*, *People Magazine*, *Good Morning America* and *Forbes*.

\* \* \* \* \*

GREG CLIMER is chair of the fashion programme at California College of the Arts. In addition to his work as a fashion educator, he maintains a studio practice. His textile work has been shown in museums including The DeYoung and The Museum of Art and Design.

\* \* \* \* \*

BRITTANY DICKINSON is a designer, educator and sustainability strategist. Her professional experience includes positions at Goodwill Industries International,

Parsons School of Design and J. Crew. Brittany holds a MA in Design Research, Writing and Criticism from the School of Visual Arts and a BSc in Fashion Design from the University of Cincinnati.

\* \* \* \* \*

JENNY LEIGH DU PUIS is a Ph.D. candidate in Apparel Design at Cornell University. Her research centres safety and function in apparel for extreme movement, and is informed by her career as a costume designer and technician in the live entertainment industry.

\* \* \* \* \*

BIANCA GARCIA is a fashion researcher who participates in fashion as a creative means of political resistance and world-building. Bianca is currently researching Filipino fashion and weaving history. She holds a MA in Fashion from Toronto Metropolitan University.

\* \* \* \* \*

RACHEL ROSE GETMAN holds a bachelor's degree in Anthropology from the University of California at Los Angeles and a master's degree in Apparel Design from Cornell University.

\* \* \* \* \*

DENISE NICOLE GREEN is an associate professor of Fashion Design, Anthropology, American Studies, and American Indian and Indigenous Studies at Cornell University. She also directs the Cornell Fashion + Textile Collection.

\* \* \* \* \*

CHRIS HESSELBEIN is an ethnographer who studies how knowledge and technology are co-constructed with conceptions of social order and self-identity. Chris received his Ph.D. in Science and Technology Studies from Cornell University and he is currently a postdoctoral researcher at the Politecnico di Milano.

\* \* \* \* \*

ALICIA JOHNSON graduated with a BAA in Fashion Merchandising from Central Michigan University in 2018. She works as an executive team leader for Target.

\* \* \* \* \*

JOFF is associate professor in the departments of Apparel Design and Jewelry and Metalsmithing at Rhode Island School of Design. He explores the image of fashion through design, creative direction, art direction, graphic design, performance, fiction and non-fiction writing, exhibitions and education. For more information, visit www.ofoffjoff.com.

\* \* \* \* \*

LUCY JONES is the founder and CEO of FFORA, a fashion lifestyle brand that primarily caters to the disability community. Jones previously worked at Eileen Fisher as a 'social innovator', with health-wear company Care+Wear, and teaches at Parsons School of Design, The New School.

\* \* \* \* \*

GRACE JUN is an assistant professor of Graphic Design at the University of Georgia. Her research explores the intersection of accessibility and inclusive design. As CEO at Open Style Lab (OSL), an award winning nonprofit organization committed to making style accessible for people of all abilities, she continues to connect her creative practice to her inclusive philosophy.

\* \* \* \* \*

CARMEN N. KEIST is an associate professor in the Department of Family and Consumer Sciences at Bradley University. Her research explores twentieth century dress history, specifically plus-size women's ready-to-wear fashions.

\* \* \* \* \*

RILEY KUCHERAN is an Indigenous scholar from Biigtigong Nishnaabeg (Pic River First Nation). Riley is an assistant professor in the School of Fashion at Toronto Metropolitan University. Riley's research supports Indigenous cultural and economic resurgence by drawing on decolonizing theories to examine, dismantle and rebuild fashion systems.

\* \* \* \* \*

MICHAEL MAMP is an associate professor of Textiles, Apparel Design, and Merchandising at Louisiana State University. His research explores fashion and textile history of the twentieth century. He teaches dress history, queer fashion, and history of textiles.

\* \* \* \* \*

KRYS OSEI is a lecturer in Cultural Studies and Fashion Media Production at Central Saint Martins and London College of Fashion, University of the Arts London. As a doctoral candidate at Goldsmiths, University of London, her research maps the world-building practices of diasporic Ghanaian women through beauty, adornment, self-portraiture and fashion film.

\* \* \* \* \*

LAUREN DOWNING PETERS is an assistant professor in Fashion Studies and director of the Fashion Study Collection at Columbia College Chicago. She is the author of *Fashion Before Plus-Size: Bodies, Bias and the Birth of an Industry* (2023) and the co-editor with Hazel Clark of *Fashion in American Life* (2024).

\* \* \* \* \*

VICTORIA PIETSCH graduated from Cornell University in 2019 with a BSc in Fashion Design Management. She was a student curator of the *Women Empowered* and *Revolution & Restraint* exhibitions, as well as a research assistant in the Cornell Fashion + Textile Collection.

\* \* \* \* \*

ANNA POLLICE is an artist and designer whose practice investigates an interlacing of fashion, image and textile. She holds an MFA in Interdisciplinary Art, Media, and Design from Ontario College of Art and Design University and an MA in Fashion from Toronto Metropolitan University.

\* \* \* \* \*

ALEXIS QUINNEY completed a BSc in Fashion Merchandising and Design and a MSc in Apparel Product Development and Merchandising Technology at Central Michigan University. She currently works in the apparel production industry.

\* \* \* \* \*

KELLY L. REDDY-BEST is an associate professor in the Department of Apparel, Merchandising and Design and the curator and director of the Textiles and Clothing Museum at Iowa State University. In her research, she examines the inter-relationships of dress, identity, consumption, regulation and the fashion system. Her work is rooted in a social justice lens.

\* \* \* \* \*

AUSTIN REEVES graduated with a BSc in Business Administration with a concentration in Marketing from Central Michigan University in 2018. He currently works as an internal communications and engagement specialist dedicated to the creation of safe space for a diverse workforce.

\* \* \* \* \*

JOSHUA SIMON graduated with a BAA from Central Michigan University in 2019 and a MSc from Iowa State University in 2022. He is currently a Ph.D. student at Western Michigan University.

\* \* \* \* \*

COLLEEN SCHINDLER-LYNCH is an associate professor in the School of Fashion at Toronto Metropolitan University. She completed a MFA at Louisiana State University and lectures on trends in fashion specifically relating to diversity and fashion illustration.

\* \* \* \* \*

BRANDON SPENCER graduated with a BSc in Apparel, Merchandising, and Design at Iowa State University in 2020. He was the editor-in-chief of *SIR* magazine, a student-run publication, and also served as the Iowa State University NAACP chapter president from 2017 to 2018.

\* \* \* \* \*

SANG THAI is a designer, lecturer and creative practice researcher at the School of Fashion and Textiles, Royal Melbourne Institute of Technology University. Drawing on extensive industry design experience, Sang is currently a Ph.D. candidate with an interest in masculinity, intersectionality and inclusive fashion design practices for social change.

\* \* \* \* \*

LYNDA XEPOLEAS is a Ph.D. candidate in the field of fibre Science and Apparel Design at Cornell University. As a member of the *WOMEN EMPOWERED* research team, she engaged in archival research methods to identify and study possible items for the exhibition.

# Index

Printed in the USA
CPSIA information can be obtained
at www.ICGtesting.com
JSHW061119030823
45845JS00005B/25